ALSO BY JUDITH MACKRELL

Out of Line: The Story of British Dance
Reading Dance
Bloomsbury Ballerina
The Oxford Dictionary of Dance (with Debra Craine)

emerge on the arm of a rich and titled husband. When she fell in love with a man who possessed neither money nor rank, she broke with centuries of tradition. She had committed herself to earning the money that would launch her husband in politics and had done so by embarking on a career that a generation earlier would have risked social disgrace.

By the autumn of 1925 all six of these women were travelling to places far beyond those that they, or anyone else, could have envisioned. They didn't do so as a recognizable group, although their lives intersected in many ways. But the journeys they took were emblematic of larger changes that were taking place around them, and which were throwing the lives and expectations of women into profoundly different configurations.

To the public eye, these changes were sufficiently vivid to inspire the branding of a new breed of women – the much demonized and much mythologized 'flapper'. Like Ardita Far-nam,[4] one of Scott Fitzgerald's early heroines, the flapper seemed to be motivated by a single aim: 'to live as I liked always and to die in my own way'. Riding the transforming dynamic of the 1920s she was seen to demand everything that had been denied her mother, from choosing her own sexual relationships and earning her own living, to cutting her hair, shortening her skirts and smoking cigarettes in public.

For Diana, the oldest of the women in this book, the determin-ation to 'live as I liked' was rooted in the harrowing dislocations of the war years. As traditional rules of class were suspended she found the nerve to defy her family, first to volunteer as a nurse, then to claim the marriage and career of her choice. Nancy, too, used the war to carve out her own rebellion, but she would push far beyond Diana in embracing the most radical elements of the Twenties' experiment in art, fashion and lifestyle. Tamara, Tal-lulah and Zelda also journeyed remarkable distances during the decade, but they not only embodied the flapper through the spirit of their personal lives they gave her a very public stamp – Tamara in the women she painted, Tallulah in the characters that she portrayed on stage and Zelda in the fictional heroines already looked like one of my paintings, so I could not ask her to pose.'[2]

Another admirer of Josephine's dancing was the poet and heiress Nancy Cunard. She, too, had left her home in England to settle in Paris, but while she frequented the same circuit of nightclubs, bars and parties as Tamara, her closest ties were with the Parisian avant-garde. That autumn she was disentangling herself from an affair with the Dadaist Tristan Tzara and falling in love with Louis Aragon, one of the founders of surrealism.

Nancy had grown up a lonely, bookish little girl but her antagonism towards her socially voracious mother had hardened her determination to make a new life for herself in Paris. Eight years later, her transformation from English heiress to Left Bank radical would appear complete. Her hair was sharply cropped, her eyes outlined with kohl, her arms loaded to the elbow with ivory and ebony bangles, and among her long list of lovers would be a black jazz pianist from Georgia.

Also in Paris during the mid-1920s was Zelda Fitzgerald. Originally a small-town Southern belle from Alabama, her 'slender supple' grace and 'spoiled alluring mouth' had famously become the template from which her husband, the novelist Scott Fitzgerald, created his exquisitely modern heroines.[3] Her former childhood friend Tallulah Bankhead had much admired Zelda, feeling herself to be the plump and truculent ugly duckling of her own Southern family, but at the age of fifteen Tallulah had starved herself into beauty and won a minor film role in a magazine competition. From there she progressed to a career on Broadway and in London's West End where, by 1925, she had become a star. Brash, witty and luxuriantly pretty, Tallulah was a novelty on the London stage.

No less exotic to American audiences was the very English, very aristocratic Lady Diana Cooper, who during the mid-1920s was touring the States in Max Reinhardt's theatrical spectacle *The Miracle*. As the youngest daughter of the 8th Duke of Rutland, Diana was only one rung below royalty and as such had grown up in a gilded cage, from which she was expected to

Her hard, supple body was celebrated as an icon of contemporary style – reflecting the glossy streamlined aesthetic of art deco and the gamine flair of the French *garçonne*.

To some of the young women who watched her dance, Josephine held out the possibility of their own transformation. In many parts of the Western world, the 1920s had been greeted as a decade of change. The Great War might have detonated the optimism of the early century, shattering millions of lives, damaging economies and toppling regimes, yet out of its carnage the modern world seemed to be reinventing itself with astonishing speed. Fuelled by the rising American stock market and the ferocious gearing up of industry, the Twenties was emerging as a decade of mass consumption and international travel, of movies, radios, brightly coloured cocktails and jazz. It was a decade that held out the promise of freedom.

For women, that promise was especially tantalizing. The war had delivered voting rights and jobs to many and it had started to redraw the social map. When Josephine Baker came to Paris, she was transported to a culture and marketplace that would have been unimaginable to her before 1914, and the same was true for the Polish-Russian artist, Tamara de Lempicka.

In Tsarist Russia, where Tamara had grown up, she had been cocooned in a life of pleasure and privilege. But when the 1917 revolution had smashed that life apart she had been forced into exile with her husband and small child. Living in a small hotel room in Paris she'd had no skills with which to support herself other than a relatively untutored gift for painting and an undaunted sense of her own entitlement. By the late 1920s she had used both to recreate herself as one of the most fashionable artists of the new decade.

Tamara's most celebrated canvases were of her contemporaries, young women whose bodies radiated a lustre of sexual independence as redolent of 1920s style as Josephine's dancing. In fact, Tamara always claimed an affinity with Josephine, even though she never attempted to paint her: 'The woman made everyone who watched her weak with desire for her body. She

INTRODUCTION

On 2 October 1925 a young American dancer from the black ghetto of St Louis stood on the stage of the Théâtre des Champs-Elysées in Paris. Her limbs were trembling from exhaustion as well as from the clamour erupting from the crowd below. People in the audience were screaming, shouting, drumming their feet; yet what seemed to her a terrifyingly hostile noise was in fact the sound of Paris acknowledging a star. Just three months earlier Josephine Baker had been a skinny chorus girl living on a modest wage and a hopeful dream. Now, repackaged as a burnished, exotic beauty, she was about to be hailed as a cultural phenomenon.

The Paris correspondent of the *New Yorker* reported that within half an hour of Josephine's debut the city's bars and cafés were talking only of the magnificent eroticism of her dancing. Maurice Bataille, a restaurant owner who later became one of her lovers, claimed that Josephine's naked buttocks (*'Quel cul elle a!'*) had simply given 'all Paris a hard-on'.[1] Yet over the following days she would be feted by artists and critics as a black pearl, an ebony Venus, a jazz age vamp with the soul of an African goddess.

Postcards of 'La Baker' went on sale, as did a range of Josephine dolls. Her shiny black hair and coffee-coloured skin, the source of so much abuse back home, were harnessed to the marketing of French beauty products: hair pomade for the glossing of Eton crops; walnut oil for the faking of summer tans.

FLAPPERS

by Jean-Claude Baker and Chris Chase; Aurum Press for extacts from *Tallulah! The Life and Times of a Leading Lady* by Joel Lobenthal; Random House for extracts from *Save Me The Waltz* by Zelda Fitzgerald; Gollancz for extracts from *Tallulah: My Autobiography* by Tallulah Bankhead; Scribner & Sons for extracts from the works of F. Scott Fitzgerald and from the letters of Scott and Zelda Fitzgerald; the Harry Ransom Center for extracts from the personal papers of Nancy Cunard; the Estate of T.S. Elliot and Faber and Faber Ltd for extracts from *The Waste Land*; the Estate of Tamara de Lempicka for extracts from *Passion by Design: the Art and Times of Tamara de Lempicka* by Kizette de Lempicka-Foxall and Charles Phillips © 2013 Tamara Art Heritage, licensed by Museum Masters NYC.

Aside from the biographers and historians who've gone before me, all of whom are listed in the bibliography, I want to thank those who've given exceptional, generous help and advice in the writing and publication of this book.

Gillian Darley and Michael Horowitz, Kate and Paul Bogan offered fantastic hospitality; many friends were patient sounding boards for my ideas, and Debra Craine in particular went beyond the call of duty in reading and commenting on the book in its manuscript stages.

Enormous thanks to my brilliant editor Georgina Morley – scrupulous, funny and challenging; also to the rest of the editorial team at Macmillan including my very patient production manager, Tania Wilde, and meticulous copy-editor Shauna Bartlett. Thanks again to the staunch support of my agent Clare Alexander.

And finally love, as always, to my family.

Judith Mackrell, January 2013

a flavour of it, for the sake of period accuracy. For the same reason I've presented quotations from letters and diaries, etc., in their original form, without tidying up oddities of spelling, grammar or idiom.

In the matter of money, which was of paramount concern to most of these women, I've tried to give a general sense of values and exchange rates, but not to track year-by-year changes. The franc in particular vacillated wildly against the other major currencies after the collapse of the Gold Standard in 1914, and its weakness against the dollar, coupled with bullish rises in the American stock market, was a major factor in Paris becoming so attractive to foreign artists and writers, and playing so central a role in this story.

The following offers the roughest of guides to the value of the money in the wage packets or bank accounts of these six women, using the Retail Price Index (RPI) to pin these values to the present day:

> In 1920, £1 was worth approximately $3.50, or 50 francs, which equates to £32.85 in today's values.
>
> In 1925, £1 was worth approximately $5.00, or 100 francs, and equates to £46.65 today.
>
> In 1930, £1 was worth approximately $3.50, or 95 francs, and equates to £51.75 today.

I would like to thank the following for their generous permission to quote from published and unpublished works: the Felicity Bryan Literacy Agency and John Julius Norwich for the Estates of Lady Diana Cooper and Duff Cooper for extracts from *A Durable Fire: the Letters of Duff and Diana Cooper*, edited by Artemis Cooper, compilation © Artemis Cooper 1983; *The Rainbow Comes and Goes, The Autobiography of Lady Diana Cooper* © The Estate of Lady Diana Cooper 1958; *The Duff Cooper Diaries 1915–1951*, edited and introduced by John Julius Norwich © 2005; Cooper Square Press for extracts from *Josephine Baker: The Hungry Heart*

AUTHOR'S NOTE AND ACKNOWLEDGEMENTS

The 1920s was a decade of exhilarating change for women and this book tells the story of six in particular, each of whom profited from that decade in remarkable ways. Diana Cooper, Nancy Cunard, Tamara de Lempicka, Tallulah Bankhead, Zelda Fitzgerald and Josephine Baker were famous in their own right; for each of them the Twenties was a moment of exceptional opportunity. Yet viewed as a group these women were also very representative of their times: they chased similar ambitions, fought similar battles, even shared the quirks of their generation's collective personality.

The world they inhabited was also comparatively small. Despite living and working in a variety of cities, these women shared lovers and friendships as well as personal concerns. They were written about by the same novelists and journalists, photographed for the same publications. But biography is essentially about the colour and detail of individual lives and in writing this book I've been fortunate to profit from the groundwork of many other fine biographers. To their research and knowledge I owe a profound debt.

In the matter of language, the 1920s was a world away from our own politically conscious era. Young women were girls, blacks were often niggers, female actors were actresses, and even though this usage can grate on modern ears, I've opted to retain

ILLUSTRATIONS

CONTENTS

❧

For Fred and Oscar

Sarah Crichton Books
Farrar, Straus and Giroux
18 West 18th Street, New York 10011

Library of Congress Cataloging-in-Publication Data
Mackrell, Judith.
Flappers : six women of a dangerous generation / Judith Mackrell. —
1st American Edition.
    p. cm.
Includes bibliographical references and index.
ISBN 978-0-374-15608-4 (hardcover) — ISBN 978-1-4299-4294-2 (ebook)
1. Cooper, Diana, 1892–1986. 2. Cunard, Nancy, 1896–1965.
3. Bankhead, Tallulah, 1902–1968. 4. Fitzgerald, Zelda, 1900–1948.
5. Baker, Josephine, 1906–1975. 6. Lempicka, Tamara de, 1898–1980.
7. Women—United States—Biography. 8. Celebrities—United States—
Biography. 9. Artists—United States—Biography. 10. Women—
United States—Social life and customs—20th century. 11. Sex customs—
United States—History—20th century. 12. Sex role—United States—
History—20th century. 13. Popular culture—United States—History—
20th century. I. Title.
HQ1412 .M1633 2014
920.72—dc23
[B]
                                                        2013035397

Farrar, Straus and Giroux books may be purchased for educational,
business, or promotional use. For information on bulk purchases,
please contact the Macmillan Corporate and Premium Sales
Department at 1-800-221-7945, extension 5442, or write to
specialmarkets@macmillan.com.

www.fsgbooks.com
www.twitter.com/fsgbooks • www.facebook.com/fsgbooks

1   3   5   7   9   10   8   6   4   2

FLAPPERS

SIX WOMEN OF A
DANGEROUS GENERATION

JUDITH MACKRELL

SARAH CRICHTON BOOKS

FARRAR, STRAUS AND GIROUX

NEW YORK

FLAPPERS

created by Scott, and eventually by herself. As for Josephine, who became internationally famous as the physical incarnation of jazz, and the free syncopated energy of the Twenties, she made the most remarkable journey of all as she transcended the poverty of her childhood to become an icon of black music, and modernist art.

Of course, the six women in this book experienced the 1920s in exceptional ways. But what made them emblematic of their time was the spirit of audacity with which they reinvented themselves. The young women of this era weren't the first generation in history to seek a life beyond marriage and mother-hood; they were, however, the first significant group to claim it as a right. And from the way the flapper was written about and represented it was clear that, to many, she represented a pro-found social threat.

During the late nineteenth century the term flapper had still carried a suggestion of innocence, evoking the image of gawky, unfledged teenage girls, but even by the end of the war the term was acquiring connotations of brashness and defiance. In October 1919, *The Times* published a column about the new flapper, warning of the restive mood that was brewing among Britain's young female population. Two million of them had taken paid work during the war and a substantial number were determined to remain in employment, despite pressures to relin-quish their jobs to returning soldiers. The following year, the same paper went on to question the wisdom of extending voting rights to women under thirty, dismissing them as a single feckless type, the 'frivolous scantily-clad, jazzing flapper . . . to whom a dance, a new hat or a man with a car is of more importance than the fate of nations.'[5] Given the terrible decimation of Britain's young men during the war, newspapers also bristled with warn-ings of the destabilizing effect these flappers might have on the country, as an unprecedented generation of unmarried and independent women appeared to be hell-bent on having their own way.

In France, women would have to wait until 1944 to get the

vote; however that didn't inhibit the power of this post-war generation to dismay and disturb. Victor Margueritte's 1922 novel *La Garçonne* created a national scandal (and sold half a million copies) by recounting the adventures of his heroine, Monique, after she has ditched her worthless fiancé to embrace a life of lesbianism, drugs and single motherhood.

At the beginning of the decade the fascinating, defiant flapper was a type more read about in novels and newspapers than encountered on the street, but within a few years, she'd become the image to which hundreds of thousands of ordinary young women aspired. Fitzgerald satirized these would-be flappers in his description of Catherine, a minor character in his novel *The Great Gatsby*: '. . . a slender worldly girl of about thirty, with a solid, sticky bob of red hair, and a complexion powdered milky white. Her eyebrows had been plucked and then drawn on again at a more rakish angle . . . When she moved about there was an incessant clinking as innumerable pottery bracelets jingled up and down upon her arms.'[6]

Catherine exists in the novel only as a construction of flapper accessories and style; and to Fitzgerald in 1925 she symbolized the degree to which the transforming dream of the 1920s was fuelled as much by economics, the appetite for consumption, as it was by the lure of freedom. Within the competitive climate of post-war capitalism the new fun-seeking flapper with her dyed hair, bee-stung lips and Charleston frocks was proving to be a wonderful opportunity for business.

After a short post-war decline, the number of working women had risen sharply across the Western world (up to 500 per cent in parts of America), and those who were young and financially independent were opening up a lucrative market for the beauty and fashion industries. They were targeted with new brands of cosmetics and depilatories; with skin treatments that promised the rejuvenating magic of crushed almonds, pine bark, rose oil and hydrogen peroxide. Celebrities like Josephine were paid large sums to endorse them, for the profits to be made were immense. In 1915 American advertisers invested just $1.5 million in the beauty industry; by 1930 that sum had multiplied by ten. In 1907 the French chemist Eugène Schueller patented a new hair dye, which by 1930 had launched him and his company, L'Oréal, into one of France's most lucrative enterprises.

Never before had so many ordinary women been told that it was their right to look lovely. Dieting fads and slimming pills flooded the market, all promising to produce the narrow-hipped, flat-chested flapper silhouette. Before the war few respectable women smoked, but numbers rocketed when cigarettes were rebranded as a route to slenderness. In 1927 Lucky Strike launched an ad campaign that featured the actress Constance Talmadge with a cigarette in her hand. The accompanying slogan, 'Reach for a Lucky instead of a sweet', generated a 300 per cent rise in sales.

The fashion industry entered a similar boom. With designers like Coco Chanel and Jean Patou pioneering narrow shift dresses and short skirts, it was possible for modern technologies to imitate their designs with unparalleled cheapness and speed. (In 1913 an average of twenty square yards of fabric went into the making of a dress; by 1928 that had been scaled down to seven.) Garments created in a French atelier could be run up in factories and sold through shops, department stores and mail order catalogues on both sides of the Atlantic.* Madelaine Vionnet was the first of the European couturiers to make ready-to-wear designs that could be shipped direct to America. For those uncertain how to wear the new styles, a barrage of tips were available in women's magazines and newspaper columns. It was, in theory, a liberating democracy, yet the pressure to be fashion-able brought its own miseries. As early as 1920 Fitzgerald wrote about the plight of a socially maladroit girl who is persuaded to cut off her one beautiful asset, her long hair.† In real life, a fourteen-year-old from Chicago tried to gas herself because

---

* Sears in America, Freemans in Britain and La Redoute in France all did big business.
† The short story 'Bernice Bobs Her Hair'.

'other girls in her class rolled their stockings, had their hair bobbed and called themselves flappers', and she alone was refused permission by her parents.[7]

To some contemporary commentators this addiction to style was the mark of a superficial and self-absorbed generation. Samuel Hopkins Adams, in the foreword to his 1923 bestseller *Flaming Youth*,* anatomized the flapper as 'restless and seductive, greedy, discontented, unrestrained, a little morbid, more than a little selfish'. As she casually spent her money on a new powder compact or string of beads she also seemed shockingly a-political. She seemed oblivious of the battles that had so recently been fought on her behalf: the right to control her own wealth, to vote and to enter professions like the law. Even to wear the clothes of her choice. For decades, adherents of the British Rational Dress Society[†] – or the Aesthetic Dress Reform movement in Europe – had been ridiculed as cranks. Yet as they correctly claimed, the freedom to wear comfortable clothes was almost as crucial a right as universal suffrage. No woman could claim effective equality with a man while her organs were being slowly crushed by whalebone corsets, and her movements impeded by bustles and petticoats that added over a stone to her body weight.

But if the flapper seemed to her critics to be passive in her politics and selfish in her desires, to others she was celebrated as a new and necessary phase in feminism. The vote had been a public milestone on the journey towards emancipation, but just as important was the unfettering of women's private emotions. The American writer Dorothy Dunbar Bromley applauded this generation's ability to disengage from the traditional feminine virtues of sacrifice and duty. To her, their embrace of an 'inescapable inner compulsion to be individuals in their own right'[8] represented nothing less than a seismic shift in female consciousness.

---

* Published under his pseudonym Warner Fabian.
† Founded in 1881, one of its modest demands was that a woman's underwear, without shoes, should weigh no more than seven pounds.

For birth-control campaigners like Marie Stopes and Margaret Sanger, the key battle was for sexual freedom. Change was slow: pre-marital sex was still far from the norm for women in the 1920s, but while only 14 per cent of American women admitted to it in 1900, by 1925 the number had risen to 39 per cent. Contraception for women was drastically enhanced with the invention of the Dutch Cap; divorce was very gradually gaining social acceptance, and much else that had been shadowy in the sexual lives of women was more openly acknowledged. The fashionable chic attached to lesbianism in the 1920s might not have been a true reflection of public opinion, but it saw many more women daring to identify and acknowledge their sexual tastes. One of the most brazen was Mercedes de Acosta, whose tally of lovers was said to include Isadora Duncan, Greta Garbo, Marlene Dietrich and Tallulah Bankhead. 'Say what you will about Mercedes,' commented her friend Alice B. Toklas, 'she's had the most important women of the twentieth century.'[9]

To Dorothy Dunbar Bromley, it was the flapper's willingness to assert her own desires that made her key not only to feminism but to the larger spirit of the age. Traditional notions of reverence, obligation and prudence had been devalued by the war. As Aldous Huxley wrote to his father in late 1923, it was as though his generation had experienced a 'violent disruption of almost all the standards, conventions and values current in the previous epoch'.[10] From one perspective that moral disruption left its survivors precariously untethered to any solid sense of principle or place. Gertrude Stein famously described them as 'the lost generation'. Yet from another perspective this ideological weightlessness felt like liberty. It gave the young permission to turn their back on the past and focus on their own brightly lit present.

The present moment was pretty much all that Zelda Fitzgerald cared about in 1920 as she rode down 5th Avenue on the bonnet of a taxi. That and her determination to be unlike all 'the little women' back home in Montgomery.

Seventeen-year-old Tallulah felt much the same as she swaggered around New York, quipping, 'I'm a lesbian, what do you do?' So, too, did Nancy as she drank jugs of cheap white wine and courted scandal on the arm of her black lover, or Josephine as she saw her image blazoned across Paris.

All these women lived many of their private moments on the public stage. Having made their names as writers, painters or performers, as well as popular celebrities, the things they said and did, the clothes they wore, were routinely reported in the press and had a widespread impact on other women. Yet stylish, talented and extraordinary as these six were, to imagine their lives now one has to look past the glamour and glare of their fame. Often they feel closest to us when they were struggling and uncertain. None of them had role models to follow as they grappled with the implications of their independence. Their mothers and grandmothers could not advise them how to combine sexual freedom with love, or how to combine their public image with personal happiness. Tallulah and Josephine, who wanted enduring love, were duped time and again by grifters and sensation seekers, interested only in their money and their éclat. Nancy, trying to live as fearlessly and frankly as a man, was dogged with the reputation of a nymphomaniac. And while all six women attempted marriage, only Diana became adept at the compromises involved. Children were even more complicated. Tamara de Lempicka could never shake off accusations from her family that, in her determination to experience everything for the sake of her art, she had become an unnatural, even destructive mother.

By the end of the 1920s and the beginning of the 1930s all six women were reaching critical points of transition in their lives. This book, too, ends on the cusp of the old and new decade. It was the point at which the experimental party spirit of the Twenties was coming into collision with economic crisis, with the extreme politics of communism and fascism and the gathering clouds of war. And just as this moment heralded the winding down of the jazz age, so too it marked the end of the flapper era. While some of that generation were settling into more traditional lives, others were simply too tired or too damaged to sustain their former momentum.

Short-lived as it seemed, however, the Twenties had created a historic shift for women. So many had tried to flex their freedom in unprecedented ways, so many had stood up against those who judged them. Some of their behaviour was self-promoting and silly – Tallulah turning cartwheels along a London pavement; Zelda throwing herself fully dressed into a fountain; some of it was destructive – Nancy breaking hearts and making herself ill as she experimented with lovers across London and Paris – but it was never less than valiant. In their various attempts to live and die in their own way, the flappers represented a genuinely subversive force. Willing to run the risks of their independence as well as enjoy its pleasures, there were good reasons for them to be perceived as women of a dangerous generation.

Chapter One

DIANA

Two months after Britain went to war against Germany Lady Diana Manners was being chauffeured across London towards Guy's Hospital and her new vocation as a volunteer nurse. It was barely four miles from her family's Mayfair home to the hospital in Southwark, yet Diana was conscious that, to her distraught mother sitting in the car beside her, it was a journey into the wilderness.

During tearfully protracted arguments Diana had tried to convince her mother that enlisting as a VAD (member of the Voluntary Aid Detachment) was not a lone, wilful act. Among the thousands of women who were queuing to serve their country, a number were Diana's own friends, and some were volunteering for much more arduous duties: driving ambulances, working in munitions factories or nursing at the Front.

Yet to the Duchess of Rutland, the idea of her daughter working in one of London's public hospitals, making tea and washing patients, was barely less squalid than her volunteering to walk the streets as a prostitute. As the family Rolls-Royce crossed Southwark Bridge and began to nose its way through grimy cobbled streets, jostled by crowds, assailed by smells from the docks and from the piles of festering rubbish, the Duchess's worst fears seemed justified. Years later Diana could still recall the detail of that stiff, silent drive. The dark drizzle spattering against the car's windscreen; the stricken expression on her mother's face; the momentary faltering of her own courage as they pulled up outside the gaunt, grey façade of Guy's.

It was not a welcoming scene. A huddle of nurses was crossing the wide courtyard, heads bowed against the blustery wind, skirts whipped around their legs. Equally drear was the expression worn by the elderly housekeeper as she opened the door and led the way silently upstairs to the room where Diana was to sleep. There was nothing as frivolous as a full-length mirror among its bare furnishings, yet as she changed into her nurse's uniform the look in her mother's eyes told Diana that, to the Duchess at least, she appeared hideous.

She felt guilty at the pain she was causing, but she was exhilarated, too. Even though the collar of her mauve and white striped dress was starched to a punitive stiffness and the coarse, regulation cotton felt harsh after the chiffon and silk to which she was accustomed, these discomforts brought a sense of transformation. When Diana tied her shoelaces and tightened her belt it was with the knowledge that for the first time in twenty-two years she was asserting some control over her life.

Apart from the death of her older brother Haddon when she was two, and the misery of being confined to bed when she was ten by a rare form of muscular atrophy,* Diana had known little beyond family parties, seaside holidays and servants whilst growing up. But there were constraints as well as privileges. Her family's expectation that she would marry into money and rank required the dowry of an unblemished reputation, and even when she regarded herself as adult, every hour of her waking life remained, theoretically, under scrutiny. She wasn't permitted to spend a night away from home, except at the house parties of approved friends; she wasn't supposed to walk by herself in the street, nor dine alone with a man. She'd developed a hundred ways of dodging her chaperones and keeping certain activities

---

* It was probably bulbar paralysis, known then as Erb's disease.

secret, yet such deceit had long ceased to be amusing. It was simply demeaning.

Life at Guy's would be very hard, with long days of menial drudgery hedged around with dozens of petty restrictions. But still it spelled deliverance. Not only would Diana be living away from home for the first time, but during her precious off-duty hours she would be free to do what she wanted and see whomever she chose.

This hunger for independence was shared by many of the other 46,000 British women who signed up to become VADs,* and by millions of others around the world. When the European powers declared war they inadvertently held out to women a momentous promise of freedom. The American journalist Mabel Potter Daggett spoke too optimistically and too soon when she declared, 'We may write it down in history that on August 4, 1914 the door of the Doll's House opened', but for many that was the great expectation and the hope.[1]

In Britain, the flood of recruits to the Volunteer Aid Detachment was a phenomenon of enormous interest to the press, with stories and photographs of the richest and most beautiful regularly featured in society columns. And Diana would rapidly become one of the most prominent. She seemed to the public to be practically a princess, having been born to one of the oldest families in Britain (the Rutland title dated back to 1525, the Crawford title on her mother's side to 1398), and also to one of the richest. In 1906, when her father, Sir Henry Manners, had inherited his dukedom, he took possession not only of thousands of acres of land, but of country houses, farms, coal mines and dozens of entire villages.

The idea of Diana emerging from this palatial life to nurse the poor and wounded was enormously appealing to the British, and throughout the war she was showcased in many, mistily sentimental press photos. D.W. Griffiths featured her in his 1918

---

* VAD's weren't paid until 1916, when the rising toll of casualties necessitated a doubling in the number of nurses, and wages became a necessary inducement to attract working women.

propaganda film *Hearts of the World* because, he said, she was 'the most beloved woman in England';[2] she was enshrined in a wartime adaptation of the music-hall song 'Burlington Bertie' with the lines, 'I'll eat a banana/With Lady Diana/Aristocracy working at Guys.'

Yet even more fascinating to the public than Diana's ancestry was her life as a socialite. Ever since she had come out as a debutante in 1910, the suppers and nightclubs she attended, the outfits she wore and the amusing chitchat attributed to her were regularly reported in magazines like *The Lady* and in the gossip columns of the press. Her reputation extended far beyond London: the *Aberdeen Journal* confidently informed its readers that 'no fancy dress ball was complete without the presence of Lady Diana' and across the Atlantic, the *New York American* described her as a necessary embellishment to smart and artistic circles.[3]

Diana's originality, her perceived cleverness and beauty were all that her mother Violet had hoped for. Despite her public commitment to family tradition, the Duchess had artistic, almost bohemian instincts, which she had passed on to her daughters. If Diana, in 1914, was restless for a life beyond her allotted destiny, it was her mother who was partly responsible.

As a young woman Violet had been a willowy beauty, the dark, pooling intensity of eyes and the pale auburn cloud of her hair lending her a dreamy, otherworldly distinction. She was sympathetic to the Aesthetic movement in dress, disdaining the elaboration of bustles and puffed sleeves for a simpler style of gown, and affecting a Romantic spontaneity, with lace scarves fluttering at her neck and wrists, posies of wild flowers pinned to her waist, the family tiara worn back to front to hold up her mass of hair. She was clever about the things that concerned her. As a key member of a group of late nineteenth-century intellectuals, nicknamed 'the Souls'*, Violet talked about art and berated the

---

* Their membership included artists, writers and politicians, including Lord Curzon, Arthur Balfour, Alfred Lyttelton and George Frederic Watts.

philistinism of the Victorian age. She was also much admired for her own amateur gifts, with several of her busts and her silver-point and pencil portraits exhibited in London galleries.

A reputation for being different, even mildly rebellious, had attached itself to her. While Violet deferred to the formal duties of a Duke's wife, she clearly preferred intimate suppers to grand dinners and court events. More subversively still she counted actors like Sir Herbert Beerbohm Tree and his wife Maud among her intimate friends. Even at the beginning of the twentieth century, this was odd behaviour for a duchess. However elevated the Trees might be within their profession, they were still theatre people, whose circle had included the scandalous Oscar Wilde. Lord and Lady Salisbury, who lived one door away from the Manners' London home, in Arlington Street, were certainly wary of moral contagion. They refused to let their children visit the house, because of the 'foreign actresses and people like that' who might be encountered there.[4]

In the raising of her three daughters – Marjorie, Violet (Letty) and Diana – Violet also raised eyebrows: she took the girls on regular trips to the London theatre and encouraged in them a precocious independence of spirit. Diana, the young-est, had been born in August 1892 and for several years had been a plain, but interestingly fanciful child. She'd imagined herself a 'necromancer', filling her bedroom with bottles that were 'coloured and crusted with incandescent sediment from elixiral experiments',[5] and because her mother liked 'only the beautiful in everything'[6] she'd been encouraged in her fancies. The governesses who'd educated Diana and her sisters (their brother John was sent off to boarding school) had been in-structed to skip over 'commonplace' subjects like mathematics and geography and focus instead on poetry, singing, embroid-ery and art.

History was also favoured, especially family history, and from childhood Diana's imagination had been shaped by stories of her ancestral past and by the imposing enchantment of Belvoir Castle, the Rutland family home. From early childhood she had

played among its castellated towers and labyrinthine passage-
ways, its vaulted roomfuls of Gobelin tapestries and Dutch paintings.* She had grown up inside a privileged kingdom, buffered
by centuries of entitlement. And despite the romantic informality
of Violet's influence, the amateur theatricals she organized, the
artistic guests she entertained, Diana and her siblings knew both
the glamour and the burden of feeling themselves to be a breed
apart.

By the time she approached her fourteenth birthday Diana
had developed into a pretty, spirited teenager, and the clarity of
her pale skin and large blue eyes promised she might even
become beautiful. That summer she was invited to holiday in
Norfolk with the Beerbohm Trees and their three daughters; to
her joy, a group of Oxford students were also staying in the
same village. Maud and Herbert tolerantly gave permission for
shared suppers and picnics, and for three weeks Diana revelled
in the company of these clever, good-looking boys. There were
games, quizzes and flirtations, during which she 'showed off
madly', and she slipped out to the chemist for a bottle of
peroxide to bleach her hair a silvery gold. Even though she felt
she was 'spinning plates' in her desperate need to impress, she
knew that among these boys she had found her métier.

Afterwards she wrote to one of them: 'Brancaster was heavenly, wasn't it. I nearly cried when I left. Do for pity's sake let's
all meet again soon ... When one makes friends, I think one
ought to go on being friends hard and not let it drop.'[7] Further
letters were exchanged, there were meetings in the houses of
mutual acquaintances and Diana, who had always been so passionately attached to family and home, now hugged to herself
the knowledge that she had acquired a circle of her own friends.
'I wanted first to be loved, and next I wanted to be clever,' she
recalled, and to make herself worthy of her boys she began

---

* Much of the castle had been recently rebuilt but to Diana, visiting her grandparents there before it passed on to her father, Belvoir seemed ancient.

begging her mother for lessons in Greek and music,* while alone
in her bedroom she practised clever, romantic bon mots in front
of her mirror.[8]

Inspired by vanity and hope, she matured fast. There were
appalling blanks in her knowledge (it was left to Iris Tree, four
years her junior, to give her the most basic instruction in the
facts of life), yet Diana's brain was teeming with poetry,
impressions and ideas, and sometimes she could appear obnox-
iously forward. One evening, playing after-dinner guessing
games with her mother's friends, she grew impatient with the
slowness of one of the players. 'Use your brain, Mr Balfour; use
your *brain*,' she snapped at him.[9] He was the former prime
minister and she was about fifteen.

When Diana met Vita Sackville-West at a country house party,
she desperately envied the older girl for her literary talent. 'She
is an aristocrat, rollingly rich, who writes French poetry with more
ease than I lie on a sofa.'[10] Feeling that she had no extraordinary
gifts of her own, she aimed instead to develop an extraordinary style. At Belvoir she painted her bedroom walls black to
contrast with her crimson bedspread; she made artful groupings
of candles, religious paintings and dried flowers; she also transformed her clothes. In 1907 'all things Greek' were in fashion,
and dutifully Diana experimented with sandals and draperies,
pinning a silver crescent moon in her hair. Dissatisfied with the
appearance of her naked feet she tugged hopefully at her second
toe, attempting to induce a more 'Grecian' length. Her new bible
was *L'Art et la Mode*, the French magazine to which her sisters
subscribed, whose pages were filled with the revolutionary designs
of Paul Poiret and Mariano Fortuny.

With a yearning intentness, she studied pictures of languid
female models, their fascinatingly uncorseted bodies draped in
silks and diaphanous gowns. She thrilled to the element of

---

* She also took a short course in Italian and German at the Berlitz language
school, to groom her into 'une petite fille modèle'.

theatre in Poiret and Fortuny's clothes, their jewel-bright colours and suggestive flavour of the Orient. Most British girls her age were still aspiring to the fresh and curvy style of the Gibson Girl – hair piled high, waist cinched tight to emphasize a full bosom – but Diana was determined that her new adult self should be far more avant-garde.

Around this time her mother was visited by the playwright Henri Bernstein and his companion Princess Murat. Diana was entranced by the Princess and her stories of sophisticated French society, which were 'totally different from anything we knew',[11] and she was even more entranced by her wardrobe. Obligingly, the Princess allowed Diana to examine her Fortuny dresses, created from brilliantly coloured, exquisitely pleated silk that shimmered to the touch. But what Diana coveted most was the Princess's Poiret-designed tunic, and she was determined to make a copy. It was a simple enough design for Diana's school-room sewing skills, and the result was so successful that she made others to sell to her friends, each with a different trim of ribbon, braid or fur. It proved to be a profitable enterprise and Diana squirrelled away the cash she earned: despite the family's ances-tral wealth, the Manners children received no pocket money of their own.

Diana continued adding to her wardrobe, designing clothes that were sometimes eccentrically experimental, but to her eyes rivetingly modish. As she refashioned her appearance, however, she became self-consciously critical of her figure. These new fluid fashions from Europe were liberating women from the corset, but they followed the line of the body so closely that they imposed a new tyranny. 'Banting' or 'slenderizing' were becom-ing de rigueur, and when Diana studied herself in the mirror she despaired at the 'round, white, slow, lazy and generally . . . unappetising blancmange' she saw reflected there.[12]

Edwardian Britain was collectively embracing the idea of physical fitness. Cycling, golf, tennis and bathing were much in vogue, part of the brisk tempo of the new century, but Diana's regime of self-improvement was unusually strenuous. She went for long runs around the grounds of Belvoir, jigged furiously to the gramophone – a precious acquisition given to her by the opera singer Dame Nellie Melba – and pounded away at an old punch bag. The following year she discovered a more creative discipline in dancing. London was newly inspired by Isadora Duncan, the radical American dancer who had become as famous for performing barefoot and uncorseted as she had become for the unfettered, expressive beauty of her movements. Feminism, fashion and the theatre all reflected Duncan's influence, and it was to a performance of one of her many imitators, Maud Allan, that Violet took Diana in 1908.

This was, in many ways, an odd choice for a mother and daughter outing, given the rumours that circulated around Allan, about her past career as a lingerie model, about her publication of a sex manual and about her many lovers, male and female. In addition, the solo she was dancing in London, *The Vision of Salome*, was a work of quite blatant eroticism. Wearing little but a transparent harem skirt and jewel-encrusted breastplate, Allan portrayed the seductive powers of her heroine with a sensuality that was advertised as more shocking than anything seen on the London stage. Publicity pamphlets circulated by the Palace Theatre promised a performance of unbridled passion: 'desire . . . perverse and amoral flames from her eyes and bursts in hot gusts from her scarlet mouth'; her body undulates 'like a silver snake eager for its prey'.[13]

Most deviant would be the climactic scene in which Allan toyed with the severed head of John the Baptist, kissing it slowly and lasciviously on the lips. To some viewers Allan was nothing more than a burlesque dancer with artistic pretensions, but to others she was a potent cultural force. The latest in a line of Salome interpreters – following on from Oscar Wilde's play and Richard Strauss's opera – she was regarded as a beautifully perverse and amoral rebuttal of Victorian prudery. To her many thousands of female fans she offered an intoxicatingly public representation of their sexuality.

In Edwardian Britain, certainly in the world that Diana

inhabited, the eroticism of women remained discreetly masked – the theories of Havelock Ellis had yet to be widely read and Marie Stopes's revelatory advice on love and orgasm had yet to be written. For those who knew, or suspected themselves of sharing, Allan's liberated tastes, it was nearly impossible to declare themselves. While lesbians were technically not outside the law (Queen Victoria had refused to believe that women could be lovers, and never approved a law to criminalize female homosexuality) it was difficult, even dangerous, for them to reveal their sexual preference in public.

Allan's Salome, a woman brazenly in control of her own desires, became a coded rallying point. Women staged private parties in which they dressed up and danced in imitation of Allan's voluptuous style (the male orchestras accompanying them remained discreetly hidden behind potted palms). When an American commentator noted that Allan had encouraged a dangerous tendency towards 'bohemianism and dancing in London', his more knowing readers picked up the sexual subtext – Margot Asquith, wife of the prime minister, was rumoured to be one of Allan's lovers. A decade later, when an extreme right-wing politician, Noel Pemberton Billing, embarked on a crusade to expose degenerate and unpatriotic elements within the British aristocracy, he accused Allan of spreading 'The Cult of the Clitoris' among the nation's women.

The Duchess was certainly not part of that cult, nor would she hear talk of it. As a general rule she shrank from anything she considered vulgar; when she suspected her oldest daughter Marjorie of using cosmetics (still frowned on before the war) she could not even bring herself to utter the word rouge, merely touching her finger interrogatively to her daughter's cheek. In art, however, Violet saw only beauty. And when she encouraged Diana to return to Allan's performances she was simply imagining her daughter being inspired to imitate Allan's expressive grace.

Diana was eager to try, and the following year she enrolled in classes to study Russian folk dance and classical ballet.* The unfamiliar discipline made her legs ache and her toes hurt, but she liked the new alertness of her body, and most of all the slender shape it was acquiring. By 1911 she had acquired the confidence to pose semi-naked for her brother John, who was a keen amateur photographer. Although she had her back to the camera, the mirror held up to her face plainly revealed her identity. Diana Manners, looking slender, elegant and defiantly self-possessed.

Diana's programme of self-improvement was yielding results, but the world around her was proving harder to shape to her imagination. By the time she'd reached seventeen she'd become furiously irritated by her childish status: she could not yet put up her hair, go to dances, or see any of her friends without the elaborate organization of parents or governesses. Her Oxford boys were graduating into the real world, and Diana's longing to join them was inscribed over and over again in her diary: 'Only one year before I'll be out – and – out OUT.'[14]

But coming 'out' did not provide the excitement she'd hoped for. The 1910 season was unusually muted, as the death of King Edward VII led to a suspension of court functions, including the formal presentation of debutantes.† Far more disappointing, however, were the people in whose company Diana found herself, during what proved to be a very long and very dull summer.

Most of her fellow debutantes were raw, shy girls: 'innocent of powder . . . deplorably dressed, with their shapeless wispy hair held by crooked combs'.[15] Most of the young men before whom they were being paraded as possible wives, seemed to her equally awkward and insipid. Diana's ideal had been formed by the men in her Oxford circle: Alan Parsons, Raymond Asquith and Patrick Shaw Stewart, who were clever, funny and read poetry. None of

---

* Her teacher was Lydia Kyasht.
† It was postponed to the following year.

the Guards officers, viscounts or earls with whom she danced that summer could compare.

Neither did they come close to inspiring the rapture Diana experienced when Diaghilev's Ballets Russes came to London the following June. She'd been spellbound by the sinuous choreography and haunting music of works like *Scheherazade* and by the blazing colour of Léon Bakst's stage designs: here at least, she felt, the world aligned itself with her most brilliant imaginings. In 1912, when she saw the Russian opera, led by the majestic singing of Feodor Chaliapin, it was as if 'comets whizzed across the unfamiliar sky, the stars danced'.[16]

That summer, too, Diana discovered another kind of theatre. She and her mother were in Venice and had become acquainted with the fabulously rich and eccentric Marchesa Luisa Casati. The Marchesa lived in a curious, low palazzo* on the Grand Canal, surrounded by a darkly overgrown garden and a menagerie of animals; and the extravagant style in which she held court was, for Diana, a 'glorious shock'[17] to her imagination.

When she and the Duchess were invited to their first party at the palazzo, they were ferried there in one of Casati's gondolas. A pair of near-naked slaves met them on arrival, one throwing oil onto a brazier to send a flare of greeting into the night sky, the other ringing a massive gong. Casati, a modern Medusa with a death-white mask of powder and red, hennaed curls, was also waiting on the Palazzo terrace. Posing with statuesque grace in the middle of an enormous bowl of tuberoses, she silently handed a waxen flower to each guest in turn.

After the predictable formalities of English entertaining, this decadent spectacle was miraculous to Diana. It was everything for which she had hungered whilst drinking fruit cup and dancing quadrilles during her season. Yet even London was finally beginning to catch up with her fantasies. There were

---

* The Palazzo Venier dei Leoni; it was later bought by Peggy Guggenheim and is now the Venice Guggenheim Museum.

changes stirring in the city, a breath of cosmopolitan energy that came with the first exhibition of post-impressionist paintings, with the radical psychoanalytic theories of Sigmund Freud, and, infinitely more exciting to Diana, the appearance of a new kind of nightclub.

The Cave of the Golden Calf, a tiny basement just off Regent Street, fashionably decorated with Ballets Russes-inspired murals, was one of several establishments that opened in 1912 that offered a doorway to the modern world. Negro bands played music that was alive with the exoticism of America – the honking stridency of St Louis; the twang of the plantation South; the yearning echo of the blues. Cocktails such as Pink Ladies were served and women were not only encouraged to drink openly, but to wear lipstick, gamble and smoke. Diana was in her element. She might have had to bribe or trick her chaperone of the evening, but once inside the smoky darkness, she felt free. Crowded onto the dance floor of a club she could abandon herself to the rhythms of the Turkey Trot or Grizzly Bear, rag-time dances that jerked invisible wires inside her body, made her hips sway and her cheeks flush. Skirts were being worn shorter this season, a few inches from the floor, and as Diana danced she noted with pride the discreet flash of her own silk-stockinged ankles.

She was equally proud of her new expertise as a smoker, although like many women she was addicted less to the head rush of nicotine than to the elegance of her cigarette holder – an accessory designed to prevent flecks of tobacco catching on painted lips, yet ripe with the flirtatious possibilities of a fan. Late at night, when the sky was just beginning to lighten and Diana drove home in a taxi with one of her admirers, the driver would often be instructed to take a detour, as she very decorously allowed herself to be kissed.

Such activities would have been considered distressingly com-promising by Violet – and that, for Diana, was largely the point. Her desire to become 'incomparable' was no longer coloured by her mother's standards; she wanted to be bold and bad – 'Unlike-

Other-People'.[18] As she remembered it, 'There was a general
new look in everything in those years before the first war – a
Poiret-Bakst blazon and a budding freedom of behaviour that
was breaking out at the long last end of Victorianism. We felt it
and revelled in it.'[19]

On the nights that Diana was able to escape her chaperones
there was not only dancing in the Golden Calf, but illegal,
moonlit swims in the Serpentine or the Thames; expeditions to
pubs in the Limehouse docks and the occasional weaving ride on
the back of a motorbike. Her new sacred texts were by Aubrey
Beardsley, Baudelaire, Oscar Wilde and Max Beerbohm, and on
their inspiration, she and her friends began calling themselves,
with only a hint of irony, the Corrupt Coterie. They coveted new
sensations and transgressive ideas whilst affecting a style of
cynicism and profanity: 'Our pride was to be unafraid of words,
unshocked by drink and unashamed of "decadence" and gambling.'[20]

In reality much of the Coterie's behaviour was little more than
cultivated naughtiness. They invented after-dinner games, like
Breaking the News – acting out scenes in which well-known
women were informed of the deaths of their children. They
staged exhibitionist stunts: Denis Anson faked epileptic fits;
Maurice Baring set his hair alight during games of Risk; while
Diana herself braved official censure by attending a formal
reception at the Duke of Westminster's with a set of fake medals
pinned mockingly to her dress.

These mild acts of rebellion, however, brought a euphoric
sense of daring and also a degree of public notoriety. The fact
that several members of the Coterie had eminent parents made
them very interesting to the press, and Lady Diana Manners was
most interesting of all. Inwardly she might feel herself to be a
'blancmange', unable to match the cleverness and originality of
her friends, but outwardly she seemed to scintillate. In a roomful of people it was Diana who held the floor in after-dinner
games of charades or parentage, who galvanized everybody into

impromptu dances to the gramophone, who scattered smart nonsense around the conversation.

People vied to secure her for their parties, because she was a guaranteed source of fun, and because she had also become beautiful, tall and very slender now, with a classical oval face and a dreamily opaque gaze (actually a consequence of mild short-sightedness) that was offset by her extreme social animation. When the writer Enid Bagnold first saw her descending a flight of stairs and sweeping the room with her 'blind blue stare' she recalled being 'shocked – in the sense of electricity'.[21] To young admirers who sent love letters and queued up to dance, Diana was 'a goddess', 'an orchid among cowslips'. Older men were no less susceptible. One of her suitors was the legendarily wealthy American financier George Gordon Moore, who insisted that on a word from Diana he would divorce his wife. He seemed to move 'in a shower of gold', courting her with such astonishing presents as an ermine coat, a gigantic sapphire (reputed to have belonged to Catherine the Great), even a pet monkey called Armide with a diamond waist belt and chain.[22]

Diana thrived on both the presents and her notoriety. In response to an ironic marriage proposal from Duff Cooper, she described herself proudly as 'very decadent, and theatrical & inclined to look fast – attributes no man likes in his wife'.[23] She was also beginning to attract malicious comment. Those who remained insulated against her electricity criticized Diana as a flirt and 'a scalp hunter', and she received anonymous letters accusing her of corrupting the young men around her.

In truth, Diana had remained far more chaste in her behaviour than some of her peers. The publication in 1909 of H.G. Wells's novel *Anne Veronica* had highlighted a trend among advanced young women to regard their virginity as a vexing encumbrance to adulthood. When the twenty-two-year-old Enid Bagnold allowed herself to be seduced by the writer Frank Harris, in 1909, she was delirious with relief. The painter Nina Hamnett wanted a plaque to be mounted on the house where she lost her own virginity. But if Diana was more cautious, she was also a far more public personality than these women. And in early 1914 the backlash against her supposed bad behaviour gathered momentum when the Coterie suffered its first brush with death. Gustav Hamel, a Swedish amateur flyer and racing driver who was close to the group, crashed his private plane during a flight from France to London. Shortly afterwards Denis Anson was drowned in the Thames during a late-night swimming party. 'Mad youth' was blamed by the press for both fatalities, and it was Diana who was identified as the prime instigator.

The report of Anson's funeral appeared under the headline DIANA'S LOVE, and rumours spread through London that both Denis and Gustav had died while showing off for her benefit. Diana, already grief-stricken, suffered her first frightening experience of social rejection. Her name was dropped from the list for that summer's Guards Ball,[24] and people who had known her since childhood joined in the general condemnation. Lady Desborough, the mother of her friends Julian and Billy Grenfell, refused for a time to have her in her house, and Margot Asquith was loud in condemning her as a heartless flirt.

All this was very alarming for the Duchess. Over two years had passed since Diana's season, and she was increasingly anxious about her youngest daughter's prospects. The acceptable gap dividing youth from awkward spinsterhood was a narrow one, and it was intolerable to Violet that Diana might be seen to be unmarriageable. She still held unswervingly to the belief that wedlock was a woman's sole source of security. If Diana could marry well and produce the necessary son and heir, she would then be free to embark on whatever private projects and love affairs she chose. Sir Henry had not been Violet's own great love, nor she his: in accordance with centuries of upper-class pragmatism the two had discreetly found passion outside their marriage, Sir Henry with his mistresses and his fly fishing; Violet with her lover Harry Cust.

This cultured, handsome man, 'the Rupert Brooke of our day' according to Lady Horner, had for several years been the adored centre of Violet's universe.[25] She saw him in the late afternoon, when she could claim to be paying social calls. And constricted though the affair was, it had suited Violet well, allowing her to compartmentalize her life between duty and love. Such a balance, she assumed, would work equally for Diana as it would for her two other daughters. Both Letty and Marjorie had already found satisfactory husbands: Ego Charteris, son of the Earl of Wemyss, and Charlie Paget, now Marquess of Anglesey. Diana was the most beautiful of the three – Prince Paul of Yugoslavia had paid court to her, as had Lord Rocksavage – and Violet believed she could secure the most brilliant match of all. The Prince of Wales might be nearly three years younger than Diana, but a long engagement was always possible. Within the royal family itself there was enthusiasm for the match, for Diana's popularity was regarded as a potentially useful asset to the throne. As for Violet, she couldn't think of anyone who might make a more beautiful future Queen.

Yet Diana seemed uninterested in anyone but her own close circle, none of whom Violet counted as brilliant matches, and anxiety made the Duchess more vigilant and critical than she intended. The rule of the chaperone was a fact of life for all respectable unmarried women – even those sufficiently independent to attend university were not permitted into public lectures on their own – but Diana believed her own levels of confinement were absurd. The only hotel she was permitted to enter was the Ritz, which was just around the corner from the family's London home. Every night the Duchess kept her bedroom door open to monitor the hour at which Diana returned, and the following day she expected an account of whom her daughter had danced with, who had accompanied her and who had driven her home.

Diana loved her mother, but her patience was running out, and by now she had acquired a piece of knowledge that made the Duchess's vigilance look absurdly hypocritical. She had been eighteen when Edward Horner blundered into telling her the truth about her mother's affair with Harry Cust and, even more startlingly, let slip that Harry was widely assumed to be Diana's biological father. The physical evidence was compelling, Diana's fair colouring and the shape of her face suggested a clear genetic resemblance, and once Diana was confronted with it she claimed to accept the revelation with barely a struggle. She had always liked Harry, and insisted that she found it amusing to think of herself a 'Living Monument of Incontinence'.[26]

Yet it was still a shock, and it left her feeling more distanced, more questioning and more restless for escape. She was by then just twenty-two. A day could still be made 'iridescent', 'intoxicating' by a new dress or a ragtime tune, she could still relish the satisfaction of love letters, compliments and press cuttings. Yet beneath it all she felt the 'grim monotony'[27] of a life where she remained as financially dependent and physically constrained as a child. It left her with a vague and discomfiting ennui that she couldn't even name, let alone address.

The notion that there might be some larger political context to her dissatisfaction was entirely foreign to Diana. As a child, she'd declared herself fervently grateful to have been born a girl because 'somebody will always look after me'.[28] As an adult she felt no identification with the suffragettes who had faced prison, even death, in their battle for the vote. At best she pitied them, at worse she mocked. During a country house party, Diana and her cousin Angie Manners staged the 'hilarious' stunt of dressing up in the purple, white and green colours of the WSPU, climbing on top of a garden gazebo and pelting male onlookers with cardboard biscuit boxes. Yet for all her political apathy, Diana would probably have concurred with the feminist Agatha Evans that there was a grim predictability in the lives of women who were 'required to be gorgeous decorative and dumb' while seeking husbands, and thereafter condemned to be 'married matronly and motherly'.[29]

There were exceptions: Diana's own mother was hardly matronly: some of the richer, more ambitious hostesses she encountered, such as the Marchesa Casati, Lady Cunard, or Lady Ripon, wielded some considerable social power. Perhaps if Diana had found a husband to suit both herself and her mother

she might have become another Lady Ripon, a patron to the
Russian ballet, or hostess to some of the key cultural circles in
London. But in August 1914, Britain went to war and Diana,
along with the rest of the population, found her life and expectations thrown drastically off course.

She had been horrified and taken off guard by the declaration
of war. Cocooned among her own small concerns she'd paid little
attention to the assassination of Archduke Franz Ferdinand, in
June, nor understood its effect on Europe's political fault lines.
She was far less well informed than the twenty-year-old under-
graduate, Vera Brittain, who pondered fearfully in her diary
what a modern war would be like: 'Attack is possible by earth,
water & air & the destruction attainable by the modern war
machines used by the armies is unthinkable and past imagination'.[30] And she knew much less than the crowd of women who
flocked to London's Kingsway Hall to denounce the war as the
product of male rapacity and aggression.

But while Diana hoped that war might still be averted (naively
wondering if the Coterie's most influential friends might persuade Asquith to organize an international peace treaty), she
couldn't help but thrill to the enormity of this new drama and its
liberating possibilities. Her first instinct had been to volunteer as
a nurse in one of the Red Cross field hospitals close to the battle
lines. Sentimentally, she cherished the idea of being near her
male friends, who were already signing up for officer training.
Competitively, she was determined not to be outdone by others
she knew who were planning to nurse in France – among them
Rosemary Leveson-Gower, who was engaged to her brother
John, and her cousin Angie. And romantically, she believed she
would have the adventure of her life.

Violet, however, was adamant in her refusal. She had never
fully recovered from the death of Haddon, her first and most
beloved child, and she could not countenance any threat to
Diana. She was convinced her daughter would end up raped
and left for dead by drunken soldiers; at the very least she would

be working in appalling conditions. Rumours were already in circulation of the horrors facing young British VADs – one volunteer wrote home of having almost no hot water or light at the Salles Military Hospital in Saumur, and of nursing alongside filthy, disreputable orderlies, most of them soldiers who were 'too mad or too bad to fight'.[31] But Diana would not be budged from her determination to volunteer somewhere, so in October, angry, stubborn and wrung out from arguing, she embarked on her new life at Guy's.

Most recruits found it rigorous. To Diana, coming from the spacious luxury of Belvoir and Arlington Street, it took all her courage to survive the first few days. From six in the morning, when the light bulb above her bed was automatically switched on, to ten fifteen at night, she was obedient to the orders of the professional nurses who patrolled the clattering, sterile wards. No allowances were made for her lack of experience as she disinfected surgical trays and handled bedpans. She was expected to work uncomplainingly through chilblains, swollen ankles, period pains and a level of fatigue she had never experienced before.

She was also thrust straight into the stink and gore of medical emergencies. Diana had tried to prepare herself by going into the kitchen at Arlington Street to watch a hare being eviscerated for the evening meal, but nothing could minimize the trauma of her first patients: a woman who'd had a cancerous tumour sliced out of her chin, another left with a post-operative wound in her side 'from which a stream of green pus oozed slowly'.[32]

For Diana, the challenge of moderating her revulsion was complicated by social factors. She'd had little contact with anyone outside her own class, aside from family servants, and she found it impossible to sympathize with the more self-pitying of her male patients. She had been raised to believe in the virtue of the stiff and stoic upper lip, and to her these clutching, complaining men appeared like 'whining Calibans'.[33] Yet despite the blinkers of her social prejudice, Diana's curiosity was captured by Guy's, with its intriguing mix of official regulation and human messiness. She submitted herself willingly to every petty rule – in contrast to Enid Bagnold who in 1917 would write a swingeingly critical memoir of her time as a VAD and would leave hospital service for the more exhilarating challenge of ambulance driving in France.[34] Diana also grew very friendly with some of her fellow nurses and was grateful to be included in their late-night 'dormy feasts'. The novelty of sharing cigarettes and sweets, of enjoying 'suppressed songs and laughter' made her poignantly aware of her restricted upbringing – of all 'the larks I had missed by never being a schoolgirl'.[35]

What her mother would have spurned as demeaning or squalid, Diana schooled herself to accept. She discovered surprising reserves of practicality and common sense, and she prided herself on her stoicism, on never taking a day off work except when she was seriously ill, on never fainting during an operation, and on no longer having 'to turn away from repulsive things'.[36] When Arnold Bennett caricatured her in his 1918 novel *The Pretty Lady* as the neurotic self-promoting do-gooder, Lady Queenie Paulle, she felt the insult keenly, believing that she had genuinely been of service as a nurse, and that she'd genuinely been changed by the experience.

The most prized aspect of her new life, however, was the autonomy it brought. Her off-duty periods were sparse – limited to three evenings a week and the occasional weekend – yet she was able to spend all of them with her friends, who took her out for taxi rides in the park or for dinner in the one restaurant in Southwark they considered decent. On those precious evenings when she 'flew' out of the hospital at five minutes past eight, 'painted and powdered and dressed (as I hoped) to kill',[37] the knowledge that the Duchess had no idea what she was doing or with whom gave these modest but unchaperoned outings a beguiling enchantment.

Not only did Diana feel purposeful and in control, but for the first time she knew herself to be part of some larger, more collective experience. Women's lives were changing, both for those like her, who had volunteered to become VADS, and for the new female workforce that was starting to tackle jobs and professions left vacant by Britain's enlisting soldiers. It was a slow trajectory, but gradually women were moving beyond the menial or domestic labour that had been their traditional employment*. By the end of the war nearly two million would have proved themselves as bus drivers, glaziers, bank clerks and cashiers, motorcycle couriers, railway porters, tree cutters, farmers, stage managers, librarians, engineers, policewomen and teachers.[†]

In ways that couldn't have been foreseen by the suffragettes, the war represented an astonishing moment for women to challenge their status as the weaker, decorative sex. Ethel M. Billborough, an affluent young Englishwoman, would write in July 1915, 'Now everyone is living and no mistake about it; there is no more playing at things.'[38] Violet, however, remained miserably resistant to this change. She hated the idea of her daughter working in so starkly uncongenial a place as Guy's, and since Diana showed no signs of returning home, she embarked on a plan to manoeuvre her back, by overseeing the conversion of their London house into an officers' hospital.[‡] Other private homes were being given over to similar use, and 16 Arlington Street was certainly one of the most commodious in London. Even with the family still in residence, its ballroom and prettily gilded drawing room would be large enough to convert to a pair of twelve- and ten-bedded wards, while the Duchess's own bed-

---

* At first the war was bad for working women: 14 per cent of those already employed lost their jobs with the closing down of peacetime industries. There was also sentimental resistance to the idea of women tackling men's work, which was only dispelled when compulsory military service was introduced in 1917 and it was clear the nation couldn't function without them.
[†] When the Endell Street military hospital opened in 1916, it was with an all-female staff of doctors as well as nurses. Even on the front line women proved their remarkable qualities: nurses refused to leave their patients, even under heavy fire; Edith Cavell became a national heroine after being executed by the Germans for helping soldiers escape from German-occupied Brussels to the safety of Holland.
[‡] The Duchess's first plan, financially backed by Moore, had been to convert a French chateau into a private hospital, but it had not been approved by the Red Cross.

room could serve as an operating theatre while she removed to a smaller room. Diana had only been at Guy's for six months before her mother offered her a perfectly kitted out and very comfortable alternative.

She felt a profound ambivalence towards this latest instance of her mother's manipulation. Even though the hospital was being run by professionals, it still had an irksome, Marie Antoinettish quality. As she later wrote, 'Hospital life kids one into thinking one is indispensable and home life after it is wanton and trivial'[39]. Friends would drop by, bringing chestnut cream cakes and even a bottle of sherry for elevenses – a preposterous contrast to the diet of tinned eggs and stale fish to which she had recently grown accustomed. Aside from traumatic spikes of activity, when a rush of emergency cases was admitted, she was only on duty for an average of five or six hours a day.

On the other hand, moving back home had not resulted in Diana giving up her hard-fought independence: there was too much going on in Arlington Street for Violet to resume her old vigilance. In fact, she was soon to be absent for long periods of time, extending her new-found patriotism to the conversion of Belvoir Castle into an officers' convalescent home. Violet had not yielded her adamantine certainties about propriety and marriage, but even she could see that talk of chaperones was futile in a world where well-brought-up young women were doing the jobs of the working classes, and where young men were being slaughtered at the Front.

During the six months that Diana spent at Guy's, the war had remained a backdrop to her life – almost an abstraction. Her energy was consumed by the demands of nursing and nearly all of the enlisting men she knew were still safely confined to officer training camp. Yet after her return to Arlington Street, as hopes of an early victory faded, the war became horribly real. One by one the lovely, clever boys with whom she had danced, flirted and read poetry were being dispatched to the Front; and one by one they were perishing there. Julian Grenfell, who had thrilled to the idea of fighting for 'the Old Flag . . . the Mother Country and . . . the Imperial Idea' had died slowly and agonizingly in a dirty field hospital, his brain shattered by a splinter of shell.[40] Diana's cousin John, and her friends Charles Lister and George Vernon, had also been killed; the last, breaking Diana's heart when she received the farewell note he'd dictated, ending with the painful scrawl he'd been determined to write himself: his initial G and the barely legible 'love'.

At Guy's, Diana had been nursing civilians, but at Arlington Street the carnage of the trenches was literally brought home to her in the maimed and shell-shocked bodies delivered to the wards. Sometimes in the middle of changing a dressing, assisting at an operation, or quieting a patient from his screaming night-mares, Diana would find herself weeping helplessly, unable to bear the senseless misery.

Hours later, however, she would be drinking and dancing. The miseries of war had released a heady fatalism in London, and with it a greed for life. Men might be dying, coal, oil and petrol rationed, food and new clothes in short supply,* yet these were times when it felt like a moral duty to grab at every available pleasure, to party in the face of death.

To Diana it was as though the pleasure-seeking principles of the Corrupt Coterie had acquired a new apocalyptic energy. Every night, as long as there were no emergencies to attend, she went out with friends: those who'd remained in London, and those who were home on leave from the Front. The press still tried to keep track of their doings, and it was with a note of desperation that a columnist would write in September 1916, 'Have you noticed that we have hardly any mention of Lady Diana Manners, Miss Nancy Cunard and their friends? This will never do.'[41] But, in truth, much of their wartime entertainment had to be kept from the papers because it was frankly illegal.

---

* German naval blockades and the diversion of resources and manpower to the war industries produced a shortage of normal peace-time goods.

One of Diana's favourite haunts was the Cavendish Hotel, a notoriously lax establishment, famous for allowing rackety parties and illicit, after-hours drinking. Frequent police raids were made on the Cavendish and on more than one night, Diana had to hide outside in the back garden until the coast was clear. She came even closer to scandal in December 1915, when she was caught drinking brandy at Kettner's Restaurant after 10.30 p.m.; she was saved from prosecution only by her friend Alan Parsons 'having a word' with Sir Edward Henry, Commissioner of the Metropolitan Police, who promised the 'matter would go no further'.[42]

She knew her behaviour was risky, but she found it addictive: the exhilaration of being 'dangerous, dissipated, desperate' kept the nightmares of war at bay.[43] In 1916 she was at an exceptionally louche party given by an American actor, and was delighted by the reaction of Duff Cooper, who bumped into her there. Duff was shocked to see her in a room full of 'the lowest kind of actress and chorus girls', and he thought she was 'probably the only virgin' present.[44] But for Diana, his discomfort only enhanced the pleasure of going slumming; carelessly she said she'd wanted to see how low she could go 'without losing caste'.[45]

The most extravagant expression of this wartime hedonism was seen in the parties that George Gordon Moore started to host for Diana and her friends in the autumn of 1914. They were on a preposterous scale. The ballroom in his enormous house on Lancaster Gate was redecorated each time with a new theme: images from the circus, the Wild West, Aubrey Beardsley's erotica or the Ballets Russes. Even the dinner tables were works of art, laden with purple orchids and the kind of rare wartime delicacies that only Moore's deep pockets could supply – avocados, terrapin and soft shell crab.

The drinking was more excessive still, with vodka and absinthe spiking the flow of champagne (whisky was still considered unacceptable for women, even behind Moore's 'barred doors'). There was dancing to ragtime and to the tropical twang of Hawaiian bands, and it continued until the breakfast eggs and bacon appeared at dawn. Or rather it continued until Diana decided she was tired and wanted to go home, at which point Moore would abruptly command the band to stop and ask the rest of the guests to leave.

Everyone knew these parties were essentially for Diana's benefit, but very few realized how very complicated and compromised her relationship with Moore had now become. During these first months of the war the financier had grown even more powerful. Money flowed to him from mysterious ventures – he was reputed to be the owner of public utilities in four American states as well as in Canada and Brazil – and his wealth gave him entrée into the highest social circles. He was especially close to Sir John French, Commander in Chief of the British forces in France, with whom he shared his house, and it was for this reason that Violet, who had always loathed Moore, now actively encouraged his interest in Diana. She was desperate to keep John, her one remaining son, safe from the trenches, and her plan was to use Moore's influence with French to secure John a staff position at GHQ.

Diana felt herself to be in an intolerable position. Before the war she had been guiltily impressed by Moore's generosity, but she had hated it when George Gordon Ghastly, as she called him, had tried to kiss or caress her. Big and loud with his 'straight black hair, flattened face and atomic energy',[46] he could not have been more physically repulsive to her. Yet her mother, in a shocking aberration from her normal practice, was now telling Diana to suppress her antipathy and be 'nice'. As she recalled, 'To get my brother to GHQ was her obsessive hope. She thought that only I could coax the boon out of Moore.'[47] Not only was Diana expected to use up some of her precious free time attending the parties Moore threw for her, she had to tolerate being seated next to him at dinner, having endearments muttered thickly into her ear as the two of them 'shuffled and bunny hugged' across the dance floor, and accepting his good-night embrace.[48]

John was due to be sent out to France in late February 1915, yet the week before, when no word of a desk job had yet arrived, Diana apparently had to coax a little harder. She was at home, recovering from the measles, when Moore came into her bedroom at about three in the morning. The Duchess certainly knew he was there, and although there is no evidence to suggest that Diana allowed Moore to make love to her, this was far more intimacy than she had ever previously granted him. It was surely no coincidence that Sir John French had just written to Violet to assure her that a 'good plan' had been formed: and that despite John's own determined resistance he would eventually be removed from his position at the Front and transferred to the safety of GHQ.

Diana felt soiled by the whole business: in a letter to her friend Raymond Asquith she had described Moore's physical advances as 'sullying . . . mutilating and scarring'.[49] Even more distasteful was the hypocrisy of her own mother who, normally so fastidious, had been willing to put her in so compromising a position. Yet if Diana recoiled inwardly, if her resentment against Violet acquired a new core of rage, she didn't alter her life. She continued her 'friendship' with Moore without any obvious break, and in some way she came to rationalize it as part of her war effort. However repellent Moore was to her, physically, his parties had become a highlight of London entertainment, especially for officers on leave. As Diana recalled, most of her generation now felt they were 'dancing a tarantella', infected by the need to keep moving to forget the horrors of war.[50] Moore's parties provided that hectic oblivion, night after night; and it was for a very good reason that they became nicknamed the Dances of Death.

If Diana's circle had become addicted to the distractions of dancing and drinking, she herself began flirting with other addictions too. When the strain of nursing and the exhaustion of partying became too much, she increasingly quieted her nerves with a dose of 'jolly old chlorers' (chloroform) from the local chemist or with an injection of morphine. Everyone was doing it. While hashish and the very new import, cocaine, had dubious associations with crime and bohemia, morphine was deemed purely medicinal. Packets of paper impregnated with the drug were marketed as gifts for the boys in the trenches, whilst to those waiting at home it was a catch-all remedy for insomnia, anxiety and every variety of physical discomfort.

Diana craved the ecstatic stillness she got from morphine, the feeling that she had become 'utterly self-sufficient ... like a Chinaman, or God before he made the world ... and was content with, or callous to the chaos'.[51] She came to crave that detachment even more urgently when Raymond Asquith, one of the dearest of her friends, was due to be transferred from officer training camp to the Front in the spring of 1916.

Raymond was fourteen years older than Diana and had long been the undisputed leader of her male friends. 'We all liked him the best,' she admitted simply.[52] He was handsome, poetic and clever, and although far out of her orbit when she was a teenager, he had been tender towards her earnest precocity and towards her star-struck parroting of his opinions. Even though he had got married in 1907 to Edward Horner's sister, Katherine, the bond between them had grown. Diana felt most naturally herself in Raymond's company, and it was almost inevitable that as she became older, their intimacy deepened into something like love.

Neither would do anything to hurt Katherine, and their relationship remained perfectly chaste, but in the destabilizing atmosphere of war, restraint was harder to maintain. Before Raymond's departure to the Front became imminent, Diana raced down to visit him at his training camp in Folkestone, careless of what anyone might think. She might have loathed Moore's groping, but she longed for Raymond's touch. They met in a local inn, and what passed between them was clearly passionate, for afterwards he wrote, 'Even into this foul and dingy inn the recollected glory of your beauty flings its unquenchable beam – and your darling darling charity of last night.' Diana responded to her own 'darling' Raymond in equally impetuous terms: 'I have loved so utterly your last two beseeching letters. I was

longing for you to claim me again, and now you have done it
fully.'⁵³ They did not become lovers; whatever 'charity' Diana
offered to Raymond, the affair was not consummated, and that
fact allowed her to believe she was doing nothing to injure his
wife. On the contrary, her love for Raymond made her feel
closer to Katherine, and it was with the latter that she shared a
desperate, pain-numbing needle of morphine on the night that
Raymond was transferred to France.

Nor did Diana let her secret emotions interfere with the
continuing drama of her public flirtations. She was constantly in
the company of other men, and while this was a diversion and a
camouflage for her true feelings, it was also part of wartime
culture. Diana believed it was only honourable to take care of
her officer friends when they were on leave, allowing men like
Patrick Shaw Stewart to kiss her, accepting their declarations of
love as though they had an actual future together.

Again, everyone was doing it. Between 1914 and 1918, across
all the social classes, there was an increase in sexual activity
outside marriage as soldiers on leave sought out physical conso-
lation and many more women seemed willing to offer it. Some
of these couplings led to hasty weddings, some to unwanted
children. With birth control remaining clumsy and inadequate,
thick rubber condoms for men, toxic douches for women, the
proportion of illegitimate births during these years rose by 30
per cent in Britain alone.

Diana, however, retained some of her former caution. Even
though she'd learned to scorn her mother's hypocrisy in matters
of sex she was scared to risk her virginity, even for the sake of a
doomed officer. She fully expected to keep this carefully tended
asset for the night of her marriage, and in moments of candour
she admitted to herself that she was rarely tempted otherwise.
Diana found sensual delight in many things, in dancing, drinking
and in lovely clothes, but while the teasing dance of seduction
was delicious to her, she recoiled from the more committed,
messy prospect of sex. Even when she liked a man enough to
allow him up to her bedroom in Arlington Street when the

Duchess was absent, she kept their love-making within very specific constraints.

Of these men it was Patrick Shaw Stewart who demanded most, begging Diana over and over again to let him into her bed, even if she would not marry him. But it was Duff Cooper to whom she permitted the most. Duff had the advantage of being constantly on hand – his government-protected work in the Foreign Office kept him in London, and out of the army. But in ways that Diana found hard to identify, he was also very attractive to her. He fell far short of Raymond's heroic beauty, his head was too large for his small feet and hands, and the downward cast of his eyes had an almost melancholic aspect. In the company of strangers he could also seem bookish and gruff. Yet, alone with close friends, and especially with women, Duff came alight with a witty, passionate ebullience and he had a power to charm that was disturbingly effective.

Duff adored women and, thanks to his close relationships with his mother and sister, he understood them well. He also prided himself on being a sexual connoisseur capable of running simultaneous affairs with a chorus girl, a titled lady, or the wife of a painter. However, he had long claimed that Diana was his ideal and, even before the war, had been writing her archly sentimental letters, in which he cast himself as her adoring troubadour: 'As for loving you best in the world, I think that might happen all too easily. I am really rather frightened that it will, for I feel that you would be terrible and have no pity.'[54]

It was in a similarly extravagant vein that he wrote to her on 23 June 1914, concluding with the unknowingly but horribly ironic farewell, 'Goodbye, my darling – I hope that everyone whom you like better than me will die very soon.'[55]

Death, of course, did come very soon, and Diana was increasingly reliant on Duff to console her as, one by one, the men with whom she had danced and flirted before the war were killed or injured at the Front. He was tenderly protective of her grief, writing to her in 1916, 'Your little face was so thin and sad tonight and I wished so to be alone with you and tell you how

I loved you.'[56] He discovered too that his initial flamboyant devotion was deepening into a more adult kind of love. After a day spent visiting St Paul's and Westminster Abbey in March that year he wrote in his diary that she had opened his imagination to 'lots of things . . . I had never noticed before . . . The pleasure of doing that sort of thing with Diana is indescribable.'[57]

And while Diana still yearned for Raymond, she began to fall in love with Duff. Even his bad habits had a charm for her. He gambled and drank too much, and incorrigibly lusted after other women, yet it gave her a pleasurable feeling of release to fight with him over his flaws. Sometimes Diana worried that she lacked passion, that her deepest emotions were blocked. Even in the most bitter wrangles with her mother, she rarely shouted or slammed a door. Rowing with Duff, however, she felt her emotions pour out in a satisfyingly clear current: during one argument in 1915 she actually hit him, and hit him so hard that his lip bled.

The ugliness of the scene aroused her, even more so the reconciliations that followed. With many people Diana was nervous of being forced into intimacy; dogged by her childhood fear of appearing shallow or dull she much preferred playing to a crowd. Alone with Duff, however, it was easy to talk and react, and with him too she felt a rare sexual confidence. He clearly desired her, but the fact that he never forced himself on her encouraged her to become more creatively responsive. One evening he came to her room as she was getting dressed for a tableau vivant – a popular entertainment during these years, in which decorative young women posed in costume to raise money for the war effort. Diana was wearing an ornate Russian headdress and ropes of pearls, and when Duff begged her to undo the bodice of her dress so that he could admire her, half-naked, in her finery, she gave him a performance worthy of Maud Allan.

Duff found Diana's combination of seduction and chastity to be very aphrodisiac: 'She . . . understands the game and how to play it . . . There is a great deal to be said for the love making that sends one away hungry.' Blind to the irony of his own double standards, he noted that her dance of withholding and yielding kept his feelings at an exquisite pitch. The women who allowed him 'excessive intimacy' inevitably produced in him a reaction of 'contempt or disgust'.[58]

Diana was grateful for Duff's tact, yet she was beginning to fret about her cautious and self-conscious virginal state. She judged herself to be lacking in poetry and generosity, especially when compared to the behaviour of some of her friends. Two in particular, Iris Tree and Nancy Cunard, were apparently using the war as an excuse to abandon all social restraint. Although a few years younger than her, they ran with the wildest crowds at the Café Royal and the Eiffel Tower restaurant in Soho. They rented a secret studio in the bohemian district of Fitzrovia, where they held riotous parties, and were often in the company of male strangers, with whom, it was said, they were recklessly intimate.

Diana was in some ways irritated by their behaviour, which she considered extreme and naive. When she visited their studio she was appalled by its squalor – the beds were unmade and the floor was littered with the detritus of parties: empty champagne bottles (broken at the neck to save the trouble of pulling a cork), overflowing ashtrays and, in the bathroom, traces of blood, semen and vomit. But she was reluctantly impressed by the number of lovers that Nancy and Iris appeared to take. 'They have more courage than me – and can seize an opportunity and hug and crush it against their palates irrespective of the taste and they are very happy while I go starved, and hesitating and checking my every impulse for fear of losing my pedestal of ice.'[59] She felt old and anomalous. Another more passionate woman would surely have yielded to Duff's seduction. Another woman would surely have made love to Raymond while she'd had the chance in Folkestone.

But such a chance would never come again, for on 15 September 1916, Raymond was shot on the battlefield of the Somme as he was leading his men out of their dugout. His was only one of hundreds of thousands of lives claimed by that summer's most bloodily futile battle. All over Europe women were receiving letters and telegrams, informing them of the deaths of their husbands, sons or lovers. Yet Diana could think only of Raymond. The pain was excruciating: 'My brain is revolving so fast, screaming, "Raymond killed, my divine Raymond killed," over and over again.'[60] After the deaths of other friends, she had been able to weep for a few harrowing hours, then stoically return to her nursing and the nightly tarantella of denial. The loss of Raymond, however, was unendurable.

In the past Diana had suffered from occasional depression – days of dark listlessness she couldn't explain – but misery now settled into her like a toxin, a 'squalid low' emotion that prevented her from sleeping or concentrating on work.[61] This time Duff couldn't help her. He had eventually persuaded her to explain why Raymond's loss had been so very terrible, and while he had been 'moved and amazed' by the revelation of Diana's secret love – he too had adored Raymond – his sympathy had inevitably been replaced by jealousy and resentment.

He grew emotionally distant, noting harshly that grief was making Diana look 'tired and worn' and he lost patience with her sexual reticence. Painfully he wondered what caresses she had permitted Raymond but denied him. When she clumsily attempted to reassure him that of course she loved him best 'among the living' he was furious. 'How', he taunted her, would he 'know that was true' since she refused him what he desired.

The two of them were actually spending more time alone together: dining in Duff's little flat in St James Street, walking through the streets of London, taking little jaunts to the countryside with picnics that Diana had carefully prepared. Yet often their quarrels made these occasions hateful, and by mid-November 1916, Diana suggested they would be better apart. 'Duff dear I cannot bear it at all you will no longer help me with my moods or be patient with my tired ways. You will not even let me lie quietly without raging at the little I sometimes needs must deny you.'[62]

They were reconciled, yet still the quarrels continued. Duff lost £170 at a single sitting of chemin de fer, and she told him despairingly that it was final, 'our relationship can never be the same again'.[63] When Patrick Shaw Stewart confided his continuing determination to marry Diana, Duff reacted with a shrug of equanimity, already wondering if he might be falling in love with another woman.

But in June 1917, he and Diana found themselves suddenly clinging to each other, as close as they had ever been. The massively depleted British army had finally introduced conscription, and was even extending the call-up to men in government-protected jobs. Duff was one of them, and when he heard the news he couldn't help a surge of wild elation. Sitting behind a desk while others fought and died, he had craved 'the experience and adventure everyone else has had'.[64] Yet excited as he was, he knew that the odds were terribly against him surviving, and the knowledge that he might never see Diana again refocused all his love and tenderness. As for Diana, the fear of losing Duff blotted out her lingering grief for Raymond. Schooled in the nightmare calculations of war, she began to count up, obsessively, the amount of time they had left together: 'I knew that for a little time he would be sent to a cadets' training college. I would see him less and less until he went to France. Then, with fair luck, once or twice on leave then Never never, never.' In real terror for her own mental state she wondered, 'Who will keep me sane,' when she had lost him, as she surely would.[65]

Diana actually had a full nine months' grace before Duff was dispatched to the Front. On 28 April, after he had marched with all the other newly recruited Grenadiers from Chelsea Barracks to Waterloo station, she bravely wrote to him that she had 'adored his glorious spirits', describing the tears she wept as 'a great pride signifying only my complete love.'[66] Left behind in London, however, waiting for his first letters to arrive from France, she felt only 'listless and crippled'.

The war had become 'a blind murderous treadmill, with no sign of the beginning of the end.'[67] A generation had been laid waste for a cause that few could even make sense of (over two hundred local men from the Rutland estate alone had been killed at the Front). The sound of bugles signifying a military funeral was commonplace, and shrines to the civilian dead were appearing everywhere as the big cities, especially London, were bombed by the enemy.

Early in the war, the bombs dropped by Zeppelin air ships had done terrifying but limited damage. It had been the done thing among Diana's set to 'lift a glass and laugh [them] to inaudibility'; people even felt a certain pride in having watched a raid. From a safe distance there was a mesmerizing spectacle in the raking searchlights seeking out the enemy's giant silver air machines, in the crack of an explosion followed by a sudden flare of fire. Now the raids were less frequent, but the new breed of German fighter planes, the Gothas and Giants, carried more lethal loads. In September 1917 Diana arrived at Arlington Street to find all the windows blown out, and 'a crater the size of half a tenis [sic] court ten yards away in the park'.[68] When caught in the middle of a raid in May 1918 she was no longer capable of 'laughing' away the threat. During a nightmarish three hours in which she was pressed among a crowd of cowering strangers 'the London Bridge gun shook our marrows and a procession of victims, dead and mangled, passed in the darkness'.[69]

In this fourth year of the war Diana felt there was an ugliness to England now. The blackout-darkened streets had become home to all kinds of 'thieving and vicing'.[70] Conscientious objectors had always been targeted, but homosexuals, modern painters, poets and foreigners were now likely to be branded as potential traitors too. The legislation passed against aliens was more strictly enforced: Rudolph Stulik, Austrian proprietor of the Eiffel Tower, had already been interned, and Duff's friend, the German-born singer Olga Lynn, whose real name was Lowenthal, lived in daily fear of being deported.

It was in this darkening atmosphere that Noel Pemberton Billing published his claims that a group of dissolute aristocrats, painters, Jews, intellectuals and female followers of Allan's Cult of the Clitoris had been identified by the German Secret Service as targets for blackmail, and as potential traitors or spies. It created a scandal – Maud Allan brought a libel action against Billing – and many in Diana's circle feared being named on the MP's list. Diana herself received a threatening letter from a man who claimed to have evidence about her 'in relation to a case now much before the public'.[71]

There was an element of grim hilarity to the affair, as she described to Duff on 5 June. The Duchess remained convinced of Allan's purity: 'True to her school, she did not believe in the possibility of vice among women.' More comically still, Diana reported, 'Lord Albemarle is said to have walked into the Turf and said, "I've never heard of this Greek chap *Clitoris* they are all talking of."'[72]

But there were few people left with whom she could share the joke. By January 1918 Edward Horner and Patrick Shaw Stewart, two of her last surviving officer friends, had perished, and her correspondence with Duff was erratic. In the long gaps between letters, she was tormented by visions of him left dead or dying. Even when letters came, the censors' deletions left her imagining unspoken horrors. Work was her only relief. Soon after Duff left for France Diana had volunteered for a second term at Guy's, hoping that the unrelenting drudgery would tamp down her terrors. It was only for a month – her mother remained fiercely opposed to public hospital life – but as a temporary distraction it had worked. The exhaustion shut down her imagination and the suffering of her patients put her own agony in perspective. She had to treat some severely burned children during this period, using the then-accepted method of pouring hot melted wax over their raw wounds. The children's pitiful screams haunted her, but it was then, Diana wrote, that she learned not to cry.

During this bleakest of periods, Diana lived tentatively from day to day. Yet she was now convinced that when the war ended she wanted to be with Duff. Previously they had only joked about marriage, each unsure of the other's feelings, but now Diana swore, 'If death will only spare him we will live our lives together.'[73] She swore, too, that she would no longer be intimidated by her mother's disapproval, even though she knew it would be formidable.

The Duchess had indeed observed the growing intimacy between Diana and Duff with alarm and had even begun to interrogate Diana's friends about the likelihood of an engagement, complaining to Katherine Asquith that she couldn't sleep at night for fear of her daughter 'marrying that awful Duff'.[74] As far as Violet was concerned, Duff was awful in too many ways to count. His father, the late Sir Alfred Cooper, had been an eminent surgeon and friend of King Edward VII, but his area of expertise – venereal disease – was something from which she could only shrink.* Duff's mother had been from a good family, but she had disgraced herself by leaving her first husband, living openly with her lover and, after the latter's death, earning her living as a trainee nurse. In fact, it was when Alfred Cooper spotted Lady Agnes scrubbing hospital floors that he had recognized her as the lovely young woman he had admired in his youth and asked her to marry him.

Had she read of this romantic coincidence in a book, the Duchess might have found it charming. It was not, however, something with which she wanted her family to be associated. She feared that Duff, with his reputation for drink and women, had inherited his mother's tainted genes, and it was hardly as if he had a compensating fortune. With an annual income of under £1,000 (his Foreign Office salary combined with his private allowance), Duff couldn't come close to offering Diana the life that Violet had planned.

She rallied her friends – Duff was 'a contemptible parvenu' opined Lady Sackville – but Diana, who before the war might have quailed at the idea of marrying so far outside her mother's

---

* Had Violet known of the nickname 'Cooper's clap trap' given to Sir Alfred's carriage, she would have been still more horrified.

expectations, had changed. And she believed that British society had changed too. As she wrote to Duff, 'In a sense the world shapes to hide our possible squalor.' With few servants and private cars available to anyone, it would be much harder for anyone to 'pity our poverty'.[75]

She framed a virtuous picture of their future lives. While Duff volunteered his willingness to 'break my champagne glasses, throw away my cigars, tear up my cards . . . study the habits of buses and the intricacies of tubes',[76] she began to contemplate money-making schemes. Her first idea was to set up a nursing home with financial backing from Moore. It was a very respectable way of earning a living, she pointed out to Duff, 'without any notoriety or convention breaking for Their Graces to take exception to'. She even toyed briefly with a scheme to launch an aviation passenger business with the backing of her new friend, the newspaper magnate Max Beaverbrook. 'Scruples must fade,' she wrote firmly to Duff, 'we must be happy.'[77]

It was hard to sustain that optimism while Duff was in danger, but against all the odds he continued to survive. In early October he was awarded a DSO for his courage in battle and given two weeks' leave in Paris. Diana gave him loving permission to take every advantage of reprieve from the Front: 'You know that I want your happiness above my own,' she wrote, although she also begged him to avoid gambling, catching a disease or making love to anyone she knew (her friend Diana Wyndham, to whom she knew Duff was attracted, also happened to be in Paris).[78]

Less than a fortnight later she was 'intoxicated' to read in *The Times* that the war was almost over, and at the end of October Duff was, amazingly, back in London and in her arms. It was a rapturous reunion for both of them: 'All that I had hoped of happiness for the last 6 months came true,' wrote Duff in his diary.[79] Yet while he had returned home unscathed, too many of their friends had perished for them to feel guiltlessly happy. On 11 November, the formal declaration of Armistice, Diana spent the day dutifully with her family, but she couldn't bear to listen to the frenzied celebrations that roared through the London streets, writing, 'After so much bitter loss it was unnatural to be jubilant.'[80]

She was worried too about Duff, who was showing symptoms of the Spanish flu that had begun wreaking carnage across Europe. Having eaten an early supper with her mother at the Ritz, she slipped away to his flat. Their mood together was sombre: 'The dead were in our minds to the exclusion of the survivors.' Yet it wasn't only thoughts of their friends that darkened their spirits. 'The war was over,' Diana wrote. 'My own battle had now to be fought.'[81] It was her and Duff now, ranged against the desires of her parents and the coercive forces of tradition and class.

Chapter Two

NANCY

⚜

W hile Diana was dedicating herself to a future with Duff, Nancy Cunard was tearing down the edifice of her own brief, unhappy marriage. Two years of being wedded to Sydney Fairbairn, an army officer and keen amateur cricketer, had left Nancy disgusted with the whole notion of matrimony. Even at her wedding party she'd felt a premonition of revulsion so acute that she had ripped the bridal wreath off her head and thrown it onto the floor.

To most of the guests assembled at the Guards Chapel, the entire event had a difficult and peculiar atmosphere. The ceremony had looked hastily arranged, lacking the traditional theatre of bridesmaids, pageboys and bouquets. There was awkwardness too about the arrangement of the family party, with Lady Maud Cunard accompanied by both her estranged husband Sir Bache Cunard and her lover Sir Thomas Beecham. And it was back at Maud's Mayfair house that Nancy, flushed with champagne and self-consciousness, had made her startling gesture. She had been talking with Evan Morgan, the elegantly dissolute poet on whose Shelleyan good looks and slender talent she'd once had an unreciprocated crush. It may have been some snipe Evan made about her newly married status, or a comment about Sydney, but the chatter in Maud's elaborately decorated drawing room suddenly faded as Nancy, her expression furious, yanked off her wreath of orange blossoms and tossed her hair free.

It had been a classic wartime wedding. The couple had met in early 1916, after Sydney had returned to England to recover from injuries sustained at the battle of Gallipoli. Little sign of what he'd seen and suffered was evident on his smooth, regular features; to the many women flitting around him at this time, Sydney appeared the handsome template of an officer and a gentleman.

Nancy for her part was normally attracted to men who appeared more foreign, poetic or louche, but Sydney had come into her life at a moment when his very English solidity was unusually appealing. The early years of the war had affected her deeply. Like Diana, she had suffered the deaths of close friends; like Diana she had been swept up in London's atmosphere of heady fatalism. Yet Nancy was three and a half years younger; she was more emotionally fragile, and more chaotically in revolt against the grown-up world. She found it harder to put limits on the wartime saturnalia of 'late hours at wild parties . . . of drinking in the Café Royal Brasserie with tipsy poets and "chaps" on leave.'[1] After a party at the Fitz, her studio in Fitzrovia, she was liable to find herself in the arms of a stranger, not knowing what she had drunk or what she had done.

When Diana and Duff came to the Fitz one morning in July 1916, they found Nancy still 'looking rather squalid' from the night before.[2] Diana 'was disgusted and saddened' and Nancy, too, was beginning to feel that she needed rescuing. Sydney might not be interested in the books she read or care for the company she kept, yet his shoulders looked broad enough to offer her a safe haven from the confusion she'd created around herself.

He also offered her a haven from her mother who, while more relaxed over the matter of chaperones than the Duchess of Rutland, could still be censorious and domineering. Nancy enjoyed a rare degree of independence, yet Lady Cunard kept a tight leash on her financially, giving her money only if she remained tolerably compliant: putting in an appearance at her dinners and opera parties, and making a pretence of listening silently when Maud launched into one of her regular excoriations of her daughter's shortcomings.

These, Maud considered, were many: the frequent disappearances to her dirty little studio, the oddity of her ideas, the peculiarities of her appearance. Lady Cunard, whose own style was meticulously and delicately fashionable, could be wounded to the quick by the sight of Nancy sauntering into the drawing room in a man's waistcoat, her mouth a blood-red slash in a mask of white powder.

By the age of eighteen, Nancy was desperate to leave home. It didn't occur to her to volunteer as a nurse as Diana had done. She already knew that she wanted to be a poet so the regulated life of a VAD would be intolerable to her. Her only alternative, as far as she could see, was a purely traditional one. Marriage would force her parents to settle some money on her and it would set her up in her own house, where she could write, entertain and dream without interference.

Poor Sydney Fairbairn was almost accidental to the equation. And even if Nancy had moments of clarity when she knew 'it was an idiotic thing to do', she couldn't resist the deliverance Sydney promised. 'It was wartime,' she later wrote in her diary. '[I] did it, went through with it all so as to get away from Her Ladyship and have a home of my own.'[3]

Her enthusiasm for the plan was reinforced by the gratifying displeasure it gave her mother. Maud had been hoping for a more extraordinary match for her only daughter, and like the Duchess of Rutland she'd dared hope as high as the Prince of Wales. More selflessly, she worried that Sydney and her daughter were disastrously unsuited, and as the wedding approached she tried, as gently as she knew how, to question whether Nancy really wanted to marry him. But already the press were buzzing with reports of a most interesting engagement between Mr Sydney Fairbairn, an officer with the Royal Bucks Hussars and 'one of the best looking in his regiment', and Miss Nancy Cunard, 'the only child of two tremendously rich people [and] one of the catches of the season'.[4] So on 15 November 1916, out of a dogged combination of honour and perversity, Nancy became Sydney's wife.

It was with hindsight, and much accumulated resentment, that she would later refer to the twenty months she had lived with Sydney as 'a detestable period', a grim 'caesura' in her life. During the first weeks of their marriage, visiting friends and travelling, the couple had managed to skate over the gulf that lay between them, but by the summer of 1918, when Sydney's leg was sufficiently healed for him to return to the war, Nancy could barely endure his company. Her nerves were grated by his talk of war and sport, and by the army friends who filled the drawing room of their little Mayfair house. She felt more confined than she ever had been at Maud's. It was almost impossible for her to focus on writing, and she possessed no skills with which to change her situation. Not only was Nancy confrontational and intemperate by nature, while she was growing up, she'd been given no example of how two people might accommodate each other. The only child of parents who had spent as little time as possible together, Nancy had scant knowledge of how to make a marriage work. She knew only how to run away.

Her parents had met in 1895 in New York, where Sir Bache had come looking for a rich and fertile American wife. He was already forty-three and feeling the urgency of producing an heir for Nevill Holt, the magnificent estate in Leicestershire that he'd inherited from his grandfather, the shipping magnate Samuel Cunard. Living quietly in the countryside with his dogs, his horses and his hobbies, Sir Bache had failed to meet a suitable wife. But with the costs of running Nevill Holt rising every year, he was now willing to follow the example of so many other British aristocrats in offering his title as a trade for American money.

Miss Maud Alice Burke was dazzlingly desirable to Sir Bache

on every count. Aged twenty-three, she was blonde, blue-eyed and spirited; her little bird-like body, piquant pink and white complexion, ready wit and inquisitive mind made most of the English women he knew appear stolid and dull. The fact that she came with a $2 million dowry, more than capable of plugging the bottomless expense of Nevill Holt, made her irresistible. The normally slow-moving, inarticulate Sir Bache was pitched head-long into the first sexual romance of his life.

As for Maud, she, too, was in a hurry to marry. Growing up in San Francisco, she'd had an unconventional family life. Her mother, widowed when Maud was in her teens, had surrounded herself with a succession of protectors, and it was to one of these, a rich and cultivated businessman called Horace Carpentier, that Mrs Burke had entrusted the education of her only daughter. Carpentier apparently made a habit of adopting young girls as protégées, and although there was no scandal attached to these relationships, they were unusual. Under Carpentier's guidance, Maud grew both intellectually and socially precocious, and, in relation to other young girls of her generation, sexually aware. By the age of twenty-one she had entered into an affair with the Irish writer George Moore, whom she'd met on a trip to Europe.

It had been a passionate experience for them both: Moore was captivated by Maud's intelligence and her unexpectedly chal-lenging sexual confidence; Maud was excited by Moore's experi-ence of the world, his distinguished literary reputation and his evident desire for her. Yet she was no bohemian: she was seeking respectability as well as love, and in her first attempts to secure a husband, she made a fatal miscalculation. Returning to America, she met the grandson of the late King of Poland, and his enthusiastic interest led her to assume they were about to get engaged. She allowed gossip to leak into the press, only to discover that Prince André Poniatowski had his sights on another, more socially elevated girl. She was forced to issue a humiliating correction and was still smarting from this when she was introduced to Sir Bache in New York. Although he was neither brilliant, like Moore, nor regal, like Prince André, she convinced herself that the shy spark of enthusiasm in his heavy features held the promise of a romantic nature. Most importantly, Sir Bache Cunard would make her an English Lady.

Less than a year later, when Maud gave birth to Nancy on 10 March 1896, she knew she had made a mistake. But she remained undaunted. Declaring with brutal clarity that motherhood was 'a low thing – the lowest', and that she would never get pregnant again, she moved on to planning a brilliant social career for herself, with Nevill Holt as her theatre of action.[5]

The house itself was beautiful, a long grey-gold building of crenellated walls, towers and cloisters. Sir Bache revered its four-hundred-year-old history; indeed, Nevill Holt was the love of his life. But Maud thought it cluttered and gloomy, and since it was her money that was being used for its upkeep, she saw no reason why she shouldn't remodel the house to suit herself. Ruthlessly, she stripped out the duller Victorian furniture; she introduced light and colour into the rooms with oriental rugs and modern silk upholstery, and she repainted walls and woodwork, including some historic oak panelling.

Maud's renovations caused Sir Bache almost physical pain. He was beginning to feel like a stranger in his own house, even more so when Maud began to entertain on a grand scale. She held large dinners, trawling the best local families, including the Manners, for her guest lists, and organized weekend parties (or Saturday-to-Mondays as she learned to call them) for the smart new friends she met on her trips to London. Within a short time she was regularly playing hostess to writers like Eddie Marsh, Max Beerbohm and Somerset Maugham, as well as leading politicians such as Balfour and Asquith. According to the ambitious San Franciscan socialite Elsa Maxwell, it had become a 'social benediction' to be a guest of the vivacious Lady Cunard.[6]

Sir Bache had little in common with Maud's new set. He disliked their loud, clever talk and the laxity of their morals. At Nevill Holt, sleeping arrangements for the guests were famously helpful to those engaged in love affairs. Increasingly Sir Bache took himself away to his workshop, where he immersed himself in the metalwork that was his passionate hobby, or disappeared on long shooting and fishing trips in Scotland. 'I don't understand what is going on in this house,' he said, after returning home early and finding Maud's guests still riotously installed. 'But I don't like it.'[7]

Maud, too, was often absent from the house, shopping, travelling or enjoying a discreet tryst with one of the many men rumoured to be her lovers. And as both parents diverged on their separate lives, little Nancy found herself stranded in the gulf between them. It was normal for children like her to be looked after by nannies and governesses, but not to be so deprived of family life. Diana Manners had grown up among a tumble of siblings, friends and relatives, and had had a doting, if occasionally distracted, mother. Nancy, however, was left on her own for weeks, even months, at a time, with only the staff to take care of her. An early photograph, taken when she was about five or six, shows her standing in the great doorway of Nevill Holt, a tiny figure, poignantly dwarfed by the grandeur of her surroundings.

Even when both her parents were home, Nancy rarely saw them outside the designated hour when she was taken downstairs in a white lace dress to be quizzed on her progress in the schoolroom. Nancy knew enough from the very few children of her acquaintance – her cousins Victor and Edward, and the Manners children at Belvoir – that this was not how other families behaved, and she harboured the guilty terror that her parents would have loved her better if she had been a boy. When Maud offered her chocolates from the lavish box that was always open by her side, Nancy sometimes averted her face, wishing for embraces, not sweets.

Later she described herself as a detached, solitary child, 'wondering much in silence how life was going to be'.[8] She didn't know how to fill the huge empty spaces around her except, increasingly, with acts of rebellion and fantasies of escape. And she became more angry and more lonely with the arrival of the formidably named, and formidably disciplinarian, governess Miss Scarth.

Miss Scarth appeared suddenly when Nancy was about nine, replacing a high-spirited young Frenchwoman who had been much loved by Nancy, but considered ineffective by Lady Cunard. The testimonials Miss Scarth brought with her, including one from the mother of Vita Sackville-West, commended her as an expert teacher, but to Nancy she seemed a tyrant, rapping out French verbs and historical dates with the aid of a steel ruler, enforcing cold baths and porridge every morning and restricting her favourite outdoor treats, such as paddling in the large pond close to the house.

Scarth became a monster, the first of many in Nancy's life, and her regime induced in Nancy an implacable hatred of authority. For the rest of her life she would associate food with punishment, haunted by the image of congealing food sitting on her plate and Miss Scarth's insistence that she could not leave the table until every scrap was eaten. Hating her governess as she did, Nancy retreated inside her imagination, reading incessantly and writing secret stories and poems. In the grounds outside the house she created a world of private places: a hollowed tree, a ditch she filled with her special treasures – a strangely shaped flint or a pretty glass bottle.

During these childhood years her closest confidante was George Moore, or GM as Nancy learned to call him. Although he and Maud were no longer lovers, Moore was a regular visitor to Nevill Holt, and to Nancy he became a substitute father. Sir Bache loved his daughter, but it was an awkward, baffled love. He had little idea how to communicate with her except on the subject of horses – at his insistence Nancy was taught to ride almost as soon as she could walk, and at the age of six she was 'blooded' in her first hunt.

GM, however, talked all the time. In his easy, garrulous way he quizzed Nancy about the books she was reading and the childish poems she was writing. When the weather was fine he took her on long walks through the grounds and local countryside. They made an odd couple – little Nancy in the absurdly smart outfits Maud insisted she wear, GM in his bowler hat and tightly laced boots – but Nancy considered Moore to be her 'first friend', and when she was old enough to understand the gossip that circulated (inaccurately) about him being her biological father, she half yearned for it to be true. Moore, too, was very fond of Nancy and worried that she wasn't happy. Much as he adored Maud, he could see that she was an unnatural mother, and it distressed him to hear Nancy announcing with unnerving calm, 'I don't *like* Her Ladyship.'[9]

But still Nancy craved her mother's presence. When Maud was away life was suspended: 'Things will not be very bright,' she noted in her diary after seeing her mother depart on yet another jaunt, 'nothing much [will] happen.'[10] When Maud returned the house was suddenly brilliant with weekend parties, games of tennis and croquet and bridge, and 'beautiful exciting ladies . . . in shot silk and striped taffeta'.[11] Nancy loved to spy on the adults and to be given her own special 'duties', checking the supplies of Russian cigarettes, books, sweets, writing paper and flowers in each of the guest's rooms. If ever Maud had a whim to show off her daughter, Nancy was ecstatically compliant. She allowed herself to be dressed up as a Velázquez Infanta in black velvet and lace; she posed for one of Maud's sculptor friends as 'the soul of childhood' with a little mob cap covering her fair hair and an owl perched on her shoulder. Willingly she showed off her prodigious stock of facts. Some smiled indulgently at this sharp-featured performing monkey, others felt her precocity bordered on the monstrous. When Nancy was older, Maud took her to London for occasional trips to the theatre and opera. Eddie Marsh was present when she saw her first performance of *The Marriage of Figaro*, and was startled by her peculiarly adult response to the production: 'Between the acts Nancy said in her high little squeaky toneless voice, "The Count is exactly like George the Second. The Countess I should put a little later – about 1790." What are children coming to?'[12]

Watchful and clever, Nancy began to accumulate other adult forms of knowledge. By the time she was a teenager, she had come to understand how barren her parents' marriage was, and how different from the hot emotional flurries that disturbed the house when Maud had certain guests to stay. When she was fifteen and Maud announced that the two of them would be leaving Nevill Holt to live in London, she knew it was because her mother wanted to be near her lover, the conductor Thomas Beecham.

Musically brilliant, clever and rich – his grandfather had made a fortune manufacturing the ubiquitous Beecham's liver pill – Thomas was everything that Sir Bache so disappointingly failed to be. Even though Maud wasn't ready for the scandal of a divorce, she wanted to live as close to him as possible, and set up her new London residence in a large rented house in Cavendish Square.*

For Nancy, the break with Nevill Holt was distressing. She identified deeply with the beauty of the house and the swathes of woodland surrounding it. She loved her father, too, despite his remoteness, and felt keenly that Maud was wrong to exchange him for Thomas Beecham, a man she could not and would not like. On the other hand, she had been speculating for years on the kind of life she might enjoy when she was delivered from the schoolroom and the barbed tensions of her parents' marriage. And when she was sent to Munich in the autumn of 1912, partly to improve her German and her music, but also to leave her mother free to enjoy Beecham, Nancy felt the first thrill of impending change. The family with whom she stayed were delightful, embracing her almost as warmly as if she had been one of their own children. Even more of a novelty was the degree of independence they allowed her. Nancy had arrived in Munich as an intensely literate, imaginative but emotionally starved sixteen-year-old. When she left she felt she had '[become] a woman' and 'tasted adult life'.

Less cherished by her were the months she spent at a finishing

---

* It was the private residence of the Asquiths, left vacant after Asquith became prime minister in 1908.

school in Paris. At seventeen Nancy felt she was too old for its 'infantile' lessons and rules, and in furious reaction she set herself a stiff and systematic reading course in Russian literature.[13] Yet even though she was continually and frustratingly in the care of chaperones, she felt the romance of the city tug at her imagination. 'My mysticism was in those streets,'[14] she wrote to GM, as she described her delight in the ancient narrow maze of the Latin Quarter and told him of her visit to La Nouvelle Athènes, the café where Moore had once mixed with artists like Manet.

Nancy vowed she would return to Paris on her own, but that summer she was taken by Maud to Venice, a city that became her second love. Diana Manners and her mother were staying in the palazzo Maud had rented, and many of Diana's friends had come out to Venice, too, including Duff Cooper and his sister Sybil, Raymond and Katherine Asquith, Billy Grenfell and Denis Anson. All members of the Corrupt Coterie, these young men and women were known to Nancy, if only by reputation, and she was fascinated by their clever chatter and capacity for fun. To her joy, they were happy to let her move in the slipstream of their brilliance as they bathed naked in the sea, swaggered around the streets of Venice in outrageous fancy dress and drank cocktails in bars down on the Lido.

This holiday was the first extended period Nancy had spent with people close to her own age, and it did much for her social confidence. By the time she returned to Cavendish Square she felt more equal to engaging with her mother's London life and more willing to be curious about it. Maud had a clever eye for what was interesting and new. She was sensitive to the changes that were happening around her in art and music,* and she understood, as Violet never could, the significance of ragtime and nightclubs. She also knew how to exploit these changes, for it was by putting herself at the centre of the new modern London

---

* In this she was also more open-minded than Diana and most of the Coterie, who were inclined to mock the more extreme intellectual currents of the avant-garde.

that Maud was able to create her own distinctive niche as a society hostess.

An American woman, separated from her husband, was always going to be excluded from the highest echelons of British society, and Maud was fully aware that the Queen had expressed her disapproval of the too-public affair with Beecham. But if most of the duchesses kept away from Maud, she could compensate by colonizing the world of culture. Her network was a bold mix of established figures like Beecham and Diaghilev and more radical iconoclasts, such as the writer and artist Wyndham Lewis, who had become a particular pet of Maud's. Inspired by Marinetti's Futurist movement and the spirit of the European avant-garde, Lewis had created a gratifying stir that autumn with the 'menacing, geometrical and disturbing' tableau* he had designed for a charity ball, featuring Eddie Marsh with his head encased in a conical tube and a box balanced on top.[15] Capitalizing on that stir, Maud had commissioned Lewis to design a line of post-impressionist knick-knacks, which she could hand out as gifts to her guests.

Another of Maud's protégés was the American poet Ezra Pound, who much impressed Nancy when she first met him, with his foxy beard, sweeping black cloak, broad-brimmed hat and checkered trousers. He dressed exactly as she thought a poet should, and as she listened wide-eared and wide-eyed to the bombastic and colourful conversations of Maud's clever young men, she caught glimpses of a world of art and ideas into which she might one day gain admittance in her own right.

Warily, she entered into a new phase with her mother. Maud was difficult to love: she remained critical and brittle, channelling more of her warmth and energy into her relationship with Beecham and her social life than into her relationship with her

---

* This was the 'Picture Ball' organized by Lady Muriel Paget at the Albert Hall. Marinetti was much in vogue in London after his series of staged lectures in London, which featured readings of his cacophonous 'phonetic poem' on the siege of Adrianople.

daughter. But Nancy recognized her qualities. Maud allowed her an unusual amount of freedom to walk around London and meet with her new friends, and much of what she cared about she recognized she had inherited from her mother: books, pictures, travel and a dedicated gift for clothes.

Maud had always enjoyed dressing Nancy up. Now, as her daughter approached her eighteenth birthday, it was clear she was going to be an even more enjoyable project. Maud's delicate fairness and Sir Bache's lanky height had combined to create a peculiar beauty in Nancy. She was slender, with long legs and long elegant hands; her features were small but finely chiselled; her skin pale to the point of translucence and her hair a thick tawny gold. Iris Tree recalled that even as a very young woman, Nancy had the 'quality of crystal, neatly crisp, gracefully turbulent, arrogantly disruptive, brave'.

She was certainly formed to wear the new fashions: in early 1914, the all-important year of her season, Maud swept Nancy to Paris to shop for her coming-out wardrobe – new dresses for balls and garden parties, hats for Ascot, and a new leopard-skin coat, which Maud also had copied for herself. They looked superficially alike, mother and daughter – both blonde, both exquisitely dressed – but even in the rare mutual pleasure of this shopping trip Nancy displayed signs of intransigence. While Maud tried to persuade her into the large flowered hats and feminine shades she favoured, Nancy insisted on berets and turbans, and on dresses with sharper, bolder colours and cleaner lines.

They were small disagreements, but in the months that followed they became more frequent and more profound. The most fundamental battleground between them was Nancy's season. Maud wanted her daughter to shine, as much for the sake of her own reputation as for Nancy's marital prospects, but Nancy decided that the whole thing was a ridiculous charade. She sulked through her presentation at court, as resentful of the demure pink dress she had to wear as the tedious hours spent queuing to curtsey to the Queen. She grew rapidly and ungraciously bored by her round of debutante parties where, she argued, the same dance bands played to the same set of girls and the same dull young men, whose bland faces were as irksome to her 'as their vapid conversation among the hydrangeas at supper'.[16]

Diana had been bored by her season, but she had been better trained to survive it. Nancy, however, saw no reason to conceal her truculence, especially once she had gulped several surreptitious glasses of champagne, bypassing the innocuous fruit cup that debutantes were meant to sip. To her delight, but Maud's dismay, she failed to secure an invitation to the crowning event of the calendar, Queen Charlotte's Ball. And the crosser Nancy became at having to endure it all, the more her contempt leaked into her relationship with Maud. She felt it was hypocritical of her mother to care about so meaningless a ritual while parading her association with radicals like Lewis and Pound.

The fragile bonds they had forged over the course of the previous year began to fray as Nancy started to disassociate herself from Maud. Her rebellion wasn't exceptional – many young women, including Diana, felt an urgent need to define themselves against their mothers. It was part of the restless sense of freedom coursing through London just before the war. Yet Nancy was drawing on a long history of resentment and exclusion, and her antagonism towards Maud was far more murderous than Diana's irritability with Violet. Around this time she was among a group of friends playing the after-dinner game Truth, in which each of them were asked to name the person they would most like to see enter the room. In a flat, cutting tone, Nancy answered, 'Lady Cunard, *dead*.'[17]

Throughout the summer of 1914 she contrived a variety of small rebellions. She turned up late for her mother's soirées and played truant from her own debutante engagements; sometimes meeting with Diana and her set to go drinking and dancing at the Golden Calf, but more often meeting with her new best friend, Iris Tree. She and Iris had known one another for years, attending a few of the same children's tea parties and coinciding at the smart girls' school in London that Nancy had briefly

attended. During those years, Iris had found Nancy stiff and
fierce, while Nancy had been cowed by Iris's puppy-like exuberance. Now, however, they recognized one another as kindred
spirits.

Iris, a year younger than Nancy, had become a student at the
Slade School of Art; dressing in peasant smocks that had been
woven at Roger Fry's Omega Studio, and wearing her white-
blonde hair in a short pageboy bob. Nancy, whose own hair was
still unshorn, much admired this audacious alternative to the
elaborate pompadours or loose, Grecian buns into which most
girls their age styled their hair. And she admired even more the
world of artists to which Iris introduced her.

Among certain girls of the middle and upper classes, art school
represented a popular escape route from home. University
places were still limited (only a thousand attended the all-female
colleges at Oxford or Cambridge, and they were not permitted
to receive official degrees until 1921). Even Diana, who had no
artistic skills, had enrolled for a term at the Slade in order to get
some privacy from her mother. Iris, however, was fully committed to her studies, as well as to the life that came with them. She
had become friendly with a crowd of painters, including Alvaro
'Chile' Guevara and Nina Hamnett, and she was on close terms
with poets Robert Nichols, Tommy Earp, Edward Wyndham
Tennant and the Sitwell brothers.

As Iris introduced a dazzled Nancy to her circle, she also
introduced her to a very new view of London, whose hub was
the Eiffel Tower. This Soho restaurant had been a meeting place
for writers and painters ever since its opening in 1896; run by
an Austrian chef, Rudolph Stulik, its menu alone – aromatic,
garlicky, Continental – seemed to waft Nancy towards a different
more authentic world. Some nights the symbolist poet Arthur
Symonds might be holding court, a veteran of fin-de-siècle
decadence with his wide-brimmed hat, glass of absinthe and
lugubrious gaze, but for Nancy, no matter who was present,
every night held a promise. GM teased her about the new
bohemian set she was seeing, dismissing their poetry and paint-

ings as 'chaos'. Yet his criticisms merely confirmed Nancy's belief that this was how she wanted to live. In her adult poem 'To the E. T. Restaurant' she paid homage to the Tower and its milieu as her 'carnal-spiritual home'; filled with 'wits and glamour, strong wines, new foods' and the 'strange-sounding languages of diverse men.'

It was with Iris that she decided to rent the Fitz, as a place where they could spend unsupervised time together, reading, writing, drawing and seeing their friends. And it was with Iris, too, that she pored over the first issue* of Wyndham Lewis's heretical magazine *Blast*. Lewis had laid out his ideological agenda by dividing the modern world into angels and devils, a 'Bless' list and a 'Blast' list. The former included a provocatively rag-taggle mix of artists, suffragettes, music-hall singers and prizefighters, while the latter featured numerous despised estab- lishment figures. Among them was 'Beecham (Pills, Opera, Thomas)' – and Nancy read that list as though it were her personal battle cry.

In those last, sunny weeks of peace Nancy was suspended between different worlds. She was still finishing her season and still under Maud's control, but she was also sneaking off to the Fitz and experimenting with a life about which her mother knew almost nothing. Initially, little changed with the declaration of war. At the Tower she listened to vigorous debates on the politics and aesthetics of war, with Lewis leading the argument that it was a necessary evil, a scourging of Europe's bloated imperial powers. At Cavendish Square, meanwhile, she was being dra- gooned by Maud into the organization of charity events to raise money for the British troops. Photos taken of Nancy, posing in a toga and slippers for an 'Omar Khayyām' gala, reveal her as her mother's still compliant, socialite daughter.

But as the predicted defeat of the Germans failed to materialize

---

* 1 July 1914.

and the casualty figures began to climb, Britain stopped playing at war, and so did Nancy. Her first published poem, which appeared in the June 1915 edition of the Eton College *Chronicle* (then edited by her cousin Victor) was an elegy for soldiers lost in battle. And if its sentiments were as conventional as its language – 'These die obscure and leave no heritage/For them no lamps are lit, no prayers said' – they were inspired by real feeling. By now many of the men Nancy knew were being sent to the Front and death was acquiring a personal face.

Like Diana and so many others, she looked for ways to numb her anxiety. She worked harder at her poetry and at night she partied to excess. Evenings that began with cocktails at the Café Royal and merged into somebody's party, somewhere, would nearly always end in a drunken haze: Nancy crooning the lyrics of her favourite ragtime song 'Oh you beautiful doll', a glass in her hand, her head resting on the shoulder of a man she'd only just met.

It's unclear exactly when she became sexually active. Even before the war Nancy had been considered fast, testing out the powers of her newly adult beauty by flirting with men like Chile Guevera. Her justification was simple: 'My mother's having an affair with Thomas Beecham. I can do as I like.'[18] Yet a young woman could be thought promiscuous simply for kissing too many men, and Nancy probably didn't lose her virginity until well into the war. When she did, however, it was with an apparently determined disregard for her reputation.

Something wild and needy in her reacted to the atmosphere of war. Her imagination was haunted by pictures of what the men at the Front, her own friends, might be suffering. Many older officers maintained a degree of discretion over what they admitted to women at home, but some of the younger soldiers with whom Nancy and Iris mixed were less guarded. They were willing to hint at terrible things on the battlefield: at the stink, the madness, the noise of the trenches; at the carnage that could be inflicted on a platoon of soldiers ordered to advance into a thicket of barbed wire and machine-gun fire. These images gnawed at Nancy, making her ashamed of her own privileged safety, and the only way she and Iris could think of assuaging their guilt was by offering themselves to the men who wanted them.

They romanticized themselves wildly as ministering angels of war. Iris would recall the two of them watching the first bombs falling over London, seeing the 'fires redden on sky and river, ourselves burnt out by the terrible gaieties of last encounters'; she would write of their 'desires heightened to a brief fulfilment before sacrifice'.[19] Given the degree to which others exaggerated the extent of their 'sexual charity', it's hard to gauge the exact nature of their behaviour, yet even if Nancy was not as intemperate as some claimed, the combination of alcohol, emotional dislocation and exhaustion had an extreme effect on her. There were days when she awoke from the previous night's debauch in despair: in her 1916 poem 'Remorse', she excoriated herself for being 'wasteful, wanton, foolish, bold', of having 'loved with grasping hands and lustful eyes'. She felt tainted as well as transfigured, and she was still only twenty.

It was in this mood that Nancy tricked herself into thinking she might love Sydney Fairbairn. He was an attractive, educated, even dashing man, and after the war he would go on to have an adventurous military career in North Africa and the Middle East. Although Nancy's perceptions were later occluded by hatred, at their first meetings he appeared to offer her a chance of security and structure.

Nancy was writing in earnest now. The war had given her material and a theme, and in 1916 she had seven poems published in Edith Sitwell's anthology *Wheels*,* one of them giving the anthology its title. Her most current writing was indebted to T.S. Eliot, whom she had just met, and whose recently published 'The Love Song of J. Alfred Prufrock' she idolized. It clearly

---

* Its theme was the grinding repetition of war, which Nancy expressed in heightened carnivalesque imagery: 'I sometimes think that all our thoughts are wheels/Rolling forever through the painted world'.

inspired the lines in her poem 'Remorse': 'I sit ashamed and silent in this room/While the wet streets go gathering in their gloom'.

If Nancy was hoping for a more ordered, productive life with Sydney, she was also compensating for the loss of Iris. Towards the end of 1915, Herbert Tree had gone to America to work on a film project in Hollywood and a Shakespeare festival in New York. Concerned for his youngest daughter's reputation, he had taken her with him. Nancy missed Iris badly, and when news came back from America that Iris had fallen in love with an artist and photographer called Curtis Moffat and planned to marry, Nancy felt half impelled to do the same. She didn't allow herself to think beyond the immediate convenience that marriage would bring. During wartime no one thought about the future. Sydney might soon be dead, and so might she.

Life with her new husband, of course, turned out to be even more trying than life at home. Sydney was very sociable, and when they had settled into the little house in Montagu Square that Maud had acquired for them, he took it for granted that his friends would all be welcome there. Many were officers on leave, and their conversations about sport and regimental matters seemed to fill every room. The few photographs taken of the newly married couple show Nancy as a blurred presence, half cancelled out by the wide shoulders, alert gaze and military moustache of her husband. They bore little relationship to the bright breezy publicity that had trumpeted the wedding, with prophesies that the very 'original' Miss Cunard was likely to be 'one of the leaders of society after the war'.

Nancy was sufficiently dutiful to hide her growing dislike of her husband. Nor did she let Sydney see her relief when, in early July 1918, he was deemed sufficiently fit to return to the Front. During the six months he was in France, she wrote to him regularly – deceptively sweet, wifely letters tucked into parcels of sweets and other treats.

Yet no sooner had Nancy's single life been restored to her than she embraced it with joy and relief. Iris was still abroad, travelling with Curtis and her new baby Ivan, but Nancy had recently become close to Sybil Hart-Davis, the older sister of Duff Cooper. Sybil was eleven years her senior, married with two children, and she appeared to Nancy to have created a fascinating balance between domesticity and independence. She was certainly a delightful mother. As Nancy watched Sybil romping in the garden with little Rupert and Deirdre she felt pangs for her own neglected childhood.

That summer Nancy and Sybil arranged to rent a house together in the Oxfordshire countryside near Kingston Bagpuize. They were anxious to escape the latest attacks from the German bombers, and Nancy hoped the tranquillity of the country would be good for her poetry too. Despite visits from London friends like the Sitwell brothers, Chile Guevara, Mary and St John Hutchinson, and despite long, shambolic parties, with jugs of cheap wine and off-duty soldiers from the local training camp, Nancy remained true to her resolve. Shutting herself away in the drawing room of the Kingston Bagpuize house, smoking cigarette after cigarette, she enjoyed weeks of productive writing.

When Nancy was working on her poetry, she felt restored to her best self. But that summer, the pleasures of creativity were also infused with the energy of her first passionate affair.

Peter Broughton-Adderley had been the only friend of Sydney's who Nancy had liked. He'd visited Montagu Square in 1917 and impressed her with his literary enthusiasm as well as his obvious sweetness of character. He was also friendly with Duff Cooper and Diana Manners – another point in his favour – and when he was home on leave that summer, she invited him to stay for a weekend.

He stayed for the rest of his leave, and the delight Nancy found in him is evident in a description she wrote of the two of them reading George Moore's latest novel together in the garden at Kingston Bagpuize: 'My love and I sitting in a tree, and under a tree, read aloud to each other several days running from *The Story Teller's Holiday*, the beauty of the writing, the mood of the book and our own and everything about those hours being unaccountably moving.'[20]

For the rest of her life Nancy associated Peter with that book, and with the belief that during the summer of 1918 she had experienced what true love was like. But at the end of that golden summer Peter was recalled to France, and it was on a chilly morning in late October that Nancy was woken by Sybil – Peter had been shot in the stomach and had died of his wounds. Her grief at the news was huge and consuming, and it may have been one reason why her hatred of Sydney grew so obdurate. He was alive and Peter was dead.

If they had had some sort of future, perhaps Nancy would have exhausted her feelings for Peter, just as she quickly exhausted her small stock of affection for Sydney and tired of so many others. Yet for years she continued to think of him as the only man 'whom I loved entirely and wanted to live with'. Some of her friends were equally convinced that a life with Peter might have settled Nancy and given her a chance of ordinary happiness. When she lost him, they believed it dealt a blow to her already fragile equilibrium, from which she never recovered.

When the war ended, just a few weeks after Peter's death, Nancy hated the rest of the world for its callous jubilation. Another grieving young woman, Vera Brittain, heard the sound of ringing bells and cheering crowds as a death knell for 'the lost youth that the war had stolen', a reminder that 'the dead were dead and never would return'.[21] Many of them were lovers, husbands, fiancés, and when the flags were put away there were women everywhere who, like Nancy, felt that their hopes for the future had been buried in the mud of the battlefield.

Ruth Holland would recall their anguish in her 1932 novel *The Lost Generation*. For her heroine, Jinnie, 'Something had snapped. Instead of a life that was like a splendid tune in her ears, with ordered sound and movement, a definite form ... she was surrounded by a mocking terrifying jumble of discords in which she could find no sense at all . . . it was as if she had lost the key and could no longer read the signs of life around her.'[22]

For many such women, marriage and motherhood had been the only life they had imagined. Yet in Britain alone, the female population now exceeded men by two million. Many soldiers were also coming home from the war with their lungs scarred from poison gas, their limbs and faces shattered, their minds traumatized. With an entire generation of men so terribly reduced, young women were warned that there was a mere one in ten chance of finding a husband.

In a very short space of time, pity for these 'superfluous' women turned to alarm. The *Daily Mail* opined hysterically that they represented 'a disaster to the human race', while in more measured terms, *The Times* judged that they presented a problem 'so far-reaching and so immense that few have yet considered its import'. Certainly there were obvious signs of instability as returning soldiers found themselves having to compete with a new female workforce for their old jobs. And with the imminent prospect of women's suffrage, male commentators began to actively censure the post-war generation. Behaviour that had been overlooked in the war – smoking, drinking, wearing make-up and flirting in public – was vilified and it was now that the idea of the flapper became evoked as a threat.

In material terms, Nancy was far more fortunate than most of her peers – she had no need to work for a living and no children to worry about – but she also had nothing to distract her from her grief. And when she succumbed to the Spanish flu virus that was sweeping through Europe, it hardly mattered to her if she lived or died.*

Death, she felt, would at least save her from the complications of disentangling her life from Sydney. He had returned from the

---

* She was lucky not to – there were 150,000 British casualties of the Spanish flu, many far more robust than she.

war in January, when Nancy was still lying feverish in her
mother's new house in Grosvenor Square. It had been communicated to him, presumably by letter, that she wanted to end the
marriage, and he had been both incredulous and furious. By
early April, when Nancy was nearly recovered, she was still
terrified of confronting him, and it was partly to dodge Sydney
that she agreed to her doctor's recommendation of a change of
scene, embarking on a long trip down to the South of France,
and accompanied by Marie Ozanne, the one friend she had
made at her finishing school in Paris.

Nancy's spirits were low, but as she and Marie neared the
Riviera she felt the tonic effect of new horizons. Poetry was still
beyond her – illness and grief had left her mind 'like a disor-
dered room littered and scattered with useless furniture; the
clumsy ungainliness of words'.[23] But she was filling her diary
with traveller's impressions, practising her eye and her pen as
she observed the texture of a stormy sea ('little black waves
tumbling on like a helpless baby and sudden patches of transparent stillness'), the quality of clouds over a mountain, the
carved cloisters of the cathedral in Arles.[24]

Stimulating as these new landscapes were, however, Nancy
still found that the simplest remedies for despair were drink and
sex. Among the several men with whom she had affairs in France
were St John Hutchinson, who followed her out from London,
and an amorous singer called Paul, whom she met in Nice.
Nancy embarked on each sexual tryst with a determined expectation of pleasure, an 'immense jolly Rabelaisian mood, strung
up to any vulgarity'.[25] Yet just as she had during the war, she
suffered extreme moments of reaction when she felt 'agitated,
flimsy, unstable'.[26]

'Oh God shall I ever get into any *mood* here, and not be
finding it forever incomplete,' she fretted in her diary.[27] The see-
sawing volatility of her emotions made her weak and queasy, and
in late May, when she returned to London, she was still in a
fragile state. Her first impressions of the city were bleak: 'Everyone dead,' she wrote in her diary: 'Denny, Edward, Patrick,

Raymond, George, Billy . . . and the lovers of last year.' When she went to the Ritz she felt 'exhausted and trembling at heart', because there was no one she recognized in the hotel bar or lobby.[28]

There were survivors, of course, and Nancy was strong enough now to return to her old haunts, the Café Royal and the Tower, and to be drawn into a new round of parties, where she could rely on getting 'buffy' or 'blind'. There were new lovers, too, among them an American called Jim McVickar, of whom Nancy grew fond and with whom she recorded precious moments of 'abandon'.

She was also recovering some pleasure in her appearance. Fashionable clothes were returning to the shops, and Nancy was one of the first women in London to get her hair shingled and to wear the new shortened skirts. She looked elegant, slightly dangerous, and wrote with appreciation in her diary of having 'a very good figure' and being 'much seen'.[29]

But every pleasure was precarious, as was Nancy's equilibrium. Scattered through her diary are anxious reminders to herself to dress or flirt or laugh in a certain way, to make sure she was still desirable to men. She was quick to feel her loneliness and lack of confidence, and frequently disguised it with alcohol: '[It] smoothes down the bitter silences and comforts the nerves, dissipates my shyness.'[30] She wished she had an occupation and even toyed briefly with the fantasy of becoming some kind of avant-garde dancer: 'masked, beautifully dressed, very original'.[31]

But she wished even more for a man with whom her 'happiness [could] be ratified and enduring.'[32] Nancy hated herself for the hopes she invested in each new lover, and for the speed with which she found them wanting: 'How odd I am in the way I pick up with people, and get to know them terribly well, seemingly . . . and then jump every time the mechanism works of itself and the doll speaks.'[33] But that seemed to be her pattern. 'I find life quite impossible as I cannot enjoy a thing without carrying it to all the extremes and then nearly dying of the reaction.'[34]

For five months she walked a tightrope of nervous tension,

with nights of 'incessant drink' followed by days of collapse. She feared she might go mad from her 'gnawing and probing and exaggerating and lacerating state of mind. I seem to want too much, hence a mountain of unhappiness.'[35] And in this state of jittery self-absorption, Nancy found it impossible to deal with Sydney, who insisted on seeing her to discuss the arrangements for their separation, and punished her with what she regarded as insufferably self-pitying rants.

Maud she found equally intolerable. Now that Nancy was effectively single again, she had not only returned to live with her mother, but also reverted to her former state of financial dependency. That was bitter to her. 'Her Ladyship gave me [only] voluntarily what she might have settled on me; I felt I could not count on it and . . . that she could and would have cut if off had she so wished.'[36] Renting a house in the countryside and writing some poetry that satisfied her brought an interlude of serenity, but it was temporary. As soon as she was back in London, she was again overwhelmed by the 'long mood of depression'.[37]

She tried to outrun it by spending three frenetic weeks shopping and partying in Paris, but in October she suffered a severe collapse. Her mind and body were both shot and even Nancy acknowledged she needed help. She admitted herself to a nursing home outside London, where for a month she submitted to a strict regime of bed rest and sobriety. It was painfully dull, but it gave Nancy the time and space to reflect soberly on the necessity for change.

'My capacity for happiness is starved,' she wrote, and she was determined to revive it.[38] On her return to London she arrived at a compromise with Maud over money and living arrangements, moving into a small rented room above the Eiffel Tower. The complicated whirl of lovers and parties gathered around her once again, and the poet Robert Nichols put a pistol to his head, luridly threatening to blow out his brains if she failed to return his love. But Nancy reported triumphantly to her diary that, for the first time in years, she had managed to survive these and other traumas, 'WITHOUT ANY DRINK'.[39]

By the end of 1919, she made a vow that she would begin the new decade in a new place and with a new spirit of independence. She would establish a home for herself in Paris, where Pound, Lewis and others had convinced her that a cultural renaissance was stirring. She would not waste her time with shops and parties, but would find the courage to dedicate herself to writing. Later, Nancy would identify this vow as the most solemn decision of her life: 'I had determined to leave England and leave I did,' she wrote. 'On 7 Jan 1920 I went to France, alone for ever.'[40]

Chapter Three

TAMARA

In 1920 Paris was reclaiming its pre-war status as the City of Light: resurrecting itself to the rhythms of jazz, the flare of new ideas, the confident bustle of cafés and bars. But it was a very different Paris from the one in which Tamara de Lempicka had arrived two years earlier. In the summer of 1918, the city's shops and cafés were still shuttered against German shelling, food was rationed and much of the city's population was frightened and tired.

Few were prepared to offer aid to the quarter of a million Polish and Russian refugees who, along with Tamara, were streaming into Paris, in flight from war and revolution at home. Tamara had managed to smuggle out a few precious items of jewellery when she left Russia. But the market was already flooded with the gems and heirlooms of other exiles, and the money they raised was rapidly exhausted by the exorbitant prices being charged for food, lodgings and fuel.

Just eighteen months earlier Tamara's life had felt limitless. She had danced all night and drunk champagne as carelessly as though it were water. Now, with her husband Tadeusz and daughter Kizette, she was cooped up in a small hotel room, with just a bed, a cot and a basin between them. That basin came to haunt Tamara: 'The poor baby, our food, everything [was] washed in that one bowl.'[1] It symbolized everything she had lost, her old St Petersburg apartment and all the lovely things it housed: the hangings, the silverware, the pictures and Turkish carpets.

It made Tamara wretched to picture her apartment now, its rooms almost certainly pressed into lodgings for factory workers, its treasures looted by soldiers, its elegance tainted by coarse voices and dirty boots. Yet her immediate problem was her husband, who seemed barely able to stir from their hotel room, a vodka bottle on the floor close by, his beautiful features slack with defeat.

When she had first met him, Tadeusz had been a careless, confident playboy. Now he was weak and querulous, shrugging off her pleas that he find a job, telling her to go and beg some cash from her relatives – her uncle and aunt, or her mother Malvina, who had also resettled in Paris.

Tadeusz remained paralysed by his former sense of entitlement. Paris was growing familiar with his type. According to Coco Chanel these once privileged exiles 'were all the same; they looked marvelous [sic] but there was nothing behind . . . they drank so as not to be afraid'.² They certainly did not care to work. Tamara's uncle, Maurice Stifter, director of the Russian branch of Credit Lyonnaise in St Petersburg, had willingly taken a more lowly post in the Paris office and had offered Tadeusz a position in the same bank. As the son of landowning gentry, however, Tadeusz could not, or would not, bring himself to become a clerk.

By the end of 1919, Tamara's jewellery had all been sold, and while her relatives would never let her and Kizette starve, her life felt intolerably drab. She looked with envy at other young women in Paris, swinging arm in arm along the street, smoking cigarettes, their futures still before them. Her own days yawned with a weary predictability: looking after Kizette, cooking the family's meals, having nothing to dress up for beyond the occasional party at her uncle and aunt's. And always the fights with Tadeusz. The more she nagged her husband, the uglier his resistance became. He hit her frequently, and when Tamara saw her family she often had to conceal bruises on her arms and neck with powder or a necklace or jacket. It was humiliating to admit the miserable state of her marriage, but one night her pride gave way and she confessed everything to her younger sister Adrienne.

'We have no money . . . and he beats me,' Tamara wept.[3] Yet the sympathy she expected was not forthcoming. The flight to Paris had been liberating for Adrienne, opening her eyes to a world where clever, spirited women might make careers for themselves. As soon as the war was over she'd secured a place at the École Spéciale d'Architecture to train as an architect. And now, as Tamara poured out the litany of her misfortunes—her useless husband, the loss of her former, lovely life—Adrienne briskly reminded her sister that she too had options. Tamara had shown considerable artistic flair as a girl, having studied painting in both Russia and abroad: even if Tadeusz was useless as a breadwinner, that shouldn't stop her from helping herself.

In the decades that followed, Tamara would point to this conversation as the single, blinding moment in which she decided to become a professional artist. In all the interviews she gave, in all the tales she recounted to her daughter Kizette, she would claim that having bared her soul to Adrienne she had immediately gone out to buy the thick white paper and sable brushes with which she worked on her first picture. She would claim that with nothing to help her but her own God-given talent, she had raised herself out of adversity.

Tamara was, however, a habitual self-dramatizer. Ever since childhood she had tailored events into crises, triumphs or reve-lations, and the reality in Paris was not the fairy tale she liked to suggest. Several things delayed her from embarking on her new vocation, including the grim duty of help182ing her mother confirm the death of her soldier brother Stanzi, somewhere on the Eastern Front. Despite her later airy claim that she achieved success single-handedly, it was the teaching and support she gained from her early tutors, as well as the financial and domestic support of her family, that aided her through the early years of her new career.

Nevertheless, her progress was remarkable. Within half a decade of completing her training Tamara was established in Paris, charging up to fifty thousand francs for a commissioned portrait, which she would generally expect to complete in three weeks. This was good money – Josephine Baker was paid roughly five thousand francs when she was brought to Paris to star in *La Revue Nègre*, while the Harlem poet, Langston Hughes, working as a doorman in a Montmartre nightclub, earned just five francs a night, plus food and tips. But socially Tamara was also on the rise, written about in gossip columns and photo-graphed in magazines. In the most well-known of her pictures, *Autoportrait*, she would paint herself as an archetype of late 1920s glamour – seated at the wheel of a bright green Bugatti, her lips gleaming a metallic red; her platinum-blonde curls just visible beneath a leather motoring helmet. She would make herself look as hard, fast and luxe as the car she was driving – an icon of the decade. The depression that had fogged her first eighteen months in Paris had long passed by then, and Tamara's charmed self-belief, fostered since childhood, was fully restored.

Girls had always been cherished in her family. Her mother, Malvina Dekler, was the spoiled and lively daughter of a wealthy Polish banker, and along with her three sisters she had enjoyed all the advantages of a luxurious family home in Moscow, holi-days on the family estates in Poland, finishing school in Switzer-land and parties throughout the St Petersburg winter season. When Malvina's brief marriage to Boris Gorski, a Russian mer-chant, had ended in scandal – he had disappeared, or possibly even killed himself – she had put the trauma aside and simply moved with her three small children, Stanczyk, Tamara and Adrienne, back into the comfort of her parents' home.

A more exact chronology of the family history is hard to estab-lish, for Tamara developed a habit of reinventing or excising crucial details when journalists and biographers started to take an interest in her life. She didn't care to make public the scandal of her absent father, and she was fashionably vague about the exact date of her birth, alternating between 1895, 1898 and (impossibly) 1902. She also distanced herself from too close an association with Russia which, after the revolution, she came to detest, claiming her birthplace was not Moscow but Warsaw.

Yet in all the stories, real and false, that Tamara told about herself, she was always consistent about the idyllic nature of her childhood. Her grandfather Bertrand Dekler was rich, and he allowed his wife Clementine and daughter Malvina to indulge the entire household. There were lavish dinners and parties, clothes from Paris, the best tutors. And if all three children thrived it was Tamara, a bossy, imaginative and greedy little girl, who thrived most vigorously.

She was always the ringleader, directing the other two children on raids to the kitchen, where they stole tiny jam-filled cakes and cream moulds that had been prepared for one of Malvina's many parties. She was also the centre of attention. At the age of eight, burning from a small joke made at her expense by one of the servants, she ran away from home, and was discovered in the street outside, selling paper flowers to support herself in her new orphaned life.

As Tamara grew older the fantasy of herself as an orphan flower girl gave way to dreams of stardom. Her grandmother was an accomplished pianist, filling the house with the sound of Chopin waltzes and mazurkas. Inspired by Clementine's example Tamara spent hours at the piano, working on her scales, yet in her imagination already a concert pianist, exquisite in black velvet and pearls, and with a vast crowd in thrall to her brilliance.

The conviction of her musical genius was eventually replaced by a vision of herself as a painter. When Tamara was twelve, she persuaded Clementine to include her on a six-month tour of Italian art treasures. Initially, she had merely been trying to escape from school, faking a cough that was sufficiently bronchial to alarm her family into agreeing that the approaching Moscow winter would be dangerous to her health. But once in Italy, she was intrigued by what Clementine showed her.

As they walked hand in hand through the galleries of Venice, Florence and Rome, Tamara absorbed her grandmother's delight in the Renaissance masters, their use of chiaroscuro, perspective, colour and line. She found she was as susceptible to beauty as she was to good food and pretty dresses, and by the time they reached their final stop, a village near Monte Carlo, she was already planning her future as an artist.

Her amused grandmother offered to hire a tutor for the short time they were there, partly so that she would be free to indulge her mild gambling habit in the nearby casinos. The tutor was a young painter called Henri, and it was possibly his romantic good looks that clinched Tamara's new sense of vocation. The closeness of Henri's body, the occasional touch of his hand as he instructed her in the sketching of mimosa blossom and the painting of sea views, were even more exciting to Tamara than the pictures she produced.

Tamara was not a pretty girl: her heavy blue eyes, broad nose and solid curves were too adult for a child's face. But in the mirror she saw herself as lovely and, convinced that Henri must reciprocate her adoration, she vowed to make herself an artist worthy of him. Back home in Moscow, around the time of her thirteenth birthday she had her portrait painted by a society painter. It was done in pastels and in a style of sentimental mistiness that was considered appropriate for a young girl. Tamara, however, dismissed it as inept: 'The lines they were not *fournies*, not clean. It was not *like* me.' Certain of her own superior skills she forced Adrienne to sit for her, working with furious determination to prove her point: 'I painted and painted and painted,' she later recalled, 'until at last I had a result.'[4]

That dogged application would serve Tamara well in Paris in 1920. But as a spoiled adolescent she was far from ready to turn her fantasy of artistic perfection into hard-working reality. There were too many other distractions in her life, especially once she was old enough to accompany her mother to St Petersburg, to stay with her aunt and uncle, the Stifters, for the winter season.

The Russian capital was magical to Tamara – a Venice of the north with its frozen canals and gilded, pastel palaces, its busy traffic of troikas and sledges on snow-etched streets. St Petersburg also offered Tamara her first glimpse of Imperial society. Moscow was a busy, commercial city, but it did not shine as St Petersburg did in the full, reflective dazzle of the Tsar's court. Attending her first grown-up parties, her first opera and ballet performances at the Mariinsky Theatre, Tamara felt she had arrived in her true element: the fantasies of her childhood realized in the crystal chandeliers, the gowns of the beautiful women and the red and gold court livery of the men.

Now aged fifteen, Tamara was also impatient for adult love. One night she was invited with her aunt to a costume ball, at which she planned to create a stir by dressing herself up as a peasant girl and making her entrance with a pair of live geese walking at her heels. As a social strategy, this proved to be a mortifying miscalculation. Alarmed by the crowds and by the highly polished floor of the ballroom, the two geese started flapping and squawking in noisy distress, and for a few stricken seconds Tamara felt the whole ballroom laughing at her.

Yet even in the middle of this humiliation she had sufficient clarity to register the presence of an extraordinarily handsome man in the room. He was tall and slim-hipped, his chiselled Slavic features given an almost insolent glamour by dark, slicked-back hair. Tamara observed the number of women hovering around him, and it was competitiveness as well as lust that made her decide that one day she would have him: 'Right away I fell in love with him because he was so good looking. And because he was alone with ten women around him.'[5]

Within the small upper-class community of St Petersburg it was easy for Tamara to discover the identity of her future husband. He was Tadeusz Julian Junosza Lempicki, a twenty-two-year-old lawyer and son of a wealthy Polish family. He was also rumoured to be a womanizer, and while his worldliness and beauty ought to have overwhelmed a fifteen-year-old schoolgirl, Tamara was already wedded to the idea of him, and willing to wait.

The next time she was in St Petersburg, she tracked Tadeusz down at the Mariinsky, and approached him with an invitation to tea at her Aunt Stefa's – she was, she reminded him boldly, the girl with 'two geese as my friends'.[6] It was simply a marker, but the following year she was able to lay siege to him in earnest when her aunt and uncle invited her to come and live with them full time.

Having no daughters of her own, Stefa had taken a fancy to Tamara. It amused her to have a seventeen-year-old girl in the house to dress up and spoil, and in anticipation of this new arrangement she had already taken Tamara to Paris to buy a wardrobe for the new season. Aunt Stefa proved to be a liberal as well as generous guardian during that visit, and Tamara was permitted to explore much of the city on her own. As she'd walked the cobbled streets of Montmartre, hearing snatches of the blaring music they called ragtime, and sat in a café on Saint-Germain, awkwardly smoking her first cigarettes, Tamara felt she was becoming a woman at last. She was ready to make good her claim on Tadeusz.

Back in St Petersburg, as she accompanied Stefa on her social rounds, Tamara studied the way other women looked and behaved. She was intrigued by the ballerina Mathilde Kschessinska who lived in one of the city's finest private mansions, and possessed an astonishingly showy collection of jewellery that, as Stefa intimated, had come to her through her many 'protectors', among them two grand dukes and the young Nicholas Romanov, before he married and became Tsar.

Just as Diana's imagination had been jolted by the spectacle of Luisa Casarti, Tamara saw in Kschessinska some blueprint for her own half-formed fantasies of a life that could be bigger and more splendid than a conventional marriage. As yet she had no idea how that life might be attained; she was determined only that it would be magnificent and that it would involve having Tadeusz by her side.

Inserting herself into her beloved's world was easier than she had dared hope. Aristocratic Poles formed a small, elite group within St Petersburg society, and several of Tadeusz's circle were known to the Stifters. Tamara conspired ways of seeing him several times a week, taking afternoon coffee with him and his friends in one of the fashionable cafés along the Nevsky Prospect, or drinking in the Stray Dog Café, where writers gathered, and where Tadeusz liked to amuse himself by listening to firebrand ideologues as they debated socialism and art. In the evenings there were concerts, parties and balls, and always Tamara stayed as close as she could to Tadeusz's side, waiting for the moment when he would ask her to dance.

So obsessive was her pursuit that when war was declared in the summer of 1914, the news barely registered. Whilst her brother Stanzi was preparing to leave Moscow for the Front, Tadeusz, the only man she cared about, was debarred from military service (or so he claimed) by a slight defect in his foot. Not only was her beloved free from danger, but he was at last beginning to pay her special attention, visiting her at home, singling her out at parties, even intimating marriage. Money had recently become a pressing issue for Tadeusz, as his formerly sober father had begun squandering the Lempicki capital on women and drink. He had little desire to put his legal qualifications to more than dilatory use, and as he cast around for other options, Tamara seemed to be one of the best. It was hard not to suppose that her banker uncle had deep and generous pockets, and she herself had definite potential. The adoring schoolgirl he'd first met was fast maturing into an attractive woman; she was lively and intelligent, she dressed well, and her enthusiasm for life carried a definite promise of sensuality.

But if Tamara quivered with hope over Tadeusz's new attentiveness, her uncle and aunt viewed him less favourably. They knew about his father's slide into dissipation and were concerned it might be a family trait. Even more worrying to them was Tadeusz's failure to settle down to responsible employment. His only serious interests appeared to revolve around a group of rich young men in the city who were setting themselves up as defenders of the Imperial order, ranging themselves against the growing threat of revolution.

The Romanovs' corrupt and antiquated rule had long been unpopular, and during the last decade St Petersburg* had been gripped by intensifying spasms of political unrest. After the mass casualties of Bloody Sunday, in 1905, when the army had shot indiscriminately at a peacefully demonstrating crowd, the city had witnessed more violent outbreaks of militancy. The war had done little to unify the people: in fact as Russia suffered a series of grave setbacks, including the loss of Poland and part of Lithuania to the Germans, the Tsar's regime grew significantly weaker. 1915 was a year of strikes and protests and Tadeusz hinted, boastfully and probably untruthfully, that he'd been enlisted by the Tsar's secret police as a counter-revolutionary spy. Tamara was riveted by his claims, but they made Tadeusz even less desirable in the eyes of the Stifters. Gently they began to urge their niece to see less of him, while in private they began to discuss whether the city was not in fact too dangerous and whether they should take her away from Petrograd altogether.

Tamara was stubborn, though, her relatives' opposition only steeling her determination to possess her beloved, and because he was still hesitating on the brink of a marriage proposal she elected to force the issue. It's not clear exactly when she and Tadeusz became lovers, but in the spring of 1916, when Tamara proceeded triumphantly up the aisle, she was already pregnant.

It was a fairy-tale wedding. Tamara glided through a chapel packed with titled nobility and foreign dignitaries; the train of her dress, or so she claimed, stretched all the way from the altar to the door, and at first the fairy tale extended to her married

---

* By now known by its new and less German-sounding name, Petrograd.

life. Tadeusz acquiesced gracefully to his capture: Tamara's
dowry allowed them to take an apartment on Zhukovsky Street,
one of the city's most fashionable addresses, and even the birth
of Marie Christine, nicknamed Kizette, in September 1916 failed
to interfere with their married life.

As soon as was decent and practical, Tamara packed their baby
daughter off to live with Malvina in Moscow, while she remained
happily occupied with Tadeusz. Life was still good in Petrograd,
despite the war and the worsening political situation. The theatres were full; the champagne flowed; women wore their Parisian
dresses and diamonds; and the city buzzed. The latest gathering
point for the smart young set to which the Lempicki belonged
was the Comedians Hall, a vast pleasure palace, whose several
dining rooms were designed in the style of a Montmartre bistro
or Venetian palazzo and whose nightly programmes of entertainment featured satirical comedians, Futurist-designed stage tableaux and bands playing the latest American songs.

All these pleasures were far more absorbing to Tamara than
bad news from the battle front or the plummeting value of the
rouble. She didn't pay much attention to the food and fuel
shortages that affected most of Russia as the country's archaic
distribution systems collapsed, nor did she register that barely a
mile from her pampered world, hungry children were scavenging in the streets. However, by the spring of 1917 even she was
forced to take notice. A succession of strikes and mass defections
from the army had finally forced the Tsar's abdication, with
power now uneasily divided between the new Provisional
Government and the left-wing Petrograd Soviet. As panic flared
among Tamara's friends and neighbours, many began packing
up to leave. Not only was their city teetering on the brink of
anarchy, but everyone feared the power of the revolutionary
Bolshevik party, led by the exiled Vladimir Lenin and waiting in
the wings of Russian politics.

By now Maurice Stifter had transferred as much money as he
could to foreign holdings and he and Stefa were preparing to
travel to Denmark, where Malvina, Kizette and Adrienne were

already heading. Urgently they begged Tamara to join them, but even though she could see the dangers around her, she preferred to listen to the confident pronouncements made by her husband and his friends, who insisted that after a short sharp struggle, the counter-revolutionaries – the Whites – would restore the Tsar to his throne. Tadeusz's posturing heroics promised Tamara the drama she'd always craved: in her eyes she was already standing by his side as he fought for the Imperial cause. By the time she was forced to accept the true peril of her situation, there was hardly anyone left in the city to help her.

All through the summer the balance of power wavered: and by October, Lenin and his Bolshevik party were able to take control of the city, quelling opposition with their secret police force, the All Russian Extraordinary Commission for the Struggle Against Sabotage and Counter Revolution. The Cheka, as they became known to a terrified city, targeted anyone in the city with right-wing connections, Tsarist sympathies or visible wealth, and not surprisingly, Tadeusz was on their hit list. When they came for him, however, he seems to have been unprepared. According to Tamara, the two of them were making love when the door of their apartment was kicked open and she had to grab a sheet to cover herself as men in black leather overcoats swarmed into their bedroom.

Immediately they began ransacking the place for incriminating papers, and even though none were found, Tadeusz was ordered to dress, and marched out of the building at gunpoint to a waiting car. Tamara ran out, too, begging piteously for her husband's release, but a blow from one of the men sent her sprawling, half unconscious, onto a bank of hard snow. By the time she recovered her senses Tadeusz was already being driven away; and to her panic and disgust she realized that she had narrowly missed being pitched onto the remains of a dead horse. Animal carcasses were a common sight in the city: dogs and horses that could no longer be fed by their impoverished owners were routinely abandoned on the street, where their emaciated bodies were butchered for remaining scraps of flesh. Tamara had always averted her eyes from them, but now the ravaged mess beside her on the snow seemed to symbolize her own pitiful situation.

Naive and blind as Tamara had been, however, she was brave in the days that followed. She knew the Cheka might return for her – wives who remained loyal to their counter-revolutionary husbands were also in danger of incarceration. Even if she managed to evade arrest, she was still alone in a city where survival was becoming more precarious by the day. Her servants had run away; she didn't know how to obtain food and coal, she didn't even know how long she could stay in her own apartment, given the campaign of targeted evictions already underway.

Her natural impulse might have been to flee Russia and join her family in Copenhagen, yet she was determined to find help for Tadeusz first. There were still foreign diplomats based in the city, several of whom she knew personally, and as she began doing the rounds of the embassies in Millionnaya Street she was, initially, hopeful of success. However, all those men who had once been so gallant and eager now had nothing to offer. Their own situation was uncertain, given that Lenin had not guaranteed to honour Russia's former diplomatic allegiances; and there was only one, the Swedish consul, who didn't turn her away.

He had been a guest at her wedding the previous year, so Tamara had expected a sympathetic hearing at the very least. His treatment of her, however, turned out to be humiliating, even sadistic. The consul was eating his dinner when she was shown in to see him, a rich succulent meal, which indicated that some people at least were protected from the city's food shortages. Half starved herself, the meaty aromas in the room made Tamara nauseous, yet the consul ignored her distress and implacably told her to sit and eat with him so that he could hear the details of her case. Just as implacably, he made it clear that if he became involved, he would expect certain sexual favours in return.

When Tamara told this story she claimed that as soon as she left the embassy she had vomited violently in the street: a reaction to the consul's food as well as to the offensive terms of his offer. Yet wretched as she was, the consul had convinced her to trust him, and grimly she accepted his help. He'd been able to reassure her that Tadeusz was almost certainly still alive. Lenin was trying to curtail the bloodletting, and as yet very few death sentences had been passed. He stood a good chance of securing Tadeusz's release, too, as long as nothing more serious could be proved against him than running with the wrong crowd. But the consul also persuaded Tamara of the danger she was in, and of the little she could do to help Tadeusz by remaining in the city. He offered to organize a forged Swedish passport, advised her to pack just a few of her most valuable possessions, and promised to travel with her on the slow train to the border with Finland and the West.

Tamara would later recall that journey through a sequence of searing images. The hammer and sickle that was newly embla-zoned on the train, in place of the Tsar's insignia. The heavy tread of the Red Army soldiers as they walked through the carriage to check everybody's papers. Her own dizzy stumble as she walked across the narrow footbridge that took her into the safety of Finland. The night she spent with the consul in the border hotel, as the final instalment of her payment.

What was done was done, however, and by the time Tamara had journeyed by boat to Copenhagen to be reunited with her family, she was almost ready to boast of her courage and her adventures. Thanks to her uncle's prudence the whole family were installed in a pleasant hotel, and Tamara could feel her old optimism stirring as she waited for news of Tadeusz and the political developments in Russia.

The Stifters still assumed, as did most of the other refugees in Copenhagen, that the revolution would be short lived. In response to Lenin's tactical withdrawal from the war, the Allies had begun an invasion across Russian borders, which was expected to restore the Tsar. Yet in the months that followed, the Bolshevik's own control of Russia spread and reluctantly Maurice Stifter was forced to make alternative plans. Settling in

Warsaw, the family's other home, was no longer an option given how politically fraught that city had also become.* Although they spent a short time there, during which they were finally joined by Tadeusz, Maurice judged that they would only be safe if they travelled as far as Paris. In the spring of 1918 he arranged for the family to make the 850-mile journey in separate groups, in order to minimize the attention they might attract (as Poles with Russian residency both their national status and their war affiliations were in doubt). By early summer, they had all arrived safely, but it was then that news came through of the Tsar's assassination. The family's exile now seemed to be permanent.

Tamara may have exaggerated her heroism in the retelling of her wartime adventures, but she had discovered a new and resilient independence in herself, and a less deferential attitude towards her husband. Even in Copenhagen, where she had been genuinely anxious for Tadeusz's safety, she had grown tired with the long wait, and been happy to distract herself with another man. By a seemingly odd coincidence, the consul from the Siamese embassy in Petrograd had appeared at the Stifters' hotel. He, too, had been a guest at Tamara's wedding, but in contrast to his Swedish colleague, the consul's physical attentions were very welcome to her. Tamara willingly entered into a brief affair with him – relishing his elegance and his worldly company she even accompanied him on a short diplomatic mission to London and Paris.

Tamara had a very clear sense of what was owing to her – it had been bred into her since she was a child – and given the traumas of her recent ordeal, she felt she deserved nothing less than the comforts this pleasing man could offer. She didn't even feel much remorse when Tadeusz finally arrived in Warsaw, haggard from weeks in prison. She was relieved that he had

---

* The Poles were fighting off both Russian and German efforts to take control of the country.

escaped, of course, and was ready to devote herself to being his wife, but the man who'd come back to her was not the husband she had known. Incarceration had broken his spirit and all he could talk about was his own humiliation and pain, showing irksomely little interest in anything his wife might have suffered.

It was a mystery to Tamara how her confident playboy of a husband could become so unattractively mired in depression. She missed the man she had married, and, because she had so little talent for empathy, his self-pity struck her as unworthy. She began to develop a germ of contempt for him and, even in Paris, where she too began to experience depression, she felt no twinge of sympathetic recognition for his suffering. It was one reason why, when Tamara found the resolve to turn her life around, she did so entirely on her own terms and without bothering to consult Tadeusz. Once she had decided to become a professional painter she immersed herself completely in the project, certain that from now on her own ambitions would take precedence over his.

Such ruthless focus would of course prove very useful to Tamara over the next few years as she forged ahead with her career. But she was also fortunate to be situated in Paris, where the art world was comparatively sympathetic to women of ambition like herself. Even though most of the French academies had only recently opened their doors to mixed students, and many female painters depended on the mentoring and support of men*, there were a significant number who had achieved highly visible success. Among them were Suzanne Valadon, who became the first woman elected to the Société Nationale des Beaux-Arts in 1894; and the Fauvist Emilie Charmy – of whom it was always said that she looked like a woman but painted like a man.

These were powerful role models, and they attracted many

---

* In London, many members of the Society of Women Artists still exhibited under male pseudonyms.

other women to Paris. Nina Hamnett studied there in 1914, and returned regularly: Gwen John, the reclusive, gifted sister of Augustus John (and mistress to Rodin) was achieving belated recognition in the city's salons. Jean Rhys, who herself came to Paris to write in the early Twenties, observed that Paris seemed to be 'full of girls' who talked of nothing but becoming painters. For Tamara, the number of aspiring women in Paris was both an encouragement and competition – and she responded well to competition.

By the end of 1919 she had enrolled herself in the Académie Ransom, a private school run by the widow of the Fauvist painter Paul Ransom. Passing Kizette over to the care of her mother, who was living in a pension close by, Tamara devoted most of her day to her new vocation. When classes were finished she went to the Louvre, filling the pages of her sketchbook with notes and copies of the works in its collection. At home she continued to sketch, ignoring the ache in her back and the strain in her eyes. Just as her thirteen-year-old self had worked obsessively at Adrienne's portrait, she was now relentless in her determination to improve her draughtsmanship, smoking three packets of cigarettes a day to keep her brain alert, and then sedating herself with large doses of valerian.

Less than a year after she entered the Académie, Tamara judged that the first stage of her education was complete. Her teachers had nothing more to show her; she could feel the confident, hard pulse of her ambition, and was ready to forge her own style. The avant-garde works that she saw displayed in Left Bank galleries were of little interest to her: the muddy earth tones used by followers of Cézanne, the abstract introspection of Kandinsky, the crazy nihilism of the Dadaists, were all equally offensive, as she later wrote, 'I was disgusted with the banality into which art had fallen.' Most of these artists seemed, to her frankly inept, unable even to draw; and much as she reluctantly admired Picasso's success, she believed it was simply because his art 'embodied the novelty of destruction'. By contrast, her own models were to be the Renaissance masters she had first discovered with Clementine: 'I aimed at technique, métier, simplicity and good taste . . . colours light and bright.'[7]

Yet reactionary as Tamara's artistic instincts were, she would be drawn, magpie like, to the bolder, more dynamic aspects of modernism. She developed a colour palette of almost unnatural lacquered brilliance; the figures in her paintings had a physical force suggestive of Leger, or of Picasso's monumental nudes. Most influential on her early work was the implosive energy and fractured shapes of cubism, whose style she principally absorbed through the work of André Lhote.

She studied privately with the painter for several months, drawn to the way he applied cubism to decorative and modish subject matter. Lhote painted attractive people framed within fragments of a stylish bar or nightclub scene; female nudes arousingly displayed.* And if many of his peers disdained his work as 'soft', or 'salon' cubism, he provided Tamara with a model she could both copy and transcend. Portraiture was to be her principle genre, portraits of beautiful, charismatic or powerful people. And her instinct for what was chic, combined with her mastery of classical techniques, created a style that chimed deeply with contemporary commercial taste. In 1922, after less than two years of study, she had a trio of works accepted for the Salon d'Automne, one of the most widely attended showcases for new art in Paris.

Her entries had been sponsored by friends on the selection committee: Maurice Denis, one of her teachers at the Academy, and her sister Adrienne who, impressively, was already acquiring a reputation as an architect. Even so, Tamara saw her inclusion in the Salon as a pure vindication of her talent. It was the first milestone on her journey towards money and fame, and she marked it with the promise that she would buy herself a new diamond bracelet with every two paintings that she sold, and

---

* Albert Gleizes, a cubist painter of portraits, was another influence, and she shamelessly plundered his smart and sexy use of the Manhattan skyline as the backdrop to his figures.

that she would continue buying them until she had diamonds stacked from wrist to elbow.

Tamara's application to her new vocation initially had a positive effect on Tadeusz, who in 1920 accepted a lawyer's position with the Banque de Commerce. The salary wasn't large, but it restored a little of his self-esteem, and it was sufficient both to engage a housekeeper to help with Kizette and to rent a decent-sized apartment. Tamara had fallen in love with a flat that had a spacious north-facing sitting room, able to double as a painter's studio. The fact that it was already occupied by the father of the concierge was no obstacle: the concierge was no match for her bullying, wheedling campaign and declared bluntly to Tadeusz: 'Votre femme elle m'a eut jusque'au trognon' (your wife sucks the marrow out of my bones).[8] The father was relocated.

The flat was on the Right Bank, but Tamara made almost daily journeys across the river to Montparnasse. This working-class area, a still-traditional mix of local grocery stores and cheap bars, was fast becoming the new artistic centre of Paris. And while she personally felt detached from many of the new trends, Tamara took care to keep abreast of them. She studied the works that were showing in the art galleries opening near the Seine and the Jardin du Luxembourg. More closely still, she studied the artists who gathered in Left Bank cafés like the Dome or the Rotonde, or in the bookshops run by Adrienne Monnier and her lover Sylvia Beach. Monnier's La Maison des Amis des Livres, and Beach's Shakespeare and Company were not only the places in which the latest art books and poetry could be found, but also the latest gossip.

Tamara knew she had to find a way into this Left Bank community. Life in St Petersburg had taught her the importance of making social contacts, of knowing how insiders dressed, talked and conducted themselves. She had already begun meeting Adrienne and her friends at Les Deux Magots; but as she made the rounds of other cafés she was often happy to sit alone, wanting simply to listen and watch.

Some of what she saw was confusing. Among the students and

artists seated around her were socialists and anarchists, parroting views that Tamara thought she had left behind in Russia. They were hideously dressed: the men in cheap suits or workers' overalls; the women in coarsely woven smocks and headscarves. Tamara couldn't understand why anyone would pretend to be a peasant. Her brief exposure to the Bolshevik terror had hardened her hatred of anything left wing or revolutionary. As she sat in the corner by herself, drinking her afternoon coffee, she felt that she had little point of contact with these strident young people.

But still she liked to be among them, imagining herself as a compelling, mysterious presence, gracefully shrouded in her own cigarette smoke, apparently deep in thought. She registered the faces of those who seemed to hold most sway over a room. And she kept her antennae tuned to the other people in the cafés, fashionable men and women who were clearly tourists in this world and who might one day be patrons of her own work.

In the early Twenties, Paris was once again a marketplace of modern culture. Before 1914 it had been the capital of the Belle Époque, home to the symbolists, decadents, post-impressionists, cubists and Diaghilev's Ballets Russes. Now it was the city of black jazz, Dada, and the emerging surrealists, avant-garde ballet and international poetry magazines. As the American stock market boomed and European economies regained their post-war momentum, art became a very desirable commodity. It was chic, it conferred status and it was a sound investment. Prices for a known artist like Picasso were rising – the most commercial of his paintings fetching up to a hundred thousand francs – and among foreign buyers there was already brisk competition to find the next significant talent. The entire oeuvre of a likely painter might be bought up by a single collector, and a new, avid breed of art tourists paid for guided tours of studios, or even visits to cafés and bars where fashionable painters might be spotted at play.

The nightclub singer Bricktop recalled that in the mid-1920s this symbiosis between money and culture seemed 'a beautiful, beautiful thing'. Paris was full of impoverished artists 'who wanted to write, who wanted to paint and perform'; it was equally 'full of people who had money but couldn't make it' and it was these 'rich ones' who began 'taking care of the ... geniuses'.[9] The commercial opportunities in Paris were all very interesting to Tamara, who saw nothing romantic in the idea of being poor or misunderstood. Financial success couldn't come quickly enough for her as an artist, and there may even have been an element of calculation in the work she opted to focus on during her early career. Portraiture was a money-making genre – many of Tamara's diamond bracelets would be bought with lucrative commissions from society figures. But certain of her canvases were particularly appealing to the 1920s art market – those that had young, contemporary and very desirable women as their subjects.

Tamara worshipped glamour. Having always aspired to it herself, she vowed 'to scent [it] out' in her models, and lavished as much care on their appearance as she did on her own – the exact shade of their lipstick and eye shadow, the styling of their hair, the cut of their clothes. Their skin was particularly beautiful: Tamara had perfected a technique of tiny deliberate brush strokes that allowed her to paint surfaces of a peculiarly glossy lustre; the classical luminosity of her models' skin would frequently be compared to Ingres.

Naked or clothed, the subjects of her portraits also possessed a liberated sexual poise: they looked like women who were accustomed to drinking in cafés or bars, who took lovers yet cherished their independence. Tamara, by instinct as much as by choice, was making herself into the portrait painter of the new woman, the flapper, the garçonne, and everything conspired to make this a highly marketable move.

Young women were much in the headlines. Victor Margueritte's novel La Garçonne* had recently been published, its narrative of

---

* Kees van Dongen's illustrations for the 1926 edition of La Garçonne represented Monique as a slender almond-eyed beauty, naked in some images, fashionably dressed in others.

lesbianism, drugs and single motherhood causing such a scandal
that Margueritte was stripped of his Légion d'honneur. The timing of its publication had been almost as controversial as its subject
matter, since it appeared in bookshops on the same day that the
French senate voted against giving women the vote.

Members of the French Union for Women's Suffrage protested
vehemently, along with the eighty or so feminist organizations
that now operated in France. Yet despite being excluded from
official politics, women in France, no less than their British and
American peers, were finding other ways to assert their presence:
through the jobs they demanded, through the independence they
claimed and, almost as significantly, through their clothes.

In the nineteenth century America and Britain had been the
principle battleground for the women's dress reform,* but it was
in Paris that the battle for emancipation joined forces with
couture style. Coco Chanel, the orphaned seamstress who
opened her own couture house on rue Cambon, went far beyond
Poiret and his generation. She created simple shift dresses,
geometric in their lines but swinging easily around a woman's
body as she walked. She appropriated the demotic uniforms of
sailors and workers for a new line of bell-bottom trousers and
striped jerseys; she replaced large fussy hats with berets, turbans
and, by the mid-1920s, closely fitting cloches that were designed
to show off their wearer's short and shingled hair. Chanel's rival
Jean Patou predicated his own most famous styles on sportswear
– the 1921 Wimbledon star Suzanne Lenglen wore his clothes
both on and off the court.

There was a liberating androgyny in these new styles – the
term *garçonne* was precise – and just as significantly a degree of
democracy. No Chanel design was cheap to buy, yet some of her
garments could be reproduced with economy and speed. The
inexpensive materials that she made fashionable – cottons and

---

* Although the Wiener Werkstätte studio in Austria had made a pioneering
attempt to incorporate fashion into a wider programme of progressive design.

jerseys (the latter formerly used for men's underwear) – were perfect for low-budget imitation. She even democratized jewellery, creating a vogue for 'illusion' pieces that were constructed out of paste and gilt.

Tamara considered fashion her natural element. She had her hair cut short in 1922, so that it curved sleekly to her head, dramatizing her broad Slavic cheekbones and the brilliant blue of her eyes. Clothes were harder for her: she was still large-boned, lushly curved and too vain to force herself into straight-cut shifts or trousers. Instead she played with more theatrical outfits, favouring draped white satin and feather trims for evening wear, and of course her diamond bracelets. Her interest in clothes was meticulously transferred to her canvases. In the double portrait *Irene and her Sister* (1925), the architectural folds of Irene's silver-grey dress contrasted with her sister's extravagant fall of golden hair and green coat. These elegantly dressed women, posed ambiguously against a dark forest background, were not merely a painterly construct, they looked like an illustration for a fashion magazine.

Tamara portrayed women as she imagined they liked to view themselves, as both chic and sexually desirable. But even more distinctive was the fact that her models' allure was directed as much, if not more, towards the gaze of other women as it was to men. Around 1920 Tamara became acquainted with one of her neighbours, a woman whom she would later casually refer to as 'a very wealthy girl across the street, a red head who sat for many paintings'.[10] Her name was Ira Perrot, and she was the model for one of Tamara's most successful early portraits, *Portrait of a Young Lady in a Blue Dress*. In this 1922 work the woman's solidly fleshed body is clearly naked beneath the cobalt blue draping of her dress, and the gaze from her kohl-darkened eyes is half accusing, half complicit. The portrait has a candid eroticism rarely seen in Tamara's earlier work and it also had a very personal resonance, for Ira was almost certainly the woman with whom she had her first lesbian affair.

Tamara liked sex, and when the opportunity allowed she had

already begun to take lovers in Paris. Tadeusz's shattered nerves and the claustrophobia of their early lodgings had made her nostalgic for the adulterous adventures she'd enjoyed with her Siamese consul. She trawled the cafés for attractive men and, as she later boasted, found it took very little to signal her availability. A slight, feline arching of her back and a glance slid from under her long eyelids would be followed by a drink and a few pleasantries. Tamara didn't waste much time in making it clear that she was happy to accompany her new conquest to his hotel room or apartment.

But it was only after she met Ira Perrot that Tamara began to appreciate the possibilities of women. Initially, she and Ira were probably just friends,* but in 1921 they went on holiday to Italy, which, for Tamara, remained one of the most passionate experiences of her life. To return to the cities she had explored with her grandmother, to enjoy the luxury of first-class hotels (at Ira's expense) felt like a precious return to her former privileged life. In the arms of her new lover, she experienced them all with a fresh pleasure.

It never seems to have occurred to her to react against these new feelings, to wonder if they were a momentary aberration. Even though the affair with Ira eventually waned, Tamara's interest in women didn't, and her work became redolent of it. *Perspective*, painted in 1923, was one of the most technically impressive canvases of her early career. Its portrayal of two embracing women combines a classical finish with a modernist dynamic – the women's naked flesh looking sumptuously golden against a turquoise cloth, the line of their bodies distorted to create an exaggerated effect of mass. But it is the physical intimacy of their embrace that dominates the picture, with one of the women abstractedly stroking the inner thigh of the other as they lie together, her head thrown back in an ecstatic drowse.

---

* Photographs of the Perrot and Lempicki couples together raise interesting but unresolved questions about how much the two husbands knew of their affair.

The scene is one of unmistakable post-coital languor, suggesting that Tamara herself could had been making love to these women before retreating to her easel to paint them. At the very least it looks as if she was painting from experience, and as critics began to identify her as a painter of 'Amazons'* Tamara encouraged that perception by gaining the friendship and patronage of a prominent circle of sapphists.

Women with money and influence played a significant role in the cultural life of Paris. As hostesses of their own private salons, they made it their responsibility to nurture careers, and broker contacts and connections. Three of the most powerful were Natalie Barney, Gertrude Stein and the Princesse de Polignac (who before her marriage had been Winnaretta Singer, daughter of the sewing-machine magnate). All were American expatriates and lesbians, and for Tamara to gain entrée into at least one of their salons was to assure herself of valuable support.

Her first attempt had been discouraging. A friend had taken Tamara to one of Gertrude Stein's Saturday salons, held in Stein's apartment at 27 rue de Fleurus. Stein herself had been a disappointment – plump and plain in her brown corduroy smock, her hair unbecomingly arranged in a cottage loaf of a bun – and while Tamara could acknowledge that this odd-looking American had an impressive art collection on her walls (Stein had discovered Picasso long before most buyers) she found the style of entertainment at rue de Fleurus impossible. It was bad enough that Stein presided over conversation that was both pretentious and dry (to Tamara's ears), but insultingly, she was allowed only a few minutes with Stein and her favoured guests before being dispatched into a corner to sit with Alice B. Toklas – Stein's 'wife' – to eat cakes and drink tea. Tamara could acknowledge the excellence of Miss Toklas's baking, but where, she wondered, was the champagne?

---

* Around this time she temporarily changed her signature to the masculine version of her name, Lempicki, though it fooled few people.

Stein had made it ruthlessly clear that she rated neither Tamara nor her painting. Later, when she was more closely infiltrated into Left Bank society, Tamara realized that Stein, on the whole, was far less professionally welcoming to women than she was to men. However, when she went to Natalie Barney's salon, Tamara encountered a completely different world, one that embraced and supported women with magnificent largesse, whether in their private affairs or in their public careers.*

Barney had embraced her lesbianism with peculiar self-confidence. Born in 1876, she said that from the age of twelve she had claimed 'the perilous advantage' of 'being other than normal'.[11] Once she had become independently wealthy, thanks to money inherited from her father, she had left her home city of Washington to settle in Paris, where she set out to create a sapphic idyll.

She was not a proselytizer for the lesbian cause. The theories advanced by Havelock Ellis concerning the natural fluidity of sexuality made little impression on her; she required neither permission nor explanation for her own desires – and while she was interested to see a younger generation living with new sexual freedom, personally she shrank from making too assertive a display of her tastes. 'I am lesbian,' she said, 'one need not hide it nor boast of it.'[12] She certainly disapproved of those who took the extreme route of cropping their hair aggressively short and wearing monocles, waistcoats and trousers.

Barney herself appeared intensely feminine, dressing in the pre-Raphaelite style that was favoured by the Duchess of Rutland and writing reams of mistily rapturous love poetry.† Yet even the most masculine sapphist of the period would have found it

---

* In 1927 Barney would launch an unofficial 'Académie des Femmes' as a riposte to the French Academy of Literature, whose list of forty 'immortals' continued to exclude women.
† The fervently sapphic imagery of Barney's poetry – 'breasts like lotus flowers', 'hearts moaning like the sea' – meant that much of it had to be privately published and distributed.

hard to equal her predatory boldness in matters of sex. She divided her affairs into three categories, starting with the long-term 'liaisons' that she had with a very few select lovers, most enduringly the painter Romaine Brooks and the writer Élisabeth de Gramont, who became known as the Red Duchess for her violently socialist views. Then came the 'demi-liaisons', which included Barney's affair with the writer Colette, and finally the 'adventures', the numerous casual encounters she enjoyed with women who, according to Alice B. Toklas, she frequently picked up in the toilets of department stores.

Those encounters had to be managed with discretion. Paris was famed for a degree of sexual tolerance – Oscar Wilde had begged his lover Alfred Douglas to flee there after their affair became public – and it was rich in transgressive haunts, from cross-dressing bars to homosexual cabarets. But in most public areas, it was impossible for two women, or two men, to openly solicit each other or behave like lovers without attracting abuse. Among the more strait-laced circles of the Parisian upper classes, a known lesbian would certainly not be accepted, which was why Natalie had to create her own private world of entertainment, from within her elegant two-storey *pavillon* on the edge of the Latin Quarter in Montparnasse.

The situation of 20 rue Jacob was marvellously discreet, hidden from the street by high walls and gates. Yet behind those gates, Natalie's sexuality was sumptuously evident, from the small columned folly in the grounds (her Temple of Love), to the profusion of gilt, tapestry, stained glass, velvet and damask within the house: 'A cross between a chapel and a bordello,' according to one much later visitor, Truman Capote.[13]

Equally feminine in style were her Friday salons. Tiny, multi-coloured iced cakes and exquisite cucumber sandwiches were served for tea to extraordinary women such as Isadora Duncan, Colette and Mercedes de Acosta. Men were regulars, too, among them Ezra Pound, André Gide, George Antheil, Jean Cocteau and Paul Poiret, yet as the young American poet William Carlos Williams realized, these male guests were incidental to the main action. The languorous glances and whispered asides of the women around him, the regular disappearance of two or three at a time, made Williams feel unsettled and self-conscious. 'I went out, and stood up to take a good piss,' he later recalled. It seemed the only way for a man to assert himself.[14]

Some of the most important friendships Tamara developed at rue Jacob were with men: including the protean artist Jean Cocteau, whom she came to love as much for his snobbishness and treachery as for his wit. But it was the women who were most important to her, including the Marchesa Luisa Casati, who was now living in France, renovating her new home, the Palais Rose in Versailles. Casati never commissioned a portrait from Tamara. Perhaps she felt that her belladonna darkened eyes and gothic, hennaed hair required the surrealist eye of Man Ray or the misty flattery of Augustus John's brush, rather than the brilliantly lit de Lempicka style. But Casati was a useful contact, giving Tamara introductions to several friends, including the influential photographer Baron de Meyer, and the Italian poet Gabriele D'Annunzio, who had once been the Marchesa's lover and mentor, and was still her close friend.

There were others among Natalie Barney's circle who both modelled for Tamara and bought her work, including the Duchesse de la Salle, whose title might be fake but whose regal asperity and mannish dress inspired one of Tamara's most compelling early portraits. Even Tamara was impressed by the speed with which Paris was opening up to her. Her friends now included prominent artists – Jean Pascin and the portrait painter Kees van Dongen – as well as a scattering of the rich and titled, among them Misia Sert, Polish wife of the painter José-Maria Sert and friend to Diaghilev, also the generous and knowledgeable Comtesse de Noailles.

Supported by such people, Tamara was growing confident of success. The three pictures she had shown in the 1922 Salon d'Automne had created a stir of critical interest with *Le Figaro* noting the 'disquieting precision' of their style'.[15] The following year, Tamara's appearance in the Salon was sponsored by André

Gide, and more group exhibitions followed in the Salon des Tuileries and the Salon des Femmes Peintres. Tamara was making her name not only in the art press; she was also being noticed by the columnists. The clothes she wore, the places she went to, the names of those invited to the parties and dinners she now hosted – all were becoming news.

Yet while Tamara basked in her success, her husband and daughter often felt themselves to be its victims. Tadeusz was not happy in Paris. He missed his family, who were now living in Poland, and although he had found a reasonably good job, he had only partially recovered his former spirit. Most nights he wanted to do nothing beyond slump in a chair with a glass of vodka and one of the detective novels to which he'd become addicted.

His depression hadn't entirely extinguished the sexual attraction between him and Tamara, yet it was only just sufficient to hold the marriage together. Tamara's obsessive interest in her work and her professional contacts left her little time for her husband, and her career increasingly represented a threat. Not only was she beginning to earn more money than him, she was starting to act like the man of the house.

It wasn't that she ignored her duties as a wife and mother. Tamara carefully allotted time to tuck Kizette up at night and to take breakfast with her in the morning. Occasionally she dedicated hours to the preparation of extravagant Polish dinners, and she always demanded the highest standards. A badly cooked meal or an ugly piece of crockery placed on the table by her unwitting housekeeper could rouse Tamara to a fury. More than one wine glass or vase was smashed because she judged it to be vulgar or bourgeois. This angry perfectionism was partly a reaction to those few, frightening years when her life had veered out of control, but it cast a net of irritable, nervous tension over the household. Kizette alternated between extravagant attempts to please her 'Cherie', as Tamara liked to be called, and resentment at her scenes. Little Nancy Cunard, averting her face from Maud's chocolates, could have sympathized with Kizette the night that she stubbornly refused to add the ritual 'God bless Mama' to her prayers.[16]

Tadeusz, however, preferred Tamara's volatile domestic presence to her increasingly regular absences. Most evenings, after tucking Kizette up in bed, Tamara would disappear from the apartment. Her excuses were always innocuous – she was going with friends to a new cabaret, the opera or a restaurant – but often she wouldn't return home until dawn. Tamara was discovering the full decadent potential of Parisian nightlife. If she was out for the evening with the Duchesse de la Salle she might go to the lesbian club, La Rose; if she was with one of her male homosexual friends she might end up in one of the gay bars on rue de Lappe, where men dressed up as women and the cabaret was exceptionally obscene.

At such places there was not only a range of drink and jazz on offer but also drugs, which Tamara discovered she enjoyed almost as much as she liked sex. Her taste was not for the anaesthetic calm of morphine, but for substances that made her feel dangerous and alive: hashish that came in tiny pellets and was swallowed with sloe gin fizzes, or cocaine sniffed from a miniature silver teaspoon. The latter was Tamara's special addiction: it was cheap and easily available, and she coveted the electric clarity it induced in her senses and the lift it gave to her physical desire.

Tamara was a greedily tactile woman: even during ordinary, daylight encounters she liked to reach forward and stroke the cheek of the person she was talking to, or cup their face in her hand. But on the dance floor, holding her partner close in a foxtrot, or circling around them in a Charleston, Tamara's caresses became demanding. Men and women who were partnered by her would feel her lips on theirs, her fingers trailing across their chest or crotch. One night at La Rose, Tamara began to undress the woman with whom she was dancing, announcing to the amused crowd that she was auditioning her as a potential model. As she caressingly assessed her victim's breasts in her hands she pronounced them to be 'round enough'; inserting her hand between the woman's legs, she judged with mock regret that she would not do, she was 'too wet to concentrate'.

These exhibitionist displays became Tamara's party trick, but they were often just foreplay to more lawless sexual encounters. It wasn't only the buzz of cocaine that fuelled Tamara's desires, but the craving for adventure. On certain nights she would excuse herself from the company of her friends and head off to an area on the Left Bank of the Seine that was notorious for its seedy, jerry-built clubs and bars. This shanty town of pleasure had flourished during the war and continued to service the appetites of the 1920s. It was an environment perfectly suited to Tamara's needs. Among sailors, students and other anonymous pleasure-seekers, she could vary and refine her sexual high: according to one unnamed acquaintance, threesomes were her favourite, allowing her to savour simultaneously the softness of a woman's skin and the muscular heft of a man.

Tamara's mantra that 'it is an artist's duty to try everything' was a cliché of Left Bank life, yet for her it had a visceral reality. The more squalid or precarious her sexual encounters, the more liberating she found them. They gave her a release from the rigid structure of her daytime life and the ambitions she'd set herself. Yet even in the random intoxication of these late-night encounters, Tamara's painterly vision was still at work. She retained a powerful sense memory of the strangers with whom she had sex: the hard or ripe texture of their flesh, the shape of their bodies. They were all potential material and when she returned home she would sometimes stay up painting until the last of her sexual and chemical adrenalin was expended, converting the sensations of the night into brush strokes and colour. Sometimes she would snatch only a couple of hours' sleep before it was time to wake Kizette for breakfast. Decades later Tamara would recall that she had 'started from nothing' with a determination to achieve 'the best of everything'.[17] By 1924, she believed she was getting close to her aim.

Chapter Four
TALLULAH

John Hollis Bankhead had always expected his granddaughter to put the family name in lights. With reluctant
admiration, the Confederate veteran and US Senator had
judged that 'Tallulah had a *force* in her from her very
childhood, and it was clear that force had to go somewhere.'[1] A
pugnacious, plump little girl, she was apparently without fear,
hurling herself out of a hay loft, her hair 'on fire' with the
excitement of pretending to be a parachute jumper.[2] She had
temper tantrums so violent that her grandmother had to douse
her with buckets of cold water, and her behaviour at school was
so delinquent she rarely stayed at any establishment for longer
than a year.

Perhaps it was inevitable that as soon as she was old enough,
Tallulah would propel herself away from her conservative
Southern family and towards the glitz and glare of an acting
career. Given the emotional hullabaloo she created around herself, the stage was her natural element. But as she was growing
up, Tallulah's attention seeking had been more than simple
exhibitionism: it had been the only strategy she knew for claiming the attention of her emotionally volatile father and compensating for the death of her mother.

Adelaide Bankhead had developed fatal peritonitis just three
weeks after giving birth to Tallulah, on 31 January 1902. Later

Tallulah would deal briskly with the tragedy, asserting that she couldn't brood over a woman she 'did not remember'.[3] Yet as a child she'd felt a haunting association between her birth and Ada's death. How could she not? Her father Will had her baptized in a ceremony that took place right next to her mother's coffin. He then lapsed into a state of histrionic mourning that continued intermittently for many years, veering between hectic high spirits and alcohol-fuelled melancholia. One of Tallulah's earliest memories was of seeing Will weaving inconsolably around the house, waving a gun and vowing to join his wife. However carefully the other adults in her life tried to shield her, she could sense from the talk about her father that some guilty train of logic connected his behaviour back to her.

Will had adored his wife. She was beautiful, spoiled and very romantic: if the mood took her she would wander down the dirt track of her grandfather's plantation dressed in her latest Paris gown. And when the mood took her to fall for the handsome young lawyer Will Bankhead, she happily threw over the man to whom she was already engaged.

For two years Will and his bride led a charmed life. They set up home in a large apartment in Huntsville, Alabama, and shortly afterwards Will got himself elected to the Alabama State Legislature, paving his way to becoming a congressman. The following year their first daughter Eugenia was born. And if the household budget was a little tight, subsidies from Will's father always ensured that there were servants, books, good food and drink.

After a cruelly short time, however, all this was taken from Will. It was evident to the family that his grief left him helpless to cope with his two tiny daughters, and so the pattern of Tallulah's childhood was set. For part of the year she and Eugenia were sent to live with their grandparents in Jasper, a day's ride from Huntsville; for another part they were with Will's sister Marie in more distant Montgomery. In practical ways it was a good solution but the girls grew up feeling that nowhere, exactly, was home. Each place had its own rules. When they were alone with their father in Huntsville, he let them stay up late and bribed good behaviour out of them with candy. When they were living in Jasper, their grandmother imposed early bedtime and any breaking of rules was met with the punishment, or the threat of it, from their grandfather.

The Bankheads were, in fact, a lively, affectionate clan. Yet without a mother or a real family, Tallulah spent most of her childhood feeling that every scrap of affection had to be fought for. Eugenia, by contrast, seemed to be fussed over by everybody. She was a delicate child, suffering acute attacks of measles and whooping cough when she was very small; she was also pretty and had a far more winning disposition than her turbulent younger sister. It seemed to Tallulah that Eugenia always had more than her fair share of their father's love, and for the whole of her life she would begrudge the fact that Eugenia had once been taken on a picnic by him, while she'd been left behind.

A photograph taken when the two girls were about eight and seven showed exactly how things stood between them. Eugenia, a neat docile girl, is seated in a chair with her hands and ankles demurely crossed, her hair tied with a large white ribbon. Tallulah, standing next to her, looks double her sister's size, her plump arms and waist unnaturally confined in her Sunday best frock and a calculating grin on her face. The hand snaking behind Eugenia's back looks ready to deal a pinch or a slap.

Tallulah suffered because she wasn't pretty, and she also suffered because she was a girl. Carelessly Will had let slip that he would have liked his second child to be a son, and so Tallulah, along with Nancy Cunard and legions of other confused daughters, grew up believing she might have been more lovable had she been male. She tried to appease Will by becoming the next best thing, the Bankhead tomboy; while Eugenia offered her father smiles and obedience, Tallulah's gifts were cartwheels, daredevil courage and a willingness to use her fists in an argument.

She also became the family clown. When Tallulah was five, Will took her to a vaudeville show to take away the pain of a trip to the dentist. She was far too young for it, but she loved every act, especially the 'risqué chanteuse' who was the star of the programme. During the ride home she mimicked the singer's routine in her husky little voice, having no idea why its innuendo-laden lines ('When he took his hat I wondered when he'd come again') should make her father laugh so. The song became Tallulah's special link with Will. If he was feeling lonely he would wake her and lift her up onto the dining table so that she could perform it again. One night he even got her to sing it for friends he'd brought home after an evening's drinking.

It was a dubious lapse of judgement on Will's part, letting his daughter sing burlesque to a room full of grown men, but to Tallulah, the raucous delight of her late-night audience was entrancing. 'The cheering of a crowd did things to my spine, to my mind,' she wrote in her memoir.[4] 'I've often tingled to applause, but never did I have such tingles as that night.' You could make people love you, she discovered, by keeping them entertained. However, she found it hard to moderate her tone. Tallulah's hunger for attention was extreme: when she was cast in a school play she ruined her scene by improvising additional lines for herself and turning cartwheels across the stage. When she told a funny story she could ruin the effect by laughing herself into a state of collapse. She was an emotional windmill at full sail. Small grievances produced torrents of tears; anger made her violent. After an argument with her younger sister, Eugenia learned it was safest to get herself behind a locked door otherwise Tallulah would 'be breaking into the room and be twisting my arm'.[5]

By the time Tallulah was ten, Will believed the only way to manage his younger daughter was to send her and Eugenia away to school. It proved difficult to find one nearby that would take them both as boarders, and the one he selected, the Convent of the Sacred Heart, was over a thousand miles away in Manhattanville, a suburb of New York. Inevitably, both children were wretched. Eugenia coped as she always did, by being biddable and working hard, but Tallulah was in trouble every day. The actress in her might have been mesmerized by the rituals of the convent – she liked to drape herself in a black shawl and sit with lighted candles in front of her mirror, trying to imitate the nuns – but the tomboy in her was floored. Restless, homesick, unable to focus on her lessons and overwhelmed by the new regime of rules, she was continually being punished.

She was also lonely. Most of the other girls in her class were from the North and were quick to judge her as a Southern outsider; her name sounded freakish to them[*] and her exhibitionism seemed absurd. Back home she might be considered naughty but she still fitted in with the gregarious spirit of the Bankheads, who for all their old-fashioned views on race and religion, possessed a colourful streak of non-conformity, what Tallulah would appreciatively call 'style and dash'.[6] Her grandfather's loud voice used to ring through the house in Jasper, mixing up Shakespeare, proverbs and local vernacular. When his wife berated him for using low words like 'ain't', he refused to listen, insisting that he would never gain another farmer's vote if he spoke like a Yankee gentleman.

Will could be equally extrovert when his mood was on an upward curve, declaiming poetry, cracking jokes, inventing games of flamboyant hilarity and sometimes offering his daughters spectacularly inappropriate treats. It's doubtful that there were any other pupils from the convent watching the Broadway melodrama to which Will took Tallulah and Eugenia after their first term at boarding school. Titled *The Whip* it wrought delicious havoc on their ten- and eleven-year-old imaginations, its highly sexed plot line involving dissolute British aristocrats and its dramatically cacophonous stagings of a train wreck and car collision, leaving both girls 'red eyed and disheveled'.[7]

The other pupils in the convent apparently came from far more decorous backgrounds. When Tallulah tried to make them laugh, by telling stories or parading naked around the dormitory,

---

[*] Tallulah was named after her grandmother, who in turn had been named after the beauty spot Tallulah Falls, which her parents had visited around the time of her conception.

they curled their lips in disdain: when she tried to join their games they regarded her simply as an annoyance. Inevitably, the more of a pariah Tallulah felt, the worse her behaviour became. At the end-of-term service, the pupils with the highest marks for conduct were given white veils to wear as they filed into chapel, and a white lily to hold. Tallulah, however, was singled out to walk in line with a black veil. Weeping, she felt like 'an untouchable'.[8]

After the convent Tallulah was sent to a succession of different schools, but she remained, intractably, a problem child. While she liked reading and was clever and inquisitive, she found it difficult to concentrate during class. Perhaps if she had been given more opportunities to perform in school plays or recitals she might have settled better. But while she loved to act and had a facility for learning chunks of poetry and dialogue by heart, she was rarely picked for anything but a minor part. Her behaviour was too unpredictable and she looked too odd. With the onset of puberty Tallulah had grown even plumper and her skin had broken out in sullen blooms of acne. With her hair still cut childishly and bluntly short, even the most flattering costume could not make her look appealing. Certainly never as appealing as Eugenia, who stoked Tallulah's burning sense of injustice by being repeatedly cast in the end-of-term shows.

By the age of thirteen Tallulah was spending most of her free time with her collection of stage and movie magazines, and with pin-up photos of her favourite stars: the haughty beauty Alla Nazimova and the adorably ringletted Mary Pickford. She was convinced she could become an actress, too, if only she were pretty like Eugenia, or like Zelda Sayre, a girl she knew in Montgomery. When Tallulah was small, she and Zelda had been rival tomboys, competing over backbends and cartwheels. But Zelda was now fifteen and had grown into a Southern belle, with beaux queuing up to dance with her and take her for rides.

Tallulah felt even more excluded from the conspiracy of attractive girls when a new rival appeared for her father's love. Having finally gained some control over his drinking and depression, Will had begun courting a young secretary, Florence McGuire, and when he announced he was going to marry her, Tallulah was outraged. She did everything she could to undermine Florence, mimicking the way she tried to conceal the Jasper twang of her accent. Yet, slowly, she began to revise her opinion as she discovered the benefits that came with a stepmother.

Florence could make things happen. It was she who persuaded Will to buy his first motor car, a shiny Hudson roadster that brought tremendous zip and possibility to the family's Sunday outings. And it was she, alone of all the family, who began to broach the subject of Tallulah's appearance. Tallulah had always assumed that her spots and puppy fat were an intractable misery; no one had ever indicated that there might be a remedy. But Florence read the health and beauty columns of all the women's magazines, and she not only suggested that Tallulah should let her dark blonde hair grow long and wavy, she also advised her to embark on a regime of diet and exercise.

Tallulah could summon draconian forces of will when she cared about something, and within just a few months she managed to shed over twenty pounds and achieve a miraculous healing of her skin. To the mild astonishment of her family, she had actually made herself lovely. And as Tallulah gazed at herself in the mirror, admiring her dewy cheeks, perfecting a mistily fervent expression in her large blue eyes, she could see herself, at last, as an actress.

The following year she moved one stage closer to her dreams. Will had run a successful campaign to be elected to the House of Representatives, and the whole family were moved to Washington, with Eugenia living in an apartment with Will and Florence, while Tallulah and her grandparents lived in the apartment immediately above. Mrs Bankhead's dearest plan was to get her granddaughters launched in Washington society, but Tallulah was focused only on finding her way to the theatres and film studios of New York, which was now just over two hundred miles away.

To some degree she'd inherited this dream from her family. Both her grandparents had been keen amateur actors in their youth, performing in plays to raise money for the Confederate cause. Will had been so caught by the acting bug that he'd come close to abandoning his legal training for a job with a small repertory company in Boston. Even poor, dead Ada had once fantasized about going on the stage. Reciting poetry in her bedroom she had confided to her friend Margaret Du Bois Smith, that she was already 'an actress in her heart'; starring in school plays she had dreamed of following in the footsteps of Sarah Bernhardt, Mrs Fiske and Eleanora Duse, all of whom she had seen perform.

As the daughter of an old plantation-owning family, Ada had no serious hope of fulfilling her ambition. It would have meant social disgrace. Yet in one generation much had changed and across America, thousands of girls were now dreaming, along with Tallulah, of becoming actors.

It was a national obsession, and it was one that had been created primarily by the film industry. A stage artist like Bernhardt could make herself known and loved by many (Henry James commented that the term celebrity would have had to be invented for Bernhardt if it hadn't already existed). On the first of her several tours to America she had performed in no fewer than fifty towns. Yet the size of Bernhardt's public was always circumscribed by her medium and until 1912, when she made her first film, most of her fans would only expect to see her act once or twice in their lifetimes.

In contrast, the cinema brought famous actors to every small town, almost every day of the week. By 1920 there were over twenty thousand movie theatres across America, in addition to the older, cheaper storefront nickelodeons that dominated the early years of cinema.[*] Young women who might never have had the opportunity to see Bernhardt or Fiske now imagined them-selves becoming another Mary Pickford or Lillian Gish.

---

[*] Prices for nickelodeons were obviously five cents; in 1915 a larger movie house would charge ten cents a ticket.

Their ambitions were also fostered by the industry's new fan magazines. By 1917 there were around fifty in publication, and if their titles were generic – *Picture-Play, Motion Picture Classic, Photoplay* – so too were their contents. Page after page featured meticulously lit and staged studio portraits of current film stars, along with stories about their homes, cars and possessions and details of their personal lives. Much of what was printed was shameless fabrication, produced by a PR industry that was becoming more and more sophisticated at peddling celebrity wares. The extravagant fictions that were spun around Theda Bara dwelt on the Arabian background of this silver screen vamp, on her menagerie of exotic pets and her wild love affairs. Yet in reality Theodosia Goodman was the daughter of a Cincinnati tailor, an intelligent woman who between film engagements preferred to live quietly with her family and friends.

The movie industry needed fantasy, not just to market their stars but to attract the lucrative advertising campaigns that came with them. Products of the new American mass market sold at a dramatically better rate when associated with a famous name. Picture cards of celebrities were given free with packets of cigarettes, and on the giant billboards that jostled for attention on American skylines and shop fronts, the eerily enlarged and blandly smiling faces of movie stars exhorted fans to buy face creams, hair pomade or mouth wash.

On the other side of world Diana Manners and Nancy Cunard existed in a world of bombs, rationing and casualty figures. And although America too had entered the war in the spring of 1917, it meant little to girls like Tallulah. The stories that dominated her imagination revolved around lucky young women like Olive Thomas, the Pittsburgh shop assistant who less than three years earlier had entered a competition to find the 'most beautiful girl in New York' and had ended up contracted to the International Film Company and married to Mary Pickford's actor brother Jack.

Olive and Jack were now reputed to be 'two of the gayest wildest brats who ever stirred the stardust on Broadway',[9] and it was in the June issue of *Picture-Play* that Tallulah spotted an item that promised her a chance to become gay and wild herself. The magazine was running a beauty contest, for which readers were invited to send in photographs; the prize was a role in a film to be directed and produced by Frank Powell in New York.

Some of these competitions could be cruel scams, the 'role' nothing more than the chance to play an extra in a crowd scene.* Tallulah was deaf to any word of caution, however. She posed for her photograph in a borrowed hat and fox stole, and such was her excitement that she sent it off without remembering to write her name and address on the back. Three months later she was sitting with Eugenia in the local drugstore, drinking a Coca-Cola and leafing through the latest issue of *Picture-Play*, when there, among the gallery of twelve winning photographs, was her own picture. Above it was the dramatic headline WHO IS SHE? And beneath it an urgent request that the 'mysterious beauty make herself known'.

Tallulah recalled that her ecstasy could be heard a street away. 'I dashed out of the drugstore, magazine in hand, screaming, "I've won it! I've won it! I'm going on the stage." '[10] As yet she'd given no thought as to whether her family would allow her to claim her prize, nor to the matter of a chaperone: Tallulah at fifteen and a half was too young, too naive and too dangerously headstrong to be allowed to head off to New York without some adult companion.

During the noisy family debates that followed, other arguments were raised. Mrs Bankhead believed the film contract would do no good to Tallulah's marriage prospects, which she considered central to her granddaughter's future. Will's objections were largely financial. His income was much reduced now that he had largely given up the law, and his congressman's

---

* Clara Bow would be offered her own film debut through a competition in *Movie Motion*, but her brief appearance ended up on the cutting-room floor.

salary had to stretch to supporting his new wife, as well as Mrs
Bankhead's plans to launch Eugenia (and possibly Tallulah) into
Washington society. Although Tallulah was supposedly being
offered a weekly salary of $25 for filming her debut role, this
would hardly cover the cost of keeping her and a companion in
New York. Especially as Tallulah had made it plain that she
intended to remain in the city once the film was made, in order
to look for other work.

Tallulah was incredulous at the opposition to her dream: she
wept, she sulked, and she threatened hunger strike – a strategy
that had served her well when she'd been trying to get herself
removed from one of her several schools. Finally her grandfather
intervened. Tallulah, he judged, was 'a peculiar child . . . self-
reliant to a fault perhaps and always thinks her plans are best'.[11]
It was clear to him that her ambitions would give the family no
peace until she found a way to satisfy them, so he offered to
subsidize Tallulah's expenses, at least for the short term, and
arranged for Tallulah's Aunt Louise to accompany her to New
York.

It's hard to know what the family were thinking when they let
her go. Louise was never a forceful woman, with less of the
Bankhead 'dash' than the rest of the clan, and she was at a
particularly low ebb at this time: grieving the loss of her youngest
son, William, to typhoid two years earlier, and the recent breakdown of her second marriage. She was hardly in a state to
contain a tornado of energy, ambition and curiosity like Tallulah,
nor to defend her from the perils of New York.

The Bankheads believed they were aware of the dangers.
They had read the headlines, and anticipated that the city might
be a snakes' nest of race activists, birth-control advocates,
women's trade unionists and drug fiends. They had instructed
Tallulah in the importance of avoiding drink and men. Yet, still,
they had very little inkling of the kind of professional pressures
she might be pitted against.

A range of abuse and exploitation was endemic in the film
industry. Aspiring starlets were routinely asked to perform sexual

favours in return for a film role, or to subsidize their earnings by working in the pornographic fringes of the business. Even in mainstream feature films, sex was a major selling point. Regulation of content wasn't introduced until 1930, and when Theda Bara starred as Cleopatra, her costume was far more shocking than Maud Allan's; her virtually naked breasts were supported by a brassiere of twisted wire snakes; the outline of her crotch tantalizingly visible behind an embroidered transparent skirt. When Clara Bow told her mother and aunt she was going into the movies, their reaction was typical of many Americans at that time – Clara would be making herself a 'hoor'. The respectable Bankheads, by contrast, had little knowledge of what their Tallulah might become involved with.

In late summer Tallulah arrived in New York 'boil[ing] with excitement and ambition'[12] as she waited for her new life to begin. She had been to the city before, on the occasional family outing to a Broadway show, but she had never lived there. To her joy, Louise had found an apartment on West 45th Street, right in the heart of the theatre district. Around her the names of her favourite actors were spelled out in electric lights, and Tallulah hummed with the knowledge that at any moment she might see one of them on the street – that one day she might even be working with them in the same studio or theatre.

Almost all her dreams were crushed as news came through that the production company with which Tallulah was meant to be working had gone bankrupt, and the film assigned to her had been cancelled. The competition organizers at *Picture-Play* promised to find an alternative, but they could not specify when that might be, and Tallulah's impatience rose to a nearly unendurable pitch when, instead of being transported to the magical world of the film studio, she was obliged to trail around the city in her aunt's wake.

Louise had her own purpose in accompanying Tallulah to New York, which was to visit some of the more celebrated spiritualists and mediums who operated there. She believed, fervently, in the possibility of making contact with her dead son William, and in that hope she had brought along his former fiancée Ola. Spiritualism was big business in America, especially among women.* Its eight million or more adherents ranged from political campaigners seeking guidance from the spirit world to the growing number of war-bereaved hoping for some message from their slaughtered menfolk. Louise had no trouble finding 'experts' in New York who were willing to take her money for the promise of a word from William. And day after day Tallulah was forced to traipse with her and Ola through a succession of dimly lit rooms, where hushed exalted women chanted and consulted with cards.

Finally, in October, she was delivered from this gloomy netherworld. A small part had been found for her in a new romantic comedy, *Who Loved Him Best?* Directed by Dell Henderson, it was a cheaply made feature, and Tallulah's character, a bohemian girl called Nell, was only one level up from an extra.† Yet every day, she and Louise took a streetcar across the river to the film studio in Brooklyn,‡ and as Tallulah learned her way around the crowds of actors and technicians, the snaking yards of cable, the painted flats and giant Klieg lights, she saw only a world of glamour and possibility.

She was lucky, too, that she came out of the filming well. In several key scenes she was positioned close to the main action, and was in shot sufficiently long for the camera to register the distinctive qualities of her face. Still not quite sixteen, Tallulah was intriguingly poised between woman and child. Her recently achieved cheekbones had brought sophisticated definition to her heart-shaped face, and there was a hint of the siren in her carefully plucked eyebrows and in the long hooded lids of her eyes. Her skin, however, was innocently creamy, and this was one of her key assets. The crudely undiffused lighting of the

---

* Initially inspired by the early nineteenth-century writings of Swedenborg and Franz Mesmer, it was popularized worldwide by a growing industry of trance lecturers, hypnotists, hack mediums and holders of séances.
† She was part of a group of friends attached to the hero, an artist called George.
‡ It was part of the Mutual Film Corporation.

early twentieth-century studios was so brutally exposing to every line, freckle or pore that most young starlets were considered old by the time they were twenty-two. Youth was at a premium, and Tallulah had it.

She herself was cock-a-hoop when she first saw herself on the screen. Making the film had been so delightful, she said it was a 'terrible thing' to be paid for it, and Will was not pleased when he heard that Tallulah had ebulliently torn up her first $25 pay cheque. She was determined to earn more, and soon, and during the early months of 1918 she scoured the trade press and pestered anyone she could find for information about work. Her family was impressed by her resolve and called in all their contacts in New York, including a business friend, James Julian, who knew the film industry. 'My dearest Tallulah,' Will wrote with pride, and perhaps some surprise, 'you are certainly going at this thing like you mean business and I am betting on you and backing you to my limit.'[13]

Without the support of *Picture-Play*, however, the audition process was a lonely, testing time for Tallulah, as she waited in line along with dozens of other girls, being stared at and scrutinized as though she were horseflesh. She was also worried that her family would withdraw their financial support if she didn't get a paying role soon; John Bankhead was an enthusiast, but he didn't have infinite resources.

It was a long and anxious three months before Tallulah got her next engagement, a walk-on part in a stage comedy called *The Squab Farm*. Frederic and Fanny Hatton's script was a satire on the new starlet culture and, ironically, it gave Tallulah her first lesson in how harshly competitive the acting business could be. There were several other young women in the cast, all with more experience than her, and they were disinclined to welcome this bouncy, privileged sixteen-year-old into their midst. While the play was in rehearsal they spoke so little to her and offered her so little practical help that Tallulah felt as though she were back at the convent, despised and unwanted. When she broke the golden rule of theatre and whistled inside the dressing room, the other girls were so savage that she went back to her room and wept.

She was unhappier still when the play opened in March and her photo appeared in the *Sunday Morning Telegraph* accompanied by a puff piece hailing her as the star of the show. Some Bankhead string-pulling had got the piece published and while she tried to assure everyone that it was 'bilge', her fellow actors refused to speak another word to her. The forty-five performances the play managed to run were professionally horrible: the reviews were bad, morale was low and she herself 'felt more lonely than ever'.[14]

By slow increments, however, her career began to advance. Two small film roles followed, along with a couple of precious mentions in the press. One line in the *Tribune*, praising her as a novice of rare intelligence and beauty, caused much rejoicing in the Bankhead family and was read with triumph by Tallulah. Significantly, too, she was beginning to make friends and contacts within the profession. Early in 1918, when Ola decided to quit New York, Louise reduced their living costs by moving them into a hotel. She had heard that Commander Evangeline Booth, heroine of the Salvation Army, had frequented a suitable establishment close by on 45th Street, and judged that she and Tallulah could find modest, respectable lodgings there.

It was only when they arrived in the crowded lobby of the Algonquin Hotel, and a couple of powdered, painted and obviously 'theatrical' women emerged from the elevator doors that Louise suspected she had been misinformed. When they were eating their first evening meal, she realized the full extent of that misinformation, as a number of startlingly familiar actors, including Ann Andrews and Douglas Fairbanks Junior, came in to dine. The hotel that Louise had so innocently selected was one of the great social hubs of New York. Actors like the Barrymore siblings (John, Ethel and Lionel) rented suites there while they were performing on Broadway, and after performances, everyone dined at the Algonquin restaurant. The following year, the hotel would also become famous for hosting the Round Table –

the New York circle of wits and media pundits that included Robert Benchley, Heywood Broun and Dorothy Parker.

Tallulah had a few tense moments watching Louise's initial reaction, terrified her aunt might insist they pack their bags and leave. But Louise shared the Bankheads' susceptibility to theatre glamour, and if she feared that it would make her task of chaperoning harder, she couldn't deny that the Algonquin was an ideal place for her niece to acquire professional contacts. As for Tallulah, arriving in the hotel was like walking into the pages of *Picture-Play*. The first time she found herself in an elevator alone with Ethel Barrymore, she had to lean against the wall for support, feeling herself in the presence of a goddess: 'Her imperious manner, the scorn in her voice, the contempt of her eyes, the great reputation in which she was cloaked, made a violent impact on me.'[15]

She was also determined to make an impact herself, and whenever she wasn't occupied with work, she hung shamelessly around the hotel's public spaces, looking out for actors to engage in conversation. When there was an after-show party or dinner being held in the restaurant, she flirted or clowned her way into the middle of it. 'I would have jumped off a cliff to gain the praise of the quality folk I met on these midnight parties,' Tallulah recalled.[16] And frequently she went too far. 'I was such an idiot I put on this big act; I was so nervous all the time they thought I was putting on airs and it was sheer nerves.'[17]

The British actress Estelle Winwood was living in the Algonquin at this time and remembered disliking her at first: 'She'd come in and flounce around. What for? Nobody cared about her then.'[18] And yet Tallulah made herself hard to resist. Estelle admitted she had never 'seen anyone so pretty', and like other of the hotel regulars she was gradually beguiled by this extraordinary looking child, with her Southern drawl and her entertaining manner. Tallulah was a wickedly accurate mimic, and she secured some of her first invitations to the dining tables of the Algonquin by imitating the very celebrities with whom she longed to be friends. Her entrée to a party hosted by Condé

Nast, the New York publisher, was given on the understanding that she would perform her Ethel Barrymore routine.

What touched these tough, cynical professionals was the ferocity of her enthusiasm. Tallulah borrowed newspapers and magazines so that she could keep up with industry gossip, and she insisted on seeing every new show or film, often more than once. Estelle Winwood was astounded when Tallulah informed her that she'd been to see her perform in the Broadway play *Why Marry Me?* eighteen times. Within a few weeks, Tallulah had become a kind of pet among the Algonquin regulars. The actress Ann Andrews had never met anyone with her vitality: 'It seemed her feet could hardly stay on the ground.'[19] Frank Crowninshield, editor of *Vanity Fair*, found her 'scorching eagerness to be somebody'[20] both remarkable and very sweet.

She was, however, too much for Louise. As Tallulah was accepted by this racy, adult community, she began to pick up its ways. She took up smoking, she learned words that would have scandalized her grandmother and she stayed out late, leaving a telephone message for her aunt, if she remembered. By the summer it had become impossible for Louise to keep up. Between the auditions, rehearsals, photo shoots and performances, the lunches, dinners and late-night parties, Louise was run ragged. She felt a failure as a guardian, and what clinched her despair was the discovery that Tallulah, desperate to earn some extra money, had gone off to a photographer's studio and posed for him semi-nude.

Louise flinched from imagining what else Tallulah might be doing, and eventually she just abandoned her task. In the summer of 1918, she joined the Red Cross and sailed to Italy to help with the war effort. Her departure created a kerfuffle of reorganization as Aunt Marie and Florence agreed to take it in turns to come and stay with Tallulah at the Algonquin. But both women were shocked by the life Tallulah was leading there. 'It was hell,' Florence claimed, and neither of them was prepared to endure the responsibility of managing it. By early 1919, the Bankheads reluctantly accepted that they would simply have to trust seventeen-year-old Tallulah to survive New York on her own.

They did what they could to control her from a distance.* Will begged the Algonquin's manager Frank Case to impose a midnight curfew – a self-defeating threat, since she simply spent the night with a friend if she arrived back late. 'I can either run a hotel or I can look after Tallulah,' Case reported back. 'I can't do both.'[21] James Julian was deputized to send home regular reports, and various members of the family kept up a stream of anxious, admonitory letters, begging Tallulah to keep on the straight and narrow. Will's focused on the need to restrict her spending and her new cigarette habit: 'I hope you are not smoking too many, as they are mighty bad for you, your nerves and looks too.'[22] Those from Tallulah's grandmother appealed hopefully to her virtue: 'I love you so dearly. It seems impossible for you ever to disappoint me and shatter my hopes.'[23]

In all the family correspondence was the unstated but clearly understood threat that if Tallulah really disgraced herself she would be ordered back home. But she did have others looking out for her. Estelle Winwood had long seen through Talullah's bluster to the uncertain, needy child beneath, and so, too, had Jobyna Howland, a six-foot blonde actress with an inventively foul mouth and openly bisexual tastes. When Tallulah had first taken up smoking she'd been startled in the lobby one afternoon by a loud voice that 'had barked, *Take that cigarette out of your mouth, you infant*'.[24] It had been Jobyna, and after Louise's departure she and Estelle appointed themselves unofficial guardians, making sure Tallulah was safely in her bed most nights and that she was not, at least, starving.

Tallulah had no concept of budgeting. Half of her $50 weekly allowance went on lodgings, but the rest was often splurged on a new hat or theatre tickets. By the end of the week she had

---

* In 1919 she was temporarily restored to Louise's care after her aunt returned from Europe. For a few weeks in 1920 she also lodged with her uncle Henry Bankhead, now in military residence on Governor's Island.

nothing left for food and depended on Estelle and Jobyna to smuggle her into parties where she could eat for free. She was acquiring a slightly ragamuffin air; her one good evening dress looked soiled, the heels on her shoes were worn and she didn't always wash as carefully as she might.

As yet she wasn't wasting any of her allowance on cocktails or champagne – Will's drinking had cast too long a shadow over her childhood for Tallulah to find it alluring – and the following year, when the new Prohibition laws made the sale of alcohol illegal, she was one of the few people in showbusiness not to be bothered. If Tallulah was keeping her promise to her family to steer away from drink, she was also being careful around men. She was still, in many ways, an innocent. One night at the Algonquin she'd been roused from sleep by Estelle Winwood knocking on her door in a desperate state. A man with whom she'd been drinking in the bar had forced himself into her bed and had not used a condom, and she needed to know if Tallulah had a douche bag she could use. Tallulah, anxious, sympathetic and wide-eyed at her friend's distress, had no idea what such a thing was. Growing up among the Bankheads, she had been kept in ignorance of the most basic facts of life, and even now she'd had no practical experience of them.

The extent of her naivety might have shocked the men who were beginning to hover around her. With her carefully made-up face and glossy pout, heavy lidded eyes and plush little body, Tallulah looked absurdly, forwardly sexual. As the actress Jane Cowl observed, there were moments when her youth already looked ripe for corruption: 'Her face is like an evil flower . . . She's so intense she vibrates. She's one of the most violently beautiful women I've ever seen.'[25]

Tallulah hardly acted the virgin, either. She was still delighted by the novelty of her beauty and by the permission it gave her to flirt. She was also genuinely curious about what sex might be like. Even before Louise's departure there had been moments when, giving her aunt the slip, she had been alone with a man in the back seat of a taxi or in a dark corner at a party. Such experiences were perilously interesting: 'More than once,' she admitted, 'I trembled on the brink of compliance.'[26]

There were forces much stronger than desire holding Tallulah back, though, and technically at least she would remain chaste for another three years. She was terrified of her family hearing rumours of scandal and 'withdrawing [her] from the tournament',[27] and she was even more terrified of getting pregnant. The episode with the douche bag had inspired Estelle and Jobyna to impart a few salient facts about babies and contraception, and they had done so in a way that warned Tallulah of the danger and unpleasantness involved.

European women were beginning to enter a modern era in birth control, with the arrival of the Dutch cap. In America, however, a puritan majority remained opposed to the general availability of contraception. For most young women in 1918, the only ways to avoid getting pregnant were using vinegary-smelling douches or the thick Trojan condoms their lovers might have picked up from a barber's – the new latex brand would not be introduced until the following year.* Both were unreliable, and at this stage of her career, when Tallulah was far hungrier for success than she was for a man, she would not run the risk.

She did, however, discover that New Yorkers had ways of enjoying themselves beyond those known to the Bankheads. As Tallulah would frequently and famously quip, 'My father warned me about men and booze, but he never mentioned a word about women and cocaine.' Caught as she was between curiosity and caution, Tallulah was soon trying both.

The first time she experimented with cocaine, Tallulah was at a party where her host had invited her to follow him into the bathroom for a sniff. She had been terrified – 'my brow clammy, my knees rattling [I was] sure I'd take off through the air like a

---

* The 1873 Cornstock laws barred distribution of contraceptive information by mail, but this was sufficient for the prosecution of campaigners like Margaret Sanger. Condoms went on sale publicly in 1918 partly due to high rates of syphilis and gonorrhoea among soldiers returning from the war.

rocket'.[28] But the effect had proved delightfully euphoric and, like Tamara in Paris, she came to rely on the drug to lift her energy and confidence. It was hard to believe there was anything wrong with a substance so easy to acquire. The medical establishment regarded it as a useful stimulant, and while its growing association with crime, especially black crime, had resulted in restrictions of its legal sale and distribution, large quantities remained in circulation. Tallulah knew of several young boys who hung around outside a tearoom on West 40th Street offering bags of 'snow' for $50. Estelle berated her for the habit, saying that Tallulah couldn't afford it and that it made her 'dirty and rude'.[29] She would routinely search her clothes for the little packets Tallulah kept knotted up in her handkerchiefs, flushing them reprovingly down the toilet. Yet Tallulah could always find someone at a party or dinner who would offer her more, and if there was none, she simply crushed an aspirin and pretended.

To equally little effect, Estelle tried to quell the rumours that were beginning to circulate about Tallulah and women. In the summer of 1919, Ethel Barrymore had introduced a young European actress, Eva Le Gallienne, into the Algonquin circle. Eva was just nineteen, pale, delicate and intense, and to Tallulah her life story was fascinating. As the daughter of the poet Richard Le Gallienne, she had been introduced to Sarah Bernhardt in Paris when she was just fourteen. Once she had embarked on her own stage career, Eva had moved from Europe to California, where she had been seduced by Alla Nazimova, one of Tallulah's first idols.

Tallulah was both flattered and uncertain when Eva began to show an obvious interest in her, sending notes and presents to her room and inviting her out for dinner. She had only the vaguest idea of what a lesbian relationship might involve, and she had to go and ask one of her friends at the Algonquin – a young man with whom she'd developed a semi-sisterly, semi-coquettish relationship – 'What is it [they] do?' The young man readily offered to show her, at which point Tallulah retreated. But there was a quality about Eva herself, simultaneously exotic and unthreatening, that emboldened Tallulah to respond to her overtures.

The affair lasted only a few months – Eva required a degree of intimacy that Tallulah found cloying and exhausting – but she very much enjoyed Eva's sexual tutelage and was interested in experiencing more. The affairs she had at this time were mostly with women older than herself. Mercedes de Acosta, who was in New York at this time, claimed she was one of them; and there was also an unidentified New York hostess to whom Tallulah would later refer as 'the only woman' she had truly loved.[30] In some ways these affairs were an extension of the vivid crushes she'd formed as a child – on the sweet-faced Sister Ignatia, for instance, who had been the only nun to show Tallulah any kindness during her first term at boarding school.

Certainly these women felt a much safer option than men. Early in 1920, John Barrymore had offered her a role in his new film, *Dr. Jekyll and Mr. Hyde*, if she agreed to have sex with him, and Tallulah had backed away. However tempting the trade – Barrymore was her idol – she had sharp enough instincts to sense that he was too obviously 'a hunter' and that she would end up as his victim.*

At this point in her career, Tallulah also found that women could be more professionally helpful to her than men.† She was trying now to direct her career towards the stage. Her last movie performance in *The Trap* had been quite successful and had yielded the offer of a contract with Sam Goldwyn's studio. Yet she had come to feel that the 'flickers' was a medium far inferior to live theatre, requiring little more of its performers than

---

* Later she would joke over the missed opportunity. Admiring a picture of Barrymore, posed nude and clearly 'well endowed', she said she would have liked to have notched him onto her, by then, extensive list of lovers.
† There was a powerful, self-selecting and mutually supporting network of women in the American film and theatre industries. In Hollywood, Alla Nazimova held her own female court, much like Natalie Barney's. In New York, actresses, writers and even producers were generous in supporting each other's careers.

mugged expressions and exaggerated gestures and she was impatient to test herself as a real actor.

In an attempt to gain more stage experience Tallulah had accepted work with a repertory company in West Somerville, Massachusetts. It was punitively hard: she was rehearsing and acting several plays in rotation while living in primitive digs – a tiny room up three flights of stairs with 'no private bath' and little heating. She lasted only a few weeks there, but it was not the work that broke her but her fear of being too far away from the centre of the action in New York and of missing out on a new role or career break.

That break came in the summer when Jobyna put Tallulah in touch with Rachel Crothers, who was one of the most respected playwrights and directors in New York. While she was discreet about her private affairs with women, Crothers was active in promoting their public careers, and she took a great interest in Tallulah – Ann Andrews considered it to be 'sort of . . . a crush'.[31] Not only did she allow Tallulah to understudy Constance Binney, the female lead in her latest play, *39 East*, she also steered her towards polishing her craft. Tallulah might have 'spark and instinct', but she had no technique, and it was on Crothers's advice that she attempted her first professional training, taking lessons in elocution, deportment and classical ballet.

With Crothers as her mentor, and Estelle and Jobyna as her guardian aunts, that summer Tallulah was being steered towards what she believed was her true destiny. As she wrote confidently to her grandfather, 'I am going to make good with a bang! Wait and see. Then you will be proud of your bad little girl with her bad little temper.'[32] For a few thrilling performances, while Constance Binney was taking weekend breaks, Tallulah was onstage as the play's heroine, Penelope Penn. And although her contract with the play was terminated by a near comic farrago of events, including an actors' strike and Tallulah being stricken with a severe case of appendicitis, it effected a crucial change in her fortunes. She was offered a second play, *Footloose*, in which her portrayal of a young woman victimized by a predatory older man earned recognition from the *New York Times* for 'her considerable power' and 'real skill'.[33] And in early 1921, Rachel Crothers offered her the lead in her next play, *Nice People*.

Tallulah's character was Hallie Livingstone, a beautiful, independent, wise-cracking flirt. A few months earlier *The Flapper* had done extraordinary business at cinemas across America, with Olive Thomas (the girl Tallulah had longed to emulate) starring as a new kind of heroine, with short skirts, a cigarette habit and a smart, independent attitude. Hallie was the same breed of heroine. Her dialogue was studded with careless, colourful slang: everything was 'divine', 'dahling', 'mad' and 'the cat's pyjamas'. She was fashionably treacherous and fashionably blasé about sex, commenting coolly to her friend Teddy, 'I adore a man who is absolutely mad about me and yet who controls himself in that perfectly marvelous way.'[34]

Hallie was, above all, an ideal role for Tallulah. The deep, throaty catch in her voice, heightened by the smoking of which Will despaired, was perfectly modulated to deliver every sexual irony and innuendo in the lines that Crothers had written for her. During the twenty weeks in which the play ran at the Klaw Theatre, *Nice People* not only earned her praise as a fine comic actor, but in the feisty character of Hallie, she had found the mould for her own offstage image.*

When Tallulah first arrived at the Algonquin she'd noted the tough, abrasive style of New York conversation. She herself had been raised never to cuss or talk dirty: yet these glamorous writers and actors made a point of using obscenities and working men's slang to give an edge to their jokes and observations. Later she observed that one of the most skilled in this idiom was the journalist Dorothy Parker. Her sly, skewering banter and provocative cynicism were her defence in a male-dominated profession and also her selling point. What Parker said at lunch at the

---

* It didn't serve Crothers so well. Normally admired for the serious social commentary of her works, *Nice People* was regarded as a sop to commercial taste.

Round Table was usually being repeated at New York parties by
the evening.

Tallulah wasn't as clever as Parker, but she noted the publicity
generated by the writer's repartee. Half consciously, half intuit-
ively she began to step up her own natural exhibitionism, adding
material from her stage roles to build a repertory of outrageous
stunts and jokes. She could, she discovered, create a gratifying stir by launching into a string of cartwheels down a sidewalk
or in the middle of a crowded room, displaying a flash of silk
camiknicker, or occasionally her naked bottom. The spinning
craziness felt euphoric – the frisson of being a child in a grown-
up place – but more importantly it made people notice and
remember her. She even developed her own signature wise-
cracks. Her affair with Eva had attracted mildly scandalous
comment, with the magazine *Broadway Brevities* alluding to Tallulah's 'close friendships' with several women.* It was now that
Tallulah began introducing herself at parties with the line, 'I'm
a lesbian. What do you do?'[35]

It was possibly a genuine mistake that inspired another of her
trademark quips. She'd been taken to a performance of Maeter-
linck's *The Burgomaster of Stilemonde* by Alexander Woollcott,
theatre critic of the *New York Times*. When asked for her opinion,
fearful that she hadn't fully understood the play, Tallulah
replied, 'There is *less* in this than meets the eye.' Almost certainly
she had meant to say, 'There is more to this,' but Woollcott had
pounced on the line and quoted it, with relish, in his column.[36]

As a result, Tallulah found herself hailed as one of the wits of
Manhattan, and she worked hard to make sure the reputation
stuck. In private, she could still be assailed by childish terrors
and weep in her dressing room from stage fright, but in public
she could launch herself into a room with a stream of slick, rude
and seemingly spontaneous one-liners: 'I'm as pure as the driven

---

* These included another young actress, Blythe Daley, who in 1925 would be
momentarily notorious for biting Charlie Chaplin on the mouth when he tried
to seduce her.

slush,' she would remark, tossing back her hair whilst taking a calculated drag on her cigarette. 'I don't give a fuck what people say about me so long as they say something.'[37]

The chemistry between Tallulah's offstage image and her performance as Hallie also attracted her first significant fans. There was a faction of American theatregoers, the gallery girls, who made cults out of their favourite actresses, returning night after night to watch them perform, greeting their entrance with hysterical applause. They were a shifting, amorphous group, many of them secretaries or schoolteachers who had travelled to the city in search of work. Often the theatre was their only refuge from the loneliness of a studio apartment or an anonymous boarding house.

Many of these women latched onto Tallulah in *Nice People*, and their numbers grew through the succession of – mostly short-lived – roles that followed. By 1922, when she appeared in Martin Brown's racy comedy, *The Exciters*, she had acquired a large and fanatical group of admirers. Tallulah played Rufus Rand, a thrill-seeking socialite with a gun tucked into her garter belt. And although Alan Dale in *The American* would compliment her on the performance of her career – 'charming . . . beautifully dictioned [with] a fine sense of comedy' – he complained that the gallery girls were in danger of wrecking it, screaming and applauding so loudly that some of her lines were inaudible.[38]

It was, Dale wrote, a real case of 'save me from my friends'. But Tallulah didn't want to be saved. Her new fans were mostly girls of her own age, and she began to invite some of them backstage to her dressing room, where she liked to chatter about the details of their lives and love affairs. She was moved by the little tributes they brought, posies of flowers or chocolates, and by the constancy of their devotion. One young woman, too poor to afford an adequate winter wardrobe, left with Tallulah's own coat around her shoulders.

In their company Tallulah was momentarily able to drop her guard. She was slowly becoming 'somebody' in New York, acquiring numerous acquaintances and admirers, but she had made few close friendships, and her family, on whose background love and support she had always counted, were beginning to fall away. In March 1920 her beloved grandfather had died from a severe case of the flu, and Tallulah had reacted badly to the loss. He was the person who had most believed in her, who saw her most clearly. And while the death of Louise the following year caused her much less sorrow, it badly affected her grandmother, whose own health subsequently declined, until she died in May 1922.

There was Will, of course, but even though he had become a more conscientious father, writing regularly and occasionally visiting, Tallulah felt his interest was primarily in her professional success and she grew distant with him. In June 1920 he wrote reproachfully, 'You know that I am willing to assist you to the very limit of my ability but what I resent is that you do not take me into your confidence, and really treat me like I was an outsider.'[39]

Eugenia was now the family member to whom Tallulah was closest. In 1921 she had come to live in New York, with her new husband Morton Hoyt, and had dramatically discarded her former role as the good older sister. Morton was a drinker and a time waster, a blot on the reputation of his late father, who had been the US Solicitor General, and lacking the talent of his literary sister, the poet Elinor Wylie. When he had eloped with Eugenia the year before, the Bankheads had succeeded in getting the marriage annulled. But the couple had simply remarried as soon as they were able and had taken an apartment together in Manhattan, on Central Park South.

Already their marriage was careening towards disaster. Infected by Morton's dissolute habits, Eugenia was running wild, and the two of them were briefly, adulterously, tangled up in the marriage of Tallulah's friend from Montgomery, Zelda Sayre, now married to the novelist Scott Fitzgerald. While Tallulah enjoyed the spectacle of Eugenia's adventures, her older sister was hardly a dependable confidante or advisor, and she was no substitute for the steadying voice of their grandparents. She also did nothing to caution Tallulah when she had embarked on her first serious love affair, with a very damaged and dangerous man.

In the summer of 1921 Tallulah had moved into a shared apartment with a new friend, Beth Martin. Among Beth's extensive New York circle was a group of sophisticated, cultured Englishmen, whom she invited to the flat for an impromptu party one night. One of them, Napier George Henry Alington, arrived in his pyjamas, with an overcoat bundled over the top and a bottle of bootleg gin in his pocket.

Tallulah couldn't help but be impressed that Naps was an actual aristocrat – the 3rd Baron Alington, whose family owned large tracts of England. He was more finely bred than any American she had met, with his bone-china accent, willowy height and languid wit. And while his appearance wasn't conventionally handsome – the dark smudges under his eyes and the pallor of his skin both symptomatic of his tubercular condition – there was a sense of exquisite contradiction about him that she found hypnotic.

Refined and witty as Naps appeared, he could also be as coarse as a navvy, with thick, sensuous lips that signalled his much-vaunted sexual appetite. His tastes ran to men and women equally, and during the short time he'd been in New York (ostensibly to study the American banking system) he'd acquired a scandalous reputation: turning up at the opera with two drunken soldiers in tow, and seducing a footman at the home of Mrs Cornelius Vanderbilt where he was staying. At their first meeting Tallulah resisted his efforts to seduce her, but within a short while she had not only yielded to him, but had fully deluded herself that the careless offer he made to marry her one day was a genuine promise for their future.

She was working hard that autumn, playing the lead in *Everyday*, another play that Rachel Crothers had written especially for her. Whenever she was free, however, Tallulah dedicated herself to her new lover. They careened around the high spots of New York, dancing at Reisenweber's Café and brunching at the Brevoort Hotel on lower 5th Avenue. In bed, Talullah found

Naps an alarming, exciting advance on her sexual education. Later she would boast crudely that he was 'big where it mattered', but there was also a streak of cruelty in his lovemaking. In contrast to gentle Eva, Naps liked to draw a little blood in bed, to bruise and be bruised in return.

In the face of that cruelty, so unpredictably mixed with tenderness and courtesy, Tallulah was helpless. Naps kept her in such a state of keyed-up uncertainty that she was never sure which version of him she would see. The man who seemed to know her every weakness and could needle her maliciously for an entire evening, or the man who would gallantly bring her presents and whisk her off dancing. Often she didn't know if she would see Naps at all, as he was capable of disappearing from her life for days at a time without a word of explanation.

This was a pattern familiar from Tallulah's childhood, when she had craved her father's attention but so often found him absent. Tallulah made herself laugh at Naps's unreliability; she busied herself with work and schooled herself to live from one moment to the next. But she had no way of defending herself when he abruptly announced his intention to return to England, offering no suggestion of when or how they might ever meet again.

All at once the fun was draining out of Tallulah's life. Audiences for *Everyday* were dwindling, despite her excellent reviews,* and the play, was about to be shut down. It was at around this time that her grandmother died, and as Tallulah mooned around New York, grieving for her grandmother and missing Naps, she was more than ready to jump at an offer that promised her a completely fresh start.

That autumn she had been introduced to the British producer and impresario Charles Cochran. He was in New York to scout

---

* Tallulah played a young idealistic woman, torn between her arranged marriage to a corrupt businessman and her love for an impoverished artist. *Variety* noted that 'Miss Bankhead looks ravishing and has a dramatic quiver in her larynx that should be worth a fortune in a reasonable play.'

for talent and Tallulah had impressed him as exactly the kind of bright, modern star that would appeal to English audiences. He didn't have a vehicle for her immediately, but in December he wired Tallulah about a play that was opening in London early the following year. It was written by the actor Gerald du Maurier, in collaboration with Diana Manners's friend Viola Tree, and its lead character was a lively North American dancer, for whom Cochran considered she would be ideal.

No actual promises were made, but Tallulah was determined she must go. Du Maurier was one of the great names of British theatre, she regarded 'a summons' from him to be a 'bugle call from Olympus'.[40] Even though a succession of urgently corrective telegrams came from Cochran, indicating that the part might no longer be available, and that she should wait in New York, Tallulah refused to pay them any regard. Recently she had been with some friends to a fashionable astrologer, Evangeline Adams, and had been told that in order to achieve fame and fortune she would have to cross the ocean. It was a standard fortune-teller's line, but Tallulah regarded it as a prophecy. Whatever Cochran was advising, she was willing to believe that fate was directing her to London.

She was encouraged in her belief by Estelle, who was not only looking forward to a reprieve from Tallulah's chaotic life, but was genuinely convinced that the move would be good for her. Tallulah had made a decent career for herself in New York, but she hadn't yet broken through to stardom. In London she would be a novelty, and even if du Maurier's play was no longer an option, Cochran would surely find her something else. The only drawback to the plan was money. Tallulah had saved nothing, and Will could offer her little, given the expensive divorce Eugenia was trying to obtain from Morton Hoyt.* Putting on her best dress and her most persuasive manner, Tallulah spent

---

* This was their second, albeit voluntary, severance, although Eugenia and Morton were nothing if not stubborn, and would attempt marriage for a third, again unsuccessful, time.

an evening with an old political friend of her grandfather's, a General T. Coleman de Pont, and somehow managed to persuade him to part with the price of a crossing as a tribute to John Bankhead's faith in her.

On the evening of 6 January 1923, Tallulah boarded the SS *Majestic*. Standing on the pier was a crowd of tearful fans, dressed in their best flapper frocks. Her own friends were fewer in number, but Estelle was there, and typically it was she who noticed that Tallulah had no warm coat for London, slipping her own mink over her shoulders as a parting gift. Tallulah was not yet twenty-one and had never left America before; the following day, the *New York Herald* would report that 'her plans concerning just what she will do in London are rather indefinite' and Will would write stoically to his sister Marie, 'If her expectations do not materialize, she will at least have had the *sight* of England.'[41] As for Tallulah, beneath her bravado she was utterly terrified. 'I thought I was going to Mars,' she later claimed. 'I was scared to death.'[42]

Chapter Five

ZELDA

At the peak of Tallulah's success in *Nice People* in 1921, she'd been visited in her dressing room by her childhood friend Zelda Sayre. Tallulah had an exact recall of Zelda as the prettiest girl in town, and of herself as the awkward outsider, but now, as the two of them kissed and exchanged gossip, she preened a little over the change in their situation. A Broadway actress with her name over a theatre, she could claim an audience far bigger than Zelda's Montgomery beaux.

However, Zelda's life had also been transformed since she'd arrived in New York the previous year. Her husband, Scott, had become the city's most talked-about novelist, and as his wife she'd become one of its most talked-about women. Stories were told of her diving fully clothed into the fountain in Union Square, and receiving guests while naked in the bath. She was said to be at the wildest parties, drinking, flirting and throwing attitudes. And to all these antics she brought the stamp of her looks. At first glance she might seem merely pretty, with a honey-coloured sheen to her bobbed hair and a candy-box curve to her mouth, but what made people look twice was the wide flare of her cheekbones and the unexpected darkness behind her grey-blue eyes.

To one of her admirers,* she had the quality of 'a barbarian

---

* John Peale Bishop.

princess';[1] and Scott, with his Brooks Brothers elegance and wavy blond hair, was her collegiate prince. Dorothy Parker said the two of them looked 'as though they had stepped out of the sun'; to the writer Edmund Wilson they possessed a combination of 'spontaneity, charm and good looks' that amounted to 'genius'.[2] After a night in the Fitzgeralds' company it might be hard to remember exactly what had been so original about their conversation, so electrifying about Zelda's dancing, so funny about Scott's drunken clowning, but people felt they had been at the centre of things.

Their celebrity had been launched by Scott's first novel, *This Side of Paradise*, which had been published in March 1920. Advertised as 'A Novel About Flappers, Written For Philosophers', it had been heralded as the voice of post-war American youth, and had sold three thousand copies in just three days.* The fact that its hero and heroine had been so evidently based on Scott and Zelda, and that their own lives threaded through its pages, enhanced their status as the couple of the moment. 'They didn't make the Twenties,' the actress Lilian Gish later recalled, 'they *were* the Twenties.'[3]

Scott's themes were those of his generation. His hero Amory Blaine was an alumnus of Princeton, a war veteran and a romantic, whose discourses on the bankrupt ideals of his parents' era resonated with the novel's readers. America had only engaged in the war for eighteen months, but parts of the nation had nonetheless borne the scars. Many men had been killed and many had witnessed degradation and suffering on just as appalling a scale as their European peers.

Yet more interesting still to readers were the details of how Amory and his student friends lived their daily lives. *This Side of Paradise* was one of the first 'university' novels in American fiction. It was a curiosity, for many, to discover what these young men did, what they read, and especially the ways in which they

---

* By the end of 1921 it had sold nearly half a million copies.

conducted their love affairs. The kisses and intimate conversations that Scott described were hardly daring – nothing like the earnest sexual epiphanies evoked by D.H. Lawrence on the other side of the Atlantic – yet the specificity of small physical facts, the sleeveless jerseys that Amory referred to as 'petting shirts', and the worldliness of the novel's tone gave it a compelling, contemporary authority. Amory's assessment 'that any popular girl he met before eight he might possibly kiss before midnight' seemed astoundingly knowing to Scott's younger readers, many of whom seized on *This Side of Paradise* as a dating manual.[4]

The women in the novel were even more appealing to those readers, especially Rosalind Connage, the flapper debutante whom he had modelled on Zelda. Rosalind was lovely and dangerous. She kissed a lot of men; she used eye pencils and rouge; she laughed at coarse stories; she smoked and drank. Yet in contrast to the sassy heroine of the movie *Flapper*, or to the images of bobbed and lipsticked girls appearing on billboards and within the pages of magazines, she also carried the suggestion of a true, individual voice.

Scott had learned much about girls when he was courting Zelda: the paradoxical mix of dependency and disdain she felt for her own beauty, the small tragedies and triumphs of her teenage life. In transferring these nuances to Rosalind, he became one of the first writers in post-war America to evoke a complex, modern heroine. Almost overnight, he was elevated to the status of expert. He was asked to lecture on the flapper, and it was reported that his audience of young women 'sway[ed] with delight' at both his appearance and his words.[5] He was repeatedly interviewed on the subject. At times Scott would wonder 'whether the flapper made me or I made her'.[6]*

Zelda found her new status as Scott's wife and muse both

---

* In 1926, the young writer Katharine Bush advertised her own literary style as a fusion of 'jazz, bobbed hair, petting and necking, flivvers, *Flaming Youth*, and Mr Scott Fitzgerald'.

delicious and disorienting. When they were out together, complete strangers would speak to her, and the sudden magnesium glare of camera bulbs would make her jump. It was far beyond what Scott had promised back in Montgomery, when he'd offered her a life in New York with 'all the iridescence of the beginning of the world.'[7] Home had been a place where barely 'a ripple' disturbed the 'lush softness of the air', and before Zelda came to New York she hadn't even been able to visualize the city, admitting in a rare acknowledgment of fear, 'I wish [it] were a little tiny town so I could imagine how it'd be.'[8]

The night before she began the two-day train journey to New York, she had been too excited to sleep. She'd wondered naively how she would make her conquest of the city, sliding down banisters, turning cartwheels along the sidewalk, making people stare. By the time she arrived in Pennsylvania Station she was in a state of high exhilaration and anxiety. The station was like a cathedral, with its vaulted glass and marble pillars, yet it was louder and busier than any place she had ever been. As a taxi drove her the few blocks east to her hotel, the scale of the city revealed itself dramatically, wide avenues thrusting north and south, tall buildings of chrome and glass, reflecting the pale sun.

The city was built to inspire awe. Louise Brooks, arriving in Grand Central Station for the first time in 1922, was wonderstruck by its size and by her own smallness: 'As I looked down at the marble floor and then up 200 feet to the great dome arching over my head, a shaft of sunlight from one of the huge, crossbarred windows pierced my heart.'[9] It took nerve for these provincials to believe that they could launch themselves here. But Zelda had been famous for diving off the highest diving board back in Montgomery, for being one of the first girls to drink gin and cut her hair. She had grown up with nerve, and nerve was what she was famous for.

From the moment of her birth, 24 July 1900, Zelda had been marked as special. Her mother Minnie (Minerva) had been thirty-nine when she became pregnant, and having long assumed there would be no more children beyond the four she'd already produced, the arrival of this lively pretty baby with her mop of golden hair had felt like a peculiar blessing. She named her Zelda, after the gypsy heroine of a romantic novel.* The little girl became a pet of the neighbourhood. *Smart as a whip, quick as a steel trap*, locals called her as she scampered around the garden with her dog and wooden cart, sped down the streets on her roller skates or hung upside down from the big magnolia tree in the garden.

To her father, however, Zelda seemed a changeling child. A hard-working lawyer of meticulous appearance and sober habits, Anthony Sayre was much admired in Montgomery, especially when he was appointed Associate Judge of the Alabama Supreme Court in 1909. He genuinely loved his children, but he was a remote, judgemental parent – 'a living fortress', according to Zelda, who protected the family but gave off little warmth.[10]

If Judge Sayre was not an easy father to his children, nor was he the romantic lover his wife had hoped for back in 1880, when she was a pretty curly-haired girl, dreaming of a life far away from Eddyville, Kentucky. Like Ada Bankhead, before her marriage Minnie had fantasized about a stage career, but like Ada she'd had her fantasies blocked by her plantation-owning father. Over the years and numerous pregnancies Minnie had learned to channel her artistic aspirations into her gardening, her reading and her five children.

Within the solid conservative establishment of Montgomery she remained an unusual mother, vague, indulgent and inclined to poetry. During the summer she allowed her daughters to bathe on the veranda of their rambling house, believing its screen of Virginia creeper and clematis was sufficient privacy. To neighbours who complained about the boys hanging around outside, trying to spy on the family bathtime, Minnie was dismis-

---

* Probably taken from Jane Howard's *Zelda: A Tale of the Massachusetts Colony*, or *Zelda's Fortune* by Robert Edward Francillon.

sive. 'God gave them beautiful bodies,' she said with romantic maternal pride.[11]

It was Zelda, as the baby of the family, who benefited most from Minnie's laxity. When she was sent to school at the age of six, she disliked it so much she was allowed to stay at home for a full year. When she pulled one of her first, legendary stunts – telephoning the fire department to report a stranded child, then climbing out onto the roof to calmly await their arrival – Minnie couldn't help but admire her youngest daughter's audacity.

While other little girls in Montgomery were learning to sit with their backs straight, twisting ringlets into their hair and gossiping with their mothers and older sisters, Zelda preferred to run with the boys. She prided herself on being able to swim as far and climb as high as any of them. Even when she began taking ballet classes at the age of nine, she cared less about her pretty pink slippers than the exhilaration of speed and dexterity, the sensation of moving 'brightly along high places'.[12] Looking back on this idyllic childhood, Zelda would claim that she 'did not have a single feeling of inferiority, or shyness or doubt.'[13] She recalled home as a place of sunshine and the smell of pear blossom. Montgomery was her playground. And it was only as she turned fifteen that both she and her world lost their innocence. Quite suddenly, the boys with whom she played became more calculating and more self-conscious in their behaviour around her, and it was at around this time that she seems to have been forced into some sort of sexual initiation.

There were two Montgomery boys, John Sellers and Peyton Matthis, who had been ringleaders of her childhood group, and it was they who took the lead in pushing their dares into more adult games. In Zelda's unpublished, autobiographical novel *Caesar's Things*, she described how these boys pressured her to go with them into the schoolyard one night. Details of the scene were merely hinted at: a 'schoolyard deep in shadows'; a 'splintery old swing'; her own 'miserable and trusting acquiescence' to the taunt that if a girl wanted to stay popular she 'went where boys told them' and was 'glad of the attention'.[14] But what

actually occurred in that yard was sufficiently close to rape for
Scott to refer, later, to Zelda having been 'seduced' and to
castigate Minnie for having taken 'rotten care' of her youngest
daughter.[15] It's impossible to know how traumatic this episode
was, but it coincided with Zelda's shift from careless tomboy to
town flirt. John Sellers and Peyton Matthis had shown her a
crude version of sexual power, and in reaction to that she began
to wield her own, making the boys of Montgomery compete for
her attention and pushing the rules of dating as far as she dared.

 'There were two kinds of girls,' recalled one of those boys,
'those who would ride with you in your automobile at night and
the nice girls who wouldn't.' Zelda 'didn't seem to give a damn'
about being the former.[16] She kissed on a first date and when
she was a little older she learned to smoke and developed a taste
for alcohol – either gin mixed with orange and sugar, or the
locally distilled corn liquor cut with Coca-Cola. Just as scandalous
was the raciness of her language. When she remarked that she
liked a boy so much he would 'probably be the father of my next
child', her shocked friends hoped very much that their parents
wouldn't get to hear of it.[17]

 Invariably they did, just as they heard about the wickedness of
Zelda's new, close-fitting bathing suit. Just eight years earlier, the
professional swimmer Annette Kellerman had been arrested on
a Boston beach for wearing such a garment. The fact that Zelda's
own costume was flesh coloured meant that in certain lights she
appeared to be swimming nude. Everything she did seemed an
affront to the Southern code of decorum. 'Alabama girls were
meant to look very feminine,' recalled one of her friends, 'we all
wore high heels . . . had long hair and didn't smoke. Later some
of us did bob our hair, but our parents would be very fierce.'[18]
Cutting her hair was one act of rebellion that Zelda delayed until
she was nineteen, but in every other respect she was the despair
of her father. He tried to lock her in her bedroom, but she
climbed out through the window; he berated her for being a
hussy when he saw her kissing boys on the veranda, but she
laughed in his face.

Zelda didn't invent her bad behaviour, she was on the rising curve of a new teenage culture. While previous generations had courted each other through a system of chaperones, calling cards and church socials, Zelda and her peers went out casually on 'dates'.* Many of them were already socializing familiarly at school: mixed education was on the increase in middle- and upper-class America, and Zelda herself went to the local co-ed, Sidney Lanier High. But as they grew older, teenaged couples enjoyed numerous other advantages that had been unimaginable to their parents.

Many homes had telephones now, and a growing number had motor cars. The Ford Model T cost just $440,† and a significant number of teenagers had access to a 'flivver' or some comparable model. That access provided a hundred different options for an evening date: driving to an ice-cream parlour, amusement park or dance hall – or finding privacy in an isolated lane or spinney. The rich lexicon of slang that had grown up around 'petting' or 'necking' was a register of the freedom enjoyed in this modern dating culture. In Montgomery, the local term was 'boodling', named after a remote stretch of road called Boodler's Bend, which was particularly popular with Zelda and her friends.

Those freedoms extended to the dance floor, as the turkey trot, shimmy and toddle migrated from the clubs of New Orleans to the white dance halls of America. The ragtime moves being mastered by Nancy Cunard and Diana Manners in London were equally liberating to Montgomery teenagers. Chaperones still attempted to patrol dances at the country club or the old wooden pavilion in Oak Park, but they could do little to intervene on a crowded floor, as couples danced cheek to cheek and swayed their hips in hot, close rhythm. They were certainly unable to curb Zelda, who regarded such events as her personal stage. She was regularly spotlit during nights at the country club,

---

* The word had been coined two decades earlier, but to many it was still considered sufficiently disturbing to require quotation marks.
† Equivalent to $10,000 in today's money.

performing solo routines of her own devising. At the ritual dance floor 'rush' no one was in such obvious demand as her, the line of young men who hoped to claim her as partner often stretching the length of the room.

Some girls would simply give up and go home if they saw Zelda arrive at a dance, while those who remained were resigned to watching her hold court over a group of beaux who were not only locals, but college students, from Georgia Tech or Auburn (where her admirers had formed a select society, named Zeta Sigma after her initials). Zelda was beautiful – on that her power depended – but she wasn't like other girls, anxiously assessing herself against the images pictured inside fashion magazines. During the daytime her skirts were boyishly hitched up, her blouse carelessly buttoned. Even though she dressed carefully for an evening's dance, painting her face and wearing ruffled organdie frocks sewn by Minnie, she still contrived to look unique: 'starry and mocking', her friends remembered, a girl from a picture book in her 'flame dress . . . gold-laced slippers . . . flirting an immense feather fan'.[19]

When Scott first met Zelda, he was fascinated by her air of certainty. She did as she pleased, regarding life as 'an inexhaustible counter', from which she seemed to be continually picking out presents for herself. She was unpredictable and apparently indifferent to anyone's opinion. She would arrive late to a dance, her feet bare and her skirt sodden, because she'd decided to go paddling in the lake. She would be flirting with a boy – glancing under the thick, dark ledge of her eyelashes, drawling nonsense into his ear – then abruptly lose interest and veer onto another topic. Young men, hoping to coax Zelda off to Boodler's Bend, would suddenly find themselves struggling with a conversation about the presence of ghosts in the old Confederate Cemetery or about the significance of the 'queerest' dream she'd had the previous night.

Beaux could sometimes be scared by the zig-zagging intensity of Zelda's conversation. Years later, when her mental health deteriorated, there would be questions about the history of psychological illness in her family and about the extremes of her own emotional states. Yet at the age of sixteen, Zelda was just an adolescent girl, vividly responsive to her own impressions, treasuring her secret ideas. 'I love being rather unfathomable,' she confided to Scott. 'Men love me cause I'm pretty – and they're always afraid of mental wickedness – and men love me cause I'm clever, and they're always afraid of my prettiness – One or two have even loved me cause I'm lovable, and then, of course I was acting.'[20]

Zelda *was* clever. At school she scored high grades in art and literature and she admired her friend Sarah Haardt, who planned to go to college and become a writer. (It was Sarah alone of Zelda's circle who went to hear a small group of suffragettes attempt to rally the women of Montgomery to their cause.) Yet work, study and the vote were irrelevant to Zelda's vision of herself. 'I just want to be young and feel that my life is my own,' she would tell Scott 'to live and be happy and die in my own way to please myself.'[21] It would be one of many lines he would give to his fictional heroines.

Yet even with all her conquests, Zelda's scope was limited. Although part of her wanted to rebel and 'to have a law to itself' she couldn't seriously imagine a world outside Montgomery. She had an instinctive desire 'to keep all the nice old things and be loved and safe and protected'.[22] Then in April 1917, the 'nice old' ways of home were jolted from their sleepy insularity as America entered the war. Two army training camps were set up outside the town, and with them came shops, restaurants and even a new hotel. For Zelda, this mass influx of young soldiers spelled an infinite variety of possibilities. The officers who congregated at the country club were graduates from Ivy League universities who 'smelled of Russian Leather' and were far more sophisticated than her local beaux. Yet they seemed no less avid for her company. Soon the whole neighbourhood was bearing witness to her popularity among the military, as uniformed officers began appearing on the veranda of the Sayre house, and rival aviators started flying their planes in the air above, performing feats of daring in her honour.*

Like London during the first years of war, Montgomery vibrated with a new and fatalistic excitement. 'A crazy vitality possessed us,' recalled one young woman, 'we couldn't afford to wait for fear it would be gone forever, so we pitched in furiously, dancing every night and riding up and down the moonlit roads. Oh we did wild, silly things, but often with the sense of tragedy.'[23] And it was partly on the wave of this collective emotion that Zelda first fell in love. She had just turned eighteen when she met Francis Scott Key Fitzgerald, a lieutenant with the 67th Infantry, at a country club dance. Scott was elegantly good looking, with large green eyes and a neat centre parting in his fair hair. He wore his uniform with freshness and style: his tunic was well-tailored, and in place of standard-issue khaki puttees, he wore a pair of yellow boots and spurs. Just as importantly for Zelda he was an elegant dance partner, moving as if he had 'some heavenly support between his shoulder blades'.[24]

At first Scott's pleasing appearance wasn't sufficient to catch her heart. When he asked if they might meet up later she dismissed him tartly: 'I never make late dates with fast workers.'[25] But she did invite him to her house shortly afterwards, to take iced tea on the veranda, and they fell into a habit of walking and talking together through the fields at the edge of town. It was Scott's conversation, then, that truly seduced her. Unlike any man she'd ever met, he didn't bore her with sports or army gossip. Rather he seemed fascinated by every detail of her girlish life, from the colours in which her bedroom was decorated to the way she imagined her future. Zelda admitted, frankly, to the narcissistic pleasure these conversations gave her. 'You know everything about me and that's mostly what I think about. I seem always curiously interested in myself and it's so much fun to stand off and look at me.'[26]

---

* A near fatal accident put a stop to this.

The more time they spent together, however, the more interested she became in Scott. He allowed her to glimpse the disappointments in his life, his father's financial failure and the embarrassment of his university career in Princeton, where bad health and nerves had caused him to flunk his degree. But he spoke with mesmerizing eloquence about how he planned to transcend these obstacles. He was writing a novel, and as soon as the war was over and he was a published author, he planned to become remarkable. He was going to live for the moment, to have 'a romantic readiness' for every experience. To Zelda, whose greatest terror was boredom, it was as though Scott was reading her soul. Not only did he understand her craving for the extraordinary, he had elevated it into a creed.

The similarity between them was hypnotic for Zelda: in her one published novel, *Save Me the Waltz*, she would describe the experience of being with him as 'pressing her nose upon a mirror and gazing into her own eyes'.[27] Yet as a new intake of officers appeared in Montgomery, she had no intention of depriving herself of other opportunities and intrigues. It excited her to see Scott's jealousy when she danced with another man, or when she kissed a rival officer goodnight. When she saw how antagonism inflamed his desire, she experienced a delicious feeling of power.

The writer in Scott could analyse his own jealous emotions: he knew that 'it excited him . . . that many men had already loved [her] – it increased her value in his eyes'.[28] He also knew himself well enough to understand that he could only seriously covet a woman who had the capacity to hurt him. Before coming to Montgomery he'd been in love with a rich and pretty girl called Ginevra King, who had shamelessly played him off against other men. She was 'selfish, conceited and uncontrolled,' Scott wrote afterwards, yet with 'a sort of passionate energy that transcended' her faults.[29] Zelda was clearly another Ginevra, but Scott also saw in her a quality of imagination and perception that was far superior to her predecessor. As he became determined to possess Zelda, his ardour was fuelled as much by the passion of a novelist discovering a new muse as by the excitement of a lover.

Scott had continued working on his novel during the summer, hoping to complete it before he was dispatched to the war in Europe. As he wrote, the heroine he had originally based on Ginevra assumed Zelda's face and personality. When he sent her a copy of the chapter in which she figured, she was as moved and flattered as he had intended, and as the date of his departure from training camp grew nearer, Zelda acknowledged that her emotions had moved beyond the familiar sweetness of a summer flirtation. She wouldn't make any promises, but in those last autumn days every shared confidence, every kiss, was freighted with romantic importance. On 26 October, when they finally parted, the last thing Scott said to her was, 'Here is my heart.'

It was a line from a vague but poetic future: Scott sailing away to Europe, writing beautiful letters from the Front, possibly dying a noble death. But before he had even boarded the troopship everything changed. The Armistice was declared and, in place of battle orders, Scott faced the prospect of returning to the training camp in Montgomery to await his military discharge. Of course he was euphoric at being saved from danger, but he felt a crushing shame, too, a shame with which Duff Cooper would have identified. He would never now acquire the badge of sweat and mud that had made heroes of other men.

Scott was also paralysed by the uncertainty of what he should do once he'd left the army. The question of how he should earn a living suddenly loomed large, and so, too, did the question of Zelda. Now that he had spent some time apart from her he began to doubt the wisdom of their marrying – if he wanted to become a professional writer, it might be folly to attach himself to so unpredictable and expensive a girl.

Back in Montgomery, Zelda was also wavering; Scott had grown more insubstantial to her the longer they were apart, and when he returned to Montgomery to await his discharge papers she felt almost hostile to his presence. By Christmas, however, their uncertainties had receded and they'd recaptured their old charged empathy. Zelda now felt so sure of Scott that she allowed him to make love to her for the first time. It was a profound step for her, despite her reputation for being fast, and afterwards it felt easy to acquiesce to all of Scott's plans. She would wait for him at home in Montgomery while he went ahead to New York – seeking out the literary fame and fortune that would permit them to marry.

'I am in the land of ambition and success and my only hope and faith is that my darling heart will be with me soon.'[30] When Scott arrived in New York, in February 1919, his first telegram to Zelda set the loving, hopeful tone of their correspondence. During the following months they exchanged letters almost daily. Zelda swore that she was longing for the moment when Scott would come and rescue her from the 'sordid, colorless existence' of Montgomery.[31] She promised that she would love no other man: 'We will die together I know.'[32] Scott, enchanted by this fantasy, imagined Zelda as his princess, locked up in a tower and waiting only for him.

Outside their letters, however, the reality of their lives was very different. Scott had taken a job writing advertising copy, for which he earned just $90 a month. Pinned to the walls of his small rented room were dozens of rejection slips, evidence of his continuing failure to sell his fiction. Meanwhile Zelda was tiring of her patient fidelity. In May, the summer party season was gearing back to its full height and she was unable to resist the lure of drives, dates and dances. After the winter's unaccustomed weeks of restraint, she grabbed at the chance to be disreputable again. She was too much even for Minnie. When she came home riotously late one night, 'stewed' on whisky and on the arm of yet another man, Minnie left her a pained little note accusing her of 'developing the habits of a prostitute'.[33]

There was a devil inside Zelda, rattling the bars of her romance with Scott. The tone of her letters sharpened. She wrote to him about the fun of trying 'my hand in new fields'.[34] Cruelly, she aimed the stories of her conquests at what she called the 'morbidly exaggerative' part of his imagination; the part that

liked to conjure 'deliberately experimental and wiggly' fears.[35] It
was possibly a genuine mistake on Zelda's part that she sent Scott
a treacherously flirtatious letter intended for one of her summer
beaux, but in a state of panic he took the next train down to
Montgomery, demanding that she renounce these other men
and marry him instantly.

It was a bad miscalculation. Scott, in his desperation, seemed
suddenly pathetic to Zelda: his speech was uncharacteristically
incoherent, his kisses felt smothering and needy. Flooded with
revulsion she handed over the ring he had sent as a secret token
of their engagement, demanding that he leave. And when he did
so she felt nothing but relief. A few days later Zelda was standing
on the top diving board at the local pool, feeling her body as
keen and sharp as a knife. Only the straps of her bathing suit
digging into her shoulders distracted her, and in a rapid movement she pulled them down and wriggled out of her suit.
Completely naked, with the sound of shocked laughter in her
ears, Zelda arced high into the air and down into the cool water.

It seemed to her that she was her old inviolable self again,
revelling in her freedom. Yet as the summer drifted towards
autumn, those moments of clear self-sufficiency became more
elusive. Zelda had assumed that word would come from Scott,
begging for a reconciliation, and when none came she started to
miss him. The officers had all left Montgomery, the students had
returned to college, and the devil inside her had retreated. In
October, when a letter finally came from Scott with news that his
novel had been accepted for publication, she wrote back immediately, inviting him down to see her. She said she was certain now
of her feelings, promising him, 'I don't feel a bit shaky and "do-
don't'ish" like I used to when you came – I really want to see
you – that's all.'[36]

Scott, however, took his time. Zelda's dismissal had pierced
both his heart and his pride, and he intended to return to her
from a position of power. He wanted to have 'the jingle of
money' in his pocket, and it was only when his short stories also
began to sell – the magazine *Smart Set* taking 'The Debutante',

and the *Saturday Morning Post* taking 'Head and Shoulders' – that he finally acted on her summons and, in late November, went down to Montgomery.

Their reunion was tender but slightly muted, as if both were cowed by their failure to live up to the large, luminous vision they had created of themselves. Yet Zelda was genuine in her assertion that she no longer doubted Scott and the future of 'ineffable toploftiness' that he was promising her.[37] The parties, the boys and the Montgomery gossips shrank to trivia: 'I am nothing without you,' she assured him, 'Just the doll that I should have been born.'[38]

Events moved fast. Cheques replaced rejection slips as Scott's tales of fast flappers and clever college boys began to sell. By mid-January he had made $1,700 from his writing; there was talk of a movie studio acquiring the rights to 'Head and Shoulders'.* With the magazines and popular newspapers that published his fiction representing a readership of several million, Scott's name was becoming known across America, and he and Zelda were ready to announce their engagement. The world didn't exactly rejoice. Zelda's family still doubted Scott's financial stability, while Scott's friends feared that she was too uneducated and wayward to be good for him, but Scott could not imagine his life or his writing without her. To one friend, he wrote that he would prefer to see Zelda dead than married to someone else. To another friend he sent a frank but impassioned justification of her power over him.

'No personality as strong as Zelda could go without getting criticism . . . I've always known that any girl who gets stewed in public, who frankly enjoys and tells shocking stories, who smokes constantly and makes the remark that she has "kissed thousands of men and intends to kiss thousands more" cannot be considered beyond reproach . . . I fell in love with her courage, her sincerity and her flaming self-respect . . . I love her and that's

---

* He would be paid $2,500.

the beginning and end of everything. You're still a catholic but Zelda's the only God I have left now.'[39]

On 3 April 1920, Zelda and Scott were married in the vestry of St Patrick's Cathedral in New York. It was the simplest of ceremonies: Zelda wore a midnight-blue suit and matching hat and carried a small bouquet of white flowers. There were only six other people present, and while these included Zelda's three sisters, her parents Minnie and Judge Sayre had declined to attend, claiming that the expense and effort of a trip to New York were too much. Zelda's sisters minded that the wedding was so reduced, feeling that it reflected some carelessness or indifference on Scott's part, but Zelda herself was already focused on the adventure that awaited her.

When she and Scott returned to their honeymoon suite at the Biltmore Hotel, there was the fizz of champagne and room service awaiting them, and the freedom to make love without inhibition or secrecy. Yet it was one trivial detail that summed up the liberating power of her new married state. When she was about to go to sleep that night, she realized that neither her mother nor father would be knocking on the door, as they had always done, to remind her to switch off the bedroom light. She was an adult now, and as she later wrote, it finally dawned on her that 'no power on earth could make her do anything except herself'.[40]

Momentarily that knowledge made Zelda dizzy; the rules she had spent so much energy rebelling against had also been her support. And during her first days in New York she experienced other moments of disorientation and drift. She was very afraid of seeming a provincial nobody: when Scott introduced her to his literary, Princeton friends, she was suddenly conscious that her gum-chewing habit appeared gauche, that her accent sounded too Southern, that her clothes were all wrong. And woundingly, on the last matter Scott agreed. Clothes mattered to him; he had an eye for what they symbolized as well as for their colour and cut, and they played an important role in his fiction. Zelda, however, was furiously offended when he suggested that his friend Marie Hersey should take her shopping for a new wardrobe. The Jean Patou suit that Marie picked out was eminently suited to the northern chic of Manhattan yet Zelda could hardly bring herself to wear it.

She was determined to figure out her own New York style, even though as Scott's novel was rushed into its second edition, she felt that the two of them were also being rushed into the social spotlight. They were mixing with very public figures now, including Kay Laurel and Lilyan Tashman, stars of the *Ziegfeld Follies*, and the influential drama critic George Jean Nathan. They were constantly out on the town, where each day promised a new party, as they and their friends gathered in hotel lobbies, chattered over telephone wires, moved in a flock between theatres, nightclubs, drinks in a speakeasy or someone's apartment. And despite her apprehension of not being elegant or clever enough for the city Zelda felt herself falling under its spell. The moment she loved best was the early evening, when Manhattan was poised in anticipation of the night to come. '[Twilights] were wonderful. They hung about the city like an indigo wash . . . girls in long satin coats and coloured shoes and hats . . . tapped the tune of a cataract on the dance floors of the Lorraine and the St Regis . . . a halo of golden bobs disintegrated into black lace and shoulder bouquets . . . It was just a lot of youngness.'[41]

A lot of youngness, and also a lot of money. Back in Alabama life was still mired in the economic decline that had followed the Civil War. New York, by comparison, was strident with cash, money generated from a bullish stock market and property boom, from movies and publishing, from bootleggers profiting by the new Prohibition laws. It was one of the cities that had benefited from the recent war, as Europe's exhausted economies had left the market open for America to drive forward its own radical modernizing version of capitalism. Some Americans were disgusted by what they perceived as their country's rampant materialism, and left for the more civilized cultures of Paris or Italy. Scott, however, believed the early 1920s was a charmed era. 'It was an age of art, it was an age of excess and it was an age of stature,' he wrote later. It was 'an age of miracles' and he and his generation were 'the great believers'.[42]

High on the buzz of their new wealth and popularity, Zelda and Scott felt their own personal miracle to be spun out of bright lights and crowded dance floors, jazz and theatre and late-night conversations. Above all, out of the illegal thrill of champagne, a Bronx cocktail or a gin fizz. Prohibition had been introduced in 1919 in order to reduce the poverty and social degradation attributed to alcohol, yet for people like the Fitzgeralds, the Volstead Act had simply created an exhilarating new culture around drinking. Young women kept silver hip flasks tucked into their garters; friendships were sealed over the recommendation of a new bootlegger or speakeasy (covert drinking places, concealed behind anonymous locked doors, or anodyne shop fronts). New cocktails were invented almost daily to cover the harsh metallic aftertaste of illegally manufactured spirits. Zelda's cocktail of choice was the orange blossom, a blend of gin and sweetened orange juice, whose sugary, chemical intensity became, for her, the taste of New York. She had drunk spirits at home, but primarily as an act of rebellion; here in the big city she was 'stewed', 'zozzled', 'fried' on orange blossoms every day.

Drink also gave her courage with Scott's friends. It had been disconcerting to realize how vacuous her famous Montgomery coquetry had appeared to them, but they seemed to approve of her more private ideas and her imaginings. The intuitive, scattered quality of her notions on life and love had a poetic novelty to their university-trained minds. To Edmund Wilson in particular, Zelda's 'fresh and delightful chatter' was alight with 'spontaneous colour and wit'; another friend Lawton Campbell would comment how 'she passed very quickly from one topic to another and you didn't question her. It wouldn't occur to you to stop her and ask her what she meant.'[43]

Like most men, Scott's friends also turned out to be sexually malleable. Safe in her position as a married woman, Zelda learned how to tease these Princeton bachelors, inviting one of them to wash her in the bath, suggesting to another that she might share his bed, if only 'to fall asleep'. Often, during the parties that gathered in their hotel suite, she was the only woman present; it was delicious to her to hold court from the sofa, the bed, or even from the bath tub, an orange blossom in one hand and a cigarette in another. Scott enjoyed these demonstrations less. While he relished showing off his wife to his friends, he was still prone to jealousy – especially when he'd been drinking. Two strong gins were sufficient to make him belligerent and paranoid. And while sometimes he paid Zelda back by turning his charm on other women (it was around this time that he made a play for Eugenia Bankhead), more often he found himself quarrelling bitterly with her.

As weeks passed, the pace of their New York existence affected them both. They were becoming captive to their own image – and trying to live up to it in ever more egregious ways. Scott took off his clothes during a performance of *George White's Scandals*, and made a boastful play of using five-dollar bills to light his cigarettes. Zelda's jokes became coarser, and her attitude to men became more overtly provocative. Observing her over lunch one day, Dorothy Parker thought there was a new petulance in her expression and an element of strain in her desire to shock. She disliked the self promotion exhibited by both Fitzgeralds, and her resentment at its effectiveness showed in her satirical squib 'The Flapper': 'All spotlights focus on her pranks./ All tongues her prowess herald./For which she may well render thanks/to God and Scott Fitzgerald.'

Scott later wrote that when he and Zelda first began their New York life together they had felt like a pair of 'small children in a great bright unexplored barn', and that it had taken only a month of drinking and partying for them to become exhausted and lost: 'We scarcely knew any more who we were and we hadn't a notion what we were.'[44] He was especially alarmed by his inability to write in New York: there was nearly always a lunch, a theatre date or a hangover to come between him and his work. If he ever managed to cloister himself at his desk for a couple of hours, Zelda grew quickly bored and nagged at him to come out with her. To recover their bearings, he suggested they leave the city for a while. If they could summer somewhere quiet, by the ocean, he believed that he would find serious time for his new novel and she would become more settled.

Zelda was happy to agree. Despite the fun she was having in New York she was mildly disgusted by the squalor which she and Scott managed to create, 'the tart smell of gin over everything [in their hotel suite], cigarettes disintegrating in the spittoon'.[45] She was beginning to miss the open skies and cool lakes of Montgomery – outdoor physical activity always restored Zelda to a sensation of being 'Blowy clean'.* After a few weeks hemmed in by the dirt and noise of Manhattan, she relished the idea of a wild shoreline and of swims in the bracing Atlantic.

In May they bought a second-hand car, a wildly unreliable Marmon sports coupé that they christened the Rolling Junk; and found a grey-shingled farmhouse in Westport, Connecticut, for rent. They were convinced they could make it an idyll, with Scott writing more and both of them drinking and quarrelling less. They would recharge their commitment to a life of significance and event. Yet in this first move of their married life, Zelda and Scott had embarked on a pattern that would become entrenched: chasing after the promise of a new start, and discovering that it always let them down.

In the case of Westport, they simply hadn't moved far enough from their problems. Just fifty miles away from New York, it was too easy for them to travel by train or car back into the city, and too easy for the city to come to them. Many Friday nights a group of friends would arrive bearing bottles of gin, and the ensuing party would drag on until early the following week. Day after day, Scott and Zelda awoke to sleeping bodies scattered

---

* Scott was very struck by the expression and gave it to Gloria Gilbert, the heroine of his second novel, *The Beautiful and Damned*.

around the house and garden, to a mess of bottles and overflowing ashtrays.

Scott had not reduced his drinking as he had hoped: in one night alone he spent $43 (now about $500) on alcohol. Nor had Zelda settled. A Japanese servant called Tana had been hired to run the house, and once the novelty of swimming and sea air had worn off, Zelda had little to occupy her. She distracted herself with a very attentive George Jean Nathan, and even though she was flirting mostly out of a desire to outscore Nathan's 'other blondes' (he'd had affairs with Anita Loos and the actress Ruth Findlay), Scott reacted badly. When Zelda smooched with Nathan at a party, or lunched alone with him in New York, he suspected betrayal, and far from finding peace together in Westport, their quarrels grew stormier, swollen by alcohol and unexamined feelings of anxiety and resentment.

One night they rowed so violently that Zelda swore she could not spend another minute with Scott. She ran down to the railway line and began weaving down the tracks towards New York. She was half hoping, in her bleary exhilaration, that a train would come roaring out of the darkness, but she knew, of course, that Scott would come running after her. The drama of their quarrels was becoming addictive; the drama of their reconciliations even more so. After the incident, Zelda wrote with almost delirious ardour to Scott: 'Nobody's got any right to live but us ... I could never do without you if you hated me and were covered with sores like a leper – if you ran away with another woman and starved me and beat me – I still would want you, *I know*.'[46]

For Scott, the rows and reconciliations were also necessary to his fiction. His new novel *The Beautiful and Damned* was a portrait of the failing marriage of Gloria Gilbert and Antony Patch. These characters were recognizable as him and Zelda: a couple determined to seize the happiness of the moment, but fatally unable to draw the line between extravagance and dissipation, between romanticism and narcissim. Gloria and Antony's failures might add up to something far uglier than the Fitzgeralds', their egotism might be more selfish and unlovable, but their characters were still drawn directly from experience. Lines from Scott and Zelda's arguments went into the novel, and so too did near-verbatim chunks of Zelda's letters and diaries. The Fitzgeralds were not Gloria and Antony yet, but the fictional couple were a warning of what their future might be.

By the autumn they were back in Manhattan, renting a small apartment on West 59th Street. Here, for the first time in her life, Zelda was responsible for maintaining some kind of domestic order, and she realized she had neither aptitude nor interest in it. It was frankly astonishing to her how quickly the chaos accumulated – dirty clothes, empty bottles, papers and books in teetering piles, dishes left over from meals they had ordered in from a nearby delicatessen.

She'd been wondering vaguely about embarking on a creative pursuit, building on her schoolgirl talent for painting or writing. She might follow the example of her sister Rosalind, who had written a society column for the *Montgomery Journal*; closer to hand was the poet Edna St Vincent Millay with whom Edmund Wilson and John Peale Bishop had recently become besotted.[*] Millay was a rival for Zelda, both lovely and accomplished, but still another woman's talents were not sufficient to drive her to any serious exercise of her own. The mess in the apartment was too oppressive for her to sit down at a table and work; and with the snap of winter in the air, it was too much fun to be outside in the city, getting her hair done in a 5th Avenue salon, or shopping for new clothes. Zelda was confident now about what suited her new Manhattan self, and she took pleasure in scouting the streets and store windows for the perfect garment. The fur coat with which she fell in love that autumn cost a shameful $750, but she nagged at Scott until he let her buy it.

---

[*] Millay's 1920 poem 'A Few Figs from Thistles' had become celebrated as an anthem to flapper recklessness: 'My candle burns at both ends/It will not last the night/But ah my foes, and oh my friends/It gives a lovely light.'

In the city, everything conspired towards the spending of money they didn't have. There were trips to the theatre followed by nights in the Jungle Club, a 'juice bar' that boasted a pre-Prohibition elegance, with a dance floor and a headwaiter in white tie and tails. There were parties too prolonged and too numerous to count. Scott's first collection of short stories, *Flappers and Philosophers*, had just been published, and both he and Zelda were caught up in another frenzy of publicity. To their friends they seemed to be everywhere in Manhattan, actively chasing headlines with Zelda's sexy dancing and Scott's clowning, with their immoderate kissing and public rows. Their friend, the writer Alec McKaig, observed that behaviour which had seemed admirably spontaneous six months ago now seemed a contrivance to 'hand down the Fitzgerald legend'.[47]

Interviewed for the magazine *Shadowland* in January 1921, Scott had emphasized Zelda's influence on the heroines of his stories. 'Flirting, kissing . . . saying damn without a blush, playing along the danger line',[48] she'd been the original model for a type he'd dubbed the 'mental baby vamp'. However, it was only one month later that Zelda was precipitated into a new and much more adult role.

There had been an understanding between them that they would have children someday. Given his Catholic background and her hazy understanding of fertility cycles, they may have been doing little to avoid it,* yet when Zelda discovered that she was pregnant in February 1921, she still felt unprepared. She had few close women friends with whom to discuss subjects like babies and motherhood; and when she realized her new condition the one thing she knew was that she didn't want to be like any of the 'little women' she'd known in Montgomery. She would not give up on her freedom, she would be pregnant in her own way.

---

* US research had only just begun to deliver accurate information about ovulation.

Zelda was all defiance when she went home to tell her family the news. The town was holding its annual masked ball, and she intended to dominate the dance floor as she always had. She dressed up in a Hawaiian grass skirt, and as she swayed her hips to the band, she languorously lifted up her skirt to expose her bare legs and silk knickers. Even with the mask she wore, it was clear to the startled Montgomery onlookers that this was the same wicked Zelda they had always known.

She was still that Zelda when she returned to Montgomery later that summer, now evidently six months pregnant. Women in her condition were expected to conceal their bodies as far as possible from public view, but it was hot, and she wanted to cool down in the local pool. With every contour of her swollen belly showing in her bathing suit, Zelda walked defiantly into the water – and felt as much triumph as annoyance when the pool guard ordered her to get out and put on some clothes.

If Zelda was determined to be pregnant on her own terms, she and Scott had initially been determined that their baby would also be born in the most beautiful of places. New York was too hard boiled a city, and back in May they'd gone to Europe to search out a more 'historic . . . romantic place'.[49] It was their first trip abroad, and they travelled in style, taking a first class cabin on the Cunard liner *Aquitaine*. But once again the fantasy of travel failed to survive the reality. Their first stop was London, where Zelda enjoyed the drama of an evening spent 'slumming' in the East End docks, for which she dressed up in men's trousers and a tweed cap, hoping to catch sight of some Limehouse criminal types. Yet pregnancy was making her feel queasy, restricting her appetite for sightseeing, and Scott proved a reluctant traveller.

He had taken slightly against London, piqued by its lukewarm attitude towards his first novel. Even when they travelled on to Paris, Venice and Rome, Scott found the cities 'of merely antiquarian interest', 'a bore and a disappointment . . . we know no one here'.[50] Although a few years later he would loftily dismiss the crass, uncurious American tourists who began flooding into

Europe, on this trip he badly missed the familiar comforts of home. When they returned to America, he suggested to Zelda that they 'play safe' and have the baby in St Paul, his own native city.*

Remarkably, when they travelled to St Paul in September, Zelda was meeting Scott's parents for the first time. She had long resisted the introduction, out of fear they would disapprove of her, and Scott had never pushed for it. He was slightly embarrassed by his family: Edward Fitzgerald was a man of old-fashioned manners who had muddled away his capital in foolish business ventures; his wife Mollie was as guilelessly loud in her opinions as she was in her taste in clothes. Scott guessed that Zelda would find his parents difficult, as indeed she did. While Edward and Mollie were warmly welcoming, she didn't care for the fact that Scott's family were such odd failures. She also took an immediate dislike to their home. St Paul architecture looked raw and ugly to her, and its attitudes remained pettily provincial – when she walked down the street smoking a cigarette, people stared and catcalled.

Not only did she miss the freedoms of New York, she was also oppressed by her pregnancy. She had always taken for granted the sleek efficiency of her body, the way it felt knit together with 'delightful precision, like the seeds of a pomegranate'.[51] Now she felt hot, hormonal and heavy. When she went drinking with Scott at the yacht club just outside the city, nobody seemed particularly ready to flirt or dance with her; she felt she had become an 'Alabama nobody', and the jokes Scott was making about her size, and the hours he was working on the final draft of his novel, made her worry that he no longer found her attractive.[52]

She would have felt lost in St Paul except for the one new friend that she made. Xandra Kalman, Sandy, was easygoing

---

* His prejudices against foreigners were also infused with the unexamined racism of his childhood. Europe had grown degenerate, Scott argued in one letter home: 'a negroid spirit had defiled the Nordic race' and the Italians had 'the souls of blackamoors'.

and sporty, a keen golfer like Zelda, and she offered the reassuring image of a mother who seemed able to enjoy herself unrestricted by her children.* As Zelda's pregnancy came close to term, Sandy offered advice about baby equipment, labour wards and breastfeeding, intimating that it would all be a breeze.

In fact, when Zelda went into labour on 26 October it was long and hard and Scott swore in anguish that he would kill himself if she died. After many hours she was delivered of a baby daughter, yet, exhausted and outraged as she was by the assault on her body, and hiccupping from the anaesthetic, Zelda was still able to put on something of a performance, murmuring dazedly: 'I hope it's beautiful and a fool, a beautiful little fool.'[53] The line was so perfect it could have been scripted, and it's not surprising that Scott filed it away for later use. (It would eventually be uttered by Daisy Buchanan in *The Great Gatsby*.) However, for Zelda, bleeding and woozy from the long delivery, it might also have been a register of her disappointment. Both she and Scott had been hoping for a boy, so much so that the name they finally gave their daughter, Frances Scott Fitzgerald, appeared to have been selected with a son in mind.[†]

If Zelda was disappointed over her baby's sex, however, she was determined to love her, and back in their rented home she spent long hours nursing and cuddling Scottie, pasting mother and baby photographs into her scrapbook. Yet, still, depression gathered. She felt imprisoned by Scottie and the bleak St Paul winter, and when a nanny was hired to relieve the drudgery of childcare, her mood did not improve. The strictness of Miss Shirley's methods took all the fun out of having a baby: 'Nanny knows best' became the unbreakable rule of the nursery, and she tutted at every hesitation or clumsiness when Zelda was handling Scottie.

---

* Scott would transpose aspects of Sandy to Jordon Baker, the professional golfer in *The Great Gatsy*.
† They havered a little. For a while the baby was called Pat (short for Patricia), then briefly Scotty, spelled with a 'y'.

The little confidence Zelda had possessed as a mother leached away. She was disoriented too by her body's failure to return to its former slenderness and snap. Fatigue and the cold weather made it hard for her to be outside, yet even with dieting she seemed bewilderingly unable to shift the weight she'd gained during pregnancy. When she overheard a man at a party refer to her as Xandra's fat friend, she felt a sickening jolt of shame. It was another few weeks before she realized she was, in fact, pregnant again.

Zelda couldn't imagine having another baby so soon. It was too gross an invasion of her body, and one that would almost certainly prolong her incarceration in St Paul. But, as determined as she was to terminate this unwanted pregnancy, it was not an easy decision. Abortion was strictly illegal in America, and the methods women were forced to use were ugly and dangerous. Of the one hundred to one hundred and fifty thousand abortions that were estimated to take place in America each year, one in six was fatal and many more left women damaged or infertile.[*]

One of the superficially less brutal options was an 'abortion pill', which could be obtained by mail order, or under the counter of a barber's shop or drugstore. These were marketed as aids to menstrual health and given blandly euphemistic names, 'Hardy's Woman's Friend' or 'Madame Drunette's Lunar Pills'. Compared to the most physically invasive methods, such as the insertion of metal hooks into the uterus, or an injection of soapy water, they seemed simpler and safer. Yet their ingredients were herbal abortificants – tansy, pennyroyal or savin – that could be dangerously toxic in the wrong combination or dose.

Fatalities among the poor were inevitably higher. Josephine Baker's younger sister died from a self-induced abortion in 1927, as she sat over a steaming tub of carbolic acid. Yet the statistics

---

[*] Britain had similarly strict laws, as did France, although the latter maintained a more pragmatic approach to abortions, turning a blind eye to a proportion of them as necessary 'family planning'.

were bad for everyone. Iris Tree had six abortions by her mid-twenties, the last of which came close to killing her. Zelda herself had already had one pregnancy scare before she was married, and Scott, terrified for both their reputations, had sent down some pills from New York. Back then, however, Zelda had refused to take them. She had said they would make her 'feel like a whore' and obstinately, naively clung to the belief that 'God or something has always made things right, and maybe this will be'.[54]

This time Zelda wouldn't trust to God or anyone. She and Scott obtained the necessary pills and booked into an anonymous hotel until the bloody business was over. It was barely mentioned between them, although Zelda's doctors later believed that the shame and loss had lodged deep inside her. Scott made just one stilted written reference to the episode in his notebooks, his use of the third person indicating an anguish too large to face directly: 'His son went down the toilet of the XXXX hotel after Dr X – Pills.'[55]

In early March, Zelda and Scott were in New York for the publication of *The Beautiful and Damned*. They were staying at the Plaza, and whatever private traumas Zelda was battling, the surface of her life was lit with the usual bright whirl of publicity. The novel's dust jacket featured a sketch of Gloria, inspired by Zelda, so that in every bookshop she saw her face flatteringly on display. There was talk of a film, with her and Scott playing the lead roles. She was even approached by the *New York Tribune* to write her own review.

As always, she thrived on the attention, but simultaneously she began to mind that it only came to her because she was Scott's wife and muse. This latest book made her feel vaguely exploited. She disliked Gloria as a character and felt tainted by being associated with her mean-spiritedness. It gratified her enormously to read John Peale Bishop's review in the *New York Herald*, in which he argued that Gloria was one of Scott's most disappointing creations, lacking 'the hard intelligence, the intricate emotional equipment on which [the flapper's] charm depends'.[56]

But Zelda was also beginning to question the degree to which Scott was mining her own letters and journals for his fiction. At first she had encouraged it. The love letters she sent from Montgomery had been full of carefully imagined descriptions that she hoped he would use. (He did: her description of the 'weepy watery blue flowers that might have grown from dead eyes' in the Confederate Cemetery, went straight into *This Side of Paradise*.)[57]

What had been a source of pride then had now, however, become contentious. Scott had recently shown Zelda's journal to George Nathan, who had considered it an illuminating document and worthy of publication. Yet without consulting her Scott had rejected the idea: the last thing he wanted was to have the precious resource of Zelda's inner life squandered and on public view. That unilateral decision smarted, and Zelda took her revenge when she accepted the *Tribune*'s invitation to review *The Beautiful and Damned*. Lightly, but deliberately, she hinted at the extent of her husband's pilfering as she quipped 'Mr Fitzgerald . . . seems to believe that plagiarism begins at home.'[58]

The review was tightly written and funny – Edmund Wilson thought it 'fine' – and it proved to be a small milestone for Zelda as other commissions followed, short stories as well as articles. Not only did these offer her the beginnings of a writer's apprenticeship, they also represented her first attempts to create a public voice that was independent of Scott's.

The first of her articles to be published was 'Eulogy of the Flapper', and it was in some ways the most predictable, a celebration of the type that she herself had helped to create. Zelda paid tribute to all those women who had ignored the warnings that men don't marry the girls who let themselves be kissed, and had instead put on their 'choicest pair of earrings and a great deal of audacity and rouge and [gone] into battle'. Yet she pointed out that a distinction had to be made between the true flapper rebel and the superficial copy. All over America

shop girls and small-town belles were painting their lips, shortening their skirts and doing a great deal of 'Flapping', but very
few embodied the careless, courageous spirit of the originals.[59]

In her second article, 'What Became of the Flappers', she
suggested that this spirit was not as easily decoded as writers and
advertisers might believe: 'The best flapper is reticent emotionally and courageous morally. You always know what she thinks,
but she does all her feeling alone.'[60] It was a telling remark. Back
in Montgomery, Zelda could write to Scott, 'You are the only
person on earth, Lover, who has ever known and loved all of
me.'[61] But during the quarrels and confusions of the last eighteen
months the distance between them had widened. There were
times when she could access their old communion, when they
talked late into the night, following the natural eddies of each
other's thoughts, but there were also subjects about which Zelda
no longer confided in Scott – her self-doubt as a mother and her
fear that she would never become more than a wife and muse.
The old conflicts were intensifying, too: his drinking, her flirting
and Scott's anxiety over money, which grew the more helplessly
extravagant they both became.

Zelda had reluctantly agreed to spend the summer of 1922 in
St Paul, because Scott insisted they could live more cheaply
there. It was a mystery and a disappointment to her that the
business of budgeting was so intrusive in their lives. Yet despite
the huge sums that came in from Scott's writing and from the
sale of film rights to several of his works, he borrowed heavily
from his literary agent, Harold Ober, and was permanently in
debt to his publishers, Scribner's, by several thousand dollars.
When Zelda suggested what she regarded as a practical solution,
that Scott spend more time on the smart upbeat stories, which
sold so well, rather than wrestling with the novels that came so
much harder, Scott reacted as if she had betrayed him.

Another wife might have economized and effaced herself,
Zelda knew. But she did not feel that was the kind of woman
Scott required her to be. She believed that he still needed the
inspiration of her free spirit, her ability to live 'the life of the

extravagant.'[62] That was what he had fallen in love with, and it had become the selling point of his fiction. Scott himself had admitted as much to Edmund Wilson when he acknowledged that it was 'the complete fine and full-hearted selfishness and chill-mindedness of Zelda',[63] that remained the most potent influence on his writing.

The next move of their marriage was to Long Island, which they hoped would be a compromise: secluded enough for Scott to focus on his third novel, and close enough to Manhattan to compensate Zelda for the dullness of her summer in St Paul. They rented a small, white stuccoed house, set back from a leafy road and close to the ocean. Yet Great Neck, the area they had chosen, proved far from modest: it had acquired the nickname Gold Coast because of its concentration of rich and famous inhabitants. Their closest neighbour turned out to be Max Gerlach, who was rumoured to be a bootlegger and who lived like a millionaire. Also living close by was the actor Basil Rathbone, and the columnist and immensely successful sports-writer Ring Lardner.

Almost every night there was a party somewhere: lights strung up in a garden, cocktails by a swimming pool, a live band and a cabaret. Alternatively, there were drinks, dinners and theatre trips to New York, which was less than twenty miles away. At certain times of the day and night the road between Great Neck and Manhattan was chock full of cars, a rush hour of pleasure-seeking commuters. It was exactly the life that Scott would write about in *The Great Gatsby*, and for all his good intentions to be frugal and productive, he and Zelda found it impossible to resist.

Journalists were constantly hovering around Great Neck and reports soon appeared of the newly arrived Fitzgeralds: the par-ties they attended, Scott's fondness for 'piquant hors d'oeuvres' and their very public drinking bouts and petting. A full-page photograph of them was published in *Hearst's International* and syndicated across America: Scott sitting behind Zelda and lightly holding her fingers; Zelda wearing a long string of pearls and with her hair unusually styled in marcelled waves. They were being presented as *the* faces of the jazz age – a term Scott himself had coined the previous year as the title of his second volume of short stories. And while Zelda was inclined to be dismissive of the photo and her 'Elizabeth Arden Face', she could still be seduced and excited by her place in the social limelight.

Some people who met the Fitzgeralds around this time attested that they still appeared to be the perfect couple. Gilbert Seldes, editor of *The Dial*, recalled lying drunk on a bed when he first saw the 'double apparition' of Zelda and Scott, 'the two most beautiful people in the world . . . floating toward me, smiling'.[64] Others spoke of seeing them locked in their own world, talking, drinking, kissing, sometimes falling fast asleep entwined in one another's arms.

The writer John Dos Passos thought them brilliant: Scott, when sober, could speak with visionary clarity about America and American culture; Zelda was simply Zelda. One night a crowd had gone out driving, and as they passed a half-deserted amusement park, she insisted that the shy, stammering Dos Passos take her for a turn on the ferris wheel. As they whirled between darkness and garish lights, Dos Passos was both unnerved and entranced by the 'strange little streak' in Zelda's conversation, the glittering non sequiturs of her ideas, the harsh satirical beat of her humour.[65]

The writer Carl Van Vechten was equally impressed. Zelda 'was an original . . . she tore up the pavements with her sly remarks'.[66] There might be trouble in her and Scott's marriage, but to Van Vechten this was part of the Fitzgerald magic. The two of them 'tortured each other because they loved one another devotedly'[67] – just like the couple Van Vechten would model on the Fitzgeralds in his own 1930 novel *Parties*.

For Zelda and Scott, however, the symbiosis between torture and love was losing its romance. Scott was again drinking too much, not simply because he was going to too many parties, but because he was depressed at the halting progress of his new book. Each novel seemed to become more difficult to write, and he woke up at nights in a cold sweat, terrified that his talent was deserting him, that he would be left with nothing but debts and a wasted life.

Zelda, too, was conscious of wasting time. She had come to Great Neck with the intention of working on her magazine commissions: in the autumn of 1923, when a journalist from the *Baltimore Sun* asked what career she would follow if ever she had to earn a living, her most seriously considered answer (after suggesting a *Follies* dancer or a film star) was to become a writer. But she had never learned self-discipline, and she lacked the determined independence of her Montgomery friend Sarah Haardt. Sarah had refused to marry, arguing that 'there is so much in life, so much for a woman to see and do'.[68] She had graduated from college and had already had several short stories accepted for publication. The contrast would not be lost on Zelda when her own first story was accepted by the *Chicago Tribune* in 1925. *Our Own Movie Queen* was published not under her name, but under Scott's infinitely more commercial byline.

Yet if Zelda had moments when she longed to experience something of Sarah's vocation, she couldn't separate herself from the person that Montgomery and Scott had made her to be: feckless, lovely and spoiled. It was easier to decide she was 'only good for useless pleasure'[69] and order in expensive seafood and vintage champagne on a whim, to telephone Nathan and the rest of the Manhattan gang to come out for the evening. She and Scott might be suckered into what John Dos Passos disdained as a 'Sunday supplement style of celebrity', but she didn't know how they could stop.

Scott wrote a summary of every year in what he called his personal 'ledger'. In the last eighteen months his situation had shown a terrifying downward slide. While 1922 had been 'a comfortable but dangerous and deteriorating year, no ground under our feet', 1923 had been 'the most miserable year since I was 19, full of terrible failures and acute miseries'.[70] Scott feared he was squandering his talents as well as his money. His new

novel still slipped and seethed out of his grasp, he was worn
down by the ugly predictability of the rows between him and
Zelda. He was humiliated by the time he was wasting on pointless
parties, and above all he was terrified by his inability to control
his finances. During the past twelve months he and Zelda had
earned $36,000 (roughly $480,000 today) between them (a tiny
proportion of that coming from her), yet every month they spent
over $600 on basic living costs, and haemorrhaged even more
on hotels, theatre tickets, clothes, drink and their second-hand
Rolls-Royce.

Scott believed that they should make a drastic move, not just
to a different town this time, but to France, where the favourable
exchange rate would make life very much cheaper. By now Zelda
was sufficiently anxious and unsettled to agree. If Scott was freed
from money worries he might drink less and he might also spare
more time from his desk for her and Scottie. If it was true that
two people could live on $5 a day in France, perhaps two people
could also find a reprieve for their marriage.

Chapter Six

JOSEPHINE

~⚜~

F reda Josephine McDonald had very little on her mind when, at the age of fifteen, she agreed to marry Billy Baker, a handsome easy-going young man from Philadelphia. Billy had fallen in love with Josephine when he saw her dancing at the local Standard Theatre. Hot licks of jazz rhythm jumped around her skinny body, her long legs were bendy as India rubber, and when she flipped into one of her comic routines the crowd went wild for her. Josephine's big round eyes glittered as she vamped her crazy grin. She strutted like a chicken, and when she exited the stage with her back arched and her butt jutting out like a feathered tail she looked as sweet, sexy and funny as any girl Philadelphia had seen.

As far as Josephine was concerned, Billy had simply been a friendly pair of arms to snuggle into after she left the theatre at night; when they first became lovers she'd had no idea of marrying him. But his father, Warren Baker, had taken a shine to her and was unhappy to think his son might be taking advantage. He suggested the two of them should make their relationship official, and so on 17 September 1921, they stood in front of the Reverend Orlando S. Watte and swore that there was no lawful impediment to their becoming man and wife.

During that short ceremony Josephine had seen no reason to inform the Reverend Watte of her exact age, nor did she think it necessary to tell anyone that she already had a husband, in another city. She'd only been thirteen when she and Willie Wells had got married down in St Louis, and they'd barely been together two months. Certainly she'd seen nothing of Willie since she'd broken a beer bottle over his head and he'd stumbled, bleeding, out of the house. He was part of another life, and Josephine had done her best to forget him.

Here in Philadelphia, with Billy Baker and his family, there were no fights. Billy's mother might disapprove of Josephine – her skin was darker than Billy's and she was a chorus girl with apparently no family to speak of – but Pa Baker treated her with affection and respect. While most people still called Josephine by her childhood nickname Tumpy, Warren referred to her as 'Daughter', clearly taking pride when he ushered her gallantly to a table in the restaurant he ran. He bought new clothes for her, a silk turban and a seal-skin coat. Sometimes, on her Sundays off, he took her on the eighty-mile train journey to Harlem, where he treated her to lunch at Dabneys on 132nd Street, followed by a matinee show.

It was just a few weeks after Josephine and Billy married that Warren Baker acquired tickets for the latest New York sensation. *Shuffle Along* was the first all-black musical to succeed on Broadway for over a decade and everything about it had been praised by the critics, from the catchy wit of signature songs like 'Bandana Days' to the brilliance of Florence Mills, the winsomely graceful lead with the extraordinary, bubbling coloratura voice.

The *New York American* had even delivered a panegyric to the chorus line – so exuberant a contrast to the stiffly drilled routines of white girls that 'every sinew in their bodies [had] danced'.[1] A few months ago Josephine herself had yearned to be one of those girls, and had auditioned for the show when it was assembling its Broadway cast. But while most cities in America didn't fuss over the age of chorus girls, in New York the rule that they had to be at least sixteen years old was strictly enforced.

Watching the show now, beside Pa Baker, Josephine's body ached to be up onstage, performing alongside Florence Mills, whom she idolized. And when she returned home to Billy and the scrappy vaudeville show still playing at the Standard, Josephine could no longer imagine why she'd been so content with life in the Baker household. A few weeks later, when she heard that a second touring cast was being put together for *Shuffle Along*, she didn't even think to consult Billy or his family before auditioning.

Josephine was good at focusing on the future. Her audition was successful (no one asked about her age) and in February she was hired to become one of the Happy Honeysuckle girls, earning what was, to her, the fabulous wage of $30 a week. In her excitement, she spared little thought for the effect her departure might have on her five-month marriage; she felt she had simply taken the necessary next step towards success.

When she arrived in New Haven for the start of the tour, the first person she saw was her friend Maude Russell, who had been working as a singer and dancer at the Standard. She was pleased to see a familiar face, but when Maude called out 'Tumpy' and held out her arms in an affectionate embrace, Josephine put up a hand to interrupt her. 'My name is not Tumpy any more,' she said. 'My name is Josephine Baker.'[2]

Names were important to Josephine. At the Female Hospital in Saint Louis where she'd been born on 3 June 1906, official records had marked the uncertainty of her provenance, identifying her father with the simple abbreviation *Edw.* Her mother, Carrie, would never commit herself to naming, unequivocally, who *Edw.* might be. Sometimes she would hint at Eddie Carson, a drummer who worked in the bars of St Louis.* But Carrie had gone with many men, and while Carson would become very eager to assert his paternity once Josephine's career took off, others doubted he'd had any hand in her making. His skin was

---

* After the early years, Carrie refused to discuss the issue of Josephine's father with anyone, neither confirming nor denying Eddie Carson.

very dark, while Carrie's was almost black, and according to the gossips, Josephine's creamier colour had surely come from elsewhere.

During Josephine's childhood she learned to feel ashamed of her uncertain origins, to believe that there was something 'humiliating and dishonorable about my birth'.[3] But as she grew older she turned it to her advantage. She invented different fathers for herself – a Washington lawyer, a Spanish dancer, a Jewish tailor – depending on the audience she was playing to. She also switched between different surnames to cover her increasingly chaotic official status: sometimes using Carrie's maiden name, Macdonald, when she filled in a form; sometimes the surname of her stepfather, Arthur Martin; sometimes that of her first husband, Willie Wells. When she decided to stick with Baker, it would be because she felt she had made the name her own.

Reinventing herself was also Josephine's way of dodging the hurt of feeling not merely obscure, but also unwanted – especially by her mother. Carrie had been an unusual child, graceful and tall, with slanting aristocratic features. She had been bright, too, the first in her family to read and write, and her adoptive parents had assumed that someday she would lift herself out of the ghetto to a better life, working in one of the city's new department stores or even becoming a schoolteacher. But Carrie developed a wild streak. She began to go out dancing and to run around with men, and when she got herself pregnant at the age of twenty-one the family were mortified. Even though Josephine was taken care of by her grandmother and her great-aunt she was, from the start, an unwanted baby, a misfit, a burden to Carrie and a symbol of the family's disappointed hopes.

Sixteen months later, when Carrie got pregnant again, Josephine's situation did not improve. The new baby was illegitimate as well, but at least the identity of his father (Alexander Perkins) was known, and his skin was the same dark colour as Carrie's. As Josephine grew a little older she was made painfully aware of how much more acceptable her brother Richard was to the family: 'He had black skin . . . he was the welcome one.'[4]

And so it remained. When Josephine was four Carrie finally settled down with a husband. Arthur Martin was a big, slow-moving, simple man, but he was fundamentally decent, and happy to be a father to Carrie's two illegitimate babies. Over Carrie, however, and her increasingly volatile treatment of her children, he had no control. On good days, Carrie could be affectionate and lively, showing glimpses of the gay laughing girl who had racketed around St Louis. She could even be sweet to Josephine. But the daily grind of ghetto life made those days increasingly infrequent. Often Carrie would be driven to fury by the lumbering presence of her husband and by the noise of her four children (two more had followed in quick succession: Margaret in December 1908 and Willy Mae in July 1910). She sought refuge in drink and occasionally disappeared for a day or two on the arm of another man, but mostly she vented her rages on her children, shouting and slapping them with a terrifyingly abrupt violence.

It was Josephine who Carrie saw as the source of her frustration – the baby who had first closed the door on her freedom. If there was a child to blame, a child to be beaten, it was her oldest daughter; if there were jobs to be done around the house, it was Josephine who was required to work the hardest. From an early age she was expected to wash the dishes and mind the smallest children; she was sent out with Arthur at dawn to forage for fallen fruit and vegetables in the wholesale market. Perhaps the worst moment of Josephine's early life was the Christmas Day that Carrie got ragingly drunk and gave Josephine one of the harshest beatings of her childhood. The blows left welts and bruises, but far more terrible were the words that Carrie shouted – that she hated her daughter and wished she was dead. Josephine was only nine.

Later, she could understand how trapped Carrie felt. Her mother worked long hours as a laundress, but the wages were low, and even though Arthur struggled hard with his own trade, hauling gravel with his pony and cart, jobs were in short supply. The best he could do for his family was a two-room apartment on Gratiot Street, in a row of tenement houses that ran parallel to the two dozen train tracks leading into nearby Union Station.

These once decent houses were now collapsing slums – freezing in winter, fetid in summer. The noise on the street was constant: babies, domestic arguments, and the roar of passing trains. Smuts and smoke from the tracks added to the miasma of dirt that hung over the street, dirtying the laundry that flapped across every courtyard. There were only the most basic amenities for every household. The Martins shared an outside toilet, got their water from a communal tap, and all four children slept together on the same thin mattress, restless from the itch of bedbug bites and the sound of rats in the walls.

Yet still the Martins were a family, and Josephine clung to her place in it, doing what she could to please her mother by playing big sister to the little ones. On Saturday nights she led Richard and a gang of friends out through the neighbourhood, where parties spilled out onto the sidewalks and the music of banjos, accordions and pianos could be heard from the Rosebud Café or the Four Deuces Salon. St Louis always claimed to be the home of ragtime. It was here that Tom Turpin and Scott Joplin had improvised their witty parodic tunes, setting classic 2/4 marches against a raggedy syncopated rhythm, creating a style that every St Louis musician was making their own.

Other evenings Josephine organized raids on the coal trucks that lined up in the station yards. She showed the smallest children how to harvest nuggets of coal that had fallen onto the ground, while she clambered up onto the cars and threw down the bigger chunks for them to collect. Over the Christmas holiday she searched the garbage bins of the wealthy white neighbourhoods, looking for discarded toys to take home. As she grew older and bolder, she knocked on doors, offering to run errands, sweep leaves or mind babies. Most of her earnings she spent on her family – Richard recalled her being 'a good sister . . . she didn't make much money, maybe 50 cents a week, and when she got it, she would buy things for us'.[5] Yet as dutiful as Josephine tried to be, when she was barely seven years old she was sent away from her family to earn her keep as a live-in scullery maid.

As far as Carrie was concerned, Josephine's departure made one less mouth to feed. Perhaps she genuinely assumed that her daughter's new employer, Mrs Kaiser, would demand only light duties from such a small child, especially as she was legally required to maintain Josephine's attendance at school. Yet Carrie had delivered Josephine into the hands of a sadist who sent her down to the cellar at night, with just a crippled old dog for company. When she wasn't in school she was working – lighting fires, emptying chamber pots, washing dishes and clothes. If Josephine lost concentration or was too weak to manage her chores, she was beaten. 'I would have loved to run away,' she wrote later, 'but I was too small.'[6]

This, at least, was the way she presented the story. Parts of it were probably true – for the rest of her life she would do anything to avoid sleeping on her own at night – yet Josephine was no less of a myth maker than Tamara, and couldn't resist exaggerating and editing her life into a more dramatic shape. According to her version of events, she was delivered from her torment only when Mrs Kaiser's brutality led to her being hospitalized. She'd left a pot of water to boil over on the stove one day, and as punishment her employer had thrust her hands into the scalding water. Her injuries were excruciating – 'My skin and my fingernails . . . boiled, ready to fall off' – and there was apparently no question of allowing her back into Mrs Kaiser's care.[7]

In truth, no one in the family could remember Josephine suffering such burns, and in all the thousands of column inches subsequently written about her, no one commented on her hands being scarred. Yet this Cinderella story made emotional sense to Josephine. Her imagination had been formed by the few fairy tales she'd been told when she was little, and in her head was a world of rescued princesses and happy endings, to which she escaped when her own life was too hard.

That fantasy world remained necessary to her, even once she was back with her family. By 1915 the Martins were sliding towards destitution. Arthur could find little work and they were forced out of Gratiot Street and into a succession of smaller, filthier apartments. For a time Josephine had just one dress to wear, held together by patchwork and darning, and she either had to walk barefoot or totter through the streets of St Louis in a cast-off pair of women's evening shoes, their high heels amateurishly filed down by Arthur.

Unlike her clever little sister, Willy Mae, Josephine neither sought nor found any escape in school. She was a poor student and spent most of her lessons crossing her eyes and pulling faces to make the other kids laugh. News of the outside world meant little to her. If papers or magazines came into the house, it was only because Arthur was using them to insulate the walls of the apartment against the cold and damp. America's entry into the war in 1917 made almost no impression on her. But the events of July that year, as St Louis was overtaken by waves of racial violence, gave eleven-year-old Josephine her first inkling of a larger and even more dangerous world that existed beyond the ghetto.

Historically St Louis had been known as a place of relative tolerance. At the beginning of the century it became a draw for thousands of blacks escaping the entrenched and still unchallenged abuses of the rural South,* and there were sufficient opportunities for work and schooling for the city to develop a small, but significant, black professional class. Of course St Louis had its own racial divisions: public places were segregated, and at the

---

* Early French settlers had brought a philosophy of relatively enlightened pragmatism, offering education to their slaves and opportunities to buy back their freedom. Josephine's grandparents and great-aunt were among the wave of immigrants to St Louis.

laundry where Carrie worked large signs assured their customers 'We Wash for White People Only'. When Josephine walked to school, the children from the all-white Catholic school nearby hurled routine insults at her: 'Hey blue gums', 'Where you goin' shine?'

All this was normal to her, and to every other child in the ghetto. Blacks were at the bottom of the social hierarchy, with quadroons and octoroons, the mixed race or 'high yellows', ranked marginally above. Further up the ladder were the white European immigrants, while at the top were the 'pure' or American-born whites. Although Josephine's inexplicably coffee-coloured skin might be disparaged within her family as a badge of Carrie's shame, many black women paid good money to acquire a more Caucasian look. Drugstores were piled high with products to whiten skin and with bottles of Mary's Congolene, or 'conk' – a noxious liquid that promised to straighten every kink in a black woman's hair and to give her a small notch up the city's racial hierarchy.

In good times, that hierarchy was a relatively stable fact of life in St Louis. However, in late 1916 a nationwide recession created a sharp rise in unemployment. White workers, paid at higher rates than blacks, were laid off first, and it was their bitterness and economic frustration that helped drive the resurgence of the Ku Klux Klan. Leaders of the racist cult were finding a newly receptive audience across America, prophesying the triumph of a rampant Negro race. And by July, St Louis had become electric with tension. It took just one incident, a white mob attacking a few blacks, to spark a wave of rioting and lynching. In the eastern part of the city, across the river from Josephine's district, entire black neighbourhoods were torched. Many were killed, thousands more made homeless and Josephine and her family watched incredulous as smoke and flames raged on the opposite shore of the Mississippi.

For several months, Carrie and Arthur were unusually vigilant about keeping the children near the house. Then, in 1918, a new danger threatened St Louis: the outbreak of Spanish flu. Schools

and theatres were shut down, a curfew was imposed and again
Carrie tried, in her irritable fashion, to keep her children close.
By now, however, Josephine was twelve, going on thirteen, and
she no longer considered herself a biddable child.

In many ways she had long been frighteningly adult for her
age – scavenging in garbage cans, scrounging money and skip-
ping school to take on extra work – but when she reached
puberty, Josephine's boldness turned to rebellion. She stayed out
late, refused to explain where she had been and began to flaunt
herself around men. In the last few months her skinny body had
acquired the provocative jut of buttocks and bust, and she had
started to style her hair in cute little spit curls. She liked the way
men looked at her now; and Carrie, who saw her own former
wildness breaking out in her oldest daughter, was terrified.

Foremost in her mind was the fear that Josephine would get
herself pregnant and bring new trouble and expense to their
already chaotic household. She attempted to impose stricter
curfews and threatened harsher beatings, but it was only a matter
of time before the situation exploded. One night Josephine came
back so late, and with such a maddeningly secretive look on her
face, that Carrie lashed out especially hard. Whimpering and
cussing, Josephine ran from the house; the following day it was
all over the neighbourhood that she had left home and gone to
live with a man.

Later Josephine would claim that this man had forced himself
on her, that she had been the victim of an exploitative paedo-
phile, yet her brother Richard remembered only that she had
been dragged back home, spitting fury at losing a safe and easy
billet. She was, he claimed, like 'a wild cat' in the house, and her
behaviour became so out of control that Carrie started threatening her with reform school. This was an institution little better
than prison, and almost certainly would have damaged and
hardened Josephine beyond repair. She was saved by the intervention of Jo Cooper, Carrie's friend and employer, who had
always taken a benign interest in Josephine and even been a
kind of unofficial godmother to her. Sensibly, Jo Cooper sug-

gested that if Josephine could no longer be contained as a child, she would have to be dealt with as a woman.

So at the age of just thirteen and a half, Josephine was married off to Willie Wells, a steelworker twice her age. How she ended up with him is unclear – some accounts suggest that Jo Cooper had heard of a decent, employed man in search of a wife and introduced Willie to the family, others that Josephine had met him at a dance. Either way, the courtship was pragmatically brief, and in late 1919 the couple were married by a pastor in Jo Cooper's house, and given a wedding supper of pork ribs and macaroni.

No one was concerned about Josephine's extreme youth. Officially, the Missouri statute allowed for underage girls to marry only if there was 'good cause and unusual conditions', yet in the black ghetto good will on both sides was considered sufficient grounds; form-filling was rarely an issue.*[8] Certainly for a very few short weeks the marriage seemed to work. Willie Wells had rented a large furnished room, which Josephine considered a wonderful improvement on her old home. And aside from a few light chores, it seemed to her that being a wife to Willie involved little beyond amusing herself and spending his money.

Reality punctured Josephine's naive contentment, however, when Willie discovered that she had not only spent her house-keeping allowance on treats and new clothes, but had run him into debt. Unable to afford the rent for their room the newly married couple were forced back into Carrie and Arthur's apartment, where they had to sleep alongside the other children. Willie was furious, and it may have been in an effort to win back his approval, or even to protect herself from his fists, that Josephine began virtuously flourishing knitting needles and declaring herself to be pregnant.

----

* Back in 1908 Arthur had 'adopted' Josephine and Richard simply by signing his name on a piece of paper.

Perhaps she was, and perhaps she miscarried, but almost as soon as Josephine had begun to make clothes for her baby, there was no longer any sign of one. This seems to have prompted her final row with Willie, who may have believed she'd deliberately got rid of their child. By her own account, Josephine feared for her life as her husband roared up the stairs, threatening to break her neck. It was in her own defence, she claimed, that she hit him over the head with a beer bottle and sent him away with blood running down his face.

With that blow the marriage was over. Yet however short-lived, it did have one very satisfactory outcome for Josephine: she was now officially a woman, no longer subject to Carrie's rules, and without consulting anyone she got herself a full-time job as a waitress at the Old Chauffeurs' Club. Malicious gossips told Carrie that her daughter was supplementing her $3 weekly wage by going with men, but Josephine didn't care what anyone said. She planned to be out of St Louis soon, and to be launched on an entirely new life.

It was about three years before her rash experiment with marriage that Josephine first became stage-struck and began slipping off to the Booker T. Washington theatre, close to her home. The Booker advertised itself as the city's premiere black venue, and by putting aside ten cents from her odd-job earnings, Josephine could buy a Sunday matinee ticket for the latest musical comedy or vaudeville programme. As a very little girl she used to sit her younger brother and sisters down on boxes in the cellar of Gratiot Street, where she performed her own impromptu shows. At the Booker, however, she was awed by the dazzle and variety of the professional talent on display – dancers who kicked their feet as high as their ears; singers; acrobats; performing dogs; comic female impersonators who strutted haughtily and ridiculously in feather boas.

Josephine was especially awed by the dancers and, with an intensity that would have astounded her teachers at school, she studied every move they made onstage. At home she practised what she had seen, trying to shimmy her bony, ten-year-old shoulders like a chorus girl, and to tap and shuffle her feet. After spending a few weeks on polishing a routine, she secured herself a spot on the sidewalk outside the Booker, from which she set herself to smiling and capering a few cents out of the people passing by.

Josephine was a cute, comic sight, and sometimes she was even thrown a nickel or two, but she faced stiff competition for the public's attention. St Louis was crowded with buskers, dancers, musicians and comics, all of whom were hoping to use their talent to escape the ghetto. Many got no further than working the local bars, or performing for the tourists, who paid thirty-five cents for an evening cruise of 'moonlight dancing and drinking' on the Mississippi riverboats. However, even as a small child Josephine was determined. Across the street from the Martins lived a family of musicians: Mr Jones, his common-law-wife Dyer and their children, who between them scraped a gypsy kind of living, playing in bars and pool halls or at country fairs on the outskirts of the city. During the winter of 1916–17 Josephine latched onto the Joneses, helping to carry their instruments from one gig to the next in return for learning their skills. Dyer Jones was a very talented musician and not only was she willing to teach Josephine the rudiments of trumpet, banjo and fiddle, she occasionally allowed her to sing and dance along with the rest of the band.* Trying to project her breathy little voice across a noisy bar, or tapping her feet on a rough wooden stage in a field, Josephine had her first experience of performing to a proper crowd.

Josephine's association with the Jones family was curtailed by the 1917 riots and the city's subsequent shutdown, but her dreams continued to grow. At the Booker she could now identify the best of the visiting performers: Bessie Smith, the blues singer

---

* When Dyer eventually disassociated herself from the Jones family band, she became a well-known trumpeter on the black vaudeville circuit. Josephine would meet her again in Philadelphia in 1921.

with a voice that tore the blood out of your heart; chorus dancer Mama Dinks, who wooed the crowd with her bowlegged walk and goofy grin; and, in the winter of 1919, her favourite was a raucous singer with a bright red wig called Clara Smith, who performed with Bob Russell's troupe, the Dixie Steppers.

Onstage Clara's trademark routine was to pick out the ugliest man in the audience and sing a melting love song direct to his face. Offstage, however, her preference was for young women. When she started going to the Chauffeurs' Club, for a meal or a glass of corn liquor, she noticed Josephine and was touched by her mix of ghetto hardness and dreamy ambition. To Josephine, Clara was a fabulously glamorous creature, even without her stage make-up and blue feather boa, and even when she was smoking the filthy corncob pipe to which she was addicted. When Clara offered to give her singing lessons, Josephine was over-joyed, and she didn't much care when it became obvious what Clara expected in return. She already knew that sex was part of the price you paid for things; better to do it with Clara than a no-hoper like Willie.

Clara grew sufficiently fond of Josephine to coax Bob Russell into giving her a trial job in the theatre. And it was this that caused the final divide between Josephine and her mother. Per-haps Carrie knew Clara's involvement with her daughter was more than professional, perhaps she believed, as many Americans did, that show business was a godless world. But even though Carrie flew into a righteous temper, abusing Josephine as a whore, Josephine simply shrugged off her mother's rage. Clara's good opinion was all that mattered to her now; that and the fact that she was about to make her first appearance on the Booker stage. Wearing a pink tunic, trussed up in a rope and harness, she was going to have a brief moment in the spotlight as a flying cupid, swung out across the stage during a romantic love scene.

Her debut was almost a disaster. As Josephine was hoisted into flight, her wings got caught in the curtain and she was left dangling in mid-air. Yet rather than being mortified by the crowd's catcalls, she seemed to know exactly what to do. Instinctively, she turned her face towards the laughter and grinned, her radiant response turning the public mockery into delight. Bob Russell could spot a natural comedian when he saw one, and by the time his troupe were due to leave St Louis he had signed up Josephine as a permanent member.

Just a few weeks later she graduated from general dogsbody and walk-on to a place in the chorus line. One of the dancers was injured, and when Josephine showed Russell her basic repertory of moves – the Itch, Tack Annie and the Mess Around – he was impressed by her potential. She also offered the hugely promotable assets of her pretty, adolescent body and enormous smile. Some of the chorus line were well into their thirties, their muscles hard and stringy from the unforgiving stages on which they had to perform. To emphasize the cuteness of his new teenaged acquisition, Russell decided to bill her under her family nickname, Tumpy. For his regular punters, she was fresh meat.

Josephine had succeeded in launching her career before she'd even turned fourteen, however life in the theatre bore little resemblance to her fantasies. Later she wrote that it was hard to have her illusions shattered so early, and to realize that most of her fellow performers worked principally because they didn't want to starve. Black troupes like the Dixie Steppers were restricted to a limited touring circuit,* whose management – the Theater Owners Booking Association – were so ruthlessly exploitative they were popularly known as 'Tough on Black Asses'. Wages were bad – even working four shows a day Josephine earned just $10 a week, from which she had to fund her own board and lodging. The Association also did nothing to address the dire inadequacies of their living and working conditions. In many towns and cities it was almost impossible to find a rooming house that would take blacks, while the few that did were so squalid many preferred to doss down in a station waiting

---

* The best theatres on the vaudeville circuit, like the Keith, were only open to white performers.

room. Everyone got sick at some point – the facilities in theatres were primitive, with no toilets and barely any running water, and many venues were filthy. Josephine recalled that the 'air was awful' from the food that audiences brought to eat during shows – 'day-old pork chops, fruit and corn patties, peanuts whose shells were lobbed onto the stage'.[9]

But if touring was hard, Josephine had endured worse; and she did at least enjoy the buffer of Clara's protective presence, ensuring that she had somewhere to bed down most nights. Clara continued to give her singing lessons, and even tried to coax her into improving her reading and writing. However tired Josephine might feel when she crawled into a filthy bed at night, however much she missed her brother and sisters, she rarely regretted leaving home. If she was hungry or fatigued, there was always the adrenalin of the stage to lift her up the next day, and the promise of a new town ahead.

Travelling was still an amazing novelty for Josephine. Back in St Louis, the trains that steamed out of Union Station had formed the daily soundtrack of her dreams, rattling out their siren song of distant places and better times. Now, riding these trains herself, she could lose herself in the unfolding drama of the other passengers – country rubes with their chickens and market produce, townsfolk with their pressed suits and leather cases. Some of the cities where they stopped seemed magical to her: New Orleans, succulent with the smell of Cajun cooking and the sound of calypsos; Chicago, a city of skyscrapers, speakeasies and dance halls.

By the time the tour wound up at the Standard Theatre in Philadelphia, it was April 1921, and Josephine had been with the Steppers for over a year. Clara had recently left, claiming her Southern blood couldn't cope with the Yankee North, but Josephine no longer needed her. She had grown used to life on the road, and more importantly she had just been promoted to the prime spot at the end of the chorus line. The dancer occupying this slot was allowed to stand out from the other girls and given fragments of her own music to which she could perform solo tricks. Maude Russell, who first saw Josephine dance at the Standard, said it was clear by now that she was destined for greater things: 'She was dressed like a ragamuffin but she killed them all the way to the peanut gallery.'[10] According to another admirer, she had a joyous comic quality that was even more beguiling than Mama Dinks, 'doin' all sorts of gyrations with her legs, trippin', getting out of step and catching up, playing marbles with her eyes'.[11]

Josephine was making such progress with the Steppers that when she went to audition for the New York cast of *Shuffle Along*, she had little doubt in her mind that she would be hired. Nor could she believe that she would be denied something she wanted so badly. Compared to the twenty-five-cent mix of vaudeville acts in which she currently performed, this was a sophisticated musical comedy, written by four of the biggest names in black entertainment: the comedians Flournoy Miller and Aubrey Lyles, and the song-writing team Eubie Blake and Noble Sissle. When Sissle himself informed her at the audition that she was too young to be employed, she was heartbroken. The composer was used to disappointing chorus girls, but he felt a rare pang at Josephine's dejection: 'Big tears filled her eyes, and with drooping head . . . she slowly turned, half stumbling down the steps to the stage door . . . without even looking back she disappeared into the rain.'[12]

Josephine was young, however, and she recovered fast. Once she and Billy were married the two of them moved in with his family, sharing a pleasant room in the little apartment over the Bakers' restaurant. And when the Dixie Steppers moved on to another city, she remained with the Standard's resident troupe, still dancing in the prestige spot at the end of the line. She became close friends with two other members of this troupe, Maude Russell and Mildred Martien, who were both very sweet to her, lending her clothes and helping her wash the 'conk' out of her hair every night before it burned her scalp.

It was Maude, though, who noticed that Josephine was never quite present, that she 'lived in her head and her dreams'.

However willingly she chatted and laughed with her new friends it was clear that everything in her life was temporary compared to her desire to see her name in lights some day. As Maude caustically observed, when Josephine got her chance to go out on tour with *Shuffle Along*, she had no qualms about leaving everybody behind.* Even Billy. 'I don't think she stayed with her husband but a hot minute.'[13]

Josephine's ambition almost got the better of her, however, on her opening night at New Haven. Dancing with the other eleven 'Honeysuckle Honeys', she was supposed to remain strictly in step; this was not a show in which comic stunts were required. Yet out on the stage, with the eyes of the audience on her, she couldn't contain herself. At the end of the first number she flipped into her usual end-of-line routine, crossing her eyes, kicking up her legs and flashing her electric grin. It was a glorious moment, with everyone laughing and applauding her, but when she exited the stage it was to an icy encounter with the stage manager, who ordered Josephine to pack her bags and leave.

Fortunately she hadn't left New Haven by the time the reviews came out the next morning. All made reference to her spon-taneous display, with one critic singling her out as a 'born comic [with] a unique sense of rhythm', and Eubie Blake, realizing he had a special asset in his cast, overrode the stage manager. Not only should Josephine stay, she should continue doing her comic routine and work it as hard as she knew how.

Josephine had secured her own little piece of limelight, but as Tallulah had discovered when she'd made her debut in *The Squab Farm*, there was a price for being noticed. The other dancers resented Josephine's promotion and took every oppor-tunity to punish her for it. They excluded her from the commu-nal gossip in the dressing room, and left her alone to manage her make-up and costume changes. After the show they didn't

---

* Maude would leave her own husband, Sam Russell, to join the *Shuffle Along* tour at the last moment. But her own longstanding marriage was unhappy, and Sam was frequently violent.

invite her to go out and eat with them and, most cruelly, they began to pick on her for the colour of her skin.

Shuffle Along might be a pioneering production for black artists, but it was still dogged by racial stereotyping. On the one hand, white audiences expected to see the usual cast of comic black characters, lazy illiterate men and eye-rolling mamas; on the other hand, they required black chorus girls and female singers to appear as attractively, tactfully pale as possible. There was an unofficial colour bar in operation for shows that played to white audiences. It was known as the 'paper bag test' and it was implacable. One of the singers in *Shuffle Along* was a superb soprano, Katherine Yarborough, who would go on to have a career in opera,* but because she was very dark skinned she was required to perform nearly all of her numbers hidden away in the wings. Among the Honeysuckle Honeys, most were 'high yallers' who, with an application of powder and paint, could almost pass for white. But Josephine's coffee colouring only just passed and the others used it against her. 'God don't love ugly,' they hissed as they turned their backs in the dressing room.[14] And when one of the chorus was required to entertain a producer, a backer, or a rich patron, it was the little 'darky' Josephine who was forced to do it.

In many respects *Shuffle Along* treated its performers well, providing sleeping cars for overnight train journeys and ensuring decent lodgings for the troupe. But there was still a hierarchy in place, by which chorus girls were routinely, and unquestioningly, expected to be available for sexual services. It was a fact of show business, white as well as black. Louise Brooks admitted to being part of a group of 'hand-picked girls' at the *Follies* who were 'invited to parties given for great men in finance and government'. They considered themselves to be above 'common whores', but only because they were fortunate enough to be well

---

* Under her later stage name Caterina Jarboro, she would become the first black singer to perform in a white opera production.

treated. As Brooks recalled, 'the profits were great. Money, jewels, mink coats, a film job – name it' were all on offer to the prettiest and most compliant.[15]

Josephine was simply trying to hold on to her job. And for a while, as she was passed from man to man during the tour of *Shuffle Along*, her life became exactly what Carrie had feared. Yet she had long acquired the skill of sidestepping pain or humiliation by withdrawing into the world inside her head, and she considered herself lucky when Eubie Blake selected her to be his special 'girl', rewarding her with small gifts and genuine affection.

Far more significant to Josephine was the fact that Blake and Sissle began to single her out for extra coaching. It was clear she had talent, and critics continued to notice her; yet while she could scintillate on certain nights, she lacked the craft to deliver her comic or virtuosic effects at will. Her 'emotions were beyond her control', recalled Sissle, and he and Noble worked patiently to persuade her that she needed technique, as well as stage magic, to progress.

Protected by Noble and Sissle as Josephine was, the cruelty of the other dancers inevitably diminished. She also gained a new friend in the dressing room, when the tiny fifteen-year-old Evelyn Sheppard was hired for the Honeysuckle chorus line. Everyone made a pet of Little Shep, with her sweet, pointed cat's face, but she and Josephine became physically very close. They didn't think of themselves as lesbian – in their world that implied perversion – but the quasi-sexual intimacy they enjoyed was nevertheless very common in show business. Young women would frequently share a bed in order to save money, and would frequently take pleasure and comfort in each other's bodies. As Maude Russell scornfully pointed out, the men in their lives were so much less appealing. 'Most of them didn't care about pleasing a girl.'[16]

Sleeping with another woman was also safer. Maude herself had an abortion when she was very young, and she made it her business to inform others of the brutal options involved. Either 'you went to some lady or old man and took your chances on them killin' you and you paid them ten or fifteen dollars', or you got yourself 'some carbolic acid and put it in a pot of hot water and [sat] over it', waiting for the baby to 'dissolve'.[17] It's possible that Josephine too had an accidental pregnancy to deal with, for when *Shuffle Along* was playing a short season in Chicago, Billy came to see it – and her. If Billy was hoping to resume their marriage, his visit was a failure. This would be the last time that he and Josephine would see one another.* But at the end of the Chicago run, Josephine took a few very uncharacteristic weeks of leave from the show, and one reason may have been due to that brief reconciliation with her husband.

This disappearance was one of several odd lacunae in Josephine's early career. But if an abortion had prompted it, she recovered fast. When she rejoined *Shuffle Along* she demanded, and received, an individual credit in the programme as 'That Comedy Chorus Girl'. When the show toured up to Canada she danced her way into even more rave reviews. A critic in Toronto wrote that she had 'burlesqued jazz until the audience nearly fell out of their seats'.[18] By the time the show was due to appear in St Louis, Josephine was ready to milk it as a triumphant homecoming.

She was appearing not at the old Booker T. Washington, but at one of St Louis's premiere mixed theatres, the American. Richard and Willy Mae were there to witness her glory, albeit from the cheap gallery seats designated for blacks. And even though Carrie had refused to come to the show – her feelings still darkened by envy, shame and anger – Josephine visited her and Arthur afterwards. Showing off her latest outfit, a brightly coloured taffeta frock and fringed shawl, Josephine's real moment of triumph was being able to give her mother a

---

* While she sent Billy money from time to time, she began divorce proceedings against him in 1925, though the case was abandoned by the American courts in 1928.

present of $75 – a full year's rent on the Martins' grimy little apartment.

Towards the end of 1923 *Shuffle Along* had played itself out and Josephine had to find a temporary new billing, dancing with the music and comedy double act Buck and Bubbles and sharing Buck's bed. But only three months later she was back with Sissle and Blake, who had devised a special solo slot for her in their next production, *In Banville*. It was designed to show off the comic, inventive range of her talent. While she would be dressed as a caricature piccaninny, in a short checked frock and clown-sized shoes, her lips whitened and her skin darkened with charcoal, the two men wanted Josephine to dance with all the vivid, wild imagination she could muster.

Those who saw that solo remembered her as a protean force of nature. At moments her body seemed to be possessed by a crazy menagerie of animals as she waddled like a duck; walked like a dog on all fours; undulated like a snake, and arched into the boxing stance of kangaroo. She could be pure comedy, crossing her eyes, puffing out her cheeks and imitating the sound of a muted saxophone; or she could be pure 'jazz babe', dancing the Charleston and the One Step, bouncing in and out of the splits.

She was vamping her own iconoclastic version of black minstrelsy and to the poet e.e. cummings the effect was both extraordinary and unsettling: 'Some tall vital incomparably fluid nightmare, which crossed its eyes and warped its limbs in a purely unearthly manner.' The *New York Times* called her a 'freak terpsichorean artist', but the *Chicago Herald and Examiner* was unequivocal in its appreciation, praising the 'comic little chorus girl whose very gaze was syncopation, and whose merest movement was a blues'.[19] The public was equally admiring and Josephine's popu-larity not only boosted her position in the troupe – her name now appearing fifth from the top in the programme – but also earned her a payrise. At $125 a week, her wage was over ten times what she'd been paid with the Dixie Steppers, four years earlier.

Still she aimed higher. The show was scheduled for a very long tour, taking in Philadelphia (where she ate Thanksgiving dinner with Pa Baker) and Canada. Josephine used that time to perfect her craft. Inspired by a friend who'd studied classical ballet, she acquired the rudiments of pointe work and started giving herself a daily class, limbering and stretching and working on her technique. Whenever she could she watched the other performers from the wings, looking out for a rhythm, a step, an effect that she could poach. She practised her singing, and even persuaded Sissle and Blake to write her a song, for which she was allowed to exchange her plantation frock for the glamour of a gold lamé evening dress.

But if Josephine was learning sophistication as an artist, the show itself was ironically being criticized for aiming too high. Reviewers panned *In Banville* for offering 'too much art and not enough Africa'.[20] They scorned Blake and Sissle for wanting to have a symphony orchestra playing alongside the band, and a chorus line that aped the high-precision 'Kick and Tap' routines of the British Tiller Girls. It was, they said, too much like a mimicking of the 'white man's' style, and the public, it seemed, agreed. Takings at the box office declined, and despite the show being renamed *Chocolate Dandies*, a title with a more obviously black spin, it folded in the spring of 1925.*

These were hard times for the black arts community, which still remained captive to the expectations and definitions of the American Establishment:† jazz music and jazz dance might be all the rage amongst white critics and audiences, but if Sissle and Blake wanted to write Broadway musicals, if Katherine Yarborough wanted to sing European opera, if the violinist Will Marion

---

* Re-packaged yet again as the *Chocolate Kiddies* it was then sent out to Europe, where it had a better reception. Its success would in fact be critical for Josephine, paving the way for the *Revue Nègre*, which made her a star.
† Also to navigate the hopeless confusion of their definitions of colour. In music hall, white singers and comedians still blacked up their faces to perform minstrel numbers, with the consequence that some black performers painted their skins even darker, in order to pass as whites in 'black face'.

Cook (a talented graduate of both the Berlin Hochschule für Musik and the National Conservatory) wanted to be more than a 'nigger with a fiddle', their aspirations were quashed. For Josephine, the closure of *Chocolate Dandies* felt particularly precarious. She was owed $1,235 in unpaid wages, and for the first time since leaving home she had no immediate prospect of work. Other cast members were heading up to Harlem, and because she had nothing better to do, she followed them there, her small cache of savings tucked into the pouch she kept tied around her waist.

In some ways she was pleased by the move. She rented a room in a lodging house on 7th Avenue and 133rd Street, owned by her former idol, Mama Dinks. Close by was Tillie's Chicken Shack, reputed to serve the best fried chicken and hot biscuits in New York state, and around her was the most entertaining community she had ever lived amongst. Harlem was exceptional in America, a black district that, despite its violence and chronic unemployment, refused to regard itself as a ghetto. Originally its wide streets and elegant brownstones had been intended for white families, but a downturn in the market had resulted in much of the area being bought up by black property developers. By 1925 blacks from as far away as the Caribbean regarded it as a place of opportunity. And with this eclectic influx came a variety of theatres, restaurants, churches, bars and beauty parlours, and an even more exuberant variety of music. During the 1920s some of the great musicians lived and worked out of Harlem, including Sidney Bechet, Scott Joplin and James P. Johnson, and on every street there were clubs and bars playing blues, spirituals, ragtime and jazz.

'It was the gayest place that America ever produced,' declared the writer Anita Loos. And that was the view of the many thousands of young white Americans, who came flocking up to Harlem during the 1920s to experience its energy and exoticism for themselves. Some were genuine music lovers, to whom jazz was the sound of the new America: writers like J.A. Rogers, who likened its restless tempo and strident harmonies to the music of 'modern man-made jungles'[21] and Gilbert Seldes who claimed that it contained 'nearly all the gaiety and liveliness and rhythmic power of our lives'.

Other white tourists sought more illicit sensations, like the tawdrily erotic cabarets that offered 'tantalizin' tans' and 'hot chocolates', or the brothels that promised 'slumming hostesses for inquisitive Nordics'. There was also the party crowd who ventured up from Zelda and Scott's Manhattan, coming in flocks to dance the Charleston and the Blackbottom amongst 'real' black people in the Savoy and Cotton Club. Ironically, even in these Harlem clubs the professional dancers who performed in cabaret slots were subject to the paper bag test – they were required to be dark enough to look authentic, but not so black that they looked threatening.

The same test naturally applied to any performer hoping to be hired by any of the venues in central Manhattan, who were also cashing in on 'the negro vogue'. The Plantation Club, located just above the Winter Garden Theater, was typical. Meticulously refurbished in a faux Southern style, it boasted a painted décor of cotton plants and watermelons, a white picket fence around the dance floor and a 'black Mama' cooking waffles in a log cabin. A changing roster of black acts played there, with headlining stars including Florence Mills and Ethel Waters. The clientele, of course, were white.

When Josephine arrived in Harlem, the revue playing at the Plantation was *Tan Town Topics*. Not only did she manage to get hired, she was sufficiently well established to get her own featured billing as 'the highest-paid chorus girl in vaudeville'. She was pleased with her new job, and also with the young actor Ralph Cooper, who had become her New York boyfriend. Ralph was handsome and amusing, and the fact that he was working temporarily as a chauffeur meant he frequently had a car in which he could pick Josephine up from the Plantation and drive her around Manhattan. She felt like a queen, roaring through the hot dusty nights in her ruffled taffeta frocks, fake pearl necklaces and big hats.

Once she stepped out of Ralph's car, however, everything was different. Central Manhattan was still aggressively white. As a black woman, Josephine was unable go into a 5th Avenue store and try on a hat, or choose where she wanted to sit in a theatre. Even at the Plantation Club she only felt secure onstage. White men, and some white women, came to the club expecting to take away a black dancer for the night, and once again Josephine found herself in a situation where she was expected to oblige. It was a brutal reminder of the limits she faced as a black chorus girl, a reminder that however hard she worked on her stage technique, however rigorously she bleached her skin with lemon juice, she was still essentially bracketed alongside the 'hot chocolates' and 'tantalizin' tans'.

She yearned for real distinction. America's decade of Flaming Youth had swept so many others to fame: Scott and Zelda Fitzgerald, Tallulah Bankhead, Clara Bow and a host of other flapper actresses. It had made gods of black musicians like Louis Armstrong and Duke Ellington. But the only black women that Josephine knew who had risen to eminence were singers like Florence Mills, Ethel Waters and Bessie Smith. These performers topped the bill of every revue or vaudeville show in which they appeared; they were nationally famous, their voices heard on the record players and radios that were becoming household staples, yet a dancer had no equivalent opportunity for fame and money. Within the formulaic conventions of American show business, the best Josephine could hope for was an occasional solo and her featured spot at the end of the chorus line.

That summer, however, she was offered a completely new platform – in Paris. Josephine had been too young to register America's entry into the European war, but it was to have a profound impact on her, given the craze for jazz and ragtime that the American forces imported with them to France. Many of the black musicians who'd fought there had opted to remain, rightly seeing it as a more liberal alternative to home.* Within a couple of years their music had spread through the clubs of Montmartre and into the bars and hotels of smart white neighbourhoods. In 1920 the song 'Jazz Partout' announced, 'There are jazz bands by day, by night/There are jazz bands everywhere'.[22] Even classical composers like Stravinsky and Auric were entranced by black music, and its hold on the city was confirmed when the Prince of Wales went on a tour of Montmartre and demanded a collection of jazz records to take back home.

By 1925 white French musicians were complaining of a 'black peril'. According to one newspaper, they were happy to 'do that jazzin' themselves', but were routinely told by dance hall managers to 'call again when you have changed the colour of your skin'.[23] There was a view in France that only black musicians could embrace the soul of jazz, its quintessential modernity and its Dionysiac spirit. Nor did this premium on blackness end with jazz. In the wake of Pablo Picasso's absorption of African influences into his art, much of French culture embraced a new black aesthetic. The spectacular Exposition des Arts Décoratifs that opened in the spring of 1925 featured an entire section dedicated to African sculpture, celebrating the vibrancy of its line and its expressive simplicity of form. African motifs appeared in textiles, in ceramics, in jewellery. Even black boxers were deemed to embody a primitive visceral nobility. Jean Cocteau, the ultimate aesthete, wrote the libretto of a ballet, *Le boeuf sur le toit*, which was set in a speakeasy and had a boxer as a lead character. He also opened a nightclub with the same name and theme.

Black culture was also in the sights of the Théâtre des Champs-Elysées, the modernist theatre which had held the violently controversial premiere of Nijinsky's *Rite of Spring* back in 1913 and had also been home to the avante-garde company Les Ballets Suédois. In 1925, its impresario, Rolf de Maré, had the idea of

---

* Around 200,000 black soldiers served during the 1914–18 war, including the all-black 369th infantry, aka the Harlem Hellfighters.

importing music-hall acts into the theatre, channelling a fashionable mix of the high and low brow that was currently so dear to
Paris. It was while de Maré was scouting for suitable material
that the painter Fernand Léger is said to have offered him a
critical piece of advice: 'Get Negroes. They're dynamite.'[24]

It was through Léger, too, that de Maré was put in touch with
an American woman living in Paris, who was regarded as a
'negro' expert. Caroline Dudley had been raised on French
novels, impressionist paintings and an unusually liberal world
view. Her father had invited black friends to the family's Chicago
house, and had taken his daughters to black vaudeville shows.
Now living in Paris with her diplomat husband, Caroline Dudley
had already been toying with the idea of bringing over a troupe
of black dancers and musicians, convinced that they would
'amaze, flabbergast [and] dumbfound' the public.[25]

Once she was offered the resources of de Maré and his
producer André Daven, her idea became practicable, and in July
she sailed to New York, looking for talent for what was already
being called *La Revue Nègre*. Her ambitions were high: she
wanted to sign up a top-ranking singer, such as Florence Mills
or Ethel Waters, to lead her cast. When both those women
demanded fees that far exceeded her budget, Caroline had to
rethink, however. And it was on a visit to the Plantation Club
that she observed a dancer who 'stood out like an exclamation
point', and became convinced she had found her star.

Others disputed her judgement. Louis Douglas, who was
already hired as a choreographer and dancer for the revue,
believed that Paris would not be impressed by Josephine. Her
dancing was too eccentric, and her voice wasn't strong enough
to be of any use in the singing numbers. Even less enthusiastic
about the plan was Josephine herself. She was very suspicious of
Mrs Dudley, who came to see Josephine in her dressing room.
She was a tiny birdlike woman, yet her intensity was alarming.
She gazed at Josephine, her voice filled with emotion as she
described the importance of bringing black art to America.
Josephine wasn't used to talking about art, nor was she used to

producers – the people with money and power – being female. Warily she wondered if Caroline Dudley was going to try and get her alone and jump her bones.

Her reluctance also stemmed from a fear of the unknown. Ambitious as she was, part of her was still a little girl from the ghetto. Josephine was unable to project her dreams all the way across the Atlantic to a foreign city, whose language she couldn't speak and whose people she knew nothing about. With untypical and largely mendacious sentimentality, she told Caroline that she couldn't possibly think of going to Paris and leaving her boyfriend Ralph.

Undeterred, Caroline returned to the Plantation night after night. She spun enticing images of the success Josephine would enjoy and promised her a weekly wage of $250, double her current earnings. She half promised that Josephine might even sing a serious number or two in the revue. What tipped the negotiations, however, was Josephine's helpless craving for lovely things. One night Caroline arrived at the club wearing a Chinese-style coat, richly embroidered with gold thread. Josephine thought it beautiful, and when she asked Caroline if she could have it, the older woman spotted her moment. She handed over the coat immediately, and by 15 September Josephine was due to board the *SS Berengaria* to France.

If Tallulah had felt as though she were travelling to Mars when she prepared to cross the Atlantic two years earlier, Josephine was no less stricken. She had never experienced a terror like it, recalling that it 'grasped my brain, my heart, my guts with such force that everything came apart'.[26] Yet she also knew the value of fresh starts. As she packed her clothes for Paris, she put aside all the letters and notes she had saved, the photographs, the tributes from fans – any memento that connected to her American life. All of them were thrown out with the garbage. When Josephine arrived in France, she was determined to leave the past behind and take only the future with her.

Chapter Seven
DIANA

Josephine's voyage to Europe was a professional break for freedom, but when Diana had crossed the Atlantic two years earlier it was America itself that seemed a land of possibility. In New York, where she was due to play in Max Reinhardt's *The Miracle*, the air wasn't clouded by issues of family and duty. Even though her name and title would bring box office dollars to Reinhardt's production, America didn't really care about the nuances of the British class system. If Lady Diana Cooper wanted to go down the extraordinary route of supporting her husband financially, and do so by appearing onstage, no one would suggest she was demeaning herself. If she wanted to economize by dining on corned beef hash in a cafeteria, she could do so without eliciting Chinese whispers of gossip and comment.

At the end of the war, battling to gain her independence and marry Duff, such freedom had been unimaginable to Diana. On the evening of Armistice Day, as she and Duff had sat together and mourned the wasted lives of their friends, she had sworn to go home and tell her parents, finally, that they were engaged. Yet it was very hard for her. She knew that the Duchess continued to hope for a more elevated match – the sight of Diana in animated conversation with the Prince of Wales could still squeeze Violet's heart with anguished expectation. And partly because she loved her mother, partly because she feared the violence of her disappointment, Diana quailed like a child at the thought of confronting her.

For days she dithered in nervous paralysis, until her friend Viola Tree – now married to Alan Parsons – took pity on her and offered to tell the Duchess herself. Diana despised herself as she hid cravenly in her bedroom, but the scene that broke out was as bad as she had feared. Her mother's voice could be heard throughout the entire house, railing against 'that awful Duff', and declaring she would rather see her youngest daughter dead from cancer than waste her life on a man of such mediocre character and prospects.[1]

Part of the problem was Violet's inability to believe that Diana actually loved Duff. Natural reticence had always prevented Diana from saying so, and when her mother challenged her to declare her feelings she was too angry and embarrassed to respond. Choked by her own emotions and trapped by her mother's demands, Diana felt isolated within her own family and turned to her old morphine habit for relief.

Nonetheless, she could match her mother for stubbornness, and as the weeks passed Diana never wavered – if she couldn't have Duff she would marry no one else. This was her trump card, and she knew it. The idea of Diana remaining a spinster was even more horrific to the Duchess than the idea of her being Duff's wife, and after a wretched family Christmas at Belvoir, the war of attrition slowly turned Diana's way. By April she'd wrung an agreement from her exhausted parents that she and Duff would be married that June.

It was the most grudging acceptance. Diana might not marry with a 'ducal curse' hanging over her head, as *Cassell's Saturday Journal* had predicted,[2] but the £300* annual allowance that her father settled on her was far less generous than Duff had hoped.

---

* Post-war inflation, hikes in wages and taxes, and a fall in the value of agricultural land were hitting the gentry hard. Many estates were being split up and many town houses sold and demolished, as families like the Rutlands struggled in the difficult post-war economy.

The wedding arrangements were made in an awkward spirit, as Diana later bleakly recalled: 'My five weeks of engagement were a little sad. My father chose 2 June for the wedding [because] he wanted to get away for Whitsuntide, before the trains were too crowded.'[3]

Yet if Diana minded her family's lack of enthusiasm, the British press were effusive. Positive news stories were hard to find that spring, as post-war recession and the ravages of Spanish flu loaded misery onto an already wearied nation. When the engagement was announced at the beginning of May, photographs of the couple covered the entire front page of the *Daily Sketch*. On the wedding day itself, the public reacted as though it were almost a state event.

Groups of the curious and expectant had begun gathering in Arlington Street early that morning, and by the time Diana and her father left to drive the short distance to St Margaret's Church in Westminster, mounted police had to clear a path through the crowd. The Duke was not a celebratory mood, 'his temper was short and his gills were white and his top hat had no jauntiness'.[4] The mob made him testier still. 'What in the name of heaven is it all about,' he protested as the car inched through the throng, apparently amazed by his daughter's popularity.[5]

Thousands more were waiting outside the church. Many were journalists and photographers, but many were ordinary women, who having followed Diana's activities in the society pages now felt a possessive interest in her wedding. They were avid for every detail: the bride's dress (made of delicate gold lamé and flowered lace); the floral decorations (rose bushes and orchids, donated from the gardens of Blenheim Palace); the celebrity of the arriving guests. Also the astonishing hoard of presents that Diana and Duff were said to have received: cheques from the Aga Khan and George Moore*, diamond jewellery from the

---

* Moore had originally offered Diana an allowance of £6,000 a year, but reluctantly she had decided it would be bad form to accept.

Royal Family, chests of fine linen, antique dinner services, rare books and paintings, and a brand-new car from the newspaper magnate Max Beaverbrook.

It was deemed by the public to be a very satisfactory event. Yet while Diana recalled that the 'day had no shadow', in some of the photographs her face registered more tension than joy.[6] The last six months had been difficult for her, and there had been an alarming moment outside the church when a man had seemed on the point of attacking her, although he was simply trying to hand her a letter. Like Zelda, she was exulting in her new freedom and the knowledge that she 'need never lie again',[7] but she was also fearful about what married life would be like.

At twenty-six Diana no longer really understood why she was still a virgin. Sexual frustration made Duff quarrelsome, and she acknowledged that her resistance to him was timid, even perverse. Yet she had been schooled by her mother to believe that virginity was a security to be given up only for a wedding ring, and deeper than that belief lay the fears of her own sexual adequacy. Diana's suspicion that she might be less physically responsive than other women made her terrified of disappointing Duff.

A decade later she would remember her wedding night as a momentous emotional transition. In bed with Duff she was over-taken by a welter of conflicting sensations: 'Nervous unhappy and elated feeling – as well as desirous too and extremely conscious of sex.'[8] She felt that she had finally become a woman, and that knowledge made the whole of their month-long honey-moon idyllic to her. Duff was apparently just as happy. The sight of his new wife, walking naked in the moonlight in the grounds of their Italian villa, struck him with poetic awe, and he claimed it was 'the most beautiful sight' in Europe. He was, however, more guarded in his sexual rapture. In his diary he noted that their wedding night had been 'very old-fashioned and conven-tional',[9] and only a few days later he caught himself lusting after another woman – a pattern that would continue throughout their marriage.

When they returned home it was to a temporary period of

limbo. They needed to find a house of their own that they could both love and afford,* and they were set back for several months by Diana breaking her leg and having to remain bedridden in Arlington Street. But in March 1920 they discovered a suitable house to rent in Bloomsbury. Even if their richer friends considered 90 Gower Street to be quaintly 'tiny' and eccentrically far off the social map, for the next twenty years it was the Coopers' home, along with their 'skeleton' staff of five servants (Diana's maid, Katie Wade; Duff's manservant, Holbrook; plus a cook, housemaid and scullery maid).

Diana liked being poised between Belgravia and bohemia. She began to entertain at Gower Street, regrouping writers, painters, musicians and young politicians into a new version of the Coterie. The more wayward of her guests, the transvestite Prince Yusopov (also a friend of Tamara's) and Curtis Moffat (Iris Tree's American husband) gave her a pleasing frisson of modernity, even if Duff tended to disapprove. In 1919, when Moffat had dined with them at Arlington Street, Duff had been annoyed when the artist not only 'forgot' to dress for dinner, but produced a 'new wonderful drug' (possibly cocaine), which was supposed to produce 'a thousand queer effects'.[10]

Set against the bohemians were their wealthy friends, who subsidized the Coopers to an amazingly generous degree. Dinners, theatre and opera tickets and holidays abroad were offered as a matter of course, and in July 1923, when Diana hosted a summer party, it was Max Beaverbrook and several others who paid for the food and drink, while the pianist Arthur Rubinstein and the singer Feodor Chaliapin entertained the guests for free. Among all those who hoped for invitations, Gower Street appeared a world away from the suburban drabness that Diana's mother had so gloomily prophesied for her.

---

* By 1922 Duff was earning £450 a year, having been promoted to secretary to Ronald McNeill, the Under Secretary of State. Combined with the £600 allowance he received from his mother, and Diana's own allowance, that gave them around £1,400 per annum.

It was Max Beaverbrook's generous wedding gift of a car that also allowed Diana the dangerous luxury of driving. Cars were not yet commonplace in Britain – just 250,000 were on the roads in 1919 – and few of their owners possessed much aptitude or experience.* Diana herself was almost as feckless behind the wheel as Mrs Stitch, the character she would inspire in Evelyn Waugh's 1938 novel *Scoop*. The day she rammed straight into a milk cart, she found it both hilarious and wonderful that the owner of a pet shop opposite had to send out his dogs to lick up the spillage.

To her it was all part of the fun of being young, married and free in London. The city was slower to recover its pre-war spirit than Paris, yet nightclubs were reopening, shops were beginning to fill, and Diana was once again in the social columns. In his 1922 novel *Aaron's Rod*, D.H. Lawrence portrayed her as the arresting Lady Artemis, holding court in a room full of admiring men: 'smoking her cigarettes . . . making her slightly rasping witty comments . . . the bride of the moment! Curious how raucous her voice sounded out of the cigarette smoke. Yet he liked her – the reckless note of the modern free booter.'[11]

Superficially Diana had achieved the life she'd fought the Duchess for, but she also wanted to work. During the war she'd grown to like herself as an active and purposeful adult; more urgently she now needed to earn the money that would subsidize Duff's eventual resignation from the Foreign Office and his move into politics. The modest salary paid to British MPs fell far short of meeting the expense of an election campaign or buffering against the vicissitudes of a parliamentary career.† Diana's 'Plan', as she confidently referred to it, was to find herself some generously paid employment that would lay the foundations for her husband's future.

---

* In America there were 7.5 million cars in 1920, and 27 million by the end of the decade, which meant one in five Americans owned a car.
† Duff's romantic old-fashioned version of Toryism was not popular with the currently modernizing Conservatives; having few influential friends within the party, he was also without financial or professional guarantees.

That confidence might easily have been misplaced – for a whole number of reasons. Unemployment remained high in Britain as the economy recovered from its wartime battering, and for a while it was particularly high among women. Despite the principles enshrined in the 1919 Sex Disqualification (Removal) Act, which for the first time permitted them to enter professions like accountancy and the law, and despite the ambition among many young women to work, there was pressure on them to remain in their homes. The Restitution of Pre-War Practices Act had specifically obliged those employed in manufacturing industries to relinquish their jobs when the war was over. Across other professions and other jobs, women were also being squeezed, and in May 1919 they constituted three quarters of the unemployed.

Diana was not like other women, of course. In some respects she was far less employable, having little training or education beyond her nursing skills. She was also hampered by her class. Although relations between her and her mother were much improved – Violet had become a regular visitor to Gower Street, bearing small treats and advice on interior design – there were few jobs that she could take without making her family, and probably her fellow employees, feel cross and uncomfortable.

But she did have extraordinary contacts, and it was Max Beaverbrook who first offered Diana a potential career as a newspaper columnist. In Britain, as elsewhere, women readers were being targeted by the post-war media, with a new style of editorial that focused on beauty, fashion and home-making tips. Beaverbrook wanted Diana as one of his new circulation-boosting writers, producing regular features for his *Sunday Express*, on subjects that would range from society weddings to the changing length of women's skirts. Even though £50 per feature was only pin money within the grand context of her Plan, this seemed to Diana a promising start. Not only did commissions follow from other papers (including Beaverbrook's main rival the *Daily Mail*), but in May 1921 came the offer of a permanent job.

The French women's magazine *Femina* was launching a British edition, and was inviting Diana to become its editor. For an annual salary of £750 – over one and a half times Duff's earnings at the Foreign Office – she would be required to do little more than write one editorial a month, reflecting the magazine's coverage of fashion, arts and news, and have her photograph featured prominently. Apparently her Plan was launched. The only problem was that Diana knew she was faking most of her credentials as a journalist. She was unable to pretend an interest in every new trend in fashion or art – she could never even see the point of Picasso – and as for her writing, while she had a vivid and idiosyncratic prose style, she had learned little about grammar and spelling in the schoolroom, and even less about structuring an argument. She panicked over every deadline and persuaded Duff to ghost much of what she wrote, including, ironically, her 'female' response to the testy misogyny of Arnold Bennett's *Our Women*. It wasn't her fault that British *Femina* folded after just six months,* but it confirmed her instinct that journalism could never be her métier.

By now, however, Diana was exploring other career options. In 1918, when she'd made her brief appearance in D.W. Griffiths' propaganda film, *Hearts of the World*, the director had believed he spotted potential in her. Her large pale eyes and fair skin had been luminous on the cinema screen, and when Griffiths was casting a new Hollywood feature in May 1919, he wanted to use her again. The sum he offered was enormous – $75,000 (or £21,000) – but while Diana gaped at it, the timing was close to impossible. She was still living at home and still not married to Duff, and when she tentatively mentioned the offer to her parents, there was a predictable fuss.

In Britain, even after the war, actresses were assumed to have a colourful reputation. The view expressed by one late-nineteenth-century critic that it was impossible 'for a woman to remain pure

---

* The publishers had wrongly assumed that much of the content could simply be translated and transposed from the French edition to the British.

who adopts the stage as a profession' still lingered.[12] And if a career in the theatre carried a taint of disgrace, acting on screen was even more dubious. It had been perfectly acceptable for Diana to perform her patriotic cameo for Griffiths (even the Prime Minister Lloyd George had made an appearance), but a commercial film was a very different prospect.

Movie making was still a mongrel industry. Certain studios did a lively business in pornography, and even the cinemas themselves had a reputation for the illicit. While the new picture houses were large and lavishly appointed, at the opposite end of the spectrum were filthy, smoky dives, notorious for the activities that took place under cover of darkness. The idea of an aristocrat willingly placing herself in such a context was a jolt to British sensibilities, and not only to those of Diana's family. When she came to make her first film a couple of years later, she would be sent hate mail by disgusted, betrayed members of the public. 'You THING,' wrote one furious correspondent. 'How can you, born in high Social position, so prostitute your status for paltry monetary considerations?'[13]

Back in 1919, the opposition to Diana's putative film career was nowhere near as sensational as the story reported in *Variety* magazine, which claimed she had been threatened with exile by her family if she accepted Griffiths's offer and even banished from court by the Queen. The Duke and the Duchess *were* strongly against it, as were other members of the Rutland family, who felt their collective dignity was under threat. But the main reason why Diana did not fight for it was that she was just one month away from her wedding, and not prepared to take on another battle.

But sixteen months later she was differently situated, and when a new offer came from the British producer and director J. Stuart Blackton, she was determined to act on it. Blackton had, until recently, been working in New York, where his development of animation techniques had brought him professional and financial success. Competition from expensive new productions emerging from the Hollywood studios had, however, forced him back to Britain. He was now hoping to relaunch his career with a new genre of films – period British dramas cast with British stars.

For this, Diana was ideal. She might not be a professional actor, but as Duff rather enviously noted in his diary, there was no one other than Kitchener 'who could equal her popularity "with the mob"'.[14] She was regularly stopped in the street by young women asking for her autograph, and when she entered a theatre she was sometimes greeted with a spontaneous round of applause. For such popularity, Blackton was willing to pay a high fee. His offer of £12,000 for two films might not match Griffiths's, but to a delirious Diana it still seemed 'preposterously big'.

She broke the news to her family with nervous defiance. Yet while there was some reflex protest, she encountered less antagonism than she had feared. It helped that the two roles for which Blackton wanted her were far from vampish: a seventeenth-century aristocrat in the first film, and Elizabeth I in the second. The money also argued her cause. In fact, as soon as Diana's mother heard the sums involved, she became a most enthusiastic supporter. The most disconcerting opposition at this point came from the Actors' Association, who delivered a formal complaint to Blackton about 'titled folk' taking work away from 'people who have to live by acting'.[15]

Diana was determined to justify herself. Silent cinema was the ideal medium in which to make her acting debut, since there were no lines to learn and her lack of voice training would not be an issue. She assumed that all her appearances at costume balls and tableaux vivants had trained her to look the part of a period character. Even so, when she began to film Lady Beatrice, the lovely, hare-brained heroine of *The Glorious Adventure*, it was much harder work than she expected. The brute physical discomfort of the process surprised her, the burning heat of the lights and the weight of the costumes. She was thrown by the enervating rhythm of filming, the long waits punctuated by concentrated flurries of action. And any illusions she'd cherished about the artistic quality of the project were dashed at a very

early stage. *The Glorious Adventure* seemed to her inexcusably full
of historical inaccuracies (she particularly minded the portrayal
of Samuel Pepys as a pimp), and Blackton seemed more concerned with meeting his studio schedules than eliciting quality
performances from his cast. One of the things that galled her
most was the age of Gerald Lawrence, her leading man – Diana
had first seen him playing romantic leads at Her Majesty's
Theatre when she was only five.

Yet she had survived far greater discomfort working at Guy's
and, according to Blackton's assistant Felix Orman, she was 'most
democratic and serious about her work . . . the least troublesome
member of the cast'.[16] The film opened to a glare of publicity:
the department store Selfridges featured it in a large window
display and crowds massed to watch the actors arrive for the
premiere at Covent Garden on 16 January 1922.* The press,
especially the Beaverbrook-owned *Express* and Rothermere's
Daily Mail, were generous in their praise. And Diana was judged
a triumph, especially by her mother and Duff, who preened over
her beauty on screen: 'her gestures . . . replete with dignity and
breeding, which of course one never sees in film actresses'.[17]

Nine months later, when shooting began on *The Virgin Queen*,
Diana was confident of delivering an even better performance,
although far more cynical about the work involved. The costumes for this production were burdensome (farthingales, ruffs
and 'collars like tennis racquets'); for the sake of accuracy, she
had to shave off her eyebrows (a fact that was unctuously
reported in Rothermere's *Daily Mail* as a 'splendid sacrifice to
her sense of art and duty').[18] And Diana was feeling particularly
irritable the day she was interviewed by an American journalist
and was hard-pressed to fake any enthusiasm for the film: 'Good

---

* The opera house had been temporarily leased out to the American film
producer Walter Wanger – one of several strategies to avert bankruptcy. Wanger
was eager to raise the cultural profile of the film industry in the UK, and was
running hand-picked programmes of high-quality films, combining them with
performances of live music and ballet.

God,' she exploded to Duff in frustration and contempt, 'it's only for money and distantly imagined fun.'[19] Yet the money was still very necessary. Duff had just forwarded a hefty bill for the rates on Gower Street, and Diana was not so disillusioned with Blackton as to turn down a possible third film with him, this one based on the historical novel *Dorothy Vernon of Haddon Hall*.* It had a resonance for her, as the real-life Haddon Hall was part of the Rutland estate and a Rutland ancestor featured as the novel's hero. She thought she might even be able to maintain control over its period accuracy. But she hadn't even begun filming when, in the summer of 1923, more elevated offer of work came to her, and Diana was able to leave the compromised world of cinema for the live stage.

Max Reinhardt was widely assumed to be a genius of the theatre, his productions a spectacular fusion of sound and light effects, drama and pageantry, and before the war his mime-play *The Miracle* had become a European phenomenon. In 1911 Diana had been one of hundreds of thousands held captive by its London staging, with a cast of two thousand dancers, actors and musicians telling the emotionally charged story of a young nun who strays from her religion and has to be saved by the miraculous intervention of the Madonna.

It was a style of ritualized, choreographed performance never seen on the Western stage before, and it developed into something of a cult, as famous and fabulous as Diaghilev's Ballets Russes. During the war, plans for an American season had stalled, but in 1923 the banker and art patron Otto Kahn backed a new revival, to be staged in the Century Theatre, New York. He was investing $600,000 in the production, and it was partly at his instigation that Reinhardt had begun looking for a new female lead who could share the role of Madonna with its original actress, Maria Carmi.

---

* Another film was made of it in 1924, directed by Marshall Neilan and starring Mary Pickford.

Carmi had trained in Reinhardt's own dramatic academy, and she enjoyed a considerable following in Europe. But the American box office required a star with a contrasting twist, a more saleable back story, and it was Reinhardt's producer Morris Gest who had suggested Diana. As he extravagantly explained to Reinhardt, she possessed a style of refinement that was guaranteed to capture the American imagination: 'She doesn't seem to touch the ground when she walks,' he claimed. 'A more aristocratic, more sympathetic and beautiful woman for the part we could never find.'[20]

Gest was so in thrall to this vision of Lady Diana Cooper that when she agreed to meet him at the Savoy Hotel, he was disappointed to see her arrive alone, without any kind of retinue. He was also surprised by how easy she was to intimidate. Diana had been greatly moved by the invitation to work with Reinhardt, but Gest, with his snappy American manner, long hair and loud clothes, was not at all what she was expecting. She was too disconcerted to protest when he told her to raise her skirts a little so that he could check the shapeliness of her calves, and she failed to recover herself in time to press for the weekly rate that she'd been hoping for: $2,000 rather than the already extraordinary $1,500 that she'd been offered.

She also accepted Reinhardt's condition that she travel out to his Salzburg schloss in order to audition for the role. It was to be one of the most intimidating experiences of her life, as she was closeted alone with the maestro for over an hour, miming the scene in which the statue of the Madonna slowly and impressively comes to life. She'd had no idea of how to prepare herself, beyond finding a skirt that she could drape over her head in a vaguely religious style, but she'd hoped her one year of dance training would sustain her while she tried to communicate a rapt, physical intensity. She was obviously successful, even though Reinhardt later intimated that what had most impressed him was the fact that when he'd talked to Diana about his vision of the story, she had burst into tears.

It seemed to her that she had done well, but during her stay in Salzburg she had her first inkling of how cut-throat the theatrical profession could be. Maria Carmi regarded her as a threat and was already trying to undermine her credibility with Reinhardt, spreading malicious gossip about Diana's drinking and drug addiction, even cabling to suggest that her room be searched for empty gin bottles and needles. However, despite Carmi's threat to sue the production for £20,000 if she had to share her role, contracts were eventually signed. On 26 October, Diana had her hair bobbed short in preparation for her conquest of New York – challenging a reproachful Duff 'to mention any woman [he] admired who still had long hair'[21] – and a month later she was boarding the SS *Aquitania* for the crossing to America.

Normally Diana relished the adventure of travel, yet she was surprisingly apprehensive about this voyage. Although she was older than Tallulah and more sophisticated than Josephine, an Atlantic crossing was no less of a journey into the unknown for her than it was for them. During the first two days she was soothed by the tranquil weather and the presence of Duff, who'd been given leave from the Foreign Office to accompany her. In contrast to her previous experience of travel – the family gyrations around Europe, for which the Duchess insisted on packing food and clothing sufficient for a year – this six-day voyage appeared all streamlined efficiency and luxury. She and Duff were childishly impressed by the spaciousness of their first-class cabin, by the Louis XIV opulence of their dining room and by the incredible modernity of the ship's amenities, which included a spa, a gymnasium, dance bands and a seemingly inexhaustible variety of cocktails and cut flowers.

All this meant nothing, however, when conditions turned stormier. Always inclined to dark imaginings, and haunted by images of the *Titanic* disaster, Diana was terrified by the steely grey waves rearing up against the horizon. She went to the ship's doctor to beg for a calmative bromide, enquiring plaintively, 'I suppose there are any amount of frightened people like me?' The doctor, too busy to concern himself with the nerves of the rich, replied brusquely, 'Sometimes a few emigrants in the hold.'[22] But Diana's nerves weren't just reacting to the weather. The closer they drew to New York, the more anxious she became about the fact that she would be spending nearly six months alone there, without Duff. She continued to suffer from periods of wavering uncertainty, when she feared that her personality lacked a solid centre and that all she amounted to was an 'aura' of social dazzle. But in their three and a half years of marriage she'd learned to anchor herself to Duff's solidity and worldliness. And just as she liked to claim that she'd been 'born to be held safely in Duffy's arms',[23] she also liked to believe that he relied equally on her, for her ease in large social situations and her ability to make him laugh.

So closely meshed had they become that she doubted her ability to survive their separation. What she feared even more, however, was Duff's guaranteed ability to do so. Much, much later, she would claim that her husband's promiscuity had never really troubled her. She would rationalize that his incurable susceptibility to sex and her own comparable lack of interest were merely symptomatic of a general law: 'like most men, Duff couldn't have enough . . . like most well brought up girls of my generation I was not much interested . . .'[24] She came to trust that his affairs were never more than passing diversions.* His mistresses might be 'the flowers' but she was 'the tree'.

This image became a true reflection of their life together, but during the early years of their marriage there were many times when Diana winced and raged over Duff's infidelities. He tried to conceal them, lying to her and even lying to himself about their number and variety. But jealousy sharpened Diana's instincts. In 1920 when Duff began seeing Diana Capel (widow of Boy Capel, Coco Chanel's former lover), Diana scented it almost immediately. Humiliated by the fact that this Diana was one of her

---

* Duff, too, would always claim that it was only 'filthiness, not unfaithfulness' of which he was guilty.

friends, she turned on Duff with a ferocity that detonated into one of the worst quarrels of their marriage: she hated him for the humiliation he brought her, and even more for making her doubt their happiness together.

When she could approve his choice of mistress, Diana tried to affect a benign indifference, but some of his women caused her profound offence. Daisy Fellowes, the expensive, competitive socialite with whom Duff had an on-off affair for many years, struck her as especially repugnant, a 'silly giggling gawky lecherous bit of dross'.[25] Duff, interestingly, was almost as dismayed by this attraction as Diana. He was fascinated by Daisy's fashionable air of depravity. As the niece of Winnaretta Singer (the Princesse de Polignac), and an heiress to the Singer fortune, Daisy was notorious across Europe for the extravagance of her sexual and social adventures.* One evening when she was alone with Duff, she smoked an opium pipe and offered to 'indulge [his] every fancy', but the excesses of what followed induced in him a spasm of self-disgust.[26] He was old-fashioned in so many ways, especially in his sexual double standards. If Diana was his necessary angel, Daisy was his whore.

What Diana found hardest to bear was her own jealousy. She regarded it as a contemptible emotion, demeaning the modern and exemplary marriage to which she aspired. Yet sex remained her most vulnerable area. However momentous her wedding night had been, it hadn't been as sensually liberating as she'd hoped. She still preferred the decorous games of flirtation to the actual reality of bed. Only in these did she feel truly confident, not only with Duff but with the dozens of other men who continued to hover round her. St John Hutchinson and Alan Parsons – 'the boys' from her pre-war circle – remained devoted, as did numerous older admirers, including the singer Feodor Chaliapin and Max Beaverbook, whom Diana found very compelling: 'A

---

* A few years later she would pay a vast sum to hire Josephine Baker to dance at one of her parties, requesting that Josephine perform naked except for a coating of gold paint.

strange attractive gnome with an odour of genius about him. He was an impact, a great excitement to me.'[27]

However, her physical attachment to these men remained minimal, and during her most vulnerable moments, she wondered if she'd been born without the natural instincts and appetites of other women. Even if Diana didn't care to read the writings of Freud, Marie Stopes or Havelock Ellis, their sexual terminology was much batted around at some of the parties she attended. People talked of orgasm and a healthy libido as essential to the pursuit of happiness and enlightenment: frigidity implied a kind of failure that Diana would surely have shrunk from applying to herself.

Certainly every time Duff was with another woman it made her question herself, and her sexual uncertainties channelled into other physical fears. In the summer of 1920, she became morbidly convinced that a tumour was forming in her breast. The mysterious illness that had kept her bedridden for months as a child had marked her with a lifetime's tendency to hypochondria. But more justifiably she was also worried about her fertility. While neither Diana nor Duff were impatient to disrupt their busy lives with babies, as the months passed she still showed no signs of conceiving. Eventually she was diagnosed with a fibroid growth in her uterus, which could have been inhibiting a viable pregnancy, but she was too fearful to be operated on and instead persuaded Duff to take her on a tonic cure in the French Pyrenees, including a superstitious detour to Lourdes.

Her support during this period was not so much Duff as drink and morphine. She'd started using the drug regularly again after breaking her leg in the summer of 1919 – she'd fallen through a skylight while watching a firework display – and by the time she'd progressed beyond any medical excuse for it she'd become emotionally dependent. Duff hated to see her withdraw into the glassy unnatural calm of her narcotic trance, yet for Diana it was a precious world away from the underlying confusion of her feelings for Duff. She was trying to make her marriage work in a sane and loving way, and accommodating his affairs felt like the modern thing to do. Even so it went against her romanticism and her determination to have something more precious than the pragmatic and unpassionate union for which her mother had settled. Like Zelda and many other young women of her generation, Diana was in experimental emotional terrain, and at moments it felt lonely.

When she and Duff finally docked in New York in early December, the roiling, noisy strangeness of the city thrust aside her private concerns. A mob of journalists was waiting with a blinding assault of magnesium bulbs and a barrage of questions. 'Was it true that Diana had just spent weeks in a convent to prepare for the part of the Madonna?' 'What did she think of Carmi?' 'Did she know whether she or her rival would appear on the opening night?' Most of these questions had been planted by Gest, who had also telegraphed instructions during the voyage about how she should reply, including one ridiculous assertion that she'd had a dream in which God had told her that it must be she not Carmi who played the Madonna first.

Diana had no intention of repeating such nonsense; what she didn't know was how dogged Gest could be in pursuit of publicity. He had already been feeding fantastical stories about her and Carmi to the press, casting Diana as an heiress in possession of $10 million and a retinue of seventy servants and Carmi as the grand wife of an exiled Georgian prince (Carmi's husband George Matchabelli was, in truth, a very minor royal whose main claim to fame would be the range of perfumes he launched in 1924). And before the New York season was out, Diana would be subject to several more of Gest's stunts.

For now the journalists were satisfied, and she and Duff were free to drive across the city to their hotel, the Ambassador on Park Avenue. Nothing Diana had read about New York, none of photographs she had seen, had prepared her for the arrogant scale of the city's skyscrapers, or for the hectic activity in the streets below, the clattering crowds, the smoky press of motor cars, the noise and variety of the food and drink vendors. Duff, who stayed in New York for a week, never cared for it. 'If it has beauty it is not the kind that leaps to the eye,' he wrote.[28] Unable to get the measure of the city's dynamic, he thought it frantic and boorish, and inevitably the Prohibition laws filled him with contempt. It seemed unbelievable that any civilized place should prevent him from drinking anything stronger than coffee with his dinner. His outrage was barely appeased by the kindness of Cole Porter, whom he and Diana had met in Venice that summer, and who sent a crate of bourbon to their suite along with the key to a personal 'liquor locker' maintained by a mutual friend at the Knickerbocker Club.

Diana's curiosity was far more deeply stirred. Their penthouse suite at the Ambassador was a marvel to her – 'the crystal New York sky a background to our high-perched luxury'[29] – and she couldn't get enough of modern American amenities: dial telephones that needed no operator, a press-button radio with a choice of channels from Buffalo to Chicago, a 'Frigid Air' machine that made 'ice by electricity'; cafeterias 'where you can see what you eat before you eat it', and a non-alcoholic 'highball' served in her local drugstore that still contrived to make her feel wonderfully intoxicated, 'an effect more powerful and delightful than anything I ever tasted'.[30]

Compared to London, New York displayed an overweening confidence in its own success. In his essay on the jazz age, Scott Fitzgerald would describe post-war America as a nation serviced by 'great filling stations full of money', and Diana likewise saw New York as a city 'paved with gold', its population engaged in heedless, happy pursuit of 'a fur coat or a better car'.[31] The blatant materialism of the culture fascinated her: after a life attuned to the minutiae of British social stratification, she found a wonderful frankness in its overruling principles of money and meritocracy. The people she met seemed more interested in the commercial value of her title than its dignity, and that was a kind of liberation.

Even so, when Duff sailed for London on 7 December, Diana found it hard not to take the next boat after him: 'My heart seems to tear my body with pain for the loss of you,' she wrote the following day.[32] She doubted her ability to find friends among the huge crowd of cast and crew she'd encountered at her first rehearsal, all apparently indifferent as they went about their business or jostled for warmth around the wooden stove that provided the only heating in the hall. Yet, within a few days, Diana surprised herself by the degree to which she became absorbed in this new world of 'rehearsals and stage jargon and the palpitating interest of "shop"'.[33]

It made every difference to her that, in contrast to Blackton's film set, *The Miracle* was directed by an artist. 'I was learning from the master of masters and falling in love with him,' Diana wrote, and she was determined to be worthy of him.[34] She had to unlearn the techniques she had acquired for the camera and acquire new skills for the stage; her toughest challenge was building up sufficient stamina for the first forty-five minutes of the production, in which she portrayed the motionless statue of the Madonna before she comes to life. Although Diana was supported by a plaster cast that mimicked the stone drapery of the Madonna's robe, her muscles cramped with the effort of remaining completely still and her face grew stiff with the effort of projecting an other-worldly emotion.

Diana worked hard, concentrating on Reinhardt's points of direction. He rarely offered praise, but she was jubilant when the maestro's assistant confirmed how surprised and impressed he was by the speed of her progress, and that compliment was confirmed when Reinhardt asked her to learn the role of the Nun, so that she could cover for the first-cast actress Rosamond Pinchot. Diana worried that she would not have the energy for both – the Nun's voyage into worldly temptation led her on a frenetic whirl through tavern and street scenes – but she took a dogged pride in her own professionalism and refused to complain when rehearsals dragged on until four in the morning. She also tolerated, as best she could, the increasingly ridiculous publicity circus being orchestrated by Gest.

The opening of *The Miracle* had been delayed by technical difficulties, and Gest was worried about sustaining the buzz of interest. As part of his press campaign, he planned a 'public draw' at which the issue of the Madonna's casting would 'finally' be resolved. In truth, he and Reinhardt had already settled that Diana would take the role on opening night, but the draw was still a humiliating farce. Carmi arrived calculatedly late, looking 'terribly flash in black and diamonds', and in front of two dozen journalists and photographers she proceeded to patronize and belittle Diana with her diva airs.[35] It shook Diana's confidence, already undermined by flutters of stage fright, and by the time the show was finally ready to open on 15 January, she'd sunk into a 'haunted desperate' state of nerves.[36]

Gest knew what he was doing, though. The first night of *The Miracle* received a full New York ovation, with flowers covering the stage and the audience standing to cheer for fifteen minutes. Thirty of the bouquets were for Diana alone. And even if the first reviews were largely obsessed with production trivia – such as the quantity of electric cable that had been required – tributes came from elsewhere. The impresario Charles Cochran, who had first presented *The Miracle* in London, cabled Duff: 'Wife's performance exquisitely beautiful unquestionable work of sensitive artist.'[37] Valentine Castlerosse, later to became famous as a columnist for the *Sunday Express*, wrote, 'It is ridiculous for me to try and describe the effect that Diana has on this enormous crowd. She holds them tight, tortures them, frightens them . . . lifts the whole thing to the sublime.'[38]

News of her success spread beyond the theatre. When she attended a Manhattan charity ball, the entire room stood up to cheer her arrival; journalists came to her dressing room asking questions about her taste in men and fashion, and about her views on the United States; articles that she (and Duff) had written back in London were recycled in the American press. From the autumn of 1924, when *The Miracle* embarked on a nationwide tour, Diana was greeted with similar levels of adulation. She was guest of honour at galas and women's club luncheons, and at a Drama League function, society women filed past to shake her hand, while speeches were made comparing her to

Sarah Bernhardt and Eleonora Duse. In Cincinnati she spoke on the radio and was heard by an audience of over 20 million.

Diana was an intriguing novelty. She looked like a contemporary flapper, with her modern clothes, short hair and scarlet mouth, and she was reputed to behave like one, drinking, smoking and staying out late at parties. On the other hand she had none of the calculated sexiness of Louise Brooks, the working-girl feistiness of Clara Bow or the Southern swagger of Tallulah Bankhead. She was a modern young woman with a cut-glass accent and an aura of old-world mystery, and Americans were fascinated to get a glimpse of her.

But it wasn't just the peculiarity of her image that helped to wing Diana towards celebrity. It was the scope of American mass media and the ease of modern travel. During the next three and a half years the Atlantic crossing became very familiar to her as she returned to the States for a further series of tours, and her growing popularity with the American public generated significant offers of new work. Such was the trajectory of her success, she could easily have found herself distanced from Duff. His own professional progress was certainly much slower; he remained dependent on her financially, and his political career was still at a formative stage. Yet throughout most of this period, Diana never worried about outstripping Duff; on the contrary, she never lost her fear of losing him.

When he'd first left Diana in New York, Duff had sent letters and poems that were both literally and figuratively stained with tears. He hated leaving her almost as much as she hated to see him go. Yet just as she anticipated, he was barely settled back into London life, before he began consoling himself with other women. Guessing at details, and probably being fed some painful gossip by their friend Olga Lynn, who was visiting New York that winter, Diana was unable to prevent herself quizzing Duff by letter. Early in 1924 she confronted him about his latest interest, Poppy Baring. She supposed he was 'in love with [her] & that's about the size of it';[39] when Duff tried to deflect her suspicions she became so tormented by the idea that he no longer cared for her that she threatened to walk out of *The Miracle* and return to London.

Duff bluffed and cajoled Diana out of her misery, but a few weeks later it was Dollie Warrender whose name appeared in the letters. When Duff wrote for extra money to cover household bills, Diana accompanied the £200 cheque with a note of delicate acidity: 'I hope it will be enough, tho I expect you to drop it on plovers' eggs and Lady Warrender.' Duff squirmed uncomfortably: 'She's on to that as I thought she would be,' he noted in his diary.[40] It was very rare for Diana to flaunt her financial power over Duff, but at moments like this it was irresistible. In the long term, too, it helped to maintain the balance of their marriage. Diana's material independence helped to ward off feelings of self-pity, shame and worthlessness – the emotions of a betrayed wife. And while it wasn't easy for her, she eventually learned to have confidence in herself, in Duff and in the very particular way they loved each other. Over time she found it easier to tidy his other women into a small and almost painless compartment of their relationship.

If earning her own money gave Diana power, it also provided her with a fascinating new game. She'd been astounded to discover that she could earn $1,000 simply by signing a testimonial for Pond's Cold Cream, and she became greedy for more profits, persuading Kahn to fund her in a property-development scheme, signing up for new celebrity endorsements and writing articles for the press.* At the same time she took proud, sometimes perverse pleasure in making economies – lunching on a ten-cent plate of macaroni cheese and seizing every perk that came with the job, including free hotel accommodation and use of a car.

Duff had been brought up to believe it was bad form to skimp

---

* Only occasionally would she draw a line. In August 1924 the Prince of Wales came to New York for a state visit, and Diana was offered thousands of dollars by journalists and editors begging for insider stories. Regretfully, she considered it bad form to comply.

on luxury, but Diana came from a class where discomfort was associated with moral fibre. When Violet came out to New York, full of interest and enthusiasm for her daughter's career, she was almost as competitive in her economizing. She took a spare bed in Diana's suite, rather than pay for a room of her own, and on nights when there were no party invitations, she would boil up a bit of rice pudding for their supper. She didn't even complain when a third-class cabin was booked for her crossing home, although Diana felt a pang of fascinated guilt afterwards, wondering how her mother would fare in her 'bolting-hole of beastliness among the lower-class barnacles'.[41] So proud was the Duchess of her powers of 'poverty and economy' that during a subsequent visit she boasted of them to a journalist – Diana had to explain that this was not what the American public wanted to hear. They didn't get free rooms and chauffeur-driven cars 'out of pity', but because their rank was seen to deserve them.*

As a result of Diana's budgeting, however, sufficient capital was saved for Duff to resign from the Foreign Office in July 1924. He was accepted as Conservative candidate for Oldham,† a solid industrial town in Lancashire, and when the general election was announced that autumn, Diana took time off from *The Miracle* to assist his campaign. After women had been given the vote, political wives had acquired a new importance; they were thought to lend a warmth to their husband's image, which would appeal to the female electorate. Of course, women MPs were a rarity still – the 1924 election would see only four returned to parliament – but although much publicity was created by Diana's arrival in Oldham (Duff noted 'an excellent paragraph in the most conspicuous part of the *Daily Mail*'), she feared she might

---

* Duff was far less docile. When Diana tried to organize a relatively cheap crossing for his return visit to New York, he called her a 'nasty cold-hearted girl' and insisted on his own 'outside cabin' on the *Berengaria*.
† The Conservative Association also contributed most of the costs of his campaign, thus easing some of Diana's financial burden.

be too grand and too ignorant to be of any use. When she and Duff went out campaigning, she fully expected the voters to 'bang the door in our silly, smirking out-to-please faces.'[42]

Yet Oldham considered her excellent entertainment. When Diana promised a group of mill workers that she would perform a clog dance if they voted for Duff, they 'mobbed me and kissed me and thought me funny'. When she told the elderly ladies of the town that Duff was a wonderful husband, and therefore an ideal MP, they adored her. 'There's no swank about her and, oh my, isn't she a beauty?'[43] said one of them to the *Daily Mail* reporter who'd been sent up from London to follow her around. Her popular touch and his election speeches delivered a small but decisive majority. On their way back to London they stopped at Belvoir where, for Diana, the real triumph was the sight of her father, waiting at the door to congratulate Duff, and the fact that they had been put in the King's Room (always reserved for Belvoir's honoured guests). 'It was a proud day for me,'[44] she wrote, and when she had to return to America she was miserable to be missing Duff's maiden speech in the House of Commons.

Yet, despite her loyalty to Duff, Diana was becoming increasingly addicted to her work. Later she would admit, 'I was always happiest with the theatre people.'[45] She enjoyed their rituals, their dramas and their gossip; they were were the people with whom she shared the daily comedy of theatre life, such as the woman in Cleveland who'd got drunk on highballs and groped Diana in the back seat of a 'Chrysler B'. Or the story of the grumpy stagehand who had taken exception to the all-female *Ballet of the Nymphs* choreographed for *The Miracle* by Mikhail Fokine. 'Fokine [just] can't get away from Lesbianism,' the stagehand had muttered darkly, 'but Lesbianism doesn't fit in.'[46]

Above all, Diana loved her work because she believed she was good at it. In New York the Russian director Stanislavsky had pronounced her to be a 'great artist',[47] and when she began to receive other offers of work, including a film in Germany, she dared to dream that *The Miracle* could be more than an isolated triumph. 'I think I must go on the stage proper in England,' she

wrote to Duff. 'I really think I could be good, if only for the
reason that I can concentrate so easily and gladly on it and am
such a good learner.'[48] Aware of her lack of formal training, she
began to study with a former student of Stanislavsky and with an
elocution coach recommended by John Barrymore.

The latter proved a step too far – Mrs Carrington turned
out to be fashionably Freudian in her theories of how to liberate
an actor's voice and Diana fled from classes that required her
to explore her dreams and unconscious desires. Nevertheless,
her ambitions were still in play. In 1925 she was complimented
on her performance by Gladys Cooper, who hoped that a London season of *The Miracle* might be organized, in which she
could alternate with Diana. Around the same time John Barrymore approached her to play Queen Ann in his production of
Richard III, and Reinhardt and Kahn consulted her over their
plan to acquire a London theatre, offering her a key role as
both performer and director's assistant. (Reinhardt had been
impressed by Diana's theatrical instincts, often agreeing to suggestions she made during *The Miracle* tour about costume and
staging.)

In March 1927, when they were performing in Hollywood,
Diana was offered the possibility of starring in a film adaptation
of *Anna Karenina*.* Greta Garbo was meant to be playing the lead
role, but had thrown temperamental objections to her contract,
and even though she was eventually coaxed back onto the set,
the offer to replace her was a significant one for Diana, and
could easily have been parlayed into other roles. Yet Diana
remained oddly unmoved by the opportunity. Hollywood
reminded her of all that she'd disliked about cinema – 'the
depressing grizzly light in the studio'; 'the snail's pace that
outwears any patience' – and even while the role of Anna
Karenina had appeared to be hers for the taking, she told Duff
that she would only accept it for a drastically high fee.[49]

---

* This was titled *Love*, the later, more famous version was filmed in 1935.

To most of her colleagues, Diana's hesitation would have seemed madness, but ambitious as she was, her commitment to acting bumped up against two obstacles. One was Duff, to whose success and happiness she dedicated so much of herself, but the other was the nagging self-doubt she'd never been able to shed. Even with the éclat she was receiving in *The Miracle* she was incapable of pushing herself beyond what she believed she could do. Faced with a choice, she would rather stick with what she was good at than risk failure at something unknown.

She had disappointed Reinhardt with her merely 'moderate enthusiasm' for his theatre project in London, and in 1928 she reacted with similar timidity when Diaghilev offered her a mime role in his company's latest production, *Ode*. The Russian ballet had entranced Diana back in 1911, yet she recoiled from the challenge of actually appearing in its ranks. She wrote back to Diaghilev, 'All my advisors say that the first time I appear in London must be in *The Miracle* . . . as they tell me that I might have been very bad in *Ode* – and that it is better to appear for the first time in London in something you can do, rather than in something experimental.'[50]

Diana had grown comfortable acting in *The Miracle*, and as the years passed it became harder for her to imagine testing her reputation in another production. Perhaps the watershed moment came when she persuaded Iris Tree to join the cast, covering for Rosamond Pinchot in the role of the Nun. Iris had visited Diana in Salzburg in the summer of 1925, when *The Miracle* featured in the Salzburg festival. With another mutual friend, Ethel Russell, the three women had shared a large room at the top of Reinhardt's schloss, and for Diana it was one of the most childishly pleasurable interludes of her life, another taste of what she had missed in the remoteness of her privileged upbringing. Every night was made 'a riot' by Ethel and Iris 'laughing talking and wrestling', she told Duff, and by the hatching of jokes and secrets and pranks.[51]

In Iris's company, Diana missed Duff less. Iris was 'a perpetual renewer of spirits', a 'dearest romantic in clown's clothes',[52] and

when they returned to America for the next stage in *The Miracle*'s
tour, the two women became inseparable, gossiping in rehearsals
and talking late into the night in each other's hotel rooms. Diana
pondered what bliss this would have seemed to her and Iris
when they were very young: 'What would we not have given for
a privacy like this, unhaunted by mothers and maidenheads.'[53]

She would always remain the more cautious of the two, berating Iris's extravagance and drinking, her unprofessional habit of
turning up late for rehearsals, dosed up on a hangover cure of
'kippers, herrings and prairie oysters',[54] but as Diana happily
admitted to Duff, 'Iris leads me to folly.'[55] She began to party
more recklessly (ending up 'flogged' at 4 a.m.), and to spend
more of her hard-earned money on herself – a $600 summer
ermine coat and a £100 Frigid Air for Gower Street, so that she
could enjoy 'well chilled drinks' and 'ice made on demand' whenever she was back in London.[56]

For Christmas that year she treated her fellow cast and crew
to ready-cooked turkey, silver-spangled candles and hot dogs.
When Diana had first arrived in New York she had winced at
the stridency of an American Christmas: 'electric trees . . .
obscene Santas and deafening carols in the shops'.[57] Two years
later, while Duff was spending Christmas at a formal country
house party, playing dull games of charades, Diana was enjoying
a 'greenroom frolic', with whisky, dancing, banjos, singing and 'a
great many imitations of absent members of the cast'.

Under Iris's influence Diana also grew thoughtful about her
sexual fidelity. Iris was still married to Curtis, but already looking
for pleasure elsewhere. The results could have been disastrous:
her first lover in America refused to use a condom, and Diana
was petrified that Iris would end up having another 'illegal'. She
had already had several and Diana wrote exasperatedly to Duff,
'Next month in all probability it will cost her her life and me
£500 in specialists' bills.'[58]

But precarious as Iris's passions were, Diana also felt they
displayed admirable verve, resurrecting her doubts about her
own passivity. Her years in America had been attended by the

usual flock of male admirers, including Reinhardt's assistant, Rudolph Kommer, and Bertram Cruger, a not-so-wealthy off-shoot of an old New York family. Also, when their paths crossed, the singer Chaliapin, who came to Diana's dressing room one day, 'red faced' and ready 'for a romp', appalling her by grabbing her hand and pressing it to his crotch. These men added to Diana's notoriety, but while she admitted to Duff that she was a 'glutton . . . for petting',[59] she rarely felt tempted to anything more.

In the autumn of 1926, however, Diana was thrown into the company of a nineteen-year-old boy, Raimund von Hofmannsthal, who had joined the cast of *The Miracle* as a temporary extra.* He was slim, sweet-natured, poetic, and when he developed a crush on Diana she was aroused in a way that was both maternal and unexpectedly erotic. Raimond's courtship was absurdly gallant: swearing he could never love another woman, he stood outside her bedroom for an entire night while she slept. The fact that his father Hugo was the librettist of Strauss's opera *Der Rosenkavalier* gave a romantic twist to his attentions. While the affair remained platonic, Diana allowed her 'Octavian' special liberties, sitting by her bedside to talk and brushing her hair. Duff picked up more than enough to become jealous: 'I do not much like the sound of Mr Hofmannsthal,' he wrote in December 1926.[60] The following month he wrote a jerky, anxious letter, questioning his attitudes towards Diana's admirers. 'I wonder how much I should mind if you really loved one of them. I wonder if you do. Don't tell me if you do, I'm with Othello on "prisoners and all".' With self-conscious virtue he assured Diana he had no comparable tales of conquest.[61]

Even though Duff had no serious cause for sexual jealousy, a shift was occurring. It was now he who complained most about their periods of separation: 'Is there to be no end of it,' he

---

* The touring production had 500 performers and crew, with additional extras hired at each town.

grumbled in February 1926. Meanwhile, Diana's letters were humming with a busy absorption. In New York the previous autumn, she had been to a dinner dance, held in her honour by Condé Nast; she had attended the premiere of Noël Coward's latest play, and the Broadway adaptation of Michael Arlen's novel *The Green Hat* (in whose London production Tallulah Bankhead had just opened). In Cincinnati a month later she improvised her way, fraudulently, through a live cookery demonstration; in Boston she went to a dance recital given by an avant-garde German who performed in a 'Picasso-designed dress, with his naked parts covered with blood'.[62] In Chicago there were dinners with Noël Coward and a visit to a preposterously rich architect, whose house boasted an Egyptian-themed dining room, with a table that 'rose from the floor loaded with caviar'; there was also a roomful of black satin-sheeted beds that prompted Coward and Diana to wonder which of them the architect hoped to seduce. Probably both at the same time, they thought.

In San Francisco, she shopped for presents and ate with chopsticks in Chinatown; she also met up with her former admirer George Gordon Moore. Moore was still impressively rich and well connected, and in his company Diana visited a house that was decorated in the style of a Persian fairy tale, with a live white peacock, white china elephants and silver espaliered trees bearing golden apples. She and Iris went out riding to Moore's country ranch, where champagne and bourbon flowed until three in the morning and the 'negro house boys [sang] in perfect harmony'.[63] Hollywood, a fortnight later, was less appealing. Mary Pickford and Douglas Fairbanks were among the local celebrities attending *The Miracle*'s opening night, yet none bothered to extend a personal welcome to the visiting troupe. Diana chafed at the lack of professional camaraderie: 'I believe they despise us for being legitimate stage,'[64] and it heightened her contempt for the swank and entitlement of Hollywood life. She was offended by the fake lawns and the swimming pools, by the money men and the bottle-dyed blondes. Most repugnant to her was Elinor Glyn, the popular novelist who in middle age had become a Hollywood screenwriter, and who was about to create the flapper movie, *It Girl*, which would make a cult of Clara Bow. After lunching with Glyn, Diana wrote to Duff with appalled distaste of her inappropriately made-up face and gaggle of gigolos. It gave her vengeful pleasure to watch Iris Tree steal away one of Glyn's 'beautiful young men', a six-foot Austrian, whom she would eventually marry.

Diana also dined with Zelda and Scott Fitzgerald (the latter was also trying to write a Hollywood script). The three of them had met previously in London, through Tallulah and Olga Lynn, and the Fitzgeralds joked that the reason they had hired an English nanny for Scottie was because they wanted her to develop an accent like Diana's. Diana found an ally in Zelda, who disliked Hollywood almost as much as she did.

Yet even if touring with *The Miracle* could be frustrating, Diana had become addicted to a life of movement and change. Back in the spring of 1925, when an unexpected gap had opened up in the schedule, she hadn't opted to return directly home to Duff, but had instead gone exploring on her own. Alan Parsons and Viola Tree were wintering in the Bahamas that year and Diana travelled from New York to Nassau to visit them. The Caribbean was a revelation of colour and beauty to her, and its impressions remained vivid for the rest of her life: 'Prisms of humming birds', and a 'peacock sea'; 'rainbow fish seen through a glass bottomed boat', and women going to market in 'white boots and organdie . . . and spotted kerchiefs topped by rakish angled hats'.[65]

Diana so relished that trip that when a second gap opened up in the tour, in December 1926, she proposed an adventure to the south-western desert with Iris. After an orgy of 'dude buying' – work shirts and 'black kangaroo cowboy boots' – they travelled to Taos, driving through mountain passes so steep and icy that they frequently had to get out of the car and travel by foot, warming themselves as they went with gulps of 'white lightning', the local corn liquor.[66] Puebla, the Indian village close to Taos, enchanted Diana as an unspoiled American 'Bethlehem'. She was astonished to meet the painter Dorothy Brett there, whom she and Iris had known before the war. Brett had followed D.H. Lawrence to Taos, in the expectation of becoming part of a utopian community, and had never gone home. She lived like a hermit, Diana reported to Duff: 'She goes once a week to Taos for provisions and . . . thinks of it as London and Paris and New York. She nearly collapsed when she heard Iris & I were on the stage.'[67]

After Taos they travelled on to the Grand Canyon and a riding trip through the desert. Guided by a 'cowboy philosopher . . . with an irresistible southern poetic voice and a rugged wistful face brimming with laughter', she and Iris lunched on steaks cooked over a mesquite fire; saw not only eagles, big red flowers and queer cactuses, but also strange pockets of twentieth-century luxury, 'with golf courses and shops round the hotel like Cannes'.[68] She adored all of it, and in her letter to Duff floated the possibility that they might even live there.

'We could be so happy,' she wrote, apparently forgetting how much Duff hated to be separated from the familiar comforts of his drawing room and club. Increasingly, however, Diana was forgetting things about home. Every time she returned to London she was ecstatic to be back in her husband's arms, yet apart from Duff and Gower Street, much of her old life had altered. The death of her father in 1925 (a cause of sadness rather than real grief) had led to Arlington Street being sold and Belvoir passing into the possession of her brother John. And while Diana kept in touch with many of her old friends, a younger generation of Bright Young Things had taken over London, with their costume balls and treasure hunts, their scandals of drink and drug taking. Diana found them entertaining and joined in with some of their exploits, but she had essentially outgrown their antics.

Her life was now centred on *The Miracle*, and when it had its final performance, during a short tour of central Europe in 1927, she was bereft. She had been clinging to the idea of a British season, but that would not take place until 1932; and so for the first time in six years she found herself without a job, or any other project to absorb her. Duff was busy – his career was advancing now, and in early 1928 he was given his first ministerial post as Financial Secretary to the War Office. But for all Diana's genius at orchestrating social events, she did not want to dedicate herself to being a politician's wife. She might hold a few dutiful dinners for Duff's colleagues but, like her mother, she preferred to mix with her own friends.

There were plenty of amusing distractions – parties where Olga Lynn sang, Duff recited Shakespeare and Maurice Baring wrote impromptu poems; holidays abroad, including a trip to North Africa where Duff was persuaded to accompany her on rides in the desert and to smoke a hubble-bubble pipe – but as Diana admitted to herself, she had got into the habit of an ocean journey at least once a year, and she resented the confines of her suddenly shrunken world. In December 1928, when the Coopers' friend Sidney Herbert invited her to travel with him to the Bahamas, she seized the chance, even though it meant missing out on Christmas with Duff for the first time in five years.

Diana claimed she was only going out of loyalty – Sidney Herbert was ill and needed a companion to care for him as he wintered in Nassau – and it may have been guilt that caused her to dwell on the negative aspects of the trip in her letters home: the toothache that plagued her and the ugliness of the new building developments on Nassau. But she couldn't suppress the delight she took in the old Caribbean magic, as she bathed naked on a coral island, watched butterflies swoop in fluttering clouds, ate freshly caught turtle and danced under a full moon.

Towards the end of her trip, however, a new topic entered her letters. Diana had missed her period and begun to feel nauseous, and while she typically jumped to the conclusion that she must be incubating a horrible tumour, she also had to consider the idea that she might be pregnant. It was very unsettling. After almost a decade of marriage, she had come to terms with what she called her 'barrenness'. Aside from a momentary fantasy that involved Iris having a 'spare' baby she could adopt, Diana had persuaded herself that she and Duff were better off without the worry of children: 'Girls were sure to be plain and without virtue, boys dishonest, even queer and certainly gambling drunkards.'[69] She had congratulated herself on avoiding the lumpen heaviness of pregnancy, the pain and danger of childbirth.

Now on Nassau she grew jumpy with panic and indecision. She wondered if she was so far beyond wanting a child that she should have an abortion, and made herself take a marginally dangerous dose of quinine to see if she would have the courage to go through it. She then wondered how disappointed Duff would be if she told him she was pregnant but turned out not to be. When she did finally gather the courage to report her suspicions, she hedged the news with foolish, pre-emptive jokes. She wrote that the baby was going to be the focus of enormous gossip: 'everybody' would be sure to suspect Sidney of being the father. Alternatively, it was certain to be dark skinned, like all descendants of those 'who went even for a trip to the West Indies . . . it must be the climate and air'.[70]

Diana was right to predict that there would be gossip. The length of time it had taken for her to fall pregnant with Duff, and the number of men who hung around her, were sufficient for several alternative names to be mooted as the father of her baby, including her old admirer St John Hutchinson. But as soon as Diana was convinced the pregnancy was real, her panic gave way to exaltation and awe. She confessed to Duff that she hadn't felt this kind of emotion since 'I lost my virginity in your arms'.[71] Startled by its intensity, she became desperate to return home and share her pregnancy with him.

Once back in London, however, her elation somersaulted with despair. Pregnancy was as inconvenient an invasion as she had always feared, and like Zelda she found her swelling body increasingly 'grotesque'. (The desire to remain slender had almost as significant an effect on lowering the pregnancy rates among certain fashionable women as the growing availability of contraception.) Diana was also genuinely scared: dying from childbirth was commonplace in those pre-antibiotic days, she was nearly thirty-seven and the fibroid in her uterus added a worrying complication. During the last days of her pregnancy, she sat by the telephone, sending out telegrams to all her friends, begging them to pray for her, convinced she would never leave the nursing home alive.

On 15 September 1929 she gave birth to a healthy baby boy, John Julius—his middle name quixotically referring to the Caesarean section that saw him delivered safely into the world. Although weak and tremulous, she herself was far from dead, and when she was discharged from the Portland Place nursing home a few weeks later, a crowd of several hundred well-wishers had gathered outside to cheer her on her way.

These crowds were a sign of the public's continuing interest in Diana, despite the years she had spent in America. Two years earlier a poll conducted by the *Sphere* had put her, along with Queen Mary and the now famous Tallulah Bankhead, among the nation's ten most remarkable women. And even after giving birth to John Julius she still expected to maintain her relationship with the public. In 1932, when *The Miracle* regrouped for its British run, Diana jumped at the chance not only to perform a three-month London season, but to slog through a six-month tour of provincial theatres, causing amusement and concern amongst the more snobbish of her friends.

Offstage, too, Diana continued to be much seen and admired. She was as famous for hosting wicked little dinner parties as for being an entertaining guest. When Cecil Beaton met her in Venice in 1932, with St John Hutchinson and Maurice Baring in tow, he considered that, even at forty, she was 'the most beautiful English woman alive today. Her lips were japonica red, her hair flaxen, her eyes blue love-in-the mist'.[72]

But Diana was also moving into a new chapter in her life. Although she was rarely in the nursery, depending on a staff of nannies and nursemaids for her son's daily care, the arrival of John Julius had changed her. She felt the gravitational pull of family now, alongside her restlessness, and from this point on, Duff's career as writer, politician and diplomat took unquestioned precedence over her own. During the following years the crowds of admirers that had followed Diana so faithfully began to disperse, and in private moments she may have regretted their passing. Yet in contrast to the driven ambitions of Tallulah or Josephine, her own impulse towards the stage had always been driven by marriage to Duff. And it was Duff who would remain the keystone of her life.

Chapter Eight
TALLULAH

When Diana was touring with *The Miracle* Duff had kept her regularly updated with London news. Olga Lynn was his prime source of gossip, and in December 1924 she passed on to him the story of a young American who had reacted with surprising vehemence to rumours of her lesbian activity. Word for word, Duff related the anecdote: 'Gerald du Maurier asked [Raymond] whether Tallulah was a sapphist, and he . . . said she was – so Tallulah came up to him and said she was going to smack his face.'[1]

In London, as in New York, Tallulah Bankhead was making her presence felt. When she'd first set out for England in January 1923, Tallulah had no certainty of finding either work or welcome there. The play in which she'd hoped to star, Gerald du Maurier's *The Dancers*, was already in rehearsal with someone else in the lead role, and the two people she most wanted to see in London didn't even know she was coming. Charles Cochran, Tallulah's contact with the great du Maurier, had told her very firmly to stay put in New York, while Naps Alington, her elusive lover, had remained out of contact since he'd left her over a year earlier.

But Tallulah possessed wonderful powers of determination and denial. On the crossing over she had found a good-looking student with whom to flirt away her fears of the ocean and had wired Cochran to inform him she was on her way. She was sure the impresario wouldn't dare abandon her once she was in London, and she guessed correctly. Not only did she persuade him to meet her train and drive her to her room at the Ritz (an excessively expensive luxury she had allowed herself, to boost her confidence and image), she also persuaded him to take her to the Wyndham Theatre to be introduced to du Maurier the following day.

Her plan for the meeting was simply to pretend that she had never received Cochran's pre-emptive telegram, informing her that she no longer had a role in du Maurier's play. She bounced into the actor's dressing room with her personality at full flourish, her eyes wide, her smile even wider as she fanfared her arrival, 'Well, here I am.'[2] The tall, fair Englishman who rose to greet her, however, was not easily bounced. Sir Gerald's manners were too perfect to point out the obviousness of Tallulah's lie, but there was steel in his voice when he insisted he could do nothing to alter the play's casting.

Tallulah had no alternative strategy and, disconcerted, she left the dressing room, blinking away tears. Cochran, however, was now warming to her cause; he enjoyed a gamble, and this American girl was proving to be an interesting wild card. He offered to arrange a second meeting, advising Tallulah that Sir Gerald had a weakness for glamorous women, and pointing out that she would stand a far better chance if she were wearing something other than her day suit and hat: 'He absolutely *must* see your hair.'[3] The following night Tallulah re-presented herself at the actor's dressing room in her one good evening dress, with her hair falling in a barely restrained tumble down her back. She looked peachy, dynamic, hopeful and by a lucky stroke, she exactly resembled the image du Maurier had always had of his heroine. Certainly she impressed his teenage daughter, Daphne, when she happened to walk in on the meeting. 'Daddy,' she blurted afterwards, 'that's the most beautiful girl I ever saw in my life.'[4]

Sir Gerald kept his feelings close, however, and the next

morning Tallulah woke in her unaffordable hotel room feeling lonely and deflated. Writing a letter home to her friend Estelle, she berated her 'foolhardy venture' and 'pigheaded pride'. 'I've got sixty dollars left. I don't know whether to commit suicide.'[5] But du Maurier had been doing some calculations overnight. He'd been having doubts about the actress he'd already cast as Maxine Hoff, his play's heroine. She was meant to be a high-spirited, sweet-tempered cabaret dancer, and Dorothy Dix, who had recently had a baby, lacked the energy he required. Although it would be expensive to replace Dix,* du Maurier thought he saw qualities in Tallulah that might translate into very compensatory box-office gold.

Tallulah had barely finished her letter to Estelle when a call came through to her room from Viola Tree, du Maurier's co-author. Viola and Sir Gerald had talked the matter over and agreed that Tallulah should be hired. She was triumphant, of course, ready to whoop and gloat over the success of her plan, but *The Dancers* was due to open in under a month, and suddenly Talullah was under immense pressure. She had to move out of the Ritz and find a flat to rent; she had a long script to learn, and she had to ingratiate herself with an unknown group of British actors, who were unhappy about Dix's sacking and very sceptical of this American replacement.

Tallulah's first encounter with *The Dancers* cast was uncomfortable. Accustomed to the casual manners of Broadway and the Algonquin, she had no idea that British actors abided by a more old-fashioned code. When she breezily asked during rehearsal where the toilets were, she was greeted by a frigid silence, punctuated only by a few nervous titters. 'The cast was horrified,' recalled Una Venning. 'This was something that was *never* said among men.'[6]

It took a little while for Tallulah to recover from that social

---

* Under the terms of her contract, Dix would stay on full pay for the length of the play's run.

misstep, and she coped, as she always did, by throwing up a smokescreen of clowning and bluster. Her irritated, critical colleagues waited hopefully for her to be quashed by Sir Gerald, who was not only directing the play but playing opposite Tallulah as her lover Tony. Yet du Maurier was rather delighted by his new protégée. He liked the gusto she brought to the rehearsal room, and he liked even better the very obvious reverence she felt for him. To Tallulah, du Maurier was an exemplar of the classic English acting style, and she was eager to learn from his direction and craft. At his suggestion, she even gave up smoking so that she could build up sufficient stamina for the dance sequences in the play.*

Pleasing Sir Gerald mattered so much that by the opening night, on 15 February, Tallulah's courage and her nerves were in shreds. She wept through the first interval, convinced she was a failure, and was genuinely surprised by her reviews, which were almost unanimous in approving 'the sincerity and tenderness' of her acting.[7] In fact, Tallulah could not have found a better vehicle for her London debut. Her own role was one she knew exactly how to play – a small-time Canadian dancer who wins her man through the sheer spark of her personality – yet the themes and plotline of *The Dancers* also proved to be of hugely topical interest.

The other 'dancer' in the play was Una, a young socialite to whom Tony has been formally engaged for several years. A 'neurotic and erratic nightbird', her passion for jazzing lures her into an underworld of nightclubs and dangerous liaisons, and when she falls pregnant by one of her dance partners she kills herself out of shame. In 1923 this was a fate that many parents had started to fear for their own daughters. The jazz culture had taken almost as profound a hold on Britain as it had on America and France, and it was met with uncomprehending resistance by

---

* She took ballet classes, too, with the Diaghilev dancer and choreographer Léonid Massine.

many in the older generation. To them, jazz represented a threat to the nation's moral identity; its warping rhythms and melodies sounded like the music of a drug addict, and the frenetic sexual angularity of its dances was no less disturbing.

The Breakdown, a 1926 painting by John Bulloch Souter, would capture the intensity of this hostility in its portrayal of a black musician seated astride a toppled statue of Minerva while a naked white girl dances the Charleston. At its most dangerous, jazz was credited with encouraging an entire generation's rebellion against God, the Empire and society. At the very least it was seen to spearhead the new American culture that was colonizing Britain, with its easy money and facile system of values. It was seen to be heralding a world in which words like 'marvellous', 'wonderful' and 'divine' were squandered on 'the colour of a new lipstick or the texture of a silk stocking' and 'life was not worth living unless somebody was having an affair with somebody else.'[8]

The fact that it was young women who appeared most captive to jazz culture made *The Dancers* appear very current. While Maxine Hoff embodied the virtues of the modern flapper – independent, charming and brave-hearted, she fully deserved her eventual marriage to the rich and aristocratic Tony – Una embodied all the flapper's failings: an object lesson for any young woman with too easy a taste in cocktails and men.

The play ran for an exceptional forty-three weeks. And during that time du Maurier continued to congratulate himself on casting Tallulah. Among a nation of Marjories, Nancys and Veras the mere sound of her name was exotic to the British public; even more appealing was her sexy Southern drawl and uninhibited energy. To the droves of young women who came to watch her from the cheap gallery seats she became a kind of heroine. These gallery-ites were as fervent a force in British theatre as their New York counterparts. Young working women who spent much of their income on following their chosen stars, they were both feared and courted by theatre managers. If they took against an actor or a production they were brutal in their condemnation, booing, laughing and leading slow, satirical hand-claps, but their approval was correspondingly passionate. Having adopted Tallulah as a new idol, they flocked to the Wyndham Theatre several times a week, following her performances with an almost sexual adulation. Innocent phrases from her lines were transmuted into a private code, eliciting giggles and screams whenever she spoke them.

A few weeks after the play opened, Tallulah decided to get her hair fashionably shingled. All of the London actresses she'd met were advising it, and Gladys Cooper steered her towards the celebrity Parisian hairdresser M La Barbe, who paid regular visits to London. Du Maurier was furious when he first saw the result: there was a particularly affecting scene in *The Dancers* that pivoted around Maxine slowly unpinning her hair in front of Tony, and now it would have to be rescripted. Tallulah's gallery-ites, however, saw her new haircut as a flapper call to arms, and a few them actually took to cutting their own hair during performances and throwing their shorn tresses down onto the stage as Tallulah took her curtain call.

With a speed that exceeded even her own 'pig headed' expec-tations, Tallulah was becoming famous. But she had not only come to London to find theatrical acclaim; she had come to track down her beloved Naps. As she was sailing to England, Tallulah had imagined exactly how their reunion would go. Naps would seek her out, filled with remorse for abandoning her in New York, while she would be cool, dignified and aloof. However, once she had managed to get hold of him by telephone, she was overtaken by love and impatience. She was still at the Ritz when Naps appeared in the lobby with a Pekinese dog tucked under his arm as a peace offering. Tallulah's shriek of 'Daaarling' could be heard throughout the hotel as she tore down the stairs and into his embrace.

It was as if the year of separation had never happened. Naps's delicate, dissolute features were still mesmerizing to her, no less his maddening elusiveness. He made a fuss over her, suggested a thousand plans for showing her London, but offered no apologies for having deserted her, nor for the fact that she would have to share him with Edward Lathan, his new boyfriend. For the moment, Tallulah was too happy to mind, and it was frequently on the arms of both men that she went out to dine at the Ivy and the Eiffel Tower, and began attending the competitively extravagant costume balls that were so much in vogue among the city's young and rich.

Tallulah found this compulsion for fancy dress extraordinary. 'At the drop of a Homburg all of London's *jeunesse dorée* would tog themselves out in masquerade.'[9] Some of these costume balls had themes (one notoriously invited its guests to dress in babies' clothes and to drink champagne from babies' bottles). Impersonating celebrities was also popular: in 1926 London would be full of Josephine Baker lookalikes and in 1927 Oliver Messel would cut a dash as Tallulah herself. Tallulah's own first costume in 1923 seemed slightly less attention grabbing: she dressed up as a courtier from Versailles, with Naps as her identical twin. But even so, she turned her outfit to flamboyant effect. As the two of them made their entrance, she gestured to her blue satin breeches, saying loudly to Naps, 'These things are all right for you. But what do I do if I have to pee?'[10]

Showing off for Naps, flush with the success of her new play, it would be a long time before Tallulah dared to question the wisdom of resuming their affair. 'He was a riddle I couldn't solve which made him all the more attractive, all the more desirable ... his contempt for the desires of others both fascinated and repelled me. Invariably I got furiously angry, only to melt into submission.'[11] In London, the contrast between Naps' affection and his withdrawal was even more blatant than in New York. He regularly disappeared for long periods, and only later would she find out that he had been down to his family's estate or on a gambling trip abroad. She had no notion of how many other lovers he might have. Loving him was 'part ecstasy, part torture',[12] and that formula was still too addictive for Tallulah to let it go.

She was only just twenty-one, and she might have felt lonelier and more vulnerable in London had it not been for her fellow cast members – among whom she had now become accepted and affectionately known as 'Tallu' – and for the handful of new women friends she had made. Viola Tree was one of them. While she struck Tallulah as eccentric, dressed like a bohemian and trailing incomprehensible literary allusions through her conversation, Viola was very sweet to her and introduced her to people she thought would be useful. Another was Audry Carten who played Una. Audry was as tightly wired as the character she portrayed, but she was funny, audacious and Tallulah and she adopted each other as soulmates, joking together in rehearsals, gate-crashing parties and exchanging confidences over bottles of wine. When Tallulah was introduced to Audry's eleven-year-old brother Kenneth, she gave the shy child an extravagant kiss and appointed herself his honorary older sister.

For purely practical reasons, her most important new acquaintance was Olga Lynn: 'The most divine woman,' Tallulah enthused to Will, 'and . . . a great friend to me.'[13] Seemingly ageless beneath her powder and rouge, and more or less good-hearted under her social ambition, Olga took a maternal interest in Tallulah's welfare, and that summer invited her to leave the poky service flat she was renting and stay in the large London house Olga had taken for the season. This move was a great relief. Actors in the British theatre were not highly paid – Tallulah's own weekly wage was just £30 – and already she had run up large debts, her habitual extravagance exacerbated by her failure to grasp the pound–dollar exchange rate. It took her years to understand that £5 for a blouse was the same as paying $20–25 back home. To live for free with Olga, and be treated to servants, hot meals and hot water, was entrancing to her: even more so the company of her fellow lodgers, Gladys Cooper and Lady Idina Sackville, about whose latest divorce the whole of London was talking.*

---

* Olga always rented a house for the London season, having both her living as a singer to earn and her reputation as an essential guest at any smart party to

At Olga's she became something of a pet and a project. The three older women enjoyed her antics – Tallulah turned some of her first London cartwheels to entertain Oggie's dinner parties – but they felt she lacked polish. Skirts were rising to mid-calf that season and dresses were cut on lines that made Tallulah's curves look unruly and unfashionable. She was put on a diet and also taken to the showrooms of the designer Molyneux to pick out a few key items for her wardrobe. (Left to her own devices, Tallulah had little personal sense of style, and her motley collection of clothes was evidence of the variety of women she'd tried to imitate, from Mary Pickford to Ethel Barrymore.)

Olga also opened up her extensive social network to Tallulah. 'To be a friend of Oggie's is a liberal education in *Who's Who* and *What's What*,' claimed the writer and music critic Percy Colson.[14] During a late summer vacation she was introduced to the Cole Porters, Maud Cunard and the ubiquitous San Francisco hostess Elsa Maxwell. In London she made the acquaintance of Dawn Farrer, the music-hall singer, Duff and Diana Cooper and Ivor Churchill. Being on first-name terms with Ivor, second son of the Duke of Marlborough, and his mother, the former New York heiress Consuelo Vanderbilt, gave her the jaunty illusion of having arrived: writing to Will she crowed, 'Not bad for a you-all miss from Jasper, Alabama.'

One of her favourite new friends was Sir Guy Laking (always known as Francis), a plump and petulantly amusing young man 'of cloudy gender' who adored Tallulah in a possessive, platonic fashion, twitted on the phone to her and sent her flowers. Another was Max Beaverbrook. The newspaper magnate had been quick to observe the beam of Tallulah's personality raking across London, and with Diana now absent in New York, he judged her to be an interesting substitute face for his papers. He steered his journalists towards her; and while Tallulah refused

---

maintain. She took in guests to amuse her, such as Idina Sackville, who was visiting London from her new home in Kenya.

his offer to lean on his drama critics on her behalf, the frequency with which her name and photograph appeared in the *Daily* and *Sunday Express* did much to accelerate her career.

Their friendship ran deeper than mutual self-interest, though. Like Diana, Tallulah admired Beaverbrook as an original: 'A brilliant conversationalist [with a] remarkable memory.'[15] And Beaverbrook was very good to Tallulah, inviting her to parties and country weekends, introducing her to everyone who mattered, from the playboy Aga Khan to politicians like Lord Balfour and David Lloyd George. It was one of the proudest moments of Tallulah's life when she was able to introduce her father to these impressive acquaintances when he sailed over to London for a short visit.

Tallulah, the actress of the moment, was judged to be an entertaining trophy in such circles. However, after *The Dancers* closed, she struggled to find a new vehicle. In London, as in New York, good new plays were scarce, and during the following eighteen months Tallulah appeared in some perilously uneven material. In *Conchita* (March 1924) she played a spirited Spanish dancer, accompanied by a live 'pet' monkey so unmanageable that Tallulah had to invent jokes and turn cartwheels to distract the audience from its antics. In *This Marriage* (May 1924) she was a funny outspoken flapper in love with a married man. Her reviews were good – few actors in London could match Tallulah's insouciance when delivering lines like, 'Conscience isn't like a liver, you can get on without it'[16] – but the play did bad business at the box office and it closed after three weeks.

More commercially popular was the murder mystery, *The Creaking Chair* (July 1924). Yet it came nowhere near the triumph of *The Dancers*, and arguably Tallulah's most successful performance during this period was in the evolution of her offstage persona. She worked as hard at it in London as she had in Manhattan, keeping her repertory of smart one-liners controversially stocked. 'Darling, I couldn't possibly go to the Marchioness's this weekend, I'm so bloody tired of three in a bed,' was one of her latest

– a reference to the sexual preferences of the Marchioness of Milford Haven. 'What's the matter, don't you recognize me with my clothes on?' was a gibe first invented for a possibly uncomprehending earl, whom Tallulah caught staring at her during a dinner at the Savoy.[17]

She enriched her range of stunts, too. Moving out of Olga's house and into a new flat in Curzon Street, she made a point of receiving her guests in provocative deshabille, and copied Zelda's trick of hosting cocktail parties from her bath. Her terrible driving skills added to her notoriety. During her first summer in London she squandered £200 on a small green Talbot, but despite dutifully taking lessons, she failed to master even the basics of motoring. What principally defeated her was the illogical layout of London's streets, and in genuine desperation she began hiring taxi drivers to guide her to her destinations. Of course, when the story was reported in the press, Tallulah was quick to realize its publicity value. To her already colourful reputation, she added the image of the delightfully incompetent motorist.

In subsequent memoirs and interviews she would confess to the fears she concealed behind her armour of provocative nonsense. 'I was not as free of inhibitions as the casual observer might have believed. On the surface all confidence, all swagger and strut, inside I churned with doubt any minute the clock might strike twelve and I'd be back in a hall bedroom at the Algonquin or, worse yet, in Grandfather's yard at Jasper.'[18] Even at the time there were some who recognized how much effort she put into her seemingly spontaneous image. Sharp-eyed Cecil Beaton observed her arrival at the Eiffel Tower one evening and was impressed by the efficiency with which she worked the room, hovering at every table in turn, being 'quick witted' at each. 'She has developed her personality to such an extent that she always seems natural. But it is only acting.'[19]

Most of London, however, was happy to enjoy Tallulah at surface-value. In a roomful of upper-class accents and manners, her American braggadocio reverberated with a delicious impact. Even the most morally blasé were taken aback by her willingness to deliver lines like, 'I've tried several varieties of sex. The conventional position makes me claustrophobic and the others give me either stiff neck or lock jaw.'[20] Tallulah had always pretended to be more sexually experienced than she was; now, in London, she was rapidly narrowing the gap between image and reality. With her family at such a safe remove it was easy to acquiesce to the many men who begged to take her drinking and dancing. Some were actors, but others, she proudly noted, were among Europe's rich and titled: 'I cut a great swathe in London . . . it was all a spur to my ego, electrifying! London beaux clamoured for my company . . . I rejoiced in this harum-scarum attention to the hilt, perhaps a little beyond the hilt.'[21] She was now drinking regularly, as well as dabbling fashionably with drugs, and both might have contributed to what she called 'my flings'. Her London beaux were also a way of compensating for Naps' fugitive affections. Tallulah was genuinely enjoying herself and was in no hurry to settle down, but she had never given up her belief that one day Naps would make good on his promise to marry her. It nagged at her that after two years in London he had still made no attempt to introduce her to his family, nor suggested any hint of a future plan.

Tallulah had no conception that marriage to Naps was never even a possibility. When his father had died in 1919 he'd inherited the Alington estate, and he took his family responsibilities seriously. If ever he chose to marry, it would be to a woman whose style and pedigree would enhance the Alington title. An American actress with a reputation for swearing and nudity would never do. Coming from New York, Tallulah didn't see how immutable this logic was. Olga's careful tuition had given her the illusion that society doors would be opened to her. 'I can say shit, darling,' she liked to drawl, '[because] I'm a lady.'[22] The fact that Edwina and Louis Mountbatten asked to be introduced to her, and that the King's third son, Prince George, came regularly to see her perform, made her believe she'd transcended the barriers of nationality and class.

But even if, in post-war Britain, actors, tennis players and newsmen could socialize with the titled elite, the underlying rules were no less implacable. When Diana's mother, the Duchess of Rutland, was asked if Tallulah had ever been engaged to Naps, her reply was crushing: 'Only she thought so. Napier was far too well informed of what he had to do for the empire to even consider it.'[23]

And so, stifling her uncertainties, Tallulah distracted herself with other men. One or two looked like serious prospects, including Michael Wardell, a handsome newspaper executive she'd met through Beaverbrook, who wore an intriguingly piratical eye patch. Most, though, were short-term diversions or, as Tallulah boasted, 'ecstatic flings', which rarely lasted more than a few nights. Few, interestingly, were with women. Tallulah knew the writer Radclyffe Hall and her sculptor lover Una Troubridge, and she was friendly with the lesbian hostess Barbara Bach. She was rumoured to have slept with the American singer Florence Mills, and she had a longish relationship with one of her understudies, a tiny, sparky gamine called Monica Morrice, who was 'flat as a board, always naked in the dressing room . . . and didn't give a damn.'[24]

Yet she didn't identify herself as lesbian in the very public way she had in New York. She had taken against London's more aggressively political sapphists – a clique dismissed by Cecil Beaton as ventriloquist's dummies for their humourless opinions and mannish suits. When Tallulah had threatened to slap Raymond de Trafford for suggesting she was a sapphist, she wasn't being coy, she was genuinely insulted. Principally, however, she seems to have found the sexual company of men more varied and interesting now – and worth taking risks for.

The first time she fell pregnant was sometime in the mid-1920s, and in a panic she turned to Olga Lynn. Oggie knew exactly what had to be done and who would do it, sending Tallulah to a nurse to have an injection of saline solution, then driving her to the house of a discreet friend. It was as slick an arrangement as could be managed, but nevertheless the abortion itself was a painful and dangerous procedure and Tallulah lost so much blood she was bedridden for two weeks. Still that didn't prevent her from going through three more procedures by the time she was thirty, and from publicizing the fact with a defiant gallows humour, a raucous raillery that made them sound like badges of honour. 'I'll never go back to that place again,' she said after one. 'They aborted me with rusty nails and old razor blades.'[25] She would never mention the clotted messes, knifing pain, humiliation and secrecy. As one friend, the actress Gladys Henson, observed, 'She put on all the hard-boiled stuff all right, but she wasn't really.'[26]

Aside from those two weeks of convalescence, Tallulah remained almost obsessively active on the London stage. Even when she knew a role was worthless she accepted it. To be out of work and invisible to her public was far more worrying to her than appearing in weak material. By early 1925, however, even she was aware that her poor choices of role were beginning to damage her career. She needed a part with 'guts and swagger and shock', and she accepted that she might have to take time off from the stage in order to secure it.[27] At the forefront of her hopes was a play that had been successfully adapted for Broadway from Somerset Maugham's short story, 'Rain'. Its central character Sadie Thompson, a young prostitute who forms a complex bond with the religious zealot who attempts to reform her, had all the guts Tallulah craved. And when 'Rain' was scheduled for a London premiere, she was ready to go to any lengths to secure the role. Ignoring all the other new scripts that were being offered to her, she sailed to America to meet Maugham and to see the play for a second time, closely studying the interpretation of Jeanne Eagles, the American actress playing Sadie.

It all looked very hopeful. Tallulah was assured she had got the role and even took part in early rehearsals of the London production. Yet when Maugham came to watch, Tallulah seemed to him to lack personality, to be mimicking Eagles rather than finding her own way into the character and he demanded she be replaced. This was a level of professional and public rejection Tallulah had never encountered and it was as piercing to her pride as it was to her ambition. She couldn't stand the idea that all of London would be talking about it, and it was partly to stage-manage the gossip that she returned to her flat, forced herself to swallow twenty aspirins and scribbled her suicide note, 'It ain't goin' to rain no moh.'[28]

Twenty pills was nowhere near a fatal dose – simply enough to put Tallulah into a deep sleep and give her a bad headache the next morning – and even though she would dwell privately on the humiliation for several months, she was saved from more public mortification by a last-minute invitation to appear in Noël Coward's latest play, *Fallen Angels*. Just a week before the play was due to open, one of its female leads had suffered a nervous breakdown and they needed to replace her. Tallulah thrived on this kind of brinkmanship, and having demanded – and secured – a weekly fee of £100, she zoomed straight into rehearsal with a vitality that a grateful Coward thought 'little short of fantastic'. Aided by her photographic memory, she delivered a word-perfect performance on the opening night.[29]

The role was classic Tallulah material. She was playing Julia Sterroll, a young married woman who shares everything with her best friend: clothes, cocktails, even lovers. And if the material was a challenge to her vocally – the speed and nuance of Coward's dialogue required a clarity of enunciation that occasionally defeated her Alabama accent – few actors could make a line sound as wanton as Tallulah. Responding to the accusation that Julia had become unhinged by alcohol, Tallulah's 'I'm perfectly hinged' was delivered with a toss of her hair, a jut of her hip and an innuendo-laden catch in her voice that suggested a hundred forms of depravity.

Tallulah's comic delivery was almost too effective on the opening night. With the pain of Maugham's rebuff still stinging, she elicited howls of delight from the audience with her extemporaneous tweaking of the line 'oh dear Rain' into the knowing 'My God RAIN'.[30] And always inclined to boredom when a play's run lasted longer than a few weeks, she found it hard to resist making more mischief. During one performance of *Fallen Angels* she

replaced the ginger beer in the actors' glasses with real champagne, generating an atmosphere of hilarity that grew ever more
precarious with each scene.

Coward, convinced she was going to wreck his play, grew testy
with Tallulah, but to her dedicated gallery-ites she could do no
wrong. *Theatre World* now judged her to have a following 'unlike
that enjoyed by any other actress'.[31] Most were clerks, shop girls,
seamstresses or factory workers, and to them Tallulah and her
characters represented a world of dreams. 'Down there onstage
she wears clothes that would cost a year's earnings,' reported
Hubert Griffith in the *Evening Standard*. 'She moves in expensive
apartments at Paris, Deauville, St Jean de Luz, young men in
exquisite evening dress are rivals in love with her. Miss Tallulah
Bankhead is on the stage what every woman in the gallery in
some degree wishes to be, the dream fulfilment made manifest.'[32]

Although Griffiths referred to Tallulah by her full name, she
would have been recognizable to his readers by her first name
alone. The gallery-ites had long called her nothing but Tallulah,
chanting, 'Hallelujah Tallulah, our wonderful Tallulah,' whenever she appeared onstage, but now the critics and commentators
were adopting the habit too. Arnold Bennett, who would write
an entire column about the Tallulah cult for the *Evening Standard*
in early 1930, found the phenomenon remarkable. 'Why is Miss
Bankhead always called Tallulah? Nobody except the privileged
Hannen Swaffer [critic of the *Express*] speaks of Marie [Tempest],
Gladys [Cooper], Sybil [Thorndyke] and Evelyn [Laye].'[33]

Even more extraordinarily, she was also being elevated into a
verb. To 'do a Tallulah' or just 'to Tallulah' had become recognized shorthand for the brand of provocative exuberance she
exemplified. As she airily explained to a New York reporter,
deployed to track her British success, 'Over here they like me to
Tallulah, you know, dance and sing and fluff my hair and play
reckless parts.'[34]

Her appeal remained a mystery to some. Bennett admitted he
was perplexed by the dedication of her fans, who seemed 'to
belong to the clerk class', yet magically appeared to spend half

their working week queuing for tickets to see her perform, and to stand patiently at the stage door afterwards, to see her walk to her car. Exactly what these 'bright youthful and challenging . . . girls' gained from their devotion eluded Bennett, beyond the competitive satisfaction of being able to boast 'to their friends about the number of hours they have waited for the thrill of beholding their idol'.[35]

Bennett failed to see the effort that Tallulah herself made to secure the loyalty of these young women. She never took for granted the money they paid, nor the discomforts they had to endure. All the seats in the gallery were unreserved, and on opening nights some of them would begin queuing forty-eight hours beforehand. Those who had to leave the queue to go to work (in answer to Bennett's conundrum) would keep their place by chaining little stools to the railings outside the theatre, with their name tags attached. Those who remained in line were served tea by the theatre management and sold sandwiches and cake by street vendors.

In return for their devotion, Tallulah showered her fans with special, small attentions. At every curtain call she reserved her first smile and bow for the gallery, and the most loyal core, around twenty or so, she invited backstage to her dressing room, where she learned their names and stories. One of them, Edie Smith, became her secretary and perhaps her most loyal and reliable friend. Edie had both the serenity and the spirit to ride Tallulah's scattered moods. She didn't mind performing menial tasks – Tallulah always depended on Edie to open the brand-new tins of her favourite Gold Flake cigarettes – but she would not be bullied. When the two of them were drinking in a bar one evening, Tallulah spotted a handsome man and instructed Edie 'to go get him for me'. Edie, whose own tastes were exclusively for other women, was unimpressed. 'I'm not pimping for you,' she retorted. 'Go get him yourself.'[36]

In September 1925, the fantasy world Tallulah inhabited onstage reached new heights with *The Green Hat*, a play adapted from the bestselling novel by Michael Arlen. Arlen had something like the status of Scott Fitzgerald among British readers. His tales of playboys and socialites, his descriptions of clothes, cars and love affairs were all frantically fashionable. And while today his style reads like a hothouse of florid literary tropes and overwrought sexual suggestion, at the time his references to abortion, venereal disease and mild erotic perversion were daring – Arlen broke taboos for a literary living.

The Green Hat was his most successful and notorious work. Iris Storm,* its heroine, was a young woman of vaguely déclassée status whose engagement to a young aristocrat, Napier Harpenden, is broken off by his family. Iris trails her broken heart through an apparently rackety lifestyle, eventually becoming engaged to a sporting hero, Boy Fenwick. Shockingly, Boy kills himself on his wedding night. And while the real reason is his shame at having contracted venereal disease, Iris chooses to defend his reputation rather than her own, by allowing everyone to believe that he died from despair at discovering she was not a virgin.

Through all this, Napier continues to love Iris, but when he again offers to marry her, she insists that his family and friends will always despise her as 'used goods'. The story ends with her striking a heroic blow against those 'shams with patrician faces and peasant minds'. Driving her yellow Hispano-Suiza into an ancient elm tree on the Harpenden estate, Iris kills herself.[37]

In some respects it was a very interesting role for Tallulah. Iris stood in a line of tragic heroines that went all the way back to Dumas's Marguerite – a fallen woman with a heroic heart – and she challenged Tallulah to a new emotional range. Even more use to her, however, was the publicity surrounding *The Green Hat* from the moment it opened. Acted out onstage, Arlen's plot and characters seemed more deviant than they had on the printed page, and when there were calls for the production to

---

* She is also referred to by her maiden name, Iris March.

be banned, Tallulah shone in the scandal's glare. To many people, Iris's story blurred with her own, and they took as literal truth the claims of one critic that Tallulah 'does not act Iris March, she is Iris March'.

Certainly Tallulah was acquainted with Arlen socially, or as Hubert Swaffen put it, belonged to the writer's 'semi-exclusive set'.[38] And this social connection lent weight to the speculation that parts of her own life had gone into the invention of Iris. The parallels between her own lover Naps and Iris's lover Napier were much commented on, and Tallulah herself claimed that at least one episode, involving a swim in the River Thames, was taken directly from her own adventures.[*]

If Tallulah benefited from the play's publicity, however, she couldn't stand the work itself. She found her lines almost unutterably pompous and Iris a humourless bore. Zelda and Scott came over from Paris and shared her dislike of both the production and (ironically) its author's relentless self-publicity. Zelda wrote to a friend, 'Just got back from bloody England where the Michael Arlens grow – hardy annuals it says in the seed catalogues.'[39] Still, there was no doubting the play's impact. The first-night audience for *The Green Hat* had been stiff with titles and celebrity: the Prince of Wales, Gladys Cooper, the Marchioness of Milford Haven (in a Russian headdress) and Lady Curzon were among the crowd at the Adelphi Theatre. A week later, when Beaverbrook took Tallulah to lunch with Lloyd George, she found the former prime minister in his living room, the floor covered with newspapers and all of them open at the pages reviewing her play.

The question for Tallulah now was how to build on her success. She still regarded acting as a serious vocation, and she wanted to

---

[*] There would also be a marked similarity between Tallulah and Ysabel, the American actress in Arlen's 1927 novel *Young Men in Love*, who cuts a swathe in London as the protégée of an older woman with more than a passing resemblance to Olga Lynn.

transcend her flapper repertoire, yet her range remained largely unproven. Directors appreciated her peculiar gifts: the intensity with which she reacted to other actors onstage; the sparkling wattage of her performances; the rare ability she possessed of holding an audience in the palm of her hand. Bennett would write, 'I have seen Tallulah electrify the most idiotic, puerile plays into some sort of realistic coherence by individual force.'[40]

And yet nearly everyone agreed that she had little or no technique. Her diction was a continuing issue. Five years in London had muted her accent somewhat, but her delivery still retained husks of her Southern childhood, and it hadn't been improved by her recent acquisition of what *The Stage* identified as 'the modern drawl'.[41] This was a vocal style made fashionable by the London crowd who in 1924 had been dubbed by Beaver-brook's *Express* as the Bright Young Things. It was characterized by fantastically drawn-out vowels and barely articulated conson-ants; *Daarling, sweeetie, loooovely* were uttered as orgasmic sighs or gently rising shrieks. Yet what was de rigueur at a Soho party was a problem onstage* and Tallulah's audiences found her lines increasingly difficult to hear.

Along with her vocal manner, Tallulah's reliance on certain physical affectations began to draw censure. At emphatic moments she would always shake back her hair; whatever char-acter she was playing, her body assumed a fashionable flapper pose – back arched like a cat, shoulders drooping forward in a languorous slouch. Tallulah's fans would not have her any other way, but critics saw her unvarying body language as symptomatic of a failure to fully inhabit her roles.

Even her finest qualities, her capacity to fizz and burn up the stage, were controversial. The drama critic of *Eve* magazine said she could be relied upon 'to discharge more emotion and give more of herself in one undisciplined half minute than almost any

---

* This was a criticism applied to several actors by the late 1920s as a modern style of naturalism overtook the old English classicism.

English actress can contrive in three acts of polite disturbance.'[42] Others, however, disparaged this gift as mere exhibitionism – a specious trick of personality that Tallulah was unable to deliver, reliably, every night. Noël Coward's former lover, Jeffrey Amherst, who had watched her closely in *Fallen Angels*, observed, 'Tuesday she might give a performance that would knock your eyes out. And then Wednesday night go off, and Christ knows what might happen.'[43]

In many things Tallulah could be a perfectionist – costumes and lighting mattered tremendously to her – yet in other respects her performances were slapdash. Dialogue that effervesced with wickedness could just as easily fall flat; it wasn't acting craft she delivered, merely the mood of the moment. Josephine, taken to task for the same weakness, worked stubbornly to overcome it, but few considered Tallulah capable of the same effort. Basil Dean, who produced many of her plays, came to the final judgement that she 'lacked a sense of dedication that alone could overcome her basic lack of training . . . approaching the theatre and indeed each aspect of her life as an experiment, quickly to be dropped when unsuccessful'.[44]

Maturing as an actor would also require Tallulah to become more selective about her roles, holding out for parts that gave her depth or cast her against type. This she couldn't do. Time and time again she returned to her default material, the glamorous fallen woman or the spirited working girl. In her defence, there weren't many alternatives on the London stage, but she had also got herself into a situation where she needed to earn a great deal of regular money. Although her fees had gone up to £250 a week by the end of 1925, and would rise to £500 by the end of the decade, Tallulah spent her money much faster than she acquired it.

She was under pressure from her fans, too. The gallery-ites had exacting views about the material in which they wanted to see her, and by now it was becoming difficult for her to disappoint them. Tallulah's next play, a slick and racy melodrama about modern marriage called *Scotch Mist* went down well, but the one that followed, in May 1926, met with unnerving disapproval from her fans. *They Knew What They Wanted* was precisely the kind of professional challenge for which Tallulah was ready. She played Amy, a young working-class girl from California who agrees to marry Tony, a sixty-year-old Italian winegrower. Amy means to be a good wife to Tony, but when he's crippled by a bad fall, she yields to the temptation of his handsome foreman Joe. Temptation leads to pregnancy but, in a rare exception to the prevailing theatrical norm, the script doesn't punish Amy with death and disgrace. Instead, it allows Tony to accept the illegitimate baby as his own, and Amy to return to her marriage.

Not only was this story unusually nuanced for the time, the dialogue in Sidney Howard's script was exceptional, compelling and poignant. Tallulah recognized its quality and was determined to do it justice. She went shopping for her own costumes, a wardrobe of modest frocks that totalled barely £6, unlike the Chanel gowns she had worn in *The Green Hat*, and spent hours talking through Amy's character and situation with Glenn Anders, the broad, handsome American actor who was cast as Joe.

Anders was impressed by her thoroughness: 'Tallulah was trying her damnedest. She would do anything.'[45] And many judged this to be the performance of her career so far. During the scene in which Amy battles between her conscience and her feelings for Joe, she evoked an anguished sexual hunger that, according to her fellow actor Cathleen Nesbitt, was far more raw and candid than Tallulah's usual romping. At the moment when Amy and Joe finally touched, a little shiver went through her body that communicated itself to the entire audience. As Nesbitt recalled, 'I've never seen anyone able to create such erotic tensions without any words.'[46]

Almost every review concurred that Tallulah had fully transcended her usual 'farrago' of trash. James Agate praised her for 'a piece of sincere emotional acting felt from the heart and controlled by the head.' St John Irvine in the *Observer* highlighted a 'nervous intensity I hardly suspected her to possess.'[47]

That night Tallulah went out dancing with Anders at the Embassy Club. He was dressed in white tie and tails, she wore a long green gown, and catching sight of their reflection in the ballroom mirrors, Anders murmured into her ear, 'God, we dance beautifully together.' The Prince of Wales was in the crowd watching, and for Tallulah it felt like a perfect affirmation of her success.[48]

Yet if she was getting the professional endorsement she craved, her gallery fans were sadly disappointed. Amy's cheap frocks and drab marriage carried no appeal for them; the dialogue lacked any kind of innuendo for them to shriek over, and there weren't the usual curtain calls at the end of each act, allowing them to demonstrate their Tallulah-love. After a few performances most had drifted away.

Going onstage without the assurance of their presence was disorienting for Tallulah, who had never lost her old childhood terror of abandonment. And she would only risk alienating her gallery-ites one more time, when she took the role of Marguerite in a 1930 revival of Dumas's *La Dame aux Camélias*. She was drawn to the role because of its associations with Sarah Bernhardt – still the legend by which she and her generation measured themselves. But she also intended this period classic to silence reviewers, who'd begun to jeer at the frequency with which she and her characters ended up in their camiknickers onstage: 'Let them say I undress in that!'[49] she retorted hopefully.

Yet as the tragic courtesan Marguerite, Tallulah pleased neither her critics nor her fans. The long literary monologues she had to deliver, the confining crinolines and ringlets she had to wear, the pose of saintly self-sacrifice she had to adopt, were too alien. Tallulah admitted that she felt a 'phoney', and her fellow actress Joan Matheson said it was as though some 'terrific vitality' in her had been 'crushed'.[50] Normally Tallulah's dressing room was the social heart of any new production, buzzing with drinks, laughter and impromptu parties, but her reviews for *La*

Dame aux Camélias were so harsh that the rest of the cast kept their distance.

No wonder she kept reverting to type. The critics might revile the predictability of plays that revolved around sex and cocktails, but the gallery never applauded louder than when Tallulah opened in *Gold Diggers* in December 1926, playing a feisty, cartwheeling chorus girl whose Charleston was acclaimed by Adele Astaire as the best she'd ever seen. When Tallulah played her final tempestuous scene in *Garden of Eden* (May 1927), dressed only in her underwear, she elicited nightly shrieks from her fans.

Glenn Anders, who had grown close to her during the run of *They Knew What They Wanted*, was one of the few people to whom she confessed the vulnerability of her situation: dependent on her fame yet also trapped by it. She feared that most of the people who clamoured for her company were attracted only by the lustre of her celebrity. And yet she couldn't resist making herself even more conspicuous. In late 1927 she bought a three-storey mews house in Mayfair, which she had designed in exquisite art deco style, silver paintwork setting off gold rug, pink upholstery and dark wood panels. There, she entertained on a lavish scale, inviting crowds of people to parties at which she served nothing but caviar and champagne cocktails. A young actor, Charles Bennett, who was invited to one, was astonished to see 'all the big stars, the most famous people in England' spilling out of Tallulah's tiny drawing room into the kitchen and up the stairs.[51] A party she gave for Ethel Barrymore went on for three days, simply segueing into yet another party that she'd arranged for yet another famous friend.

Tallulah had set in motion a social cyclone. And even if she feared that it was all glitz and opportunism, she had no idea how to bring it to a halt. She was as caught by the mechanism of celebrity as Zelda and Scott had been in New York. One clear register of her éclat was the degree to which she was courted by the Bright Young Things. Obsessed with getting as much press coverage as possible, these aesthetes and exquisite rebels would tip off gossip columnists (often their friends) with the location of their next stunt: ramping up the extravagance and campery of every new costume ball. For them, having Tallulah on their guest lists was the surest guarantee that the newspapers would take an interest.

So well known was she that if she went to the theatre as a member of the public, half the auditorium would get up to crane a look at her. It was gratifying to her ego, but even Tallulah recognized how unfairly it drew attention from the actors she'd come to see. In 1927 her celebrity reached its apotheosis. It was the year she was voted one of Britain's ten most remarkable women;* the year that Oliver Messel went to a fancy dress ball dressed as the character she played in *Garden of Eden*; the year in which stories of her rumoured engagement to Prince Nicholas of Romania were reported avidly on both sides of the Atlantic.

But to Cecil Beaton, Tallulah appeared to be turning into a parody of herself. He observed that the dewy sheen of her beauty had hardened to a more artificial brilliance: 'Her cheeks are huge acid-pink peonies. Her eyelashes are built out with hot liquid paint to look like burned matches, and her sullen discontented rosebud of a mouth is painted the brightest scarlet, and is as shiny as Tiptree's strawberry jam.'[52] Her girlish recklessness had hardened, too, into something more predatory. It was by then an open secret that any handsome actor in the same cast as Tallulah would have to run the gauntlet of her sexual advances. One young man, invited to her house for tea, was placed directly opposite her as she sat with her legs spread and angled, so that he could see directly up her skirt. Godfrey Tearle, her co-star in *Scotch Mist*, was coerced into rehearsing a love scene of such blatant realism that his watching wife was reduced to tears. Basil Dean wrote later, 'It was as if her Godfrey was being raped

---

* Also on the list were Lady Astor, Diana Cooper, Olga Lynn, Edith Sitwell and, of course, the Queen.

before her eyes.' As she left the stage, Tallulah commented with callous joy, 'Good thing I had me drawers on, wasn't it?'[53]

The tone of her voice was one that would have been recognized, immediately, by Eugenia Bankhead. She had heard it throughout their childhood as Tallulah had channelled her insecurities into baiting and bullying her older sister. Even now, the old rivalries could still surface – and they did so with a vengeance when Eugenia arrived in London in the spring of 1928, announcing that she planned to join Tallulah on the stage.

For the past few years Eugenia and her husband Morton had been living a nomadic life between New York and Europe. Much like the Fitzgeralds, they'd been travelling to escape their problems. Recently, however, their marriage had reached a point of crisis and Eugenia had walked out on Morton, determined to forge a new, professional life for herself. Initially, Tallulah hadn't felt threatened by her sister's decision to do this on the London stage. Although Eugenia had secured a part with unusual speed, as a dancer in Kenyon Nicholson's new play *The Barker*, it was only a very small role. And Tallulah was confident that she had largely been given her chance because of the Bankhead name, a name she had personally made famous.

Perhaps Eugenia realized that, too, which might also explain why she also deliberately set out to seduce the man Tallulah was seeing at the time. Tony Wilson was tall, blond and, just nineteen years old, was as overwhelmed by Eugenia's flattering advances as he was innocently unaware of the trouble he would cause by responding. He had no idea that for Tallulah, Eugenia's treachery would awaken the resentment she had suffered as a child, during all those years when her older sister had absorbed so much of their father's love and attention.

If Tallulah had been mean and angry then, her rage as an adult was implacable and it sent Eugenia scurrying back to Paris (and into Morton's arms), creating a breach between the two sisters that lasted for several years. Eugenia's betrayal was, however, only a prelude to a far deeper pain. For a while Tallulah had been seeing Naps only intermittently, but she still hadn't

abandoned her dream of a shared future with him. The previous
year they had met up in Paris, where she'd been having costumes
fitted at Molyneux for her role in *The Gold Diggers*. They'd had a
delirious few days together of drinking, dancing, lovemaking
and chatter. And when Naps said he had to leave – he was
travelling on to Lake Geneva for treatment of his chronic tuberculosis – he delighted Tallulah by suggesting that she follow him.
As usual, he was typically dilatory about the arrangements and
took a detour to a casino in Venice, leaving her hanging around
in Lake Geneva for two days, ignorant of his whereabouts. Yet
when, finally, he did arrive, it was for another 'two magic weeks'
of happiness.

This on-off relationship with Naps was a cruel conundrum for
Tallulah. At moments when she felt unhappy and 'hag-ridden by
ambition', she longed to settle into marriage. Recently she had
been wondering if she might like a child – women with babies
were often surprised by the tender interest she took in them.
She'd even wondered about leaving the stage. After nearly a
decade of striving and working she was tired, and as she admitted rather wistfully in a column she wrote for the *Sunday Express*,
she longed to have a break from the 'exciting and harrowing'
strain of her career.[54]

Ideally she would do so with Naps, who still aroused her,
amused her and interested her in ways that no other man could.
She knew that she could never love anyone as intensely as him,
and yet he continued to treat her with the same carelessness as
he treated his money at the roulette table. On her journey back
to London she wept over her inability to keep him and her
inability to let him go. She was terrified that eventually it
wouldn't matter either way, and that his health or his perverse
instincts of self-destruction would kill him. 'I knew he was
doomed. I had a feeling he welcomed that doom.'[55]

What Tallulah did not predict was that she would lose Naps to
another woman. But in September 1928 it was announced that
he had become engaged to Lady Mary Sibell Ashley-Cooper,
eldest daughter of the Earl of Shaftesbury and exactly the kind

of titled young woman his family expected him to wed. Tallulah could not help but be wretched at this final, absolute desertion. Nor could she help but be vulnerable to a man who very shortly afterwards presented himself as the ardent opposite of Naps: 'a rugged Romeo' who was masterfully determined to sweep her off her feet and into marriage.[56]

A few weeks after the news of Naps's engagement, Tallulah went to Brighton for the weekend and met Count Anthony de Bosdari. A handsome and apparently wealthy Italian, he seemed to fall so possessively in love with her that by the time she'd returned home she found a note from him, announcing his intention to marry her. Three days later he arrived on her doorstep, insisting that he wouldn't leave until she agreed to be his wife.

Tallulah was used to extravagant posturing from her lovers but Tony was in a different league. He appeared quintessentially and romantically European to her, with his brilliantined wavy hair, elegant manners and flamboyantly assertive masculinity. He claimed to be a cousin of the King of Italy and a graduate of Winchester and Oxford; and the arrogance of his background seemed to be channelled into the masterful way in which he walked into her house, instructed the butler to take the day off and told Tallulah to close her eyes as he slipped a diamond necklace around her throat.

Tony made her feel feminine and protected, and she interpreted his pursuit as genuine ardour. When he talked about their future together, the children they might have and the career he might pursue in politics, she allowed herself to dream of a blissfully restful life under his control. She agreed to his insistence on an early wedding, and her letter informing Will that she was likely to be married before Christmas painted a bright and hopeful future. She promised him that within a 'decent space of time' he might 'expect a grandson'; he might eventually see her returning home.[57]

But it was still mostly fantasy – Tallulah barely knew her fiancé or even her own mind. Sara Mayfield, an old friend from

Montgomery, was visiting London at the time, and she observed Tallulah veering back and forth in her enthusiasms, at some moments full of Tony but at others joking that she had other 'bigger game' on the romantic horizons.[58] She had sufficiently pressing second thoughts to ask Tony for the marriage to be postponed for a month or two, and her doubts became more clamorous still when, early in the new year, she briefly accompanied him on a business trip to Berlin. At close quarters, Tony's charm started to look suspect: he 'oozed small gallantries',[59] and his motives for taking her to Berlin seemed 'crafty and a bit twisted', as she discovered that, without consulting her, he had offered her services as an actor to the film company with whom he was trying to finalize a deal. Clearly Tony had a loose relationship with the truth. And it was around this time that Tallulah discovered he had not only been married before meeting her, but that the divorce he'd obtained from his first wife might be shaky under British law. When she returned to London her friend Francis Laking presented her with even more disturbing information. He'd been digging around in Tony's background and discovered he was much less wealthy than he claimed, so much less wealthy that the diamond necklace he'd given her with so much flourish had not yet been paid for. Far from having caught herself a rich and aristocratic businessman, Tallulah had been duped by a clever grifter.

Tallulah placed a telephone call to Berlin to tell Tony she would never see him again. Yet even though her friends congratulated her on a lucky escape, she smarted at the humiliation. Once again she had been abandoned, let down, and with her spirits already lowered by the loss of Naps, she found it hard to rally her usual defensive wit and defiance. As soon as there was a long break in her schedule, she ran away from London to take an extended holiday in the South of France.

Here she dedicated hours of consoling narcissistic attention to herself. If she couldn't control her lovers, she could at least control her appearance. She tanned herself to a chic olive brown and dieted herself into thinness, observing with satisfied self-love the severity of her hip bones and the sleekness of her legs. Feeling that the short flapper hairstyles had become commonplace, she grew her hair longer 'à la Greto Garbo' and booked herself in for cosmetic surgery to slim down the bridge of her nose.*

The past continued to hurt, however, and that autumn, when she sat for Augustus John, it showed in her portrait. John gave her an almost martyred quality, her cheekbones looked flayed, her eyes haunted under drooping lids. When the portrait was exhibited at the Royal Academy, many who saw it complained that it was hideous, but Tallulah insisted to the *Sunday Express* that John had captured 'the Real me'.[60] Her readiness to claim this troubled image may also have been fed by other problems in her life. The Inland Revenue had recently been alerted to the fact that Tallulah had paid no taxes during the seven years she'd spent in London, and they were now demanding thousands of pounds – money she didn't have. To add to her sense of persecution, she was also being targeted by some unusually scurrilous press.

By the late 1920s, the public's addiction to celebrity gossip had become consuming. Journalists were encouraged to write about sexual or financial scandals with a detail that would previously have been merely hinted at: if they could find nothing genuinely outrageous to report, they followed the example of the American press and invented it. Tallulah had first fallen victim to this trend in 1927 when she was still friendly with Tony Wilson. The two of them had driven down to visit Tony's younger brother at Eton, and taken the boy and some friends out to lunch at a nearby hotel. It was a minor infringement of the school rules, but when the press got hold of the incident they turned it into an inflammatory story. One report claimed that Tallulah and Tony had hired an aeroplane to snatch the boys away from Eton; another, more luridly, had suggested that

---

* It was her second operation.

there had been a sexual romp at the hotel involving Tallulah and five underage boys.

Her reputation had become so extreme that the public were willing to believe anything, and the story was so widely circulated that the police were forced to investigate. No scandal was uncovered, but that didn't prevent a derogatory report being filed at Scotland Yard. It noted that Tallulah Bankhead had not only appeared in a 'sex play', but had a reputation as 'a sexual pervert' – presumably a reference to her affairs with women.[61] Ultimately she was judged to be of sufficiently disturbing moral character to justify some low-level surveillance, with a view to possible deportation.

The contents of that report were to prove poisonous. Six years later, when she was living and working in America, she applied for permission to join a five-week tour of British music halls. From the response of the official in charge, it was clear her visit would be strictly limited to that period: 'Knowing what we do of this woman I think it is undesirable that she should be allowed to stay here.'[62]

Tallulah, of course, knew nothing of the file, but she could sense an atmosphere around her. Even in the theatre, she felt under siege. The antics of her fans were becoming destructive: When she had opened in *Her Cardboard Lover* in August 1928, the mob outside the theatre grew so rowdy that police were called. As Tallulah drove up to the stage door her car was nearly rocked onto its side. Even inside the theatre, the crowd remained hysterical, shouting and chanting so loudly that much of the dialogue was inaudible. Tallulah's female devotees were becoming a liability, and actors and directors were beginning to say they would not work with her. She was accused of encouraging her fans' behaviour, and insinuations were made in the press about her relationship with them. One journalist, noting that Tallulah had stripped to her underwear in yet another play,* commented,

---

* *He's Mine*, 1929.

1. Diana, *c*.1915: 'painted and powdered and dressed (as I hoped) to kill'.

2. Diana in costume for the musical tableau *La Damoiselle Elue* at the French Embassy, London, June 1914. *From left to right:* Felicity Tree, Nancy Cunard, Violet Charteris (Diana's sister Letty) and Diana.

3. Diana in VAD uniform collecting for a war charity, October 1916.

4. Diana and Duff holidaying in Italy, August 1923.

5. Diana in the London production of *The Miracle*.

6. Diana posing for Iris Tree's husband, Curtis Moffat, 1925.

7. Front cover of *Blast*, War Issue, July 1915.

8. Nancy as a published poet in 1921, living independently but still using her married name.

THE AUTHOR OF " OUTLAWS " : MRS. SYDNEY FAIRBAIRN, FORMERLY MISS NANCY CUNARD.

Mrs. Sydney Fairbairn, the daughter of Sir Bache and Lady Cunard, is well known as a poet, and used to contribute to " Wheels," the yearly production of the smart intellectual set, which contains the work of such authors as the Sitwells, Aldous Huxley, etc. She has recently published a new book of poems entitled " Outlaws."—[*Portrait-Study by Bertram Park.*]

9. 'Miss Nancy Cunard ... who admires eccentricities in dress and appearance [and] carries out her ideas with success'.

10. Nancy working at the Hours Press, late 1920s.

11. Nancy and African bangles, from the Cecil Beaton series, 1929.

12. Tamara – fashion-plate in life, dressed by Marcel Rochas, Paris, *c*.1931.

13. And in art, *Autoportrait (Tamara in the Green Bugatti)*, 1929.

14. Tamara in one of her many designer hats, this by Rose Descat, Paris, 1932.

15. Natalie Barney amidst Duncan-style nymphs during the early years of her Sapphic idyll.

16. Tamara de Lempicka, *Four Nudes*, *c*.1925.

17. Gertrude Stein and Alice B. Toklas, *c*.1925.

18. Tallulah in *The Dancers*, 1923.

19. Tallulah in a 1928 portrait by Paul Tanqueray.

20. Tallulah conducting a charity treasure hunt in the grounds of the Royal Hospital Chelsea, June 1930.

21. Tallulah stripping down to cami knickers and silk stockings in *Her Cardboard Lover*, 1928.

22. Tallulah (*left*) in *The Garden of Eden*, 1927.

23. Zelda Sayre, Montgomery belle, posing in dance costume in her mother's garden, *c*.1918.

24. Zelda and Scott escaping New York celebrity in Westport, summer 1920.

25. Zelda with baby Scottie, early 1922.

26. Zelda, Scott and Scottie celebrate Christmas, Paris, December 1925.

27. Zelda in practice clothes and pointe shoes, 1928.

28. Josephine (*centre*) and chorus line in a promotional picture for *Chocolate Dandies*, 1924.

29. Josephine in faux ragamuffin guise, Les Folies Bergère, 1926.

30. Poster for *La Revue Nègre*, designed by Paul Colin.

31. *Below left:* Josephine in the 1927 rhinestone-studded variation of her iconic banana skirt, 1927.

32. *Below:* The Ebony Venus – one of a series of dynamic nude portraits taken by Lipnitzki, *c.*1926.

'I am told that these rather feeble attempts at immodesty are for the benefit of the feminine element of the audience. Well, well,' sniggered the writer, 'girls will be boys!'[63]

It was an ambivalent moment in British culture. As the popular press grew more sensationalist, the official forces of reaction and prudery were also gaining momentum. In 1928, the year before Tallulah's fans were mocked for their sapphic tastes, the Home Secretary banned publication of Radclyffe Hall's lesbian bildungsroman *The Well of Loneliness*. Alongside suggestive adverts of flappers wearing short skirts and smoking cigarettes were newspaper articles voicing grave concern about the frivolous amorality of the nation's young women. In 1930, when suffrage was extended to all women over the age of eighteen, the flapper vote was greeted with fear and derision by large sections of the male establishment.

The General Strike of 1926, when British workers joined forced with the miners to demand better pay and working conditions, had already revealed the limits of the nation's party spirit. Jazz, cocktails, easy money, lax morals and experimental art looked suddenly irrelevant given this sudden baring of class hostility. The following year when Tallulah's London friends staged a 'Beggars' costume ball, the spectacle of these rich young men and women gaily drinking champagne while aping the dress of the poor aroused sharp condemnation from a formerly indulgent press.

Tallulah herself had typically ignored the strike. Taxis had been unavailable, but when she needed a lift she'd simply flagged down a passing motorist, announcing sweetly, 'I'm Tallulah, could you drive me to my rehearsal.' However, by the end of the decade even she sensed that life was changing. Crashing markets spelled an end to a culture of fast credit and unbridled excess: the publication in 1930 of Evelyn Waugh's *Vile Bodies* portrayed the butterfly brevity of London's gilded youth. That same year Tallulah's own irksome but irreplaceable gadfly Francis died – she claimed the cause was 'drinking too much yellow chartreuse', although it was more likely to have been diabetes. In his will

Francis left 'my friend Tallulah Bankhead all my motor cars',[64] but in fact he possessed none, and that same echo of loss and disillusionment reverberated through the play in which Tallulah opened that summer, written by her former New York mentor Rachel Crothers. Its title, *Let Us Be Gay*, sounded like a paean to a decade of pleasure, but its message was elegaic.

Tallulah's character, Kitty Brown, was a young and very modern divorcee. Putting aside the hurt of a failed marriage, Kitty transforms herself into a flapper, taking lovers and making a career for herself as a fashion designer. She flaunts her new independence: 'When I'm paying my own bills, men may come and men may go.' And to her husband Bob, who is trying to win her back, she boasts of becoming as hard as any man 'amusing myself with anything and everything that comes my way'.[65] Yet an older friend of Kitty's suspects that this lifestyle is not the magic formula it seems: 'Women are getting everything they want now, but are they any happier than when they used to stay at home – with their romantic illusions?' The play's closing scene supplies the answer. As Kitty agrees to return to her husband she admits that her independence was never so much fun as she claimed. 'I've been so gay,' she admits, 'so – so full of – so empty.'[66]

It was a line that Tallulah delivered with poignant conviction. She, too, was running on empty, barely able to deal with her mounting debts, unpredictable career and shiftless love life. She had no loyal husband to rescue her as Kitty did, so when a new man appeared, bringing with him the offer of a new start, Tallulah was more than ready to listen. Walter Wanger was an independent producer at Hollywood's Paramount Pictures. He had a famously creative commercial touch – his film credits boasted Valentino's *The Sheik* – and it was he who had successfully converted Covent Garden into a temporary cinema during the early 1920s, screening the premiere of Diana's debut film. Now, in bed with Tallulah, Wanger seduced her with talk of a second film career. Hollywood, he told her, was on the hunt for fresh stars, actors with sufficient vocal skills to meet the demands of the new 'talkies'. Tallulah was ideal – she had stage experience as well as glamour – and he promised that Paramount would market her as their next Marlene Dietrich; offering her a starting contract for five films and a weekly rate of $5,000, rising to $8,000 if the contract was extended. (Even in the turbulent economy of 1930, the film industry could still offer lavish induce-ments to its stars.)

Wanger waved this offer in front of Tallulah like a conjurer's wand. At a stroke he would get rid of the creditors dunning her for cash and remove her from the stalemate of her stage career. For a day or two Tallulah demurred. She had grown to despise filming back in New York, and her one reluctant foray into a British studio had been a disaster – *His House in Order* was judged by *Film Weekly* to be 'almost destitute of entertainment'.[67] Yet Wanger's terms made too much sense for her to turn them down. By the end of the year she had put her little house on the market, thrown her last party and played her last gig (a comedy sketch that ran for two weeks at the London Palladium).

Tallulah was ambitious enough to want to return to America as a conquering star: she lost weight through a reckless abuse of laxatives and prepared stories of her London career with which to impress her family and the press. Even so, she hated having to leave. Most of her adult life had been played out in London and she would always refer to her years there as 'the happiest and most exciting in my life'. Whatever treacheries and setbacks she had suffered, whatever moments of nostalgia she had felt for America, the city had been her home. On 1 January 1931, as she boarded the *SS Aquitania*, she sobbed miserably. Her friend Audry had come to wave her off, and piteously Tallulah begged her to stay on board and come to America, too. Who did she have waiting for her? Aside from Will, most of her blood relatives were now dead or dispersed, and she feared her old theatre friends would have moved on. She suspected, too, that America in this new decade would be a very different country from the one she had left. She had first made her name as a fledgling flapper actress, when America was poised on the brink of the jazz age. Now, nearing thirty, she was returning to a far harsher climate; jazz was giving way to the depression era.

Chapter Nine

NANCY

When Tallulah made her debut in *The Green Hat*, she was not the only woman in London reputed to be the inspiration for its lovely, errant heroine, Iris. Idina Sackville, with whom Tallulah had lodged at Olga Lynn's, was mooted as one possibility, but an even more likely candidate was Nancy Cunard. The physical match was compelling—Nancy was tall and blonde like Iris—and both women regarded themselves as fugitives from society.* More compelling still was the fact that Nancy had been romantically involved with Iris's creator, Michael Arlen.

Nancy had known Arlen slightly during the war, but it was early in 1920 that she began to fall in love with him. He was Armenian by birth, a small, tightly strung man with dark liquid eyes and a very flamboyant, un-English style of dress. To Nancy's male friends, Arlen appeared gaudy and meretricious. 'I really can't see why you like this ghastly Oriental rug merchant,' griped St John Hutchinson. Yet their contempt only made his foreignness more beguiling to her.[1]

It was Arlen's writing that most attracted her, however. Nancy

---

* In Arlen's description, Iris had 'outlawed herself . . . she wasn't any of the ghastly things called "society", "county", upper, middle and lower class. She was, you see, some invention . . . of her own.'

had always fantasized about a life of shared literary endeavour, and the Baron, as she called him then,* had already published several essays, short stories and a play, and was halfway through his first novel. She was awed by his output, believing it would be a spur to her own poetry, and after she had vowed to start a new life in Paris, it was Arlen she took with her on long, exploratory visits to the city.

He was, it seemed, the perfect companion, matching Nancy's own inquisitiveness and delight: 'It was always champagne,' she recalled, 'and our heads were often swimming.'[2] They liked to walk the maze of gravel paths that criss-crossed the Jardins du Luxembourg, or watch the busy river traffic on the Seine. They dined among Pigalle prostitutes at their favourite restaurant La Perle, and after jazzing in the clubs of Montmartre they wandered back to their hotel room in the misty flush of the Paris dawn. Yet Nancy's romance with the city could not soften the critical, edgy reaction that always set in with any man who wasn't Peter. By the autumn she was finding fault with every aspect of Arlen. He was proving irksomely proprietorial as a lover: becoming 'sullen as distant thunder ... brooding and brewing' if another man showed an interest in her.[3] He was talking of marriage, enraging Nancy as much by his presumption that she would accept him as by his obliviousness to the fact that marriage to Sydney had made her swear she would never again be anyone's wife.

Even his role as an outsider was becoming an irritant. Nancy had felt shocked sympathy for what Arlen's family had suffered when they'd been exiled by the Turks in 1901, but she couldn't understand the exhaustingly personal grudges he continued to hold against the world. One long, winter evening, when he launched into a litany of the insults he had suffered, the queru-

---

* By this point he had yet to switch from his birth name, Dikran Kouyoumdjian to his English pseudonym. Nancy was told that his nickname, the Baron, was connected to an actual title, but in fact it was merely an anglicization of Baaron, the Armenian for 'Mister'.

lousness of his tone grated so badly that she realized she was shredding the pages of the new book she was meant to be cutting.

But above all Nancy could not overlook Arlen's literary flaws. When he gave her the draft of his first novel, *Piracy*, to read, she was impressed by its 'beautiful gift for observation'[4] and its courage in charting the sexual and social issues of their generation. Yet Arlen was squandering his talents on a fantasy of London life whose banality and snobbery made her wince. 'You go on and on writing about Cocktails with a capital C,' she berated him, 'and ladies and gentlemen of Mayfair the likes of whom never existed.[5] Even more disconcertingly, it was her own life that he was using to flesh out this fantasy. On almost every page of *Piracy* she met an exaggerated but recognizable version of herself. Virginia Tracy, the novel's heroine, was her blonde, aristocratic and rebellious twin. During the war she had escaped from her socially formidable mother to a restaurant virtually identical to the Eiffel Tower, where 'tawny haired women of almost barbaric fairness [toyed] with their food and their poets'. She acquired a reputation for 'glamour and a rottenness' that meant even 'decent men [took] licence with her name'.[6]

Nancy was conscious that Arlen had to make a living, and initially she tolerated his literary plunderings, but they continued long after *Piracy* was published and their affair was over. When *The Green Hat* first appeared in the bookshops in 1924 she was furious to see that yet again Arlen had rifled her personal life. To her friend Janet Flanner she complained that everyone was talking about it – a complete stranger, a 'perfect swine', had come up to Nancy at a party and begun interrogating her as to 'whether or no I was the Green Hat'.[7]

On a very fundamental level she was not: despite their shared reputation for social and sexual deviancy, Iris lacked Nancy's intellectual stringency and wit. Yet however quick she was to brush off the connection, Arlen's borrowings remained a violation. Some were only a betrayal of small intimacies, such as the scene in which Iris, alone with her lover, dreamily traces her name in candle smoke, just as Nancy herself had once done. But one in particular was a brutal invasion of her privacy.

In December 1920, when Nancy's affair with Arlen was coming to an end, she was admitted to a private clinic in Paris for a curettage or scraping of the uterus lining. The procedure may have been to terminate a pregnancy – the high surgeon's fees suggest that discretion was part of the price – or it may have been related to an underlying gynaecological condition: Nancy always complained of painful periods. But either because it was badly botched, or because she was suffering from something more serious, in early January a second, more drastic operation followed, in which the whole of Nancy's womb was removed.

In 1920 a hysterectomy was a major surgical event, and afterwards Nancy developed a series of near-fatal infections. She made little of the episode afterwards, referring to it in the baldest of factual terms in her diary:

Dec, Jan, Feb. in the hospital in Paris

1st Op Curettage
2nd Op Hysterectomy
3rd Op Appendicitis, Peritonitis, Gangrene with 'a two per cent chance of survival'.[8]

Arlen, however, helped himself freely to the details of her suffering, first in *Piracy* and again in *The Green Hat*. It must surely have been horrible for Nancy to revisit his melodramatic embroiderings:

'It hurts,' she whispered '. . . Frightful . . . There's things inside me,' she said with a sob. 'Steel things. They've left them in there . . . holding things together . . . Look,' she said pitifully. And she lifted up her hands under the clothes, and he saw that they were tied together with a handkerchief. 'That's to stop me tearing the things out and killing myself.'[9]

A decade later Nancy would suggest that she had happily embraced the hysterectomy, which put an end to all cumbersome contraception and fear of abortion, but in truth it was a blow to her always precarious health, leaving her physically scarred and with her hormones harrowingly askew. In 1951 she would admit to her friend Solita Solano that she believed her lifetime of bad 'nerves' had been caused by 'those operations of 1921 – gland deficiency of some kind'.[10] And even though she had rarely expressed any interest in being a mother, apart from when she had fantasized about a life with Peter, twenty-five was still a very young age for Nancy to have her reproductive future taken away from her; a very young age to have yet another door slammed on her chance of ordinary happiness.

When Nancy recovered, she seemed to resume her old busy life. In Paris, she moved between different hotels, looking for a place to settle. She danced at the Plantation Club and Le Grand Duc, where Bricktop sang and the Harlem poet Langston Hughes worked as a waiter; she drank at the Dingo and the Jockey. She grew familiar with the Left Bank crowd, who drifted between the bookshops owned by Sylvia Beach and Adrienne Monnier, and the little art galleries, bars and cafés of Montparnasse. She may have noticed Tamara, smoking and watchful at her solitary table, minding her centimes and planning her career. But mostly Nancy would have been too busily in the thick of café conversation, talking about Freud, Diaghilev or jazz, her curiosity and intellect at full stretch.

The *Daily Mail* delighted in tracking her new lifestyle. 'Nancy vows she wont stand us anymore. Whenever she can she leaves us for Paris . . . As a rule, Nancy affects the Society of Futurist Artists and Highbrows, whereas the friends of Lady Cunard are either statesmen, brilliant Society beauties, or operatic celebrities who don't bother their heads about books and things.[11] Other papers were assiduous in tracking Nancy's travels around Europe as she moved with the summer flock of tourists.

The image she presented was rich and confident, one of the

cleverest and most stylish of the new decade's flappers. The *Daily Express* fanfared her arrival in Monte Carlo in March 1922 with the promise of many interesting outfits to report: 'Miss Nancy Cunard . . . who admires eccentricities in dress and appearance . . . carries out her ideas with courage and success. She was one of the first to adopt the Eton crop.' The *Sketch* supplied further details of the 'mauve tulle scarf tied across her eyebrows, with floating ends under a big grey felt hat, which looked, oh, so Spanish'.[12] Yet however confident Nancy appeared, those who watched her closely saw a driven quality in her social gyrations. Leonard Woolf noted the vulnerability behind her smart opinions and clever clothes, while Mary Hutchinson, wife of St John, equally saw dark shadows moving behind her bright veneer. Everyone commented on how thin she was becoming.

Nancy looked 'burned to the bone', said William Carlos Williams, observing that some days she appeared to survive on little beyond champagne or cheap white wine.[13] If she was not clinically anorexic, she was sometimes very close. To the poet Brian Howard, her 'thinness . . . was a sort of thing in itself in her', going far beyond fashionable slenderness. It was as though she were making herself as light and steely as possible, a thin blade of a woman cutting away her past, clearing her way towards a future.

Certainly she was putting as much distance as she could between herself and Maud. Year by year she grew more critical of her mother: despising the way she reduced art and ideas to trivial dinner table talk; finding her fashionable caprices increasingly contemptible. In 1926, when Maud changed her name to Emerald on the advice of a numerologist, Nancy refused to acknowledge it. She couldn't bear to imagine that, among the several traits they shared, she had in any way inherited her mother's flightiness. Three years later, when she responded to a literary questionnaire that invited her to list the qualities she most prized in herself,*

---

* It was compiled and printed in the *Little Review*, 1929.

Nancy chose to describe herself as 'impervious, concentrated, secret and unquestionable'.[14]

Financially independent, ferociously well educated and fearlessly stylish, Nancy could easily give the impression of moving imperviously through the early years of the decade. She took many lovers, some of whom were fleeting diversions, some of whom, like Wyndham Lewis, were important to her. 'Dear dear Lewis,' she wrote to him in 1923, 'I get warmed when I am with you – you are a sort of black sun, dark earth, rich and full of new things, potential harvests, always dark, *plein de sève*,* oil, blood, bread and comfort . . . I cannot get a nearer word than Rich.'[15] Yet whatever the seriousness of her affairs Nancy appeared to pursue them without fuss or guilt. She didn't brag about them like Tallulah, nor did she elevate them into a feminist cause. She seemed almost wilfully not to care how other peopled judged or interpreted her.

But other people did judge, of course. While a man like Duff could run dozens of mistresses and be applauded for his vigour, a woman who took as many lovers as Nancy was either a hardened nymphomaniac or fascinatingly damaged. William Carlos Williams inclined towards the latter view: he saw a martyred quality in Nancy's promiscuity, as if she were seeking a form of spiritual purity through physical excess. It was true, certainly, that beneath the casual trafficking of her love affairs, Nancy's relationship with sex remained complicated. To every new relationship she brought the hope of finding an emotion as large and pure as the love she had felt for Peter, but she also brought an equal terror of becoming trapped, as she had been with Sydney. Hope and fear alike made her restless, critical and self-conscious, and these emotions were compounded by her difficulty in finding a lover who could satisfy her in bed.

Orgasm was very hard for Nancy; to experience any kind of arousal she needed to feel a degree of physical pain, and some

---

* Literally 'full of sap'.

men were made queasy by her demands. Wyndham Lewis, for instance, admitted to a friend that he had to break off with Nancy because he found her requests for anal penetration perverse. Far more sympathetic was Raymond Michelet, the young surrealist writer with whom Nancy had an affair in 1931, who understood that the physical scarring left by her gynaecological history had affected her sensitivity, making pain an essential stimulus to pleasure. Between Lewis and Michelet there were many other men who, while confused by the riddle of Nancy's sexuality, were also bewitched by it. They fell in love with her because they wanted to understand her.

Aldous Huxley became one of the bewitched when he had a brief affair with Nancy in the spring of 1922. Touchingly earnest in her desire to be a poet, terrifyingly assured in her beauty and wealth, infuriating in her fashionable mannerisms, she seemed a maddening enigma, and he became obsessed with the need to solve it. Initially, she was receptive to his interest. She'd met him briefly during the war, when they had both been published in the same anthology. And while he'd then been a poorly paid schoolteacher, rarely able to afford his few 'whizzing' trips to London, now, with the publication of his debut novel, *Crome Yellow*, he was being talked of as the new comic-philosophical voice of English fiction. It was his writing more than any physical attraction that caught Nancy's interest. Pale and lanky Huxley was not a type to appeal to her – although the writer Anita Loos thought him beautiful: 'A giant in height – with a . . . magnificent head; the head of an angel drawn by William Blake.'[16]

Yet as casually as she allowed Huxley into her bed, Nancy was ready to discard him. Socially he was of little use to her: he despised the sloganizing and philosophical hot air of the literary Left Bank; he found the smoky atmosphere of bars and clubs deleterious to his weak lungs and he liked to be in bed early. And bed, unfortunately, was the place where Huxley was even less use to Nancy. He adored her body and was aroused to a tender reverence by her sharp-edged fragility, yet the sensitivity of his love-making was almost repugnant to her. Later, without mercy, she confessed to a friend that it was 'like being crawled over by slugs'.[17]

It was a point of honour to Nancy that she would never fake desire or a sentiment she did not feel, and she tried to convince Huxley that the affair was over. He could not accept it, however, continuing to write her letters and importune meetings. On one desperate night he paced outside her window like 'a dim haunting ghost'.[18] Even after his wife, Maria, finally dragged him away to Italy, Huxley was unable to sever himself from Nancy. She was an idée fixe, an obsession lodged inside him, and he wrote about her and niggled away at her again and again in his fiction.*

His first literary portrait of Nancy appeared in *Antic Hay*, a satire of post-war London that skewered the intellectual vacuities and artistic pretensions of the age. Myra Viveash was a brittle society beauty whose cultivated smartness and atrophied heart were symbolic of the world in which she moved; to the extent that she was Nancy, it was a cruel lampooning. Yet despite Huxley's satiric intent, the portrait remained charged with his first fascinated adoration of her. He described Myra-Nancy with a lover's attentive detail: her 'palely brightly inexpressive eyes', the eerie grace of her dancer's walk: 'placing her feet with meticulous precision one after the other in the same straight line . . . Floating she seemed to go, with a little spring at every step.'[19]

He was also conscientious about excusing her deadened affect through the sufferings of her past – Myra, like Nancy, had lost her first, great love. However, the more distant from Nancy Huxley became, the fewer redeeming qualities he gave her fictional incarnations. Barbara in *Those Barren Leaves* (1925) was a crass artistic snob; Lucy Tantamount in *Point Counter Point* (1928) was the sexually depraved and intellectually lazy product of 'too much money and leisure'. When Lucy recollects being half raped by a stranger, her account hums with perverse excitement: 'He

---

* The details of their relationship don't appear in Nancy or Aldous's surviving correspondence, but were circulated by friends like the writer Sybille Bedford.

came at me as though he would kill me. Letting oneself be hurt, humiliated, used like a doormat – queer. I like it. Besides the doormat uses the user. It's complicated.'[20]

Arlen and Huxley's fiction set in motion a literary mythologizing of Nancy, and it was a process continued by many others. The writer Harold Acton later commented that she had 'inspired half the poets and novelists of the twenties'.[21] Some were her lovers, others more distant acquaintances, including Evelyn Waugh, who would scatter a generalized Nancy-glitter over several of his fictional characters. In *Unconditional Surrender* (1961), she would inspire the figure of Virginia Troy, who was presented as the emblem of a fascinating generation, a ghost of romance, 'exquisite . . . doomed and . . . damning . . . we shall never see anyone like her again in literature or in life'.[22]

Later, Nancy lost interest in her own artistic celebrity, but when she was young it was simultaneously flattering and disruptive to be cast as muse to so many – there were painters and photographers as well as writers. During the early 1920s she still felt unformed and uncertain of herself: as she groped to find a poetic voice and to create a life in which she could believe, it didn't help to see herself in the distorting mirrors of other people's fantasies.

It wasn't simply the puzzle of her behaviour that challenged so many to write about her. Raymond Mortimer, then an aspiring novelist, found her beauty heart stopping when he first met her in 1921 on a boat crossing the Channel. 'Everybody old, it is hoped, can look back to one person who was incomparably bewitching: and I have never met anyone to equal Nancy Cunard.'[23] Writers scrabbled for adjectives to capture the essence of her uncompromising beauty. To David Garnett it was the brilliant pallor of her skin, 'as white as bleached almonds';[24] to Harold Acton it was the shapeliness of her small head, 'carved out of crystal', and the arctic brightness of her unwavering blue-green gaze. To Carlos Williams it was the tapering length of her legs and the delicate poise of her ankles, a 'tall blond spike of woman';[25] to George Moore it was her beautiful back, 'as long as a weasel's' (and given to Brigit, a character in his 1926 novel *Ulick and Soracha*).

Nancy's distinctive appearance was equally appealing to journalists and photographers. Fashion was being marketed on a mass scale after the war, but the more widespread its reach, the higher the premium placed on individual style. People wanted to be seen in the latest trends, yet they also wanted their clothes to be an expression of their personality. A woman who spent her wages on a cape of vibrant chevron design, or an art deco powder compact, believed she was making choices that were no less creative than the bright young aesthetes fashioning outfits for a costume ball, art students adopting gypsy skirts and headscarves or sapphists in their tailored suits and green carnations.

Few, however, dressed more creatively than Nancy. The turbans and scarves she customized in the early 1920s, the geometric fabrics she commissioned from the artist Sonia Delaunay, the enormous African earrings and ivory bangles she began wearing in the mid-1920s, all looked astonishing on her and were seized upon by journalists as the possible start of a trend. Even her make-up was different – eyes elongated with a dramatic line of kohl, her lipstick a slash of scarlet that gave her mouth a determined, even savage tension. During these years any publication that made use of Nancy's face could guarantee itself a frisson of modernity.

Certainly there was barely a photograph in which she didn't appear perfectly in control of her image, from casual snapshots taken by friends to the formal portraits of Cecil Beaton. In the famous series he shot in 1929, Nancy's pose had the quality of an abstract artwork – sharp chin resting in the palm of her hand, thin arms loaded with ivory and ebony bangles. Yet while she lavished time and passion on her physical appearance – and many would say she had a genius for it – Nancy was wary of being defined by it. It was never her clothes for which she wanted to be famous, only her writing.

*

During the first half of the decade, Nancy worked hard on her poetry. As she moved from hotel to hotel she kept her notebooks and pens close by; even when she was holidaying across Europe she maintained a writer's discipline, using her diary entries and letters to hone her eye and her style. By April 1921 she had had her first volume of poetry published, and received some encouraging attention. The tone of *Outlaws* might be marred by traces of Nancy's old adolescent posturing, with lines in which she cast herself as 'the perfect stranger/Outcast and outlaw from the rules of life', but as a collection it was welcomed by the *Nation*, who judged it a volume of 'entirely genuine and strangely individual, if imperfect poems'.

George Moore, writing in the *Observer*, thought Nancy showed signs of 'genius', 'a special way of feeling and seeing', even if he demurred over a lack of 'handicraft, tact [and] judgement'.[26] But Moore of course was tenderly biased, and Nancy was given a far more relentlessly objective assessment of her work when she sent a poem to Ezra Pound, hoping for help in getting it published. Pound's response was personally affable, but he made it clear that Nancy was still a novice, with much to learn, and that her voice, if she had one, was hard to discern under the muffling influence of her favourite childhood poets.

> *Lovely Nancy,*
> *I will take the poem to the Dial this evening, but, my dear, why why the devil do you write in that obsolete dialect with the cadences of the late Alfred Tennyson . . .*
> *Iambic pentameter is a snare because it constantly lets one in for dead phrases . . . rhyme is no good unless you use it without letting it disturb the order of the words . . .*
> *Damn it all, midnight is midnight, it is not 'this midnight hour'.*[27]

The list of her shortcomings was hard to read, but Nancy stuck the letter into her poetry scrapbook and kept it. Pound's editorial toughness had the status of holy writ amongst writers

she revered,* including T.S. Eliot, with whom, according to one
biographer, she'd had a brief sexual encounter the previous
year. There was another reason for cherishing the letter however – the sweetness of its tone and the hint it contained of
something more intimate. Pound was now living in Paris (Nancy
had written to him from London) and there was a kind of
invitation in his closing paragraph: 'I wish you would come back
and deliver me from the ferocious mercies of wandering American females.'

Nancy had had a slight crush on Pound ever since he'd come
to tea with Maud in 1915 – the sartorial brio of his gold earring
and green baize trousers as impressive to her as his intellect. And
there is some evidence to suggest that after her return to Paris,
she began an affair with the poet. It could only ever have been
intermittent. In his own fashion, Pound remained committed to
his wife, the English painter Dorothy Shakespear, and the longest period Nancy ever had him to herself was a walking holiday
in Southern France in 1922, which they took while Shakespear
was away. To Nancy it seems to have been a near perfect time.
Large landscapes were always liberating to her, and Pound, with
his vehement opinions and boundless curiosity, was their human
equivalent. The fact that she couldn't ever possess him only
made him more desirable.

She tried to arrange other rendezvous, taking an apartment
in Venice in the autumn of 1922, where they might write poetry
together. 'Do come. I can see us at breakfast splitting a fig,
muttering over the foulness of the tea . . . There will be hours
devoted to the two typewriters.' She believed she might be a
better poet, even a better person, if only she could have more
contact with him: 'I am dull without you . . . I have no application. I am getting so drunk on this Bianco Vermouth alone,
surrounded by the Paris nostalgia.'[28]

---

* Hilda Doolittle, for a while Pound's lover, felt her own voice overwhelmed by
his influence.

But Pound never came. He cared for Nancy, but he preferred his mistresses to be less complex, less hard work, and their affair, such as it was, petered down to an exchange of letters and occasional meetings. Even so, Nancy's second collection of poems, *Sublunary*, was charged with his presence.* Memories of their holiday in France were filtered into 'Pays Hanté'; in 'You Have Lit the Only Candle' she paid homage to Pound's cleansing effect on her sexually, his 'straight flame' of desire, 'absolving' her from the muddle and 'shame' of her own.

This 1923 collection paid homage to Pound's critical influence, too, as Nancy laboured to tighten her style. But it was in her third and most important work, *Parallax* (1925), that she attempted her own version of his modernist poetic. This extended work, written in multiple voices and registers, was very evidently inspired by the structure of T.S. Eliot's *The Waste Land*, which had been published three years earlier and had been closely edited by Pound.† However, the landscapes in which Nancy placed her poetic voices and the issues she broached were very personal to her. Parts of *Parallax* read like extracts from her diaries, vivid travelogue jostling with confessional self-doubt and earnest, intellectual argument.

It was her most experimental, and her most intensely visualized, poem. Raymond Mortimer saw in it 'a desolate sort of beauty . . . particularly poignant to my contemporaries'; the *Times Literary Supplement* admired it as the 'creation of a resilient mind'.[29] Yet others could not see past its debt to Eliot, and continued to question the individuality of Nancy's style. And this was a doubt that was slowly, unhappily, beginning to grow in her mind too. She might be able to create brilliant, original effects with make-up and clothes, yet that same flair eluded her with language and form.

---

* James J. Wilhelm's research into Pound's years in Paris provides the basis for this account.
† It was also published by the same publishers as *The Waste Land*, Leonard and Virginia Woolf's Hogarth press.

Eliot himself had already passed judgement on Nancy's poetry. An early draft of *The Waste Land* had included the voice of a rich socialite, Fresca, whose literary pretension far outweighed her 'mishmash pourri' of talent. It was almost certainly Nancy who was satirized in the lines: 'When restless nights distract her brain from sheep/She may as well write poetry, as count sheep'. Pound thought so too: in 1921 when he read the draft through, he crossed out those lines, advising Eliot to cut the entire Fresca section.

Nancy would have been mortified to read those lines, but in a self-flagellating moment she might have acknowledged their point. She was mixing with many professional writers now, and in contrast to Fitzgerald, Hemingway or Pound, she knew herself to be a privileged dabbler, too easily distracted from her desk by a new lover or by the prospect of a new city or landscape. She was still frequently in transit. There were regular trips back to London to see Maud, to whom she remained bound by habit and a reluctant need, and some of her old friends like Iris Tree, Diana and Duff Cooper, Tommy Earp, St John Hutchinson and the Sitwells.

Nancy still loved England, but more and more it was to Europe that she felt bound. She'd inherited Maud's passion for the Venice season, and for several weeks each summer rented a palazzo apartment in the city. Like the Marquesa Casati, if on a less expensive scale, Nancy became a local attraction. Dressed in her remarkable outfits and surrounded by her often remarkable entourage of friends, the sight of her feeding pigeons in St Mark's Square, or shopping in the Rialto market, would frequently draw a small crowd. Bar owners begged for her business, artists pleaded to paint her portrait.

As well as Venice there were trips to Monte Carlo, Rome and Florence, where Nancy was almost always guaranteed to meet someone she knew, including the writer Norman Douglas, to whom she had become very close. The Twenties were a decade on the move: there were passenger flights between London, Paris and Berlin; the Train Bleu whisked fashionable holiday-makers down to the French Riviera; ever faster, more luxurious liners criss-crossed the Atlantic. Although passports, introduced during the war, remained mandatory, Nancy and her circle regarded themselves as citizens of a newly accessible world.

As a traveller she also cherished the discovery of little places – the fishing port of Sanary on the Mediterranean coast; the remoter villages of Normandy. She craved the solitude and exhilaration of empty spaces. And there are lines in her early poem 'Voyages North' that evoke a very different Nancy from the tormented heroines depicted by Huxley or Arlen – an invigorated, independent Nancy, standing alone 'on a northern hilltop/shouting at the sun'.

Nancy regarded such moments as a necessary escape from urban life; even so Paris, her adopted city, remained her base for most of the 1920s. It was in early 1924 that she found the perfect apartment, a ground-floor flat on the Ile Saint-Louis. This elegant sliver of old Paris, with its narrow houses shadowed by high trees, was, to Nancy, purely romantic. The view from her window opened out to the river and Notre Dame, and the interior of the apartment, though small, was elegantly proportioned.

Rue le Regrattier was her first real adult home, a place where she could assemble all her precious belongings – her books, African carvings and a growing art collection that included works by de Chirico, Tanguy and Picabia. She could also entertain, holding regular soirées with the help of her new maid, Anna. Nancy's guests reflected the interlocking circles in which she now moved. There was the party crowd, centring on Jean Cocteau; the avant-garde artists, revolving around Brancusi, Marcel Duchamp, Man Ray and his green-eyed lover Kiki de Montparnasse; there was also her growing number of literary friends, including Pound, Carlos Williams, Kay Boyle and Ernest Hemingway.

Nancy looked splendid at 'the Grattery': thin and animated against the backdrop of her books and paintings; bracelets clacking on her arms as she gestured with her cigarette; dancing to a snatch of jazz playing from her gramophone. And talking, always talking. Brian Howard wrote, 'She is the only woman I know who can be really impassioned about ideas almost continuously';[30] Carlos Williams equally admired her 'courteous cultured and fearless mind'.[31]

Two of Nancy's most regular visitors at the flat were an American couple, Janet Flanner and Solita Solano. Both were writers and they became her first close female friends since Iris and Sybil. With Janet and Solita she could talk seriously about books and poetry, but equally she could spend intimate, hilarious evenings talking about sex, food and clothes. Maud was still buying beautiful couture for Nancy, wanting to believe her daughter was dressing well, even if her life was going to bohemian rack and ruin. Often when Janet and Solita arrived at the Grattery to pick Nancy up for an evening in the city, she would spread out her new bounty from Poiret or Vionnet for the three of them to wear – Janet sometimes sporting the addition of Sir Bache's old top hat. They made a piquant trio: Solita small and precise, with her clear assessing gaze and dark bell of hair; Nancy sharp-boned and blonde; Janet sardonically handsome. Solita recalled that painters were always 'begging' to use them as models.

In 1925, when Janet was hired to become French correspondent for the *New Yorker* magazine, Nancy and Solita accompanied her as she trawled clubs, parties and gallery openings for copy. By the mid-1920s, every fashionable American wanted to know about Paris, and Janet's fortnightly letters, written under the pen name of Genet*, were required reading. It was through Janet's column that Nancy was introduced to Isadora Duncan, still a legend despite the maudlin alcoholism into which her life had unravelled, also the lesbian grande dame, Mercedes de Acosta.

Janet herself had had a brief affair with de Acosta back in New York; when they met again in Paris in 1926 Mercedes was involved with Tallulah's first love, Eva Le Gallienne, but also

---

* A pun on the French pronunciation of her name.

with Alla Nazimova – Gallienne's original lover and Tallulah's early stage idol. This international lesbian coterie and its Parisian hub at rue Jacob intrigued Nancy, but she had no desire to become part of it.* Sexually she had little interest in women and she certainly had no intention of complicating her bond with Janet and Solita. She hadn't learned the trick of successfully combining sex and friendship, and no one else could give her the simple steadiness these two provided. Solita fondly avowed that the three of them were a model of 'modern female fidelity'; they referred to each other as 1, 2 and 3, signing off letters with the symbol of a three-legged stool.[32] And although some of the demands that Nancy made on that fidelity were extreme – she swore she would never forgive Janet and Solita if they allowed themselves to be annexed by Maud – the two women were as close to family as anything in her life.

Rue le Regrattier became Nancy's settled base, but around her Paris buzzed in what she described as 'an extraordinary and permanent state of avant gardism'.[33] Writers and artists were drawn to the city from all over Europe, America and England; the cafés and bars were noisy with the competing languages of Freudians, Communists, Dadaists and Surrealists. London could not compare. Even though its post-war gloom had lifted by the mid-1920s, Nancy saw nothing like the joyful proliferation of experiment she encountered daily in Paris. The shrieking baby flappers and the exquisite drawling boys who were Britain's Bright Young Things seemed like bored children to her, indulging in nursery-room naughtiness with their treasure hunts, fancy dress parties and car races.

Nancy had left all that behind. It was intellectual and political rebellion that interested her now, and in 1924 she found them with her new lover, the Dadaist Tristan Tzara. Slender and

---

* In Djuna Barnes's thinly disguised portrait of the salon in *Ladies Almanack*, Janet and Solita appeared as the admirable couple, Nip and Tuck.

dandified – Tzara always sported a monocle – he was the most buoyant of cultural terrorists. On the one hand he passionately avowed the fundamental Dadaist tenet that truth and civilization lay in ruins, yet he enjoyed himself with what, to Nancy, was an irresistible and eclectic vitality.

In his company she went to the tiny surrealist galleries opening up near the Jardins du Luxembourg, she jazzed at Cocteau's club, Le Boeuf sur le Toit, and attended one of Etienne de Beaumont's costume balls – annual bacchanalia for the rich, aristocratic and deviant. She was photographed by Man Ray wearing a silver trouser suit, a mask and her father's top hat; and with Tzara kneeling to kiss her hand she radiated pleasure and anticipation. She took a dancing role in one of his theatrical events *LECMOM 3rd Diens* and inspired another (Tzara claimed he'd written *Mouchoir des nuages* after he'd suffered a sneezing fit, showing off to Nancy by eating an entire pot of mustard).

'Lord how we laughed,' she wrote. The affair with Tzara was one of the most purely joyous periods of her life.[34] Yet however much she delighted in his sweet-natured anarchy, the old restlessness gnawed at her, and by early 1926 Nancy had moved on again – to an affair with Louis Aragon. Aragon was tall, dark and thin, his searching blue eyes set in a finely drawn face, and Nancy thought him one of the most inspiring men she had ever met. The surrealist movement he had founded with André Breton two years earlier combined experimental art, revolutionary politics and Freudian theory in a way that to her made captivating emotional and intellectual sense.

Freud's theories of the unconscious were much in vogue now, cited as explanation for the forces of destruction that had been unleashed during the war, as well as for the pleasure-seeking, taboo-breaking culture that had emerged in its wake. Nancy herself had been reading Freud since 1919, searching for clues to her own precarious mental health and to her unresolved antagonism to her mother. Through her new lover, however, she felt she was encountering larger views of psychoanalysis, as Aragon explained how techniques of dream study and automatic

writing might unlock the collective unconscious, providing a
route to the political transformation of human nature.

For many months Aragon seemed a man as close to Nancy's
ideal as she had ever met. She was spellbound by his literary
facility as he poured out poetry, journalism and theory. 'He is
delicious,' she admitted to Janet and Solita, 'in perfect training,
always to write at will any place, of any thing.'[35] They shared
other pleasures, too, hiking in the countryside, travel, jazz and
African culture. Some of their happiest times together were
trawling through the clubs of Montmartre in search of the most
authentic black pianist, or visiting port towns to buy African
masks and carvings that sailors had brought back from the West
Indies. Even if Aragon, as a good surrealist, lectured Nancy on
the superior authenticity of black culture, on the decadence of
Europe, he didn't judge her more frivolous concerns: the African
jewellery with which she was now beginning to decorate herself;
the Charleston lessons she was taking from the nightclub singer
Bricktop.*

Some of Aragon's comrades in the surrealist movement, however, were wary of Nancy's fashionable shimmer. She might have
rebelled against her class, but the fact that she still lived off her
mother's money, and spent some of it on trivial pleasures, made
the most intransigent among them distrust her. Above all, they
disapproved of her emotional independence. Despite the surrealists' theoretical commitment to female emancipation, they
expected their women to be faithful helpmeets to the cause. By
her own standards, Nancy remained loyal to Aragon – this affair
was one of the longest and most intimate of her life – yet by 1927
she had become sexually and emotionally fidgety and was running several other affairs in tandem.

She knew she was giving in to old destructive habits: 'He is a

---

* Aragon tolerated Nancy's devotion to fashion, but he resented it when Paris
began appropriating surrealist art as a new style trend. When Ernst and Miro
created designs for Diaghilev's Ballets Russes in 1926, it was Aragon who
organized a group of comrades to heckle the first performance.

very sweet person,' she wrote to Janet. 'Were I not myself so irreducibly myself I should be very happy. I am as far as can be.'[36] Yet according to the ever-forgiving Raymond Michelet, Nancy was always trying to find some new way to out-run her demons: she 'forged ahead, fleeing from something, never stopping to consider, never turning back, burning everything behind her, things she had loved, people she might have loved'.[37]

Aragon, however, found her infidelities difficult either to understand or forgive, and their relationship would probably have ended by the summer had Nancy not found a new and practical way to channel her energies, which gave them both a reprieve. For some time she'd been thinking of buying a house in the country, a refuge from the nervous intensity of Paris. In 1927 she found it in an old farmhouse, sixty miles north-west of the city. Le Puits Carré, named after the ancient stone well in its front courtyard, was set just outside the village of Chapelle-Réanville in a small hectarage of fields and orchards, surrounded by a tangle of wild flowers. It was a modest building, constructed in classic peasant style, and Nancy did little to change it beyond stripping the walls of her bedroom back to the original stone, painting the walls of the dining room green and moving in favourite pieces of furniture from Nevill Holt, along with books, paintings and her by now enormous collection of ivory bracelets.

There was room in the house for Aragon and her friends to stay, and when the nights were warm Nancy establised a supper-time ritual of setting up table and benches in the front courtyard, and hanging lamps from the ancient lime trees. Less romantic were the freezing winter nights when the smoking fires gave out inadequate warmth and Aragon's grouchier comrades came to drink all her wine. But Nancy was planning to do more than make a rural retreat for herself. After the mixed reviews of *Parallax*, she had begun to ponder alternative possibilities to poetry, and a plan was slowly forming in her mind to launch herself as a small, independent publisher. The Twenties and early Thirties were a golden age for such enterprises. The proliferation of literary magazines, political manifestos and experimental writing had created a demand for non-commercial presses, and to Nancy this kind of business seemed the perfect way of remaining in the literary world she so revered.

Other women were thriving in similarly practical endeavours: Sylvia Beach had expanded her bookshop into a publishing venture, producing the first English edition of Joyce's *Ulysses* in 1922. And in 1928, when the Paris-based Three Mountains Press was put up for sale, Nancy saw her opportunity. She was able to purchase a magnificent nineteenth-century hand press, with leftover stock of Vergé de Rives paper and Caslon Old Face type from the press, and its former owner, William Bird, also introduced her to a French printer, Levy, who would be willing to instruct her in her new craft.

Impatient to begin, and enthusiastically supported by Aragon, Nancy made the necessary preparations at Le Puits Carré, and early that summer she was ready to start her apprenticeship. Levy, a political radical and a proudly traditional craftsman, was inclined to patronize his Parisian pupil, informing her she would require a seven-year apprenticeship before she could go into business. But Nancy was wilfully quick to learn, and within a few weeks declared herself, and The Hours Press, ready for production.

The money for this press, and perhaps a little of its inspiration, had come from her father. By the mid-1920s she was seeing very little of Sir Bache: after the divorce from Maud necessitated the sale of Nevill Holt, her rare visits to her father were an ordeal for both of them. The world they had shared during her childhood had shrunk to a remote memory: 'It seems fantastic now to think of the scale of our existence then, with its numerous servants, gardeners, horses and motor cars,' and she couldn't begin to explain to him the way she lived in Paris.[38] But Nancy loved her father, and when Sir Bache's health started to fail in autumn 1925, she went to watch over him. It was 'rather terrible', she wrote to Sybil Hart-Davis, but sitting beside him as he died brought Nancy closer to her father than she had been during his lifetime. His instructions for the simplest possible funeral – 'I would prefer to go to my grave in a farm wagon rather than a hearse,' moved her deeply, as did the bequest to her of all his remaining capital – £14,500.[39]

In some ways The Hours became Nancy's tribute to her father. Living and working in the Normandy countryside, she was nearer to his spirit than to Maud (who disdained both the countryside and manual work). Just as Sir Bache's happiest hours had been spent in his metal workshop, Nancy discovered an unexpected peace and fulfilment working long days with Aragon or Levy. A photograph shows her hefting the handle of the giant nineteenth-century press like a natural, despite being elegantly dressed in a high-collared shirt and heeled shoes. From the start she felt an affinity for her craft. The slow, shaping process of assembling type for a poem was almost like giving birth: 'Letter by letter and line by line, it rises from your fingers.'[40] The special visual alchemy between font, paper and cover design came easily to her, and The Hours publications were always beautiful – their covers in vermilion, yellow, or duck-egg blue, with illustrations by Man Ray or Tanguy. She even came to prize the permanent 'slight ingrain of grey' that the printing left on her fingers: 'The smell [of the ink] pleased me greatly, as did the beautiful fresh-ness of the glistening pigment. There is no other black or red like it.'[41]

Nancy had hoped to make The Hours a platform for new and experimental writing, but initially she had to take her commissions where she could find them. Her first publications were a pamphlet by her friend Norman Douglas, a short story by George Moore and Aragon's translation of Lewis Carroll's *The Hunting of the Snark*. During the three years in which she was in business, however, the list grew impressively. Nancy would publish the first editions of works by Robert Graves, Havelock Ellis and Arthur Symons, as well as a one-volume edition of Pound's *Cantos* (1930). She would give a platform to young writers and her greatest coup, although it would take her some time to know it, was to publish, at her own expense, one of the very first works by Samuel Beckett.

Nancy could not claim to have discovered Beckett – he'd been working in Paris as James Joyce's assistant, and had already published some work in translation – but her publication of one hundred beautifully printed copies of 'Whoroscope' (the poem he wrote in response to a poetry prize she launched) raised his profile considerably. So, too, did his association with Nancy. Dissimilar as they were in situation and ambition, Nancy and Beckett became friends. There was an odd physical kinship between them, both so very tall, pale and thin, and Nancy thought his face exceptional, with 'the fierce austerity of the Mexican eagle'.[42] It's even possible that they were lovers for a night or two, though Beckett had little interest in matching Nancy's sexual or social drive. The night he got swept into a Montmartre club with her, he berated himself miserably: 'What in God's name am I *doing* here.'[43] And while they continued to correspond for years, and spoke of each other with affection and loyalty, their worlds inevitably ceased to coincide.

The months during which Nancy was setting up The Hours were among the most satisfying of her life. The ink stains on her fingers, the ache in her muscles, were all solid evidence of the structure she had found for herself. Even so, this settled period of productivity was doomed, as always, by the sheer rage of frustration that descended on Nancy. She began heading off to Paris for days on her own, needing to prowl around the city and be away from Aragon. When Nancy was in this state, her moods were impossible to predict. According to Michelet, she could switch in an instant from being 'as hard as an independent woman, used to playing with men' to a 'tremulous romantic' who would 'weep with emotion . . . like a young woman taken by surprise by unexpected and suddenly burgeoning love.'[44]

Aragon couldn't stand the strain. That summer they were locked into a second downward spiral: both drinking too much and both very angry. Nancy, at flash points, could turn unrecognizably violent, her small, white face contorted and savage as she lashed out with her fists. Yet despite the mutually degrading misery of their fights, they were still not done with each other, and Nancy insisted that Aragon accompany her on her summer trip to Venice.

This was yet another punishment, for Aragon had no money to spend on holidays. At the beginning of their affair it hadn't mattered that Nancy paid for most of the food, drink and travel, or that she subsidized much of Aragon's work. Now, however, he squirmed at the extent of his financial dependency, and would only agree to accompany Nancy to Venice when some money of his own came through from the sale of a painting. Perhaps he hoped that a change of scene might restore her to her old sweetness and generosity. But while for Nancy that holiday was 'a hell of a time, gay and mad, fantastic and ominous', for Aragon it was simply hell.[45]

He had believed that the cash from his painting would guarantee him a modicum of financial dignity, but Nancy's impossibly expensive round of restaurant dinners, drinks and dawn revels at the Lido meant he either had to ask for money or stay in the palazzo on his own. He felt himself to be in 'a false position perfectly intolerable', and Solita, who was among Nancy's guests, overheard terrible rows, with Aragon threatening to commit suicide and Nancy taunting him that he lacked the courage.[46]

She was wrong. One night, after yet another brawl, Aragon stormed out and failed to return. This was not his usual pattern, and as the hours passed even Nancy became alarmed. A search began of the local hotels, and eventually Aragon was found unconscious, having taken an overdose of sleeping pills. He was resuscitated and there was no serious damage done, but he swore that if he remained near Nancy he would try and kill himself again. Leaving for Paris as soon as he was fit, he composed a heartbroken reproach in his 'Poème à crier dans les ruines'.

Aragon was venomous in his despair: 'Let us spit if you want/ On what we have loved together.' But in Venice Nancy appeared almost indifferent to his loss. She had recently counselled the writer Richard Aldington through some emotional difficulties with the advice: 'Never mind darling you'll [just] solve those complications by getting into others.'[47] This was what she'd always done herself and it was what she did now. While Aragon grieved in Paris she was already moving on, towards the next set of complications, the next lover and the next project.

September drew in, and as Venice began to empty Nancy fell into a routine of going with her cousin Edward Cunard for evening drinks in St Marks Square. She'd taken a fancy to the black jazz quartet playing at the Hotel Luna, and one night, as the musicians were packing up to leave, she invited them to her table for a drink. It was the pianist who most interested her, a man in his late thirties, tall, broad-shouldered and neatly dressed. His round face had a natural sweetness, but there was a craggy authority in his wide cheekbones. His name was Henry Crowder, and over the next few weeks Nancy would fall in love with him – attracted as much by the difficulties he had overcome in his life as for his looks, personality and talent.

Henry had grown up in a poor but devout family in Georgia, learning his music in the church choir and playing piano for the YMCA. Like Josephine Baker he had yearned to live in a world where colour would not define him, and when he left home, he worked his way up to the more liberal cities of the north, washing dishes, taking handyman's jobs and playing piano in a brothel. By the time America entered the war Henry had made a new life for himself – he was a married man, a father and a respected name on the Washington jazz scene.

The war, however, brought a run of bad luck. With many of America's musicians drafted to Europe, the jazz business went into recession, and by 1918 Henry was unemployed and his marriage virtually over. He drifted between contracts in Chicago and New York, until finally his luck changed and the new band in which he was playing, Eddie South and his Alabamians, were offered the chance to perform in Europe.

To Henry, the peeling, listing grandeur of Venice was a revelation, as were the people he observed around the city. One woman who came regularly to drink at the Luna he regarded as most 'peculiar [and] striking'. Normally Henry tended to distance himself from the bawdy comments made by the other band members about the women who listened to them play. But when they were invited to drink at Nancy's table, he was fascinated by her appearance, 'so thin, so white and so fragile', and by the articulate passion with which she spoke to him about his music.[48] When she invited him to dinner and began writing him romantic letters, he had no power to resist. As he later acknowledged, he became 'infatuated beyond all reason'.[49]

Even so, becoming Nancy's lover was a profoundly difficult step for Henry. Down in Georgia a black man could be lynched for being with a white woman. Even in the more tolerant cities of Chicago and Washington, where he had experimented with a couple of affairs, he felt as though he were 'running with the devil'. The taboos of race ran deep, and in one early letter to Nancy he tried to explain the combination of terror and euphoria that their relationship induced in him: 'It seems that I am bridging centuries in writing to you.'[50]

In Europe, too, those taboos had power. Nancy chose to linger in Venice after the summer crowd had departed, and she and Henry were much more exposed when they were out together in public. Children shrieked insults at Henry's black skin; knots of black-shirted fascists watched them closely. Even at the hotel where Henry was lodging, the formerly accommodating proprietor turned hostile, clearly wanting to be rid of him. This kind of bigotry was familiar to Henry; he knew how to blank those looks and jeers, to sheer away from provoking trouble. What, for him, was a far more troubling issue was predicting how Nancy's attitude would develop. His experience of other racially mixed relationships had taught him that the black man always ended up subservient to the white woman; they could never be equal. He had barely been Nancy's lover for a fortnight before it became clear that, with her, it would be no different.

Nancy genuinely adored Henry – that much was evident to her friends when the two of them returned to Paris in October. He was unlike anyone she knew, his stories and opinions so interesting to her that she would always claim he was the one man who never bored her. Henry also possessed a touching natural gravitas and the strength to absorb her emotional storms. When Janet Flanner met Henry one day with bruises on his face, inflicted by Nancy's fist and bangles, he mildly waved aside her concern: 'Just braceletwork, Miss Janet.'[51] Above all, Nancy loved Henry because he was black and a musician. She felt it was a rare privilege to sit alone with him as he improvised at the piano, conjuring jazz out of the keyboard just for her.* She felt she had been granted a special, insider status as he introduced her to the other black artists with whom he was now playing at the Plantation club and Le Boeuf sur le Toit.

Yet however much Nancy delighted in Henry and Henry's world, she had no intention of changing, and shortly after arriving in Paris she started seeing Aragon again. She was piqued that he had found a new lover, a tiny red-headed Russian called Elsa Triolet, whom he would eventually marry, and it brought back a rush of her own feeling for him. Triolet was bewildered by the ease with which Nancy reeled Aragon back to her, the combination of 'tenderness and snake-like power' he seemed unable to withstand. After every meeting Aragon would return 'in pieces', yet he always went back for more.[52]

Henry, even less accustomed to such games, was similarly bewildered. But what hurt him more was Nancy's new affair with his friend Mike, the cockily handsome banjo player in the Alabamians. Everyone was gossiping. Richard Aldington smirked that black musicians had now become Nancy's 'stronger sexual drug': that she'd adopted the *culte des nègres* and was 'no longer interested in poor white trash'.[53]

For Henry, this very public cuckolding marked the end of his unconditional infatuation with Nancy. However, he loved her

---

* In some ways Nancy overestimated Henry's talent. In 1930 she persuaded him to compose the music for a series of poems written by herself and others, which she published. Henry, however, had only ever aspired to improvising in clubs, and after he left Nancy and returned to America, he gave up the piano completely.

sufficiently and was pragmatic enough to accommodate himself to this new state of affairs. He realized that Nancy would always be more powerful than him, that he would always be 'a pawn upon her chessboard of life',[54] but he believed that he could also choose to play the game on his terms. His motive for coming to Europe had been to enrich himself, culturally as well as financially, and it was clear that Nancy's breadth of experience and 'independence of thought' were the best education he could hope for. Finally, he accepted that it was a privilege to be part of her life, for the 'innumerable new things' she could show him.[55]

He didn't like everything he saw, though. Oliver Messel, arriving at a party with his 'eyelashes done in silver' disgusted him, and at first he was deeply affronted by Janet and Solita's lesbian relationship, which offended every principle of his Baptist upbringing. Yet Henry's inquisitiveness and intelligence were stronger than his prejudice; he grew fond of Janet and Solita, he learned how to flirt safely with the queers. And as Nancy took him round Paris he began to feel himself a figure of interest, even of fame.

For a couple of months the relationship remained in this state of equilibrium. But just before Christmas, Henry and the Alabamians were put out of work after Mike, the banjo player, was thrown into jail following a brawl with another musician that had escalated into a gunfight. New gigs were hard to find in the winter season, and Nancy suggested that Henry come down to Réanville, where she was continuing to work for half the week at The Hours Press. At first it was almost idyllic: during the evenings Henry played piano while Nancy read and did her accounts; during the days he helped work the press and made repairs to the house. But being at Nancy's beck and call, as well as being financially dependent on the small assistant's wages she paid him, made his situation increasingly uncomfortable.

Nancy could be tactless and very cruel about money. She had grown up in a world where wealth was equivalent to status, and despite her passionately held egalitarian theories, she found it hard to respect Henry, who had nothing. Despite the guilt she felt at living off her family's capital, she inherited Maud's tendency to use money as a weapon and means of control. In Réanville, if Henry angered her by making a mistake at the press, or simply inflamed her with his imperturbably patient manner, she accused him with breathtaking unfairness of being too lazy to go out and earn a proper living.

This was one of the few insults that could get a rise out of Henry, who was acutely sensitive to any suggestion that he was Nancy's gigolo. It made him feel his situation at Réanville was untenable in every way, not only financially but sexually (the knowing look on the face of Nancy's driver spoke insolent volumes of the casual fling she had previously had with him). By the spring he could stand the atmosphere no longer and moved back to the city, where he found a job playing piano at the Bateau Ivre nightclub.

Nancy, too, was keen to leave Réanville. She was tiring of the weekly commute to Paris and believed she could secure more business for the press if she relocated it to the city. She had already found a suitable shop and workroom at 15 rue Gueneguad, and over the spring and early summer she transported the whole of The Hours' operations there. In commercial terms it was a clever move: the shop window and interior were strikingly dressed with Miro paintings, Brazilian headdresses and choice African art, and Nancy's sales figures rose as a result. However, now that she was living in the city, without the relative calm of her interludes at Réanville, her health began to suffer.

As Harold Acton observed, she was working and playing like a woman possessed: 'The clock did not exist for her: in town she dashed in and out of taxis, clutching an attaché case crammed with letters manifestoes, estimates, circulars and her latest African bangle . . . A snack now and then but seldom a regular meal; she looked famished and quenched her hunger with harsh white wine and gusty talk.'[56] She was ricocheting between affairs, the latest of which was with another black piano player called Dan. Richard Aldington thought she was behaving atrociously, even by her standards: 'She lacks not only elemental common sense but the capacity to love with any purpose, continuity, tenderness.' Henry, too, was reaching the limits of his patience; increasingly mortified by a sense that people were 'laughing at me and considering me a fool', he was threatening to return to America.[57]

Yet as hard as Nancy seemed to be pushing Henry away from her, she did not want to let him go. Later she would claim that he was the man she had loved most, his sweetness and humour, his music and physical attraction retained their power however much she abused them. She saw him as both an artist and a noble savage. And by the end of 1929 he had begun to embody something even more necessary, an ideological cause and a political commitment. At first Nancy's fascination with Henry's colour had centred on her romance with jazz and African art. She had badgered him to travel with her to Africa to discover his cultural roots, and had been disappointed to discover how little he shared her curiosity. Partly, he'd foreseen the world of trouble that would await a black man and white woman travelling around Africa together, but as he pointed out to Nancy, that aspect of his heritage meant little to him: 'I *ain't* African, I'm *American*.'[58]

It was only gradually that Nancy came round to appreciating what being a black American meant. During the winter that she and Henry spent in Réanville, she began to question him closely about his past, and as he explained to her in detail about segregation, race riots and the re-emergent Ku Klux Klan, she felt a huge and intoxicating anger. It was from this point on that all the vague political sympathies she'd held in the past began to focus on Henry and the injustice meted out to his race.

She was now alert to every narrowed, hateful glance shot at Henry by the redneck American tourists who seemed to be everywhere in Paris in the late 1920s. She was mortified by the ignorance that even her close friends displayed about what it was like to be black. And by the summer of 1930 she had come up with her own means of restitution. She planned to publish an anthology of black art and history that would not only open the world's eyes to the richness of black culture, but would chart the terrible centuries of persecution that blacks had suffered.

Negro became a heroic obsession, eclipsing all of Nancy's interest in The Hours, which she abandoned in 1931. It absorbed her energy and much of her money as she researched and commissioned the essays, stories, poetry, music and photographs that would fill its eight hundred and fifty pages. When the project took her to New York, the press portrayed her as a depraved English lady with a taste for black flesh; she received hate mail accusing her of being a 'hoor' and a 'nigger fucker'. One threat came with the signature of the Klan, 'I hope that when you try to free the lousy niggers down in Alabama the white people will lynch you.'⁵⁹

Negro also had the effect of alienating Nancy from many of her friends, and it dealt the final, fatal blow to her relationship with Maud. Nancy had, for a while, attempted to keep Henry a secret from her mother, knowing the exhausting and humiliating fuss that would inevitably ensue. However, Maud had finally been forced to confront the gossip circulating about her daughter when her old friend and rival Margot Asquith had enquired loudly after Nancy at a lunch party, 'What is it now – drink, drugs or niggers?'⁶⁰

Margot's jibe was humiliating, but the timing was even worse: Nancy was about to arrive in London, with Henry in tow. She was trying to organize a private screening of the surrealist film *L'Age d'Or*, which had been banned in Paris as both blasphemous and obscene. To Maud, the knowledge that her daughter would be walking openly around London with a negro lover was intolerably shaming, and she hired private detectives to shadow the couple and find evidence of anything that might get Henry arrested and deported. Maud also set in motion a campaign of harassment, including anonymous phone calls being made to Rudolf Stulik, who had rented rooms to Nancy and Henry at the Tower, threatening him with jail unless the latter was evicted.

Nancy was sickened by her mother's behaviour, and although Henry tried to calm the situation, begging Nancy not to quarrel on his account, she was beyond any possibility of compromise. The febrile energy with which she had been working and partying in Paris now channelled into this single issue, and it was from this moment that she began, obdurately, to see the world solely in terms of those who were with her and those who were not.

Friends were urged to take sides. After she returned to Paris in January 1931, she wrote an emotional letter to George Moore, begging for his support and demanding to know 'how YOU feel'. Moore, aged seventy-nine, couldn't find it in his heart to make a choice between the two women he had loved for so long, and refrained from replying. Nancy's agitation intensified when she heard intimations that Maud was planning to disinherit her. It would be a disaster, not only curtailing her lifestyle, but making it impossible for her to continue with *Negro*. In truth, Maud was merely planning to reduce Nancy's allowance, blaming the recent collapse of the American markets, but Nancy was already consumed by righteous anger. To punish Maud, she wrote two vitriolic essays, both directly aimed at her.

The first was a short, satirical squib, attacking the stiff-upper-lipped bigotry of the British upper classes, and it concentrated most of its poison in the title, 'Does Anyone Know Any Negros?' – a direct quote from Maud.* The second, however, entitled 'Black Man and White Ladyship', was a devastating personal attack. Ostensibly this eleven-page pamphlet was a history of institutionalized racism, but Nancy had devoted nearly a third of it to a list of her mother's perceived sins: her snobbery, her extravagance, her intellectual timidity and her prejudice.

Nancy's hatred coursed through the essay, relentlessly mocking 'her Ladyship's snobbery': 'If a thing is *done* she will, with a few negligible exceptions, do it'; her extravagance: 'I have not the faintest idea how much I spend on clothes every year. It may run into thousands';[61] the vapid nature of her social life: 'She is so alone – between little lunches of sixteen, a few callers at tea and two or three invitations per night'.[62] The pamphlet was sent out, not only to her own friends but to all of her mother's, including,

---

* It was published in *Crisis* magazine, September 1931.

allegedly, the Prince of Wales. It horrified almost everyone who read it. Janet and Solita squirmed, Henry thought it 'atrocious' and the general feeling was that Nancy could only be excused by the fact that her health was in such a bad state. Brian Howard, who had holidayed with her and Henry in February that year, had thought she was close to becoming unhinged, even then: 'She talked so much, seemed unable to stop. The whispery, disjointed voice goes on and on. A kind of sober drunkenness. Drinking is now fatal to her.' Howard also noted that she was 'bickering' constantly with 'the infinitely patient, stupid Henry', whose impassivity was almost as intolerable to witness as Nancy's agitation.[63]

In fact, Henry wasn't so much patient as numbed: 'My reaction . . . was an absolute blank,'[64] he wrote. He knew now that Nancy was ill, possibly close to a breakdown, and even though he didn't fully break off their relationship until 1935, he had almost given up believing he could help her. Even Maud understood that Nancy was barely answerable for her actions. With careful restraint she refused to react to the insults her daughter had published, commenting only that 'one can always forgive anyone who is ill'.[65]

Nancy, however, did not want to be forgiven. Publishing 'Black Man and White Ladyship' had been a deliberate act of matricide, killing off her relationship with Maud. She never saw her mother again and refused even write to her, putting her away with the rest of her past: the unhappy, privileged limbo of her childhood, the burnt-out excesses of the war, the flapper frivolity of Charleston lessons and of Parisian café chatter. Thin-skinned and angry, Nancy believed the time for playing was over. Others might have considered her to be the most stylish muse of the 1920s, but she herself was turning her face towards a new decade – and a new life of political activism.

Chapter Ten

ZELDA

When Zelda and Scott came to Paris in May 1924, they were as hopeful for new beginnings as Nancy had been four years earlier. Sunshine filtered through late-blooming horse chestnuts, and lovers drank wine in pavement cafés as if Prohibition had never been invented. With the exchange rate at nineteen francs to the dollar and rising, the Fitzgeralds felt themselves to be rich and free. As they walked together down the Champs-Elysées, Scott flourished a jaunty silver-headed cane and Zelda wore a simple blue frock of her own design. She called it her Jeanne d'Arc dress.

They had arrived with an introduction to an American couple said to know everybody in Paris. Sara and Gerald Murphy had been among the first wave of artists and intellectuals to flee the aggressive materialism of post-war America: the 'lurid billboards' and the 'automobiles that swarm[ed] everywhere like vermin.'[1] During their three years in France they had formed a web of connections that stretched from cultural grandees like Picasso and Stravinsky to young expatriates like Ernest Hemingway. And as soon as Zelda met the Murphys she acknowledged them as fellow thoroughbreds. Sara's creamy prettiness was edged by a confident, clever chic, yet she was also a woman who seemed to hold her life in enviable balance. She and Gerald had come to Paris to paint, taking lessons with the Russian futurist Natalia

Goncharova, yet Sara still had time to be an easy, affectionate mother to her three children, and to maintain an apparently unruffled marriage.

Sara, and Sara's Paris, offered a glimpse of how Zelda's own doubt-strewn life might gain an equivalent shape. But the plan was not to stay in the city, not yet. Scott needed to finish his novel, and they had agreed to give themselves a recuperative period of calm, somewhere inexpensive by the sea. The Murphys suggested the Mediterranean coast, where they themselves would be holidaying. Inspired by the promise of an unspoilt Provençal landscape and a warm turquoise sea, Scott and Zelda took the long train ride south with Scottie, their new British nanny Lillian Maddock, and seventeen trunks packed with their former American life.*

They ended up in Sainte-Raphaël, a town of whitewashed walls and terracotta roofs, where they found a large villa to rent for just $79 a month. Not only was the Villa Marie cheap by American standards,† it seemed to Zelda and Scott a foothold in paradise. Fragrant with lemon trees and jasmine, and shaded by dark umbrella pines, it was perched high on olive-planted terraces, its blue and white tiled balconies giving wide views of the sea. As soon as they arrived Zelda went shopping for beach umbrellas, espadrilles and bathing suits: she gave herself up to a trance of pleasure, swimming and tanning herself, and, as she later wrote, it seemed that she and Scott had achieved the most lucky of escapes: 'Oh we are going to be so happy away from all the things that almost got us.'[2]

---

* The French Riviera had not yet become the spoilt summer playground of the rich. Its traditional season was late winter and early spring, when people came to take the sea air and, like Tamara's grandmother, to gamble at the casinos. The Murphys themselves had been told about the area by Cole Porter, whom Gerald knew from their student years at Yale and who was well known for his 'great originality in finding new places'.
† In *The Great Gatsby*, the narrator Nick Carraway pays $80 a month for the 'simple cottage' that huddles in the shadow of Gatsby's enormous mansion – itself boasting a rental price of $15,000.

For Scott certainly, this summer felt like a critical last chance. He was desperate to complete the great novel he knew was inside him: 'A purely creative work,' he assured his editor Max Perkins, 'not trashy imaginings as in my stories but the sustained imagination of a sincere and radiant world.'[3] In some ways *The Great Gatsby* was turning into another fictional re-working of the Fitzgeralds' lives, with Daisy Buchanan a richer, sillier, but still 'thrilling' version of Zelda, and Jay Gatsby, a farm boy turned millionaire who lived by Scott's faith in the necessary magic of illusions: 'Illusions that give such colour to the world that you don't care whether things are true or false.'[4] But if the origins of *The Great Gatsby* were personal, Scott's focus was widening, moving towards the portrayal of a larger collective illusion, the American dream.

Gatsby lived the jazz age with more extravagance than any of Scott's other heroes. His wealth was an art deco fantasy of elaborate parties, 'yellow cocktail music', expensive clothes and cars.[5] The nickel and cream opulence of his Rolls-Royce 'terraced with a labyrinth of wind-shields that mirrored a dozen suns' was a symbol of the shining absurdity of his life.[6] But rather than merely glamorizing that fantasy, Scott presented it as an exquisite bubble, floating on the dirt and corruption of modern American capitalism. As a writer, his vision was maturing. He could see that Gatsby's desperate wish to reclaim his perfect love with Daisy was part of the bright, precarious dream of his own generation, a dream that confused the ownership of beautiful things with happiness and freedom.*

Scott knew very well, too, what damage that confusion had wreaked on him and Zelda. And for several weeks at Villa Marie he tried to maintain a simple, sober and productive routine; writing to his editor Max Perkins, that he was determined to recapture the purity of his artistic conscience. He could feel he

---

* His ideas were partly formed by Oswald Spengler's *The Decline of the West* and its thesis of a modern Faustian culture driven by the twin engines of yearning and entitlement.

was writing well, symbolism and description, romance and irony all tightly pitched. Yet for Zelda, Scott's artistic conscience soon began to feel like very dull company. 'What'll we *do* ... with ourselves,' she complained, as one heat-hazed day blurred into the next.[7] Servants took care of the villa, Nanny Maddock took care of Scottie and, although Zelda tried to occupy herself, improving her French by reading a Raymond Radiguet novel, she grew very bored.

She also missed having an audience, and her tone was only half ironic when she wrote to Edmund Wilson that 'everything would be perfect if there was somebody here who would be sure to spread the tale of our idyllic existence around New York'.[8] Although the Murphys had recently arrived in the area, they were staying further along the coast at Antibes. By the time Zelda struck up a friendship with some French aviators stationed at a nearby air base in Fréjus, she had become desperate not only for company, but for the admiring gaze of men.

The aviators were around almost every day, and Zelda and Scott fell into a routine of standing them dinner at a local restaurant, then drinking and gambling along the seafront bars and casino. Scott enjoyed their conversation, while for Zelda it felt like a return to the old Montgomery days, when she'd been so pleasantly surrounded by handsome young men in uniforms, all competing for her attention.

Her favourite was Edouard Jozan. Scott rarely danced any-more, but Edouard partnered her with an easy, athlete's grace; during the day he took her for drives along the winding moun-tain roads or lazed with her on the beach, telling her the local gossip in his attractively slanted English. In contrast to Scott, with his book deadlines and bothers about money, Edouard's company was delightfully relaxing. And in the heat and intimacy of their long hours together, Zelda began to find him very attractive.

Years later, when she incorporated memories of Edouard into her fiction, she wrote about him with the erotic recall of a lover: his dark olive skin 'smelling of the sun and the sea ... the blades of his bones carving her own',[9] and it's very probable that in real life, too, the friendship became sexual. Scott's own suspicions may have been aroused when Edouard, in a gallant tribute to Zelda, flew aerial stunts in his plane high above the Villa Marie. He could not have known what memories he was stirring of Scott's former rivals in Montgomery, but they precipitated the ugliest fight so far in the Fitzgeralds' marriage. On 16 July Scott wrote grimly in his ledger, 'Big Crisis,' and from that point on Zelda and Edouard never met up with each other again.

Edouard himself would always maintain that his friendship with Zelda was innocent, but he seems to have been protecting either her reputation or his own. Zelda herself would refer to their relationship explicitly as a 'love affair',[10] and cite it as one of the profound emotional experiences of her life. Scott would claim that she had gone as far as to ask him for a divorce, and that he had felt such murderous anger that he had locked Zelda in her room at the Villa Marie, taunting her to wait there until Edouard came to claim her like a man.

But if there are conflicting accounts of the affair, the truth remained that Zelda and Scott had long reached the point where their marriage depended on these quarrels for cathartic release. By August Scott was able to write in his ledger, 'Zelda and I close together.' Yet in comparison to their previous rows, this crisis was not so easily contained. With Edouard, Zelda had threatened more of a betrayal than with any of her other flirtations, while Scott had said things that lodged more deeply than any of his former accusations. Later he acknowledged that his optimism had been premature: 'I knew something had happened that could never be repaired.'[11]

Zelda, although outwardly calm for the rest of the summer, manifested odd, disturbing tics of emotion. Gilbert and Amanda Seldes came to stay at Villa Marie for a few days and were unnerved by the way that, during the drive to the beach, she always asked Scott for a cigarette at the exact point where the road curved into a dangerously precipitous bend, as though she were deliberately distracting Scott in order to court danger.

When Sara and Gerald Murphy met up with the Fitzgeralds they sensed a 'spooky' reserve of feeling in Zelda's eyes. Or they thought they did, given what happened in early September when they were woken up in the night by Scott, 'green faced, holding a candle, trembling', and afraid that Zelda had taken an overdose of sleeping pills. When they got to Zelda, she was not yet unconscious but she was in a frighteningly altered state. As Sara fed her sips of olive oil, trying to get her to vomit up the pills, Zelda mumbled incoherent protests, 'Don't make me take that, please. If you drink too much oil you turn into a Jew.'[12]

It's possible that the Murphys' chronology was a year out, as some evidence suggests that this episode occurred the following year.* It's also very unlikely that Zelda took a fatal dose, as she had a history of scaring both Scott and herself with melodramatic gestures. But there is no doubt that that summer marked a miserable falling away of the bright resolve with which Zelda and Scott had first arrived in Europe.

By October, the heat had gone out of the sun and the Fitzgeralds prepared to travel down to Rome, where the lira was even cheaper than the franc. Despite their best economizing intentions, the summer had been bewilderingly expensive: the servants had fiddled the accounts (taking advantage of their poor grasp of French); the cheap price of alcohol along the seafront bars had spurred Scott to reckless generosity, standing drinks for everyone when the mood took him. He was shocked by his continuing inability to budget, and a few months later he admitted the depth of his panic to Max Perkins: 'I can't reduce our scale of living and I can't stand this financial insecurity.'[13] If *Gatsby* turned out to be a failure, Scott swore he would have to abandon serious fiction for a scriptwriting career in Hollywood.

---

* Zelda's biographer Sally Cline points out that the Murphys' hotel was fifty kilometres away from the Villa Marie, which makes the events of that night problematic, unless they all four happened to be staying the night in the same place. In 1925 the two couples were geographically closer, and it was in August that year that Scott entered the brief note in his ledger, 'Zelda drugged.'

Rome would, of course, be another change of scene, holding out the promise of yet another fresh start. But while Zelda spent her first few days as a contented tourist, taking herself off on solitary walks around the city, enjoying the romantic pleasure of getting 'lost between centuries in the Roman dusk', an unusually difficult winter lay ahead.[14] She had begun to suffer from recurrent pelvic infections, telling her doctors that she had got sick 'from trying to have more children', which suggests she may have had a miscarriage, and she was anxious about her chances of having another viable pregnancy. Even before coming to Europe she and Scott had talked about giving Scottie a brother or sister. Although Zelda had been exhausted and depressed by early motherhood, Scottie had grown into a charming toddler. The two or three hours a day that Zelda spent alone with her were now a delight to her, a shared world of simple pleasures: telling stories, drawing pictures and inventing games of make-believe.

She was ready to try for another baby, but when she was admitted to hospital for investigative surgery, the findings were bad. The infections had damaged one of her ovaries and Zelda's chances of conceiving again were significantly reduced. In the past her body had rarely failed her, and this setback not only distressed her but made her feel physically insecure. Scott was not in much of a mood to comfort her either: their hotel room in Rome was damp, a bout of flu had left him with a persistent cough, and he was fretting over the proofs of his novel. Zelda found some distraction in an American journalist attached to the film crew shooting Roman scenes for Fred Niblo's *Ben-Hur*, but it was only a reflex flirtation. When Scott retaliated with the actress Carmel Myers, the quarrels that ensued were tedious, spiritless affairs that did little to disperse the tension.

They were still irritable and unwell in February the following year, when they packed up to move further south to the island of Capri. But the island's vertiginous rocky landscape and its improbable wealth of semi-tropical shrubs and flowers acted as a tonic: Zelda felt the dank claustrophobia of the Roman winter lift. She also encountered Romaine Brooks, the friend and former lover of Natalie Barney, who was wintering on Capri among a group of female artists. Zelda was interested to see this group of women, all creatively absorbed in a life without men, and as she began to spend time with them, she accepted their encouragement to start painting herself. It was a novel experience for her, losing hours each day in the study of shifting light and sea, of rock formations and flowers, but also detaching herself Scott and the complications of their marriage.

Scott, however, hated Capri. He felt sidelined by Zelda's new hobby and her new friends; he grumbled hatefully to Max Perkins that the island, historically a haven for male, as well as female homosexuals, was 'full of fairies'.*[15] But the foulness of his mood was primarily due to writer's nerves. He genuinely believed that *Gatsby* was his best novel yet: 'My book has something extraordinary about it,' he wrote to John Peal Bishop. 'I want to be extravagantly admired again.'[16] Yet until it was published and the reviews came out, Scott's head buzzed with a white noise of worry and self-doubt.

Later he would recall that period on Capri as a time when 'there seemed to be nothing left of happiness in the world anywhere I looked'. In April, however, just as he and Zelda were preparing to return to Paris, he assured Bishop that the two of them were 'enormously in love'.[17] There were still days, even weeks, when they could believe in the uniqueness of their bond, when Scott, for Zelda, was the one person who could give words to her deepest feelings, and when Zelda, for Scott, was the core not only of his life but of his writing.

Even Max Perkins, his staunch and sympathetic editor, did not understand his work as Zelda did. In Rome, when Scott had been working on the final edit of *Gatsby*, it had been her mem-

---

* Nancy's friend, the writer Norman Douglas, was also wintering on Capri. He lived principally in Italy, having fled England in 1916, when he was charged for sexual assault on a boy. He, too, was surrounded by a colony of friends and admirers, many of them homosexual.

ories on which he drew to finesse descriptions of the landscape, and inhabitants of Great Neck, and to sift the emotional truth of his dialogue. When Max Perkins commented that he could not fully 'see' Jay Gatsby yet, it was Zelda who prompted Scott's imagination by drawing sketch after sketch of Gatsby until she had caught the exact cast of his features and expression. It was Zelda, too, who helped decide on the title, rejecting Scott's wordier and far more clumsy alternatives, like *The High Bouncing Lover*. His dedication – 'Once again to Zelda' – was more than a sentimental tribute.

The first reactions to *Gatsby* were disappointing, however, with poor sales that Perkins blamed on its brevity. But then came the 'extravagant' admiration. T.S. Eliot praised the novel as 'the first step that American fiction has taken since Henry James'; Gilbert Seldes's review in *The Dial* argued that Scott's talent had 'gone soaring in beautiful flight' leaving behind 'everything dubious and tricky in his early work'.[18] In June the stage rights were sold, and although Scott made a point of being modest in public, in private he was jubilant, allowing himself to believe that he had become 'the biggest man in the profession'.[19]

This was the mood in which Zelda loved him best, optimistic, buoyant and lucky. It was also the mood in which the gears of their public image clicked back into beautiful efficiency. To Sara and Gerald Murphy they seemed 'flawless' on their return to Paris. Zelda, thinner from her recent illness, looked lovely in the new season's sheer dresses. She wore them in 'her own personal style', recalled Sara, favouring reds and hot pinks that set off her dark blonde hair. But essentially Zelda's beauty was 'all in her eyes', Gerald thought; 'she had an outstanding gaze, one doesn't find it often in women, perfectly level and head on. If she looked like anything it was an American Indian'.[20]

Gerald thought Scott almost as rare: his 'head was so fine, really unbelievably handsome'.[21] And, along with the aura of their beauty, the Fitzgeralds set out to impress Paris with the perfection of their marriage. On a shared instinct they had re-written their recent troubled past, recasting Edouard as a tragic suicide whose love for Zelda had been so passionate, yet so unrequited that he had killed himself. Of course he had not. But to those who listened to the Fitzgeralds, the only apparent flaw in their story was the frequency and intensity with which they seemed to need to tell it.

One couple who heard it several times were Ernest and Hadley Hemingway. When they first met Scott and Zelda, the Hemingways had seen no reason to probe beyond their surface image – Scott the successful novelist and Zelda the exceptional beauty. Ernest admitted that Zelda's 'dark gold hair . . . hawk's eyes . . . clear and calm . . . and light . . . long "nigger legs"' had aroused him to an erotic dream.[22] But he and Hadley soon began to sense something strangely theatrical in the way the Fitzgeralds kept returning to Edouard's story, Zelda looking 'beautiful' and 'solemn', Scott 'pale and distressed'. 'It was one of their acts together,' Hadley recalled. 'Somehow it struck me as something that gave her status.'[23]

But to others, the Fitzgeralds seemed to be celebrating their arrival in Paris, and Scott's success with *Gatsby*, in high careless style. They jazzed in Montmartre, taking Charleston lessons from Bricktop; they drank at the Dingo, the all-night American bar on rue Delambre whose bartender Jimmy Charter claimed to mix every known cocktail, a smile spread like butter over his broad boxer's face. It was said you could always be certain of meeting someone you knew at Dingo's, either on their way to a party or on their way back home. To Sara Murphy the whole city 'was like a great fair . . . you loved your friends and you wanted to see them every day',[24] and that was how it seemed to the Fitzgeralds, too. As Scott recorded, 1924 was the 'summer of 1000 parties'.

Through Ernest Hemingway, they were introduced to the key Left Bank institution, Getrude Stein's salon at rue de Fleurus. Scott revelled in the occasion: Stein praised *Gatsby* and was almost coquettish in her attentiveness. Zelda, however, hated it. Just like Tamara, she was shooed off briskly to sit in the wives' corner and drink tea with Alice Toklas, while Stein talked serious art with the men. This kind of sexual apartheid was unknown to Zelda (unless she herself was enforcing it) and she took profound offence. Ignoring the proffered tea, she stalked off to study the paintings that hung on Stein's walls and afterwards scoffed to Scott that what she'd overheard of their hostess's famous literary conversation had been 'sententious gibberish'.*[25]

Zelda sought alternative cultural experiences with Sara, who took her shopping for clothes, exploring the maze of little Left Bank art galleries, and to performances of Diaghilev's Ballets Russes. With Sara, too, she was taken to Nathalie Barney's salon, where she discovered that women were far more prized than men. When Zelda had been growing up in Montgomery, she had only ever been aware of women holding power in the home or on the dance floor. At rue Jacob, however, the female writers, painters and actors were all apparently successful, all apparently supportive of one another. Partly on their inspiration Zelda enrolled for a second course of painting lessons. Although there was no room for her to put up an easel or create a mess of oil paints in their over-furnished rented apartment, she bought gouache and watercolours and commandeered the dining-room table to begin a series of studies for her own self-portrait.

Zelda was genuinely interested in carving out an independent space for herself, outside of her marriage and apart from Scott's writing. Yet even as she drew closer to Sara and her new painter friends, and even as she became genuinely absorbed in her art studies, she was motivated, in part, by resentment towards Scott and his new best friend. Ernest Hemingway was a man who lived up to his nicknames, Hem, Hemmy, the Champ. He was built like a sportsman, square across the jaw and shoulders, with a warm flush to his skin and a boyishly crooked smile. He boxed, he hunted, and the slight limp in his walk bore witness to the shrapnel wounds he'd suffered during war service in Italy. Even as an author he was a man's man: his stories of travel and

---

* When Scott was invited to have tea with Edith Wharton, who lived twelve miles outside Paris, Zelda refused to go, saying she had no interest in being patronized by another 'grande dame'.

bullfighting written at wine-stained tables in bars (unlike Scott, who preferred his own desk); his prose style stripped to the bare essentials of dialogue and action.

Scott always yearned for close male friendship, and he listened with a sense of fascinated privilege to Hemingway's stories of women and war. Despite his natural preference for cocktail lounges, Scott willingly accompanied his new friend on tours of the 'real' Paris, of working men's bars and neighbourhood *bals musettes*, where music from cracked accordions drifted from windows and the air smelled of sour wine. Everything Scott admired, however, Zelda reacted against. She felt crowded by Hemingway's physical swagger, she scorned his affectation of working-class tastes and she particularly resented the coarse way he spoke about women.

'All they talk about is sex,' she complained to Sara, 'sex plain, striped, mixed and fancy.'[26] While others were starting to regard Hemingway with awe, a tough, authentic literary voice, Zelda was convinced he was bogus. 'No one is as masculine as you pretend to be,' she later taunted him, and she dismissed his debut novel, *The Sun Also Rises*, as a fake parade of 'bull fighting bull slinging and bullsh[it] . . .'[27] Zelda hated that Scott was unable to see through Hemingway's machismo, and unable to see how bad an effect this new friendship was having on them both.* Ernest was famous for an ability to hold his alcohol, but after the long nights he and Scott spent at Dingo's – nights for which Scott almost always paid – Scott would wake up belligerent and frowsty. After a few weeks in Paris his face was acquiring the puffiness and greenish tinge that always signalled he was drinking beyond his limits. More upsettingly, he was beginning to parrot Ernest's views about wives, women and marriage.

Hemingway had decisive opinions on all three. Like the sur-

---

* Picasso also considered Hemingway's pose as a bullfighting 'aficionado' and left-wing radical to be fake. In 1959 he observed Hemingway salute the playing of the 'Marseillaise', then, when no one else joined in, stuffing his hand back into his pocket. *'Quel con,'* was Picasso's verdict.

realist comrades who baulked at Nancy's relationship with Aragon, he believed that a woman's essential role was to support the struggles of her husband. His own wife, Hadley, was exemplary in that regard. Intelligent and musically gifted, she was still happy to devote herself to the care of Ernest and their new baby, and to the diligent managing of their tiny income. But while Hadley rarely interrupted Ernest with complaints about the lack of hot water or electricity in their apartment, and while she was happy to dress in plain, sturdy clothes, Zelda appeared to be her greedy, flighty oppostie. Hemingway blamed her extravagance for the money worries that niggled at Scott, her volatile moods for his lack of concentration. And ignoring his own role in Scott's almost daily hangovers he believed that it was Zelda, resentful of her husband's superior talent, who deliberately provoked the drinking jags that kept him from his desk.

Later, in print, Hemingway would make the implacable judgement that Zelda had represented the 'terrible odds' against which Scott was forced to write.[28] In Paris, he arrived at that verdict more slowly, but his disapproval became apparent as, over the next eighteen months, he began to level criticisms at Zelda, especially at the company she kept. Hemingway detested Natalie Barney, partly because she was rich and partly because she was a lesbian. He had a visceral aversion to homosexuality, both male and female, and aside from Stein, whom he admired, he regarded the cultural influence of American sapphists as especially pernicious. For a complex variety of reasons he began intimating to Scott that it was dangerous for Zelda to spend so much time at rue Jacob. It might provoke gossip that she was a lesbian herself; it might even draw out tendencies of which she was unconscious. And both, he suggested, could do serious damage to Scott's reputation.

It's hard to know how much credence even Hemingway gave to this nonsense, but sex was becoming a sensitive issue between the Fitzgeralds, and Scott was susceptible to any suggestion that Zelda and he were not compatible. Over the last year alcohol and ill health had resulted in them making love less frequently, and while Hemingway drip-fed suggestions to Scott that Zelda might prefer women, Scott was also wounded by gossip that was circulating about his friendship with Hemingway. It was probably the poet Robert McAlmon (a friend of Nancy Cunard) who started the rumour that the two men were gay, and it might have been only a simple act of malice, but it took hold. Tamara de Lempicka was one of many who believed it; she claimed that Hemingway had always protested his masculinity too much, bracketing him with Gertrude Stein as two 'boring people who wanted to be what they were not – he wanted to be a woman and she wanted to be a man'.[29] When Zelda taunted Scott with the same rumour – 'Ernest is just a pansy with hair on his chest'[30] – he was violently angry, telling her she must never repeat such 'slanderous things'.

These were all slow-festering issues. But as Zelda later acknowledged, Paris was 'the perfect breeding ground for the germs of bitterness' between her and Scott.[31] It was an unnatural life they were leading, at home neither in the elegant, unreadable world of the native Parisians nor in the gossipy competitive expatriate community. As Zelda wrote in *Save Me the Waltz*, the two of them were unable 'to sense the beat of any other pulse half so exactly'[32] as the world they had left behind. Scott certainly never came to love Paris. Unable to speak good French or find much poetry in a city afflicted by bad plumbing and eccentric cooking, a part of him remained stubbornly homesick. Zelda, too, had flashes of feeling at a disadvantage. Her French was better than Scott's, but not fluent, and at times she felt excluded from the chatter about art, books and ideas that dominated every bar or party. Sara thought that Zelda could be extraordinarily intuitive in her perceptions, but that she had 'no intellectual talk' and could speak 'only of things that came into her mind at the time'.[33]

Already sensitive to her 'lack of accomplishment', Zelda's confidence was further undermined by a flare-up of the pelvic infection from which she had previously suffered.[34] By the time the summer heat began to bear down on the city, she was hugely relieved to leave Paris and head down to Antibes, where the

Murphys were overseeing the extensive re-modelling of their new holiday villa. The sea was a restorative, as always, and she spent happy days lazing in the sun with the Murphys, Gerald slender and charming in his elegant knitted sun cap, Sara laughingly stylish in her bathing suit and string of pearls, which she wore looped in a style she copied from the Duchess of Rutland on a visit to England before the war. Scott, who had just embarked on a new novel about expatriate life on the Riviera, was writing optimistically and well, and Zelda was finding contented occupation in the games of make-believe she invented for Scottie and the three Murphy children.

The nights, however, were more volatile. The Riviera was crowded that summer as fashionable Parisians took advantage of Le Train Bleu, the luxury express that ferried them south to the Mediterranean.* Staying close to the Murphys were Etienne de Beaumont, the cabaret singer Mistinguett, Jean Cocteau, Marie Laurencin, and the Picassos (the Fitzgeralds and the Picassos met several times but didn't much take to each other – Picasso found Zelda too strange). There were also American friends of the Murphys, such as Archie McLeish and his wife, and every evening a party inevitably began. Zelda was only half joking when she wrote to a friend back home, 'We went to Antibes to recuperate, but all we recooped [sic] was drinking hours. Now once again the straight and narrow path goes winding and wobbling before us.'35

Zelda's own self-assurance could wobble, too. One night, when she and Scott drove out with the Murphys to a restaurant in the mountains, they were seated at a table alongside Isadora Duncan and some friends. To Zelda's eyes the dancer looked middle-aged and raddled, thickening at her waist, her hair badly dyed. Scott, however, was enchanted and went over to pay homage, charmingly sitting at Duncan's feet and allowing her to run her

---

* This was becoming so iconic a feature of modern French life that in 1924 it inspired a new work by the Ballets Russes, with designs by Coco Chanel.

fingers through his hair. Flirtatiously and loudly, Duncan told
Scott the number of her hotel room. Yet what looked like a
harmless piece of theatre to everyone else was unbearable to
Zelda, who felt negated and eclipsed.

It was still key to Zelda's belief in their marriage that she and
Scott had privileged access to each other's moods. Gerald used
to watch for those moments when the two of them became
suddenly 'inseparable', tuned into a 'fantastic' emotion that was
theirs alone. For Scott to be so oblivious to her feelings in so
public a place was intolerable to Zelda. A steep flight of steps ran
from the restaurant terrace down to the sheer mountainside
beneath; without a word she stood on her chair and threw herself
down them into the darkness below. The restaurant was shocked
into silence. Yet when she reappeared, her dress torn and blood
running down her legs, she offered not a word of explanation.
When Sara tried to look after her, she shrugged dismissively.
Later the incident would be cited as evidence of Zelda's unravel-
ling mental state, but at the time her friends assumed it was just
one of her odder scenes.

The following few months were a period of limbo. Zelda was
desperate to find a cure for her chronic pelvic infection, and she
hadn't given up hope of conceiving another child. In the early
months of 1926, possibly following the advice of Diana Cooper,
she went to a curative spa in the Pyrenees, then in June she had
her appendix removed. By the time they returned to the Riviera
the following summer she was physically much fitter, but in every
other way she was restless. Scott seemed to have spent much of
the year either fretting over his new novel or drinking with
Hemingway. Meanwhile, she herself had written nothing since
she'd arrived in France, and had similarly allowed her painting
to lapse, too.

The Murphys, by contrast, radiated achievement. The Villa
America had been completed, and that summer everyone came
to admire it. The art deco interior was designed in an immacu-
late palette of black and silver, with a few brilliant splashes of

colour from the roses, camellias and oleander that were picked every morning from the gardens. Even the beach close to the villa was perfect, its sand cleared daily of seaweed, so the Murphys and their friends had only exquisite views as they sipped their late-morning sherry from crystal glasses and the children tumbled in and out of the waves.

Gerald had developed into a gifted artist* and along with Sara, had channelled his considerable talent into the orchestration of this Riviera fantasy. John Dos Passos, however, claimed it was too exhaustingly beautiful: 'I could only stand it for about four days. It was like trying to live in heaven. I had to get back down to earth.'[36] And to Scott and Zelda its perfection was a constant reproach to their own chaotic domestic world.

Scott was frustrated. He was trying to move into different territory with this new novel, using two recent murder cases to plot a sensational crime tale about a young film technician who is driven to murder his mother. But he couldn't find a voice for it, and as he faced yet another summer of blank pages and squandered hours, he condemned himself as 'futile, shameful, useless'.[37] In such a mood the marmoreal beauty of Villa America looked intolerably smug. One night, after too many gins and with his face set in a grimace of buffooning hilarity, Scott began lobbing Gerald's precious Venetian glasses over the terrace and onto the rocks below – a protest that was too much even for the tolerant Murphys who refused, for a while, to have him in the house.

Zelda, too, was strained. Sometimes her restlessness felt like a sickness, as she waited for something significant to happen, or for something significant to do. In a letter to Scott, Sara later remembered the barely suppressed ferocity that was evident in Zelda's gaze 'black – & impenetrable – but always full of

---

* Gerald would create a small, but acclaimed, body of work; his coolly objective still life *Razor*, composed of a safety razor, fountain pen and matchbox, was much admired by Léger, who regarded Gerald as the only American ex-patriot painter to respond in depth to the Parisian avant-garde.

impatience – at *something* – the world I think – she wasn't of it
anyhow – not really . . . She had an inward life & feelings that I
don't suppose any ever touched – not even you – She probably
thought terrible dangerous secret thoughts – & had pent-in
rebellions. Some of it showed through her eyes – but only to
those who loved her.'[38] Zelda partied as she always had, but that
summer her gaiety had a cracked quality. One evening she
pulled off her knickers while dancing and tossed them to the
theatre critic Alexander Woollcott, who was visiting from New
York. There was laughter, but it was nervous; the people watching Zelda were less amused than anxious about what she would
do next.

With Scott, their former intimacies were now increasingly
deflected into battles of will. Near the beach was a rocky outcrop
used for diving, and one day Zelda challenged him to a contest
in which they would each dive off higher and higher points, until
they reached the top, about thirty foot above the sea. Zelda took
her final dive without hesitation, knifing cleanly into the waves
below. Behind her, however, Scott trembled and looked sick,
and everyone watching was appalled by the risk she was inciting
them both to take. Afterwards, Sara remonstrated, but she
recalled that Zelda seemed lazily indifferent: 'But Sayra [sic] –
didn't you know, we don't believe in conservation,' she drawled,
as though their deaths could have no emotional significance,
representing nothing more than a dispersal of tissue and bone.[39]

The battles were played out in private, too. Several times Zelda
threw her belongings into a trunk and threatened to leave, yet
every time she had to have the trunk unpacked. She wasn't ready
to leave Scott, and the truth was she had nowhere to go and no
sense of what she could do. Later that year, when she was
interviewed by an American reporter about her views on modern
women, she could only reiterate her old flapper attitudes: 'I like
the jazz generation and hope my daughter's generation will be
jazzier. I think a woman gets more happiness out of being gay
. . . than out of a career that calls for hard work, intellectual
pessimism and loneliness. I don't want [Scottie] to be a genius. I

want her to be a flapper because flappers are brave and gay and beautiful.'[40]

Zelda was twenty-six, however, and she no longer felt as brave, gay and beautiful as when she had conquered Manhattan six years ago. In late 1926, when she and Scott returned to America, she encountered a new generation of women whose collective independence chilled her with an inkling of her own redundancy. Scott had been offered a contract to script a comedy for the actress Constance Talmadge, and despite his very vocal disdain for Hollywood he'd been happy to take it. He needed the money and he needed something to distract him from the difficulties he was experiencing with his novel.* Zelda, despite mixed feelings about leaving Scottie with her Fitzgerald grandparents, was interested to see first hand the glamour of the movie world.

They were installed in a luxury compound of villas, swimming pools and manicured gardens, and at first Zelda was enchanted by the ease of Hollywood, a life of sunshine and stucco, without the chatter of foreign voices or the smell of drains. She wrote long letters to Scottie about their occasional encounters with celebrities and about meeting Diana Cooper, a fond acquaintance of Sara's, who was performing in *The Miracle*. But once Scott knuckled down to his script, Zelda had too much time to herself, and she grew very conscious that Hollywood was filled with accomplished and ambitious young women, who put her own dependent idleness to shame.

They were a new breed of flapper, modelled on actors like Louise Brooks and Clara Bow. And while Zelda wanted to be dismissive of their uniformly scarlet lipstick and glossy bobs, of their manufactured sass and smart opinions, she couldn't ignore that so many of them were busily in control of their own destinies. 'Everybody here is very clever,' she wrote wistfully to

---

* Fitzgerald's first six years as a full-time writer had been prolific: three novels, a play, forty-one stories and twenty-seven pieces of journalism, but for this one script he would earn $3,500, rising to $12,000 if it was filmed.

Scottie, 'and can nearly all dance and sing and play and I feel very stupid.'[41]

One young starlet stood out, a lovely innocent-looking seventeen-year-old called Lois Moran, and when Scott became obviously infatuated with her, Zelda felt unusually threatened.* Scott had always flirted with other women; he was half in love with Sara. But Lois was so very young, and Zelda feared the light in his eyes when he talked to the girl about literature and life – it was exactly the way he had once talked to her. Even though Lois was carefully chaperoned by her mother, Zelda went on a pre-emptive attack. She mocked Lois's provincial girlishness, trying to shake Scott out of the stunned reverence he appeared to have for her. Scott's response, however, was a brutal contempt that she had never experienced from him. Lois might be young, he argued, but she was already making her way through talent and hard work. Zelda by comparison had achieved nothing.

This was an accusation that Zelda had already levelled at herself many times, but the sudden baring of Scott's scorn made her wince. Recently she had returned to designing her own dresses. Now, in her hurt and self-disgust, she threw every one of her creations into the bath and incinerated them. The episode could have precipitated another crisis, but although Scott shouted at Zelda, accusing her of being childishly melodramatic, she herself felt unexpectedly braced and purged. They left Hollywood shortly afterwards. Scott had made the mistake of assuming that writing for the screen would be easy, and the script he delivered was not worth filming. Rather than returning to France, however, he and Zelda agreed to look for another fresh start, this time in America's suburbs.

They found it in Wilmington, Delaware. Ellerslie House was an old colonial mansion of high square rooms and enormous gardens that ran down to the banks of the Delaware river. Its tranquillity

---

* Lois became the model for Rosemary Hoyt, the young starlet in *Tender is the Night*.

and spaciousness energized Zelda, who launched into a sustained burst of creative activity. She filled the rooms with new furniture, designed by herself and made up by local craftsmen; she painted screens and lampshades with scenes from the places where they had lived; she designed and built a doll's house for Scottie and produced an exquisite array of paper dolls, portraying characters from history and fairy tales. These dolls were her own personal folk art, beautiful and inventive, and as Zelda cut and painted she was determined to reapply herself to her adult art studies as well. Signing up for a course of painting lessons in nearby Philadelphia, she converted one of Ellerslie's many empty rooms into a studio, and embarked on her first oil painting.

For Scott, however, the space and silence of the house became an echo chamber of his anxieties: he was smoking incessantly and struggling to write. Yet to Zelda, his difficulties acted as a further spur to her confidence, and she now began to write seriously, as well as paint, and over the next few months produced four articles, three of which were bought by magazines. Her prose style had matured and in 'The Changing Beauty of Park Avenue'* her descriptions of Manhattan street life were a vivid synaesthesia of detail, 'crystalline shops, lying shallow against buildings . . . disciplined, cool smells . . . of hot motors and gusty dust – of violets and brass buttons'.[42]

Her attitudes had matured too. In the other three articles, 'Looking Back Eight Years', 'Who Can Fall in Love After Thirty'? and 'Paint and Powder', Zelda wrote about her old subjects – flappers and the jazz age – but with a more analytic edge. She surmised that her generation's gaiety was losing its sheen: that the powder compact and the marcel iron had not, after all, proved such wonderful novelties for women – the hours spent perfecting their flapper style had often been more of an oppression than a liberation.

But if Zelda's perspective was more adult, it was also being

---

* It was published in *Harper's Bazar* in January 1928.

coloured by a new and very disciplined vocation. She was more determined than ever to make some kind of artistic career for herself; but much as she cared about writing and painting, she was beginning to accept that they might not be fields in which she excelled. Her articles were still being published with Scott's name next to her own, and she knew she could never equal his reputation as a novelist, just as she knew her painting could never match the genius of Picasso, Goncharova, Léger and all the other artists she had met in Paris. What Zelda needed was a field of her own, and that summer she began to think about ballet.

Based in Philadelphia, a short train ride away, was a young dancer and teacher, Catherine Littlefield. Aged just twenty-one, she had taken over direction of the ballet chorus attached to the city's opera company, which she was transforming into a disciplined classical ensemble.* Even though Zelda was almost twenty-seven and hadn't taken a formal class since she was a teenager, she dared to believe that if Littlefield could achieve so much, so fast, she too might make equivalent progress. Everyone had always said she had a natural talent, and if she worked hard, she believed she might even now make herself 'a Pavlova, nothing less'.[43] She might even recapture the girl with whom Scott had first fallen in love, dancing at the Montgomery Country Club.

Zelda started to work as she had never worked in her life. In between her three weekly classes with Littlefield, she practised for hours every day, converting Ellerslie's large front room into a ballet studio, screwing a barre onto the wall and purchasing a full-length gilt mirror. Each day, as she sweated earnestly over her exercises, she cherished each precious increment of progress, the extra pliancy in her spine, the suppleness of her legs as she forced them higher into *battements*, *developés*, *attitudes*. Even when

---

* Philadelphia was one of the few cities in America with a long history of ballet activity, having several schools and a lively ballet audience. Littlefield both directed and performed with the ballet chorus attached to the opera, and in 1934 would elevate it to an independent ballet company – one of the first in America.

visitors came to the house, Zelda frequently continued to prac-
tise, working her body as she talked.

At times it seemed to her that she had never been so well.
Dancing demanded a clean, orderly space in her life, and it
demanded detachment. Zelda had always been dependent on
the admiring gaze of an audience; now she cared only for the
judgement of her mirror, studying herself critically against the
standards of her new art form.

But if Zelda felt liberated, Scott grew increasingly irritated.
The sound of her practice music, drifting self-righteously into
his study, grated on his nerves. He hated the intensity with which
Zelda gazed at herself in that 'Whorehouse Mirror', as if she had
forgotten he and Scottie existed,[44] and he was genuinely afraid
that Zelda was setting herself up for disappointment. Her expectations seemed to Scott to be crazily high. Even though he knew
nothing about ballet, he assumed that she must have started too
late to achieve the greatness of which she spoke.

In the autumn, Celia, the daughter of one of Scott's cousins
came to stay with them for a few days, and after taking her on a
sightseeing trip to New York it was agreed that they would break
their return journey in Philadelphia, so that Zelda could take
her class. Celia, who'd studied a little dance herself, asked if she
might come and watch, and Scott agreed to accompany her, both
curious and anxious to see how Zelda measured up in public. It
was far, far worse than he feared. Surrounded by younger
dancers, several of them more highly trained, Zelda appeared to
Scott to be struggling badly. Ever since he'd met her, Zelda had
always been the most striking woman in the room: in Littlefield's
studio, she looked shockingly stiff and exposed.

Celia was also disconcerted by Zelda's performance, and her
embarrassment was too much for Scott to bear. He left the studio
in search of a drink, and by the time they met up to catch the
train home he was weaving and staggering, barely coherent. To
Celia's surprise, however, Zelda seemed barely to notice Scott's
condition; she was still in a state of heightened preoccupation,
musing over the class she had just left. More and more their

marriage seemed to be surviving through distance as they hived off small parts of themselves, creating compartments for work, for drinking, for parenting, as well as for their separate dreams.

Zelda tried hard to live inside the space of her dancing, but the accumulating resentments of their marriage were always waiting for her. The flirtation with Lois still rankled. It was, as Scott later acknowledged, his own revenge for Zelda's affair with Edouard, and back in May he had actually invited Lois to stay at Ellerslie, to join a weekend party of guests. Zelda had managed to maintain a veneer of politeness, but only by drinking as much as everyone else, which was a great deal. At one point the party was gathered around the radio, listening to news of Charles Lindbergh's successful solo flight from America to France. It had been a heroic trajectory, and to Zelda it seemed to inhabit a sphere shamingly different from the 'putrid drunkenness' in which she and her guests were mired down below.[45]

The tension of holding her marriage together and being a good mother to Scottie, whilst also focusing on her work, took its toll on Zelda's health. A raw itching rash spread over her neck and in the creases of her elbows, a warning flare-up of the eczema that would increasingly plague her. One night she wound herself into such a hysterical state that a doctor had to be called to administer a shot of morphine. Yet she would not admit to outsiders that anything was wrong. In February the following year, she and Scott stumbled into one of the worst rows of their marriage. He was drunk, unhappy and easily goaded, and they ended up trading insults so hateful that Scott, very unusually, hit her.

Zelda's sister Rosalind was staying; and at the sight of Zelda's bleeding nose and the purple bruise swelling around her eye, she tried to persuade her to leave Scott. Zelda refused to hear a word against her husband or her marriage, though. They loved each other, she said; they lived as they chose. And when they returned to Paris a few weeks later she still clung to the hope that the city might work some redemptive spell.

*

Zelda's hopes for Paris were not only for her and Scott. She believed she had made sufficient progress at her ballet barre to be accepted as a pupil by Lubov Egorova, the former Russian ballerina who had taught Littlefield. As soon as she and Scott had settled into their new apartment, close to the Luxembourg Gardens, Zelda went to Egorova's studio to beg for admittance to her class. Egorova was tiny and perfect, with huge serious eyes and exquisite hands; she had danced for the Tsar's Imperial Ballet in St Petersburg as well as for Diaghilev's Ballets Russes, but was now retired from the stage, living in Paris with her husband Prince Troubetzkoy. She listened quietly to Zelda's petition and, moved by her determination as well as her money (Zelda was prepared to pay $300 tuition fees a month), she agreed to take her on.

From this moment on, Egorova's bare, unheated studio over the Olympia Music Hall in rue Caumartin became the sacred centre of Zelda's world. She believed she was undergoing a spiritual transformation in Egorova's class, finally able to 'drive the devils' that had controlled her in the past,[46] and to discipline herself into a pure conduit for her art. Later she tried to explain to Scott, 'I wanted to dance well so that [Egorova] would be proud of me and have another instrument for the symbols of beauty that passed in her head.'[47]

Yet the higher Zelda aspired, the more frustrated she became with her own limitations. She hated her body for its gross physical resistance, its stupidity, its age: her 'legs felt like dangling hams', her breasts 'hung like old English dugs'. Revulsion spurred her to work harder, and her body acquired a flayed, bruised look as she lost weight and accumulated small injuries. Even at night she continued to battle with her body, sleeping with her feet wedged through the bars of the bedstead, her toes 'glued outwards' in order to improve her classical turnout.[48]

Her friends grew afraid of the unreal expectations she was setting herself. That summer Gerald and Sara went to watch Zelda in class, and were as upset by her performance as Scott had been in Philadelphia. The Murphys understood something of ballet –

they had spent a great deal of time among Diaghilev's dancers – and they saw how disproportionate Zelda's efforts were to her talent. 'There was something dreadfully grotesque in her intensity,' Gerald recalled. 'One could see the muscles individually stretch and pull . . . It was really terrible. One held one's breath until it was over.'[49] Yet it was impossible to reason with her, for she said simply that she was no longer able to function without her 'work'. At home she seemed to have become a phantom presence, uninterested in either her family or the world outside ballet. Even Zelda herself acknowledged the extent of her withdrawal into 'a quiet, ghostly, hypersensitised world of my own'.[50]

Scott and Zelda's quarrels, when they had the energy for them, no longer had the power to shift the stalemate of their marriage. Sara Mayfield, Zelda and Tallulah's friend from Montgomery, was in Paris at this time, enrolled on a course at the Sorbonne, and she was one of the few people to whom Zelda confessed how things stood. After one fight Scott and she hadn't spoken to each other for days: 'When we meet in the hall, we walk around each other like a pair of stiff-legged terriers, spoiling for a fight.'[51] Each felt betrayed by the other. Zelda was hurt by Scott's refusal to take her dancing seriously; Scott felt he had been deserted. He had recently exulted over an invitation to meet his literary hero James Joyce at dinner; but although Zelda had compliantly accompanied him, she had participated little in the evening – her thoughts drifting back to the ballet studio. Scott barely recognized her as the woman he had married: 'She no longer read or thought or knew anything or liked anyone except dancers and their cheap satellites. People respected her . . . because of a certain complete fearlessness and honesty that she has never lost, but she was becoming more and more an egotist and a bore.'[52]

That autumn they returned to Ellerslie, where the lease on the house still had six months to run. If Scott hoped that detaching Zelda from Egorova would diminish her obsession, however, she had no intention of giving up her studies. She simply transferred to the studio of Alexander Gavrilov, another former Diaghilev dancer, now based in Philadelphia. She was painting again, too, experimental oils in which she attempted to express in thick urgent brush strokes the sensations of ecstasy and exhaustion she experienced in the ballet studio.

Within the calm of Ellerslie, she also resumed her writing. The magazine *College Humor*, which had already published two of her articles, had approached her with a commission for half a dozen short stories, about 'girls' of the modern type. The fictions that Zelda began to write were in some ways variations of her own story: in each she portrayed a different woman whose attempt to fulfil herself was blocked by some essential failure of nerve, or by the constraint of her husband. But while she found character and dialogue difficult to master, her descriptions of place and atmosphere were a rich sensual swarm of words, evocations of velvety nights and organdie-dressed girls in 'Southern Girl' and of a vibrating New York in 'A Millionaire's Girl'.

Scott was generous in his appreciation. It was one of his more lovable traits that even when he despaired over his own gifts, he was able to recognize and nurture those of others. The following year he told Max Perkins that he thought Zelda's style had 'a strange haunting and evocative quality that is absolutely new'. Later, he would even go so far as to admit that she was 'a great original, her flame at its most intense burned higher than mine'.[53] But having two writers at work in Ellerslie proved difficult. At one level Scott welcomed the feeling that their marriage was, once again, a shared project. He willingly involved himself in the practicalities of her commission, using his own agent, Ober, to write her contract. He gave Zelda advice in the shaping and focusing of her prose. But to see her writing so easily was a rebuke to his own struggles. While he was turning out his own short stories with profitable facility, his new novel continued to slip away from him 'like a dream'.[54]

And if Scott couldn't but be competitive with Zelda, she felt a comparable rivalry with him. Her editor, H.N. Swanson, was insistent that Scott's name should appear as co-author. Part of her acceded to the financial logic, as it doubled, even trebled, the fee for each story, and at this point she required the money to pay for her ballet lessons. Even though Scott gave her a generous allowance, she wanted her dancing career to be hers alone, not something gifted to her by Scott. Yet another part of Zelda was furiously diminished by the sharing of her byline. On the original manuscripts of her stories she crossed out Scott's name, writing in angry black pen, 'No! Me.' And when the last of the stories was sold to the *Saturday Post* in March 1930 and appeared under Scott's name alone, it was a bitter blow. Scott's agent argued that the *Post* had wanted to distinguish it from the stories published by *College Humor*, and had paid well for the privilege, but Zelda felt only the betrayal.

Trust and communication were fragile threads in their marriage now, hard to forge and easy to break. That autumn, when Hemingway came to stay at Ellerslie, it took very little time for him to inflict a great deal of casual destruction. He was no longer married to Hadley – somewhat counter to his own principles, he'd fallen in love with a lively, stylish American journalist, Pauline Pfeiffer, with whom he had recently had a son. To Zelda, his visit was an all-too-predictable violation as Ernest and Scott got drunk together and Scott lent Ernest money they could ill afford. But even more stressful was the presence of Patrick, Hemingway's sunny, robust little boy.

The sight of this baby, and of Pauline's maternal pleasure in him, was a painful reminder that she herself had failed to conceive again. It was months since she and Scott had made love, and often they were simply too exhausted and preoccupied to care. But when Ernest boasted about Patrick's adorable temperament, and joked that he was always available to sire the perfect child, the issue became a treacherous one. They began to argue, dangerously, about sex. Zelda baited Scott by saying that he was unimaginative in bed and that his penis was too small,* and in

---

* In his memoir *A Moveable Feast* Hemingway recorded a possibly apocryphal incident when Scott expressed his anxiety that 'he wasn't big enough'. They

retaliation he said she could not possibly be satisfied by him or any other man because she was in love with Egorova and with half the women at rue Jacob.

These were wincingly sensitive areas, but by the time the two of them were headed back to Europe the following March, they had passed beyond all bounds of reticence. During one argument on board ship, Scott accosted a female passenger to ask if women preferred men's penises 'to be large or small'. Zelda furiously rounded on him, calling him a pathetic embarrassment, and he punished her shortly afterwards by forcing anal intercourse on her. It was the lowest point in their marriage, she later told him, 'the most humiliating and bestial thing that ever happened to me'.[55] And as she recoiled from Scott, Zelda also began, half consciously, to fulfil his fears.

Once they had arrived in Paris, in the spring of 1929, she found herself turning to women for the sympathy and understanding that she had formerly got from her husband; she felt their 'eyes had gathered their softness . . . from things I understood'.[56] At the ballet studio she grew very friendly with two or three of the other students, and at rue Jacob her new receptiveness to women suggested to some that she might be ready for an affair. Nancy Hoyt – sister of the poet Elinor Wylie and of Eugenia Bankhead's husband Morton – began paying her marked attention, and so, too, did Dolly Wilde. Zelda was particularly flattered by Dolly, whose extravagant gold lamé scarves and pungent wit marked her out as the true niece of Oscar Wilde. Even Scott admired her as a genuine original. But while she enjoyed this nuanced, feminine flirtation Zelda was afraid. Growing up in Alabama her sexuality had been predicated on the clear-cut definitions of Southern beaux and Southern belles. Deep down, the idea that she might be a lesbian repelled her.

Despite the decade's new, theoretical openness about sexual

---

went to the men's urinals, where Hemingway was able to assure Scott that he was 'perfectly fine'.

identity, few individuals were as bold as Tamara or as clear-minded as Natalie in acknowledging their desires. A survey conducted among 2,200 middle-class American women in the late 1920s revealed that many had experienced lesbian impulses: nearly half of those interviewed said they'd experienced a close emotional relationship with another woman, while a quarter admitted to those relationships being sexual. In a generation that had suffered the loss of millions of young men, many women had turned to their own sex for physical contact. Yet this contact was still rarely displayed in public. Within most communities, the taboo against lesbians remained rigidly in place and even Tallulah, who'd flaunted her own early relationships with women, would find herself in situations where she felt the need to pretend she'd never been anything but heterosexual.

Zelda's own confusion was brought to a crisis when Scott accompanied her to Barney's salon and caught Dolly making a very obvious pass at her. Possibly it was mischief on Dolly's part, but he saw it as a challenge to his marriage and his masculinity. It led to another round of sexual accusations and recriminations: Scott accusing Zelda of being attracted to a 'hysterical rotten lesbian'; she accusing him of being a fairy. Zelda, however, was desperate for Scott's help, wanting his guidance to untangle the muddle of her feelings. She felt that Dolly was pressuring her into taking a step for which she was 'morally and practically unfitted',[57] but when she begged him to talk to her rationally he was too bewildered and antagonistic to respond. Zelda found a packet of condoms among his things, and when she accused him of being unfaithful, he said that he'd wanted to have sex with a Parisian whore in order to prove to her that he was a man.

By the time they went south for the summer, they had inflicted all the damage they were capable of. Both were convalescent, exhausted and guilty. Scott described himself to Hemingway as 'leaking' tears and gin.[58] The Murphys worried about both of them: Scott's pallor was frightening and Zelda looked haggard, her complexion pale and papery, with little spasms of emotion twitching at the corners of her mouth. Gerald noticed that her laughter had a new random quality, a sound of 'unhinged delight' with little humour in it. She was retreating further inside herself and it was in this precarious state that she was faced with an opportunity that might redefine her life.

They were staying in Cannes and Zelda was taking classes with a ballet master at the Nice Opera. Through him she was given one or two very minor roles to perform with the opera chorus. And while the work was technically undemanding it placed Zelda on the first rung of a potential career. It might well have prompted the invitation that came to her in late September from Julie Sedova, a former St Petersburg ballerina who was now directing the ballet ensemble at the San Carlo Opera in Naples. Sedova wrote to say that she was short of a dancer for the company's autumn production of *Aida*, and to ask if Zelda was interested.

Again, the work would not be taxing. Ballets in opera productions were little more than divertissements, short and usually formulaic in their choreography, but Sedova's invitation was still significant. Not only was she offering Zelda a solo role in the *Aida* ballet; she was also suggesting that Zelda remain in Naples for the rest of the season, picking some more minor roles and gaining some invaluable stage experience. After just two years of study Zelda was being given the chance to turn her aspirations into a professional reality, yet she simply didn't know how to respond.

Training with Egorova she had focused only on the daily detail of her practice, and had never had to face the potential limits of her talent. She'd been able to cling to her fantasy of a ballerina career, imagining that soon she would be invited to dance with a company like Diaghilev's Ballets Russes. Such was her naive absorption in that fantasy that when a man had come to see her dance at Egorova's studio a few months earlier Zelda had imagined he was a talent scout for Diaghilev.* Her disappointment

---

* That blow had been followed shortly afterwards by the news of Diaghilev's sudden death in August, and of the imminent disbanding of his company. For a

had been crushing when she discovered the man had been sent by the Folies Bergère to see if Scott Fitzgerald's wife might be useful as a 'shimmy dancer'. Now Zelda feared that if she accepted Sedova's offer to perform with a mere opera company, it would be tantamount to giving up on her dreams of ballerina greatness: an acceptance that she could never, ever attain the level of Egorova, Pavlova and the other idols she had erected for herself.

Even if she did take her chances with Sedova, Zelda agonized over her ability to survive in Naples on her own. She had wistfully confided to Sara Mayfield of her longing to start her life over and recoup her wasted years. But at the age of twenty-nine she had no practical experience of life – Scott had always dealt with money, travel and houses. Perhaps if he had agreed to come to Naples with Zelda, she might have attempted the move, but by now he had accumulated such a history of grudges against Zelda's dancing that he couldn't make such an offer. He also genuinely believed it was dangerous to encourage her. Later, when she was ill, Zelda pressed Scott to ask Egorova for an objective assessment of her talent, and he flinched from letting her see it. As Scott had always believed, Egorova wrote that Zelda was naturally gifted but had made far too late a start to become a serious ballerina. At best she could have worked with a Broadway ballet ensemble, such as the one that Léonide Massine was directing at the Roxy Theatre in New York.

Later Zelda would rejig in her mind the way this episode had gone. The Naples offer had been 'the great opportunity' of her life – an invitation to become a 'premier dancer with an important company' – and she claimed that Scott had forbidden her to accept. But the short story she wrote soon afterwards, 'The Girl who had Some Talent', suggested a greater self-awareness. Her heroine, a dancer from New York, is offered an equivalent,

---

few days Zelda had been unable to put on her ballet shoes, saying with dumb anguish that there was no point any more.

career-changing opportunity, but at the moment of decision she ducks away from it and goes with her lover to China.

When the summer crowds departed and the time came for her and Scott to return to Paris, Zelda could feel none of her former excitement at being reunited with Egorova and her studio. She was still too conflicted by the implications of Sedova's letter. Driving home along the steep mountainous road with Scott, she suddenly grabbed the steering wheel, almost sending the car in a violent swerve over the cliff. Afterwards she shrugged the incident off – the car 'had acted wildly' she said – but Scott believed she had wanted them both to die. Back in Paris her mood was still jangled. She returned to her ballet classes, but was also socializing again, ricocheting from lunches to dinners to parties at Maxim's. 'Nobody knew whose party it was,' she wrote, 'it had been going on for weeks. When you felt you couldn't survive another night, you went home and slept and when you got back, a new set of people had consecrated themselves to keeping it alive.'[59]

Sometimes in the middle of the frenzy she would experience a feeling of such weightlessness and detachment that she had to hold onto the table where she was sitting to anchor herself in place. The city itself seemed alien to her now. It had filled up with Americans during the summer, tourists who were aggressively bullish with their strong dollars and market capital; in October, as the US stock market went haywire, Paris was also infected by manic uncertainty. Scott, deeply interested in the systems of money, was haunted by the spiritual as well as the financial implications of the see-sawing market, and was convinced that it heralded the end of the American dream and, very specifically, the end of his own dream with Zelda.

The entry in his ledger at the end of that year was stark: 'Crash. Wall Street. Zelda.' Certainly Zelda's mental state was now deteriorating badly, her behaviour was erratic and she seemed to have trouble connecting to people and events around her. Early in 1930 Scott took her on holiday to North Africa in the hope that new surroundings would restore her natural curiosity. But the moments of slippage, when Zelda seemed frighteningly disengaged from the world, became longer and more intense. She spent much of her time in Algiers feeling herself 'on the other side of a black gauze'.[60]

At times Zelda experienced her detachment as exalted and extraordinary: 'Colours were infinite, part of the air and not restricted by the lines that encompassed them.' She could sense her body filling up with music, beating behind her forehead, welling up through her stomach. But at other times she felt trapped inside a nightmare. She heard voices, flowers talked at her, the bodies of the people around her swelled and shrank, their faces seemed to be concealed by masks. After she and Scott returned to Paris, Michael Arlen came to their flat, and when Zelda came upon the two men in conversation she became violently agitated. Although they smiled and greeted her warmly she was convinced they hated her and were plotting to get rid of her.

The only place that she felt safe was Egorova's studio, and her need to be there grew more and more intense. Once, Egorova had to practically force Zelda to her feet after she dropped to her knees in front of her teacher, as if she would never move from the spot. Scott was terrified. Much of the time he could get little sense out of Zelda, who was either mumbling unintelligibly to herself or locked in silence. He knew she was ill, but he now wondered if she was mad. Arlen, having witnessed her fraught behaviour, advised that she should take a rest cure in a clinic just outside Paris. Zelda agreed to have herself admitted on 23 April, but after just ten days she signed herself out again, insisting she had to see Egorova, who was like 'the rays of the sun' to her 'shining on a piece of crystal'.[61]

By now Zelda was beyond any clarity that Egorova could bring. She was in the middle of a breakdown so extreme that she was hallucinating half the day, and at night having dreams so violent that she awoke from them shaking and crying. Only morphine could calm her, although neither she nor her doctors realized it was doing more harm than good, exacerbating her anxieties to the point where she was suicidal and a genuine danger to herself. By now Scott accepted that drastic treatment was necessary. On 22 May he got Zelda admitted to a clinic in Switzerland, and from there transferred to a psychiatric hospital on the shores of Lake Geneva.

It was less than a year since *College Humor* had advertised, jubilantly, its forthcoming series of short stories by the fascinating Zelda Fitzgerald. The magazine editor had conjured up the entitled, beautiful flapper whose image had been created by Scott, the media and Zelda herself. 'I cannot imagine any girl having a richer background than Zelda's, a life more crowded with interesting people and events. She is a star in her own right.'[62]

Even though Zelda would grope her way painfully towards a new life, recovering sufficiently to write two novels and to paint, she was no longer part of that crowded, starry existence, and she would never again be an object of envy, a muse or a role model. For much of the remaining eighteen years of her life she would remain hidden away, suffering from a series of misdiagnoses and mistreatments for a mental condition that no doctor was able to cure. Her body was slackened by drugs, her beauty almost extinguished and her world bounded by institution walls.

She wrote, 'I believed I was a Salamander, and it seems I am nothing but an impediment.'*[63]

---

* It was assumed by many doctors that she suffered from schizophrenia: today Zelda would probably be diagnosed as bipolar.

Chapter Eleven

TAMARA

During the first two years of Zelda's illness, she wrote down long therapeutic accounts of her life, trying to understand what had happened to her. In some versions she blamed her breakdown on Scott, his drinking, his self-involvement and – above all – his failure to support her creative aspirations. 'Horrible things have happened to me,' she wrote, 'through my inability to express myself.'[1]

There were many occasions when Tamara de Lempicka, too, had accused her husband of being drunk and insensitive, but never once had she let him interfere with her art. By the mid-1920s the arguments between her and Tadeusz had escalated into an operatic violence as he berated her selfishness and greed and she dismissed him as an embittered failure. One night she returned to the flat to find him riled up to an exceptional, drunken self-righteousness: she was a whore, a bad mother, a lousy wife. A few years earlier he would have used his fists as well his tongue to abuse her, but Tamara had long taken control of their arguments. When Kizette awoke to the sound of shouting, and crept out of bed to observe her mother emerging from the kitchen with a knife in her hand. As Tamara began to chase Tadeusz round the apartment. Kizette was convinced that her father only escaped serious injury by darting into the lift in the corridor outside.

It incensed Tamara that Tadeusz should dare to accuse her of selfishness. She was beginning to receive important commissions and her paintings were starting to sell. She saw herself as the saviour of the Lempicki family, raising them out of their humiliating dependency on her relatives. Beyond the good she had done her husband and daughter, she also regarded herself as an important painter – and as such above reproach.

Kizette had long learned to accept Tamara's mantra. Her mother, her Cherie, 'was an artist always, before anything else.' She had accepted that most of the time she would be cared for by her grandmother Malvina, while Tamara was walled inside the ferocious concentration of her painting. She learned to treasure the occasional days when Cherie left her easel and announced that they would take a walk in the Bois de Boulogne, a trip to the open-air skating rink at the Palais de Glace or even a rare holiday. But when Tamara was on vacation, Kizette still accepted that her mother never stopped thinking about her work.

During one trip to Italy, Tamara, Kizette and Malvina were eating lunch in a restaurant in Rome when Tamara suddenly halted the conversation. She was struck by the quality of the sunlight as it slanted through the window and onto their checked tablecloth. Needing to see its effect more clearly she swept aside their plates of food, sending antipasti flying, and snapped imperiously to the startled diner opposite to get out of her line of vision: 'There is an unforgettable light coming through the window opposite. Please move, monsieur, so that I can study [it].'[2]

Tamara's addiction to her work was genuine. She sought to capture the perfect image no less intently than Zelda sought to master the perfect jump or the perfect balance in the ballet studio. But she also wanted to be judged by the same standards as a man. Picasso and the other male painters in Paris all took mistresses and lived as they chose – their behaviour justified in the name of art. Tamara believed it was her right, even her duty, to claim the same freedom.

The further she progressed with her career, the more conscious she became of the battle to hold her professional ground. Unlike Marie Laurencin, who'd had the support of her lover Apollinaire, or Emilie Charmy with Matisse as a mentor, she lacked powerful male allies. Nor could she claim membership of a politically influential group, such as the surrealists. As a painter of portraits she earned good money, and she was acknowledged to have a perceptively original eye. In her 1923 portrait of André Gide, Tamara stylized the writer's features into an almost tribal mask of intelligence, his eyes two black glittering slits in the carved planes of his face. In the 1927 portrait of her friend the exiled Grand Duke Gabriel Constantinovich, she caught a combination of nobility and dissolution that was both arrestingly personal yet profoundly evocative of the Grand Duke's class. But however impressive Tamara's achievements, there were those in the art world who regarded commercial portraiture as a hangover from the past, almost irrelevant to the great modernist enterprise of European painting. As a genre it earned her little status.

There was one movement to which Tamara would later become very profitably affiliated – art deco or art moderne* – but in 1925 deco was regarded principally as a movement within commercial design. Its name was taken from the Exposition Internationale des Arts Décoratifs et Industriels Modernes, which had opened in Paris in April that year. Its exhibits ranged from furniture and kitchen equipment to clothes and architectural design, and it proffered the vision of a shiny, confident lifestyle, tailor-made to the post-war era. Products came in bold colours and efficient, geometric forms, they radiated a cosmopolitan assurance in their fusion of cultural and historic references – a radio shaped like an Aztec pyramid, a bourgeois dinner service patterned with an African tribal motif. Few of the visitors who crowded into the exhibition could afford to build a deco villa like the Murphys and live the full deco lifestyle, but most

---

* The term art deco did not acquire popular currency until the 1960s.

had the money to buy themselves a small piece of it – a chrome coffee pot, a scallop-edged powder compact, or a bevelled bottle of perfume.

The connections between Tamara's painting and the deco aesthetic would later become very obvious: in 1978 she would even claim that she had been a prime mover in deco, dating it from her own 1925 painting, *Irene and her Sister*, and referring to it as the greatest of her achievements. But at the time it was of little use as a platform for her work, and in order to push her career forward she was casting round for some kind of external sponsorship and support. The salons where she had already been exhibited – the Salon d'Automne and the Salon des Indépendants – had shown her work to a large public. But within the Parisian art world, power had begun to shift to the smaller independent galleries, and by 1925 Tamara needed to find one that would nurture her own career.

Her instinct was to look beyond the crowded marketplace of Paris. On the way home from her Italian holiday with Kizette and Malvina, she broke her journey in Milan to visit the wealthy collector Count Emanuele Castelbarco. Later she would spin this meeting as a spur-of-the-moment encounter between a nervous young artist and a formidable grandee, but in fact she had prepared for it very carefully, taking a portfolio of photographs to show him her pictures and formulating a determined line in negotiation. She came away triumphant, with the Count offering her a two-week solo show at his Milan gallery, Bottega di Poesia.

It was due to open at the end of November, in just four months' time, and Tamara returned to Paris flooded with adrenalin. She bullied her friends and family into sitting for her, experimented with painting still lives, and by the time she travelled back to Italy she had over fifty works ready. Meanwhile the Count had commandeered the Italian art press as well as all his friends to welcome her. Tamara hadn't felt so happily the centre of attention since the day she had floated up the aisle in her wedding dress in St Petersburg. In Milan, everybody seemed to notice and

admire her. The foreword to her exhibition catalogue, written by
the French critic Jacques Reboud, made flattering allusions to her
'genius' for form, her role as an 'evangelist' for cubism. The
Italian critics were equally enthused, and no less encouraging to
Tamara was the hospitality she received from Castelbarco's rich
and cultured circle of friends.

They were mostly cosmopolitan and aristocratic, the kind of
people with whom she felt instantly at ease. In Paris, there were
so many networks for her to navigate – the writers and the
painters, the Left Bank and the Right Bank, the socialists and the
surrealists – and she had worked hard to gain a foothold in most
of them. She had got herself introduced to Left Bank figures
like Hemingway and Lucia Joyce at the chaotic parties thrown
by Jules Pascin (the famously eccentric artist who painted in a
matador suit and dined in a dressing gown and bowler hat). At
Nathalie Barney's salon she had become acquainted with Casarti,
de Acosta and the writer Colette. She was on nodding terms with
Janet Flanner, Nancy Cunard, Zelda Fitzgerald and Sara Murphy.
She was close to Jean Cocteau, who knew everybody; she called
Coco Chanel and Jean Patou her friends; she boasted of sharing
cocaine with André Gide. But she had few intimates among these
people, especially the American and British expatriates, in whose
language she was not yet confidently fluent.

In Milan, however, she was introduced to men and women
very much like herself: privileged by birth, instinctively right
wing in their politics, but also very hedonistic in their tastes.
Among her new best friends was the Marquis Guido Sommi
Picenardi, an exquisite young man who knew everyone in
Europe, from the Polignac family to Alice Keppel and her
daughter Violet Trefusis (one notoriously the mistress of Edward
VII, the other notoriously the lover of Vita Sackville-West).
Picenardi became an important patron of Tamara's work, and
possibly even her lover. 'I refused myself nothing,' she later
boasted, 'I had always had *innamorato*, always. For my inspiration,
I liked to go out in the evenings and have a good-looking man

tell me how beautiful I am or how great an artist I am – and he touches my hand . . . I loved it! I needed it.'³

Tamara lingered in Milan for several weeks, working her new contacts and enjoying her new lovers. She only just kept her promise to Kizette to return home for Christmas, and she was so keyed up by her achievements that she barely paused for family festivities before getting back to her career. The November 1925 issue of *Harper's Bazaar* had featured an entire page of photographs of her and Kizette 'playing hoop' in the Bois de Boulogne. Tamara claimed these shots had been a happy accident and that a passing photographer had asked them to pose. But the photographs have a staged look, which suggests that it was Tamara herself who orchestrated it. Both mother and daughter are immaculately dressed, Tamara in a striped wool coat with luxuriously deep velvet cuffs, Kizette in bright white gloves and socks and a checked coat. Tamara's hand is lightly placed on the hoop circling Kizette's waist, balancing it so that it can be clearly seen, and both of them are smiling happily at the camera, as though nothing could be so natural or normal as the two of them playing together all day.

At that moment, however, Kizette was seeing very little of her mother. On her return Tamara had successfully used her Milan debut to secure an exhibition at a Parisian gallery run by the serious but commercially successful dealer Colette Weil. Once again the pressure was on her to produce new work, and once again she was working long days to produce it. She had become obsessed with nudes, relishing the challenge of their formal composition, of capturing light on skin, but also taking an almost narcissistic pleasure in the beauty of the female form.

One of her most seminal recent works had been *The Model* (1925), and in it Tamara had begun to explore the expressive impact of physical distortion. A single standing woman takes up almost the whole canvas; the lifted arm with which she shields her face from the viewer has a massive heft, and her left leg has a correspondingly voluptuous thrust. In formal terms these exaggerated elements combine to create an S-shaped rhythm through the picture. But more significantly they lend it a concentrated physical inwardness, making the woman appear fully absorbed in the drama of her own body.

In *Group of Four Nudes* (1926), Tamara went further in the balance between form and sexuality. The surface of the picture is theatrically glossy, the four women's faces lustrously made up, their skins luminously perfect. Yet the intimate clustering of their bodies implies an inward compulsion, a secret life. Along with *Le Rythme*, which Tamara painted as a companion piece, *Four Nudes* received some of the finest reviews of her career so far, with critics acclaiming her twin debt to Ingres and cubism.

Another, more elemental aspect of Tamara's fascination with nudes was the thrill she derived from seeking out new models. Her hunting ground was Paris, the bars, theatres, parks and streets, and while some of the strangers she approached had the look of professionals – artists' models or prostitutes – others were riskier propositions. Late in 1931, when she was working on her painting *Adam and Eve*, she spotted a policeman on duty who seemed to be her quintessential Adam, and she regarded it as a professional coup when the young man agreed to pose, coming to her studio when he was off duty and showing no embarrassment whatsoever as he 'took off his things, and folded them neatly on the chair, placing his big revolver on the top'.[4] He was, he claimed, an artist too.

Another prized find was the stylish woman she noticed in the audience at the Théâtre de Paris. Tamara had been struck by the elegance of her profile and the slope of her naked shoulders in evening dress: she seemed an ideal fit for the fifth and final figure in the painting she was working on, which was probably *Le Rythme*. Expecting rejection, she nonetheless touched the stranger on the shoulder and asked if she would model for her. To her surprise, the woman looked at her 'with level eyes' and agreed. Over the next three weeks she sat for Tamara wearing nothing but a transparent green mousseline shift. Tamara recalled her as one of her favourite models – 'Perfection of body, beautiful colour of skin, light and gold'.[5] In her gratitude she'd tried to offer gifts of flowers, chocolates, even money but the woman had declined. 'Thank you, no ... I knew and admired your paintings' she'd said, before taking her final leave. 'She was gone. I never knew who she was.'[6]

Tamara may well have embellished this story – the number of rich, respectable women in Paris who would be prepared to model nude was limited, and she would probably have known or recognized most of them. But the fantasy was revealing. She liked to think of herself as an undercover agent, seeking out people as audacious and exceptional as herself, as a woman operating on the 'fringes of society', equally at home in a palace or the gutter, but always at a remove from everything 'bourgeois, mediocre or just *nice*.'[7]

Tamara's sense of herself as a solitary hunter was one reason why she now visited rue Jacob less frequently. She found Nathalie Barney's salons too whimsical, too safe; now that she had money to spend (her paintings were selling for an average of fifty thousand francs each) she began to host her own private parties in her own more outrageous style. It was difficult to be shocking in mid-1920s Paris, a city inured to most forms of outrage. Zelda and Scott found their own antics had less impact this side of the Atlantic; when they jumped into the pool at the Lido cabaret they elicited little more than an elegant, collective shrug from the Parisians present. Hardly more successful was Caressa Crosby, wife of the American aesthete Harry Crosby, who once hired a baby elephant to transport her to an artists' ball, which she attended as an Inca princess, her naked breasts barely concealed by her long blue wig.

Tamara's soirées, however, were more grown up, and far more deliberately choreographed. She was a commanding hostess – immaculately dressed, her large eyes gleaming, her gestures rapid and authoritative – and she found it easy to impose her will. At certain parties the waitresses she hired to serve her guests were required to wear seductively scanty costumes, copied from the Folies Bergère. At others they would begin the evening fully dressed, but would be required to remove an item of clothing every time their tray of canapés was emptied. Tamara's favourite stunt was to lay out food on the naked body of a young woman, then invite her guests to compare, with relish, which parts were most delicious to eat from.

Those who were present at her parties recalled the atmosphere as self-consciously wicked, but not threatening. Drugs were routine – cocaine or little pellets of hashish (as common as 'breath mints' according to one friend), which were stirred into cocktails.[8] The servants were often as high as the guests, and were apparently selected for their willingness to participate in whatever sexual activities ensued. This was the kind of fantasy Tamara adored: meticulously orchestrated, but with a frisson of danger; ritualized yet ripe with sensuality.

Nevertheless, it was not a beautiful woman whom she stalked most obsessively at this time, but a man in his early sixties. Gabriele D'Annunzio, the celebrated Italian poet, had none of the athletic lustre Tamara admired. He was short, barely five foot four, with a bald head, pale skin, pointed waxed moustache and insinuating lizard eyes that, according to one fascinated but repulsed mistress, 'were like caca'.[9] But 'Il Comandante', as he liked to be known, was a legend: Italy's unofficial national poet and national hero,[*] and also the Don Juan of the age.

During the last four decades D'Annunzio was said to have had every woman of beauty, rank or genius: the actors Sarah Bernhardt and Eleonora Duse, the dancer Isadora Duncan and the astonishing Luisa Casati were all his trophies. When he'd met Tamara in Milan in late 1925 he had seemed very interested in adding her to the list, and she was sufficiently impressed by his reputation to play along with his overtures. What the sixty-three-year-old poet lacked in beauty he made up for in power, and Tamara itched for the opportunity to capture his peculiar hyp-

---

[*] Just after the war he had led the capture of the disputed territory of Fiume in an attempt to prevent its annexation by Yugoslavia.

notic presence on canvas. It would be a most interesting artistic challenge, and it would bring her a great deal of kudos.

D'Annunzio's initial suggestion that she paint his portrait had been offered more as a flirtatious advance, but in the summer of 1926, when Tamara was again in Italy, working on a portrait of Picenardi, she received an invitation to lunch at the poet's palatial villa on Lake Garda. Right up until the moment she arrived at Il Viattoriale, she assumed she would be able to brush aside the poet's amorous game-playing and pin him down to a serious commission. Once there, however, she realized the kind of person she was dealing with. Here was a man who made her own ego and willpower seem almost modest.

Tamara saw that everything about the villa was contrived to aggrandize its owner. Within the grounds was the hangar that housed his famous biplane (during the war D'Annunzio had flown over enemy troops, dropping pamphlets to exhort their surrender). Inside were rooms devoted to the most stagily monumental of art collections: statues of Buddha and the Virgin Mary, plaster casts of Michelangelo sculptures and of the Parthenon friezes. One blood-red room contained the trophies of his love affairs, pairs of gloves belonging to all his former mistresses. There was a music room that could be hung with either scarlet or black drapes, depending on the mood of the evening, and the ultimate coup de théâtre was the chamber, containing D'Annunzio's own coffin, in which he claimed to sleep in order to prepare himself for death.

Such gothic memento mori were favoured by other celebrities of D'Annunzio's generation – Sarah Bernhardt also famously kept a coffin in her rooms. While the flappers of Tamara's generation considered it shocking to host cocktail parties from their baths, sleeping in coffins was a leftover from true fin-de-siècle decadence. Even Tamara was thrown. And she felt further wrong-footed over lunch, as D'Annunzio plied her with charming questions about her life and work, yet flickered evasively whenever she attempted to broach specific details of the portrait. By the end of the day she was forced to leave the villa with nothing other than the poet's compliments and his vague promise that they would meet again.

Tamara was nevertheless determined to coax something more definite out of him, and later that autumn, when she was once again in Italy, she wrote to suggest that she call in to see D'Annunzio on her return journey. Believing she now had the measure of her prey, she laced her note with flattering innuendo, suggesting that her interests in him were as much sexual as they were professional: 'Would you like me to pass your way, too? (In the good sense of the word?) I'd like to – how about you? I send you, my brother, all my thoughts, the good ones, and the bad ones, the mischievous ones and those that make me suffer.'

When D'Annunzio agreed to the visit, Tamara wrote again, absurdly exaggerating the flutter of her own girlish excitement: 'I'm so glad – and afraid. What are you like? Who are you? And me, will you like me looking like a little student without my Paris gowns, my make up, etc. Etc.?'[10] But if she thought she was close to getting the poet to sit for her, what actually followed was a comedy of crossed purposes, two forceful wily egos, each trying to get what they wanted, and failing.

Tamara had no intention of letting D'Annunzio make love to her. Even with models to whom she was genuinely attracted, she now kept sex and work distinct. 'The man who sits for the portrait is, for me, like a statue,' she once explained. 'The flirt can be in the evening with somebody else. But never with the person that is sitting.'[11] D'Annunzio, however, had no intention of being Tamara's statue. And when she went to stay with him in December 1926 she appreciated just how formidable and peculiar an opponent she had taken on.

D'Annunzio was in the habit of consuming large, daily quantities of cocaine, and as a result he slept and ate at very unpredictable times. Everyone else in his household was expected to do likewise, and Tamara, who depended on routine, even when she was playing to excess, began to feel seriously unwell. Both her digestion and her sleep patterns were being sent haywire, yet the more she pleaded discomfort the more energetically

D'Annunzio pressed his attentions. She could never find a quiet moment to rest and consider her situation without the poet appearing by her side, attempting caresses and murmuring insinuating suggestions. Any time she proposed a suitable opportunity for their first sitting he brushed the idea of the portrait aside. After several fraught days and exhausted nights Tamara was defeated. She packed her bag and slipped out of the house, without daring to say goodbye.

The game was far from over, though. D'Annunzio pursued her with a flurry of telegrams and letters, their tone sufficiently ardent for Tamara to agree to return. Perhaps she believed that she could successfully wear him down this time, tolerating his advances without actually letting him into her bed. Certainly she managed to sustain her second campaign for a full ten days. She listened with pretended fascination to D'Annunzio's rambling discourses on sex and the soul, and while she allowed him to kiss her she concocted a dozen different reasons why he could go no further – from fidelity to her husband, to her fear of contracting venereal disease (D'Annunzio was deeply insulted). She even put up with the ignominy of having to listen to the poet enjoying noisy sex with his housekeeper, Aélis, in the corridor right outside her bedroom door.

It was ugly, however, and at times frightening. D'Annunzio harangued and insulted Tamara, complaining that she had his entire household 'hanging by a hair of her cunt';[12] he offered her quantities of cocaine to unsteady her resolve and came very close to raping her when she had taken to her bed with a slight fever. But it became clear to them both that they were engaged in an unwinnable and unprofitable battle of wills. If D'Annunzio couldn't have Tamara in his bed, he had no intention of letting her have him on canvas; equally, Tamara would not accept D'Annunzio on any terms but her own.

She left Il Vittoriale worn out and disgusted, but underneath their mutual rancour she and D'Annunzio acknowledged one another as worthy opponents. And even if Tamara didn't get her portrait, she did receive the gift of a large topaz ring, which she wore in tribute to the poet until she died. She also found no difficulty in erasing the memory of his creepily staged advances. Before returning to Paris, she spent a delightful few days in the arms of one of her 'innamorati' – possibly Picenardi or his Venetian friend, Count Marcello Vettor.

When she arrived home she was wearing an expression of sleek and, to Tadeusz, infuriatingly obvious satisfaction. For several months he'd been aware of Tamara's games with D'Annunzio, having read most of the florid love letters she'd received from the poet and never bothered to conceal. Assuming that she had just come from the latter's bed, he raged bitterly at her, refusing to accept her protestations that the entire visit had been chaste and that she had only stayed in the villa for the sake of her art and, ultimately, for the family's good.

Tamara didn't much care what Tadeusz believed. She was used to his jealous eruptions and often rather enjoyed them, believing they kept the sexual charge of their marriage alive. It never occurred to her that one day her husband might find his situation intolerable. Yet this time, when she arrived back from Italy, the recriminations with which Tadeusz greeted her did not end as they usually did, either in bed or with her stalking out of the flat to meet her friends. Instead he turned on her with the triumphant announcement that he was leaving her for another woman. During a recent business trip to Poland he had met a wealthy divorcee called Irene Spiess, who had fallen in love with him and wanted him to come and live with her in Warsaw.

For Tamara the news was so unexpected and the shock so great that it knocked all the natural fight from her. She watched Tadeusz pack up his things and move out of the apartment, and in the days that followed she barely had strength to dress herself, let alone paint. Kizette, who was used to being ignored for hours at a time, was alarmed by the intensity with which her mother now clung to her. Tamara was so fearful of the emptiness in the flat, without Tadeusz, that for a while she wouldn't even let Kizette go to school.

Throughout her life Tamara had been prone to extremes of elation and self-pitying collapse, and the loss of her husband triggered one of the most extreme depressions of her life. It's possible that it also triggered an emotional recall of her past sufferings, for the nightmare of the Cheka in St Petersburg, and the misery of her first months in Paris still haunted Tamara. The diamond bracelets she ritually purchased with her earnings weren't simply for show, they were insurance against loss, portable capital that she could take with her if ever her world imploded for a second time. During these last few years she'd felt such triumph and relief in making herself financially secure, that she'd never imagined the possibility of her marriage being taken from her.

For a few weeks Tamara was enveloped by fear and loss, but she had fought to have Tadeusz when she was a fifteen-year-old schoolgirl, and as she emerged from the fog of depression she was prepared to fight for him again. She travelled to Poland to see him, convinced that she could seduce, argue or simply will him to return. And while he resisted her on the first visit and continued to resist her on the second, the third time she played her trump card and took Kizette with her.

Tadeusz was a genuinely fond father and, as Tamara had hoped, the sight of a wan-faced Kizette pleading with him to come home, had an effect. He agreed to take a holiday with them both at Lake Como, and to attempt a possible reconciliation. Yet he and Tamara were too angry for it to work. On 21 May 1927, the day that Charles Lindbergh landed at Le Bourget airfield after completing his Atlantic flight, Paris was full of cheering crowds. The Lempicki, however, were in Lake Como, locked in an argument so loud and abusive that the hotel management were threatening to evict them.

In Kizette's recollection, Tadeusz had justified his affair with Irene by listing every betrayal and insult he'd received from Tamara over the last five years; Tamara, unable to accept any responsibility, had flipped back into her old, angry contempt:

'Who do you think you're talking to. I'm an artist. You're a nobody who's too dumb even to have an affair with a pretty girl instead of the first mouse who runs across your path.'[13]

Not surprisingly, Tadeusz walked out, assuring Tamara that nothing she could say or do now would prevent him seeking a divorce and marrying Irene. Again, Tamara was crushed, and again poor, bemused Kizette had to look after her mother as she huddled on the floor of her hotel room, moaning over and over again, 'Oh God, how I love him.'

It wasn't just the loss of Tadeusz that assaulted Tamara, it was the wound to her pride and her carefully constructed public image. She had expended a formidable amount of energy on presenting herself as a woman who could accomplish everything, in her work and in the home. An article published in the February issue of *Vanity Fair* had delighted her by praising both the 'momentous event' of her debut show in Milan and the 'exquisitely novel' style in which she had decorated the family's current apartment in rue Guy de Montparnasse.[14] In 1979 Tamara would acknowledge how proud and competitive she had always been. Not only had she wanted to be the best artist, she had wanted 'to have the best husband, the nicest house, the best dresses',[15] and it was intolerable to her that people might now regard her as a deserted wife, an object of pity, rather than envy and adulation.

Nevertheless, Tamara still couldn't acknowledge the degree to which she had brought Tadeusz's desertion on herself. At Lake Como she not only blamed him for the failure of their reconciliation, but even heaped abuse on Kizette for failing to give her proper support. Compromise and sympathy had never really counted in the family narrative constructed by Tamara; Tadeusz and Kizette had been given their allotted roles, and when they didn't play them as expected she was furious.

Tamara could be selfish, narcissistic and cruel, but she continued to justify her behaviour on the grounds that her life was essentially in the service of her work. It was her duty, she believed, to bend the world to her creative will. And she was far from alone in that notion. In this decade of rapid social change, the borderline between freedom and selfishness, ego and egotism was hotly contended ethical ground.

For male artists and writers, the supremacy of the individual over society was one of the clarion themes of the Twenties. The question of what constituted the moral self had taken on a new urgency after the war. Scott Fitzgerald argued that 'character was the only thing that did not wear out' in the face of collapsing ideologies and broken dreams; for D.H. Lawrence the self was a mystical flame, set against a disintegrating modern world.

Most women, however, were experiencing the dichotomy between individual liberty and society in far more practical, problematic and domestic ways. In theory they were living in an era of emancipation – many had the vote, many were attaining financial independence and every flapper image that featured in the movies or magazines seemed a celebration of their freedom of choice. Yet women were presented with few narratives of what to do with those choices. Most of the feckless flapper heroines of the 1920s, from Betty Lou in *It Girl*, to Monique in *La Garçonne*, ended up being rewarded by – or corralled into – marriage. And at that point their stories typically came to an end. If ever a liberated girl failed to get her man, the alternatives were nearly always tragic, like Iris March driving herself into an ancient elm tree in a last, lonely gesture of integrity.

The practicalities of how grown-up, married flappers might balance independence and family life were much less documented. Zelda might be commissioned to write an article or two on modern marriage and in Britain an assortment of writers from D.H. Lawrence to Violet Bonham Carter penned newspaper columns on the same subject. But these barely touched on how hard and confusing a project it was for women to combine the ambitions of their single selves with the compromises required by husbands and children. Diana and Zelda knew they didn't want to be like their mothers, but they had no other blueprint on which to model themselves. As for Tamara, she had lost Tadeusz because she had conceded to so few of his needs.

And however self-righteously she had tried to justify her behaviour, she still felt diminished and exposed by his departure. She had been bred to believe that any woman abandoned by her husband was a failure.

The only thing she could do to counter that sense of failure was to make herself a better painter. During this period Kizette recalled Tamara veering between listless depression and 'frantic' work;[16] she was already exhibiting symptoms of the bipolar behaviour that would worsen in middle age, although, unlike Zelda, she could still turn her 'manic' phase to professional advantage. Significantly, one of the best portraits she produced during this period was of Tadeusz himself. It was both a homage and a critique, for while Tamara made her husband look dangerously handsome, capturing the dark, charismatic beauty with which she'd first fallen in love, the left hand, on which he would have worn his wedding ring, was left deliberately unfinished. The title she gave the canvas – *Portrait d'homme inachevé* – implied all her dissatisfactions with Tadeusz as a weak man and an inadequate husband.

In late 1927 or early 1928 they began divorce proceedings. And with Tadeusz definitely out of her life, Tamara focused more attention on her daughter – at least on canvas. She was now painting Kizette more frequently, and for her part Kizette was an apparently compliant model, grateful to spend more time with her mother, anxious to please as she attempted to pose motionless during each forty-five minute session. They are uncomfortable paintings, though – one in particular, which shows Kizette sitting on the balcony of their apartment, suggests an unacknowledged but powerful resistance in her relationship with Tamara. While Kizette's hand is placed quietly in her lap, her blue gaze is staring half sullenly, half challengingly at the unseen woman painting her. The art world judged it to be a powerful painting, winning Tamara first place at the 1927 Exposition Internationale des Beaux-Arts in Bordeaux, but it was not a happy one.

Certainly as far as Kizette was concerned, Cherie was reverting hurtfully to her old patterns. 'She stayed out late and came home with so much energy she would paint for twelve hours non-stop. Then she'd take her favourite medicine, valerian, so she could get some sleep.'[17] Tamara was painting to exorcise Tadeusz, but she was also galvanized by the discovery of a new model. Sometime in 1927 she had been walking in the Bois de Boulogne when she had noticed a curious activity in the crowd ahead of her. People were pausing or breaking stride, turning their heads, and the reason was a young woman heading in her direction. It was one of those moments, she later recalled, when her perceptions were heightened and she felt the pulse of her vocation quicken.

The woman was astoundingly beautiful and when Tamara peremptorily begged to paint her, she was more than happy to comply. Rafaela turned out to be a professional, working as a model and part-time prostitute, but while that made her a very familiar type, she had a physical ripeness, a glossiness of colouring, that Tamara had never seen. She would have taken Rafaela to bed if she hadn't wanted to use her as a model so badly, and the quality of the three portraits she went on to paint may well have been charged with the intensity of deflected desire. In *La Belle Rafaela*, the softly lit curves of the young woman's body, foreshortened and exaggerated, have a perfumed heaviness, a bruised and satiated quality. In *The Dream*, or *Rafaela with Green Background*, a rare moment of intimacy is caught on canvas: Tamara has used unusually soft skin tones, making Rafaela's flesh look vulnerable, and captured an equally vulnerable expression in the model's eyes, an expression of darkness clearing, as if she has just awoken.

Professionally and socially Tamara was now working towards the peak of her success. British art critics were joining the European interest in her work, with the *Sunday Times* comparing her favourably to Wyndham Lewis, and the magazine *Graphic* publishing a flattering reproduction and review of *La Belle Rafaela*. In 1928 she was commissioned to paint a series of cover images for *Die Dame*, the German fashion magazine, which was one of the most significant commissions of her career. Not only did it bring her exposure to a mass market (and a lot of money), but one of the images she produced for the magazine, *Auto-Portrait* or *Tamara in the Green Bugatti*, became her most widely reproduced painting. It showed a woman driver, gloved and helmeted for speed, her blonde hair and long, heavy-lidded eyes quite recognizable as Tamara.

She had painted herself as an icon of the decade, and as her stock rose on the social register, Tamara's life moved closer to the perfection she created on canvas. She had honed her appearance to a sleek, expensive look: her short blonde hair was styled in marcelled waves, and her scarlet lipstick and nail varnish were balanced by thick false eyelashes. She wore evening gowns by Poiret and the young Schiaparelli, whose artful folding and draping flattered her body's curves. She also wore the designs of the newly launched Marcel Rochas, who loaned or gifted her several outfits. She had many lovers, both male and female, and as her estrangement from Tadeusz moved towards the formal severance of divorce, she developed an increasingly close relationship with one of her patrons.

Baron Raoul Kuffner had begun collecting Tamara's work sometime in the late 1920s, and in 1928 he commissioned her to paint a portrait of his mistress, the Spanish dancer Nana de Herrera. It's not clear at what point Tamara began to consider Kuffner as a potential husband. At this point he was still married to his first wife, and with his thick-set body and thinning hair he wasn't particularly attractive to her, but he was very rich, cultured and kind, and she seems to have wanted to manoeuvre herself into a possible future with him. The portrait she painted of de Herrera was strategically unflattering – her thin shoulders hunched and her smile so tense as to resemble a snarl – and certainly, when Kuffner's wife died in 1934 Tamara moved swiftly to secure him and his fortune.

Even though she claimed to have made over a million dollars by the end of the decade, Tamara never felt she was rich enough or enviable enough. She was still consumed by the need to shore up her life. In the late 1920s she was approached by the wealthy scientist Pierre Boucard, who had made his fortune patenting the indigestion remedy Lactéol. Boucard wanted her to paint portraits of himself, his wife and his daughter and, in addition, he wanted first rights of purchase over all her work. The terms that Tamara negotiated were such that she was finally able to create the home of which she had dreamed since coming to Paris – a public showcase for her achievements and a monument to herself.

In 1929 she bought a three-floor apartment on rue Méchain, big enough to double as both living space and studio, and hired the celebrated architect Roger Mallet-Stevens and her own sister Adrienne to remodel its interior. She wanted its style to reflect her own vision of contemporary luxe, with the airy chrome and glass structures of the staircases and mezzanine landings, the streamlined windows and radiator grilles, all complemented by a more theatrical glamour. She had a pair of vases made to her own design, with electric lights in their base that showed her favourite calla lilies to stagey effect; her large sofa was upholstered in a plush grey fabric that had her initials woven into the pattern.

The centrepiece, of course, was Tamara herself, and photographs of her painting at her easel, in jewels and an elaborately draped evening gown, appeared in the press. It was the apotheosis of the image to which she had always aspired: rich, famous and beautiful, in charge of her own created kingdom. And the following commission she received felt like the inevitable next step in her career, allowing her to extend her reach across the Atlantic.

A young American millionaire, Rufus Bush, had invited her to paint his wife's portrait in New York, for which he was offering a fee of forty thousand francs, plus lavish expenses. In early October, Tamara made her first voyage to the United States in high style, ensconced in a first-class cabin and dining at the captain's table every night. She was met by Bush and his wife with not one, but two Rolls-Royces standing by to transport her and her luggage, and she was booked into the recently opened

Savoy Hotel on 5th Avenue, an art deco temple to beauty and excess.

From her first day in Manhattan she felt as if she had come home. The city was living the American dream to the hilt, with the ever-rising stock market promising a season of even more extravagant parties and consumption. Tamara was enchanted by this vision of a city at play, of 'women who ... flirted and laughed as their men heaped fortune upon fortune and gave away mink coats and diamond bracelets and thousand-dollar bills as party favours'.[18]

But then, nine days after Tamara arrived, the market began to crash.

All that summer Wall Street had witnessed exceptional speculative activity. An interview with the financier John Jakob Raskob had been published in August under the title 'Everyone Ought to be Rich'. Its promise that a market investment of just $15 a month could accumulate $80,000 (close to a million dollars by today's values) in the space of two decades was taken as holy writ by many ordinary Americans, and by early September the Dow Jones share index was driven to a record high of 381 points as Americans avidly exchanged market tips.

On 24 October, however, concerns about rising personal debt and lax market regulation contributed to a rash of nervous selling. The market lost 11 per cent of its value at the opening bell, and over the days that followed terrified investors were suckered into the panic as the Dow slid faster and deeper. Attempts were made to steady it, with a few of the very wealthy buying up huge quantities of stocks, but by 13 November the market had plunged to just under the 200-point mark.

Tamara, who had only modest fluency in English and little sense of formal economics, could not follow the details, but couldn't fail to see the panic. Those who stood to lose most were those who'd borrowed heavily to buy stocks. Yet business also suffered – from the loss of capital, from the contraction of credit and from the massive decrease in outside investment. Over the following months a hundred thousand American companies would close, and five thousand banks would fail, ushering in a decade of economic depression.*

The mood in Manhattan was febrile, almost like a war zone, with people alternately retreating into despair or partying with fatalistic excess. As far as Tamara was concerned, it was vexing but not calamitous – she lost a sizable chunk of her American earnings by depositing them in a bank that subsequently failed. But there were still people in America whose fortunes were sufficiently large or well managed to consider the market crash a temporary hazard. Tamara received several lucrative commissions during this time and even managed to organize an exhibition of her work in Pittsburgh.

As far as she was concerned the party hadn't really ended. She continued to write letters home extolling the wonders of Manhattan: the 5th Avenue department stores, the perfect deco skyline and the nightclubs of Harlem, which, she informed Kizette, were the 'best . . . in the world'.[19] In mid-December she met a handsome ranch owner, who gave her a train ticket for New Mexico and an invitation to visit him. She had promised Kizette and Malvina that she would be back for Christmas, but the adventure was just too tempting, and it was late January before she finally returned to Paris.

Kizette, who was now boarding at a Catholic girls school, had been yearning for a festive holiday with her grandmother and Cherie. When Malvina saw Kizette struggling to overcome her disappointment, she was enraged by her daughter's callousness. There was a cupboard in the new apartment in which Tamara kept her by now enormous collection of hats – a collection that ranged from the large theatrical models she had favoured in the early 1920s to the close-fitting cloches she now preferred, dozens

---

* It would be over two decades before it fully recovered (in April 1932 the Dow Jones would slide even further, down to just 41.22 points).

of them in different colours and styles. Malvina emptied the cupboard and took all the hats downstairs where, one by one, she tore them to pieces and threw them onto the fire.

There's no record of how Tamara reacted to the destruction of her hats when she returned home. It was a busy time for her. Paris was already suffering from the fallout of the market crash, especially in the steady exodus of its American population. As Janet Flanner reported in the *New Yorker*, orders for expensive jewellery were being summarily cancelled, art collectors had stopped buying and in the bars of expensive hotels, the 'pretty ladies' were suddenly having 'to pay for their cocktails themselves'.[20] Yet Tamara's client list continued to expand. In Paris, as in New York, those who still had money seemed determined to continue spending. Among the numerous social events she attended that year was the 'silver' party given by Jean Patou, held in a roofed garden where every surface, including the trees, was covered with foil. Giant stuffed parrots hung in silver cages and three lion cubs were led on leashes through the crowd of conspicuously fashionable guests.

None looked more fashionable than Tamara. To be in possession of her beautiful apartment, her extensive wardrobe and her lovely social life was all balm to her. To see herself not only survive but triumph during the economic crisis, while others failed, was proof of her talent and spirit. In 1934, when she married Kuffner and his enormous fortune, she could safely consider herself immune from danger for the rest of her life. And yet for Tamara, too, something significant had ended with the turn of the decade.

From 1930 onwards she started to suffer prolonged bouts of anxiety and depression. Her robust health faltered and she developed severe stomach pains. She missed Kizette, whom she had sent to boarding school in England, believing it offered a better education and better care than her convent in France. She missed Ira Perrot, with whom she had quarrelled irrevocably, and she was distraught over the death of Jules Pascin in June 1930, which seemed to be a grim exemplar of the passing decade: drunk and unhappy he had slit his wrists and hanged himself in his Montmartre studio.

But it wasn't just her personal life that seemed to be slipping out of control. When Tamara visited friends in Berlin in 1934 she was seriously alarmed by her first vision of Hitler's Germany. She claimed she could smell the fear on the streets, and when Nazi uniformed officials had demanded to see her travel papers she felt a shuddering reminder of her past encounters with the St Petersburg Cheka. It seemed that the world was heading towards another catastrophe, and as it did so Tamara was far less confident now that her talent would allow her to transcend it. She was feeling her age, and also her vulnerability to changing trends.

The 1920s had created Tamara; they had provided her with her style, her subject matter and her marketplace. Even if her painting had never, objectively, attained the greatness she had hoped for, it had been exceptional as a register of its time. It had captured the tempo and colours of jazz, deco, of Coco Chanel and *la garçonne*; it had evoked the café culture of the Left Bank and the monied luxury of the Right. But in a rapidly changing world she began to sense that she was adrift. Over the decades that followed she tried to experiment with different techniques and subject matter, yet again and again the results turned out to be kitsch, sentimental or coarse. With the passing of the 1920s, it was as though she had lost some instinctive accord with her material, and when she and Kuffner moved to Hollywood, Tamara became known merely as the eccentric baroness who did 'these amusing paintings'.[21] While she lived long enough to see her early work making a return to fashion in the 1970s, it was also long enough to know that as a painter her golden age had been disappointingly brief, ending shortly after the decade that had formed her.

Chapter Twelve

JOSEPHINE

When Josephine Baker arrived in Paris on 22 September 1925, the city was still inventing itself as the capital of the *années folles*, and all the elements that had limited her career were about to be repackaged as something Dionysiac and new. She was to be presented as a Harlem jazz babe, a black modern flapper, but also as the most primitive of sexual fantasies, an African goddess. As the Paris historian Jean Prasteau would write, the timing was perfect: 'She arrived exactly at the moment we needed her. With her short hair, her free body, her coloured skin and her American accent, she untied the tendencies, tastes and aspirations of that epoch.'[1]

Josephine herself was alight with expectation when, along with the rest of the troupe, she stepped off the train at the Gare Sainte-Lazare. Her terror of the Atlantic crossing had been distracted by an on-board romance with the band leader Claude Hopkins, and by Caroline Dudley's promises of what awaited her. Even though the city was misted in a grey autumnal drizzle as the troupe were taken by bus to their lodgings, Josephine stood on the observation platform to catch every passing view: the jaunty taxis honking through the streets, the pavement cafés under bright awnings, the massive stone boulevards as grand as Manhattan museums. Approaching Montmartre and its steep, cobbled streets, she witnessed her first astonishing sight of white people and people of colour talking easily on the pavements and drinking together in bars. Paris looked like a kind of paradise, and when she fell asleep that night her mind was filled 'with the idea of conquering [it]'.[2]

Conquest was not, however, what an unhappy Rolf de Maré predicted when he watched the troupe's first rehearsal. The assortment of jazz, tap and Charleston numbers that had been assembled for *La Revue Nègre* seemed to offer little that would excite his sophisticated home audience. The troupe didn't even look very 'nègre' with their hair straightened, their cheeks powdered and rouged and their performance style honed to suit white American audiences. De Maré looked in vain for the blue-black skin, the tight African curls, the exotic 'dynamite' he had imagined selling to Paris.

With little more than a week to go before opening night, he tried to imagine a more original way of restyling the show. His producer, André Daven, had been impressed by the troupe's gregariousness when he'd first met them at the Gare Sainte-Lazare, spilling off the train in a 'rocking, boisterous, multi-coloured [crowd] all talking loudly, some roaring with laughter. Red, green, yellow shirts, strawberry denims, dresses in polka dots and checks. Incredible hats – derbies – cream coloured orange and poppy.'[3] This Harlem energy was new to Paris, and with the help of Jacques Charles, a famously canny veteran of the music hall, de Maré decided to make it key to the revue. New costumes were ordered in an exaggerated, motley design – Louis XIV hats were combined with overalls and straw hats paired with furs; scenic backdrops of New York and Mississippi steamboats were to be lit with carnival-bright colours. Charles also trawled Paris for darker-skinned performers to augment the cast, including the Antillean dancer Joe Alex. Finally, Charles identified the crucial missing ingredient. Erotic images of black women were widely peddled in France, ranging from the tropical fantasies of Gauguin's paintings to the postcards of half-naked Algerian women on sale in the street. Charles was clear: 'We need tits. These French people, with their fantasies of black girls, we must give them *des nichons*.'[4]

Naked breasts were already key to the marketing of the famous, and white, Folies Bergère, as well as productions that were less obviously burlesque. Parisians were accustomed to discreet views of flesh: ever since a 1908 court ruling had drawn a legal distinction between the 'aesthetic' and the 'obscene' nude, audiences had become used to the flash of a naked breast or buttock slipping from artful drapery. But Charles was right to assume that de Maré's audience would hope for more from this black American troupe. He planned strategic moments at which the chorus line would appear topless, and suggested a duet for Josephine and Joe Alex to be titled La Danse Sauvage, in which she would be virtually naked, except for a decorative belt of feathers and minuscule briefs.*

If Charles hoped that these improvements would create the necessary oomph of sexual bravura, the dancers were tearfully resistant. Onstage nudity was a rarity in legitimate American theatre, and for them to show their breasts in Paris, in what they had assumed was an upmarket show, seemed like a professional insult. Josephine, too, was angry and confused. She had come to Paris in the expectation of a sophisticated new platform for her career – Caroline Dudley had half promised her the chance of developing her singing – and to perform a 'savage' dance in nothing but a few feathers sounded like a step backwards into the theatrical ghetto.

But Charles was good at his job. In the face of Josephine's reluctance, he promised her that the duet with Joe Alex would be purely artistic, that it would be the climax and talking point of the entire show. And in truth, Josephine had little choice but to comply. She was in a strange city whose language she couldn't speak, and she had no money with which to buy a ticket home.

As the remaining days blurred into a frenetic schedule of rehearsals and costume fittings, she continued to feel very

---

* Josephine's appearance was also meant to arouse echoes of Fatou-gaye, the bewitching, erotic black girl in Pierre Loti's popular novel Le Roman d'un spahi.

unsettled though. André Daven's publicity had made an attempt to trumpet the revue's novelty: 'You will see these twenty-five Negros, in typical scenes and in their crude state. We haven't changed or altered anything. It might not appeal to everybody, but all the same, Negro art is really something. The greatest artists in the world have praised its . . . force.'[5] But despite this fanfare negative rumours were circulating: people were already suggesting that the dancing girls were not up to Parisian standards, and that the music was too wild for Parisian ears. The singer Mistinguett insisted that her own adoring public would never accept these American mongrels.

By opening night everyone's nerves were ragged. Although there were sold-out notices plastered outside the Théâtre des Champs-Elysées and flowers were heaping up at the stage door, many of the venue's two thousand seats were unoccupied when the curtain rose on the first half of the show. This was not the revue itself, but a music-hall programme of singers, dancers and Japanese acrobats, yet even so, as Josephine warmed up backstage, she was convinced she'd come to Paris only to fail.

During the interval, however, crowds began to fill the theatre, and by the time Josephine came onstage to dance her first number, a comic Charleston, she could sense their warm, excitable presence. Clatters of applause greeted her high kicks, and laughter rumbled round the theatre as she rolled her eyes, yodelled, puffed out her cheeks and exited the stage on all fours, her bottom arched high in the air. The excitement in the auditorium pitched even higher when Sidney Bechet started to play the music for 'Big City Blues', a number set in the streets of New York. Afterwards, Caroline Dudley swore that with the first searing notes of his clarinet, she could feel the public's reaction vibrating through the building: 'It was like the trumpets of Jericho, the house came tumbling down.'

All this was familiar territory for Josephine. But when she was back in the wings, waiting for the music of her Danse Sauvage, she felt drawn towards a very different place. She and Joe began their duel of seduction: their bodies coiling and retreating, their feet thrumming a fierce rhythm, and as she later recalled, a kind of ecstasy possessed her: 'Driven by dark forces I didn't recognize, I improvised, crazed by the music, the overheated theatre filled to bursting point, the scorching eye of the spotlights . . . Each time I leaped I seemed to touch the sky and when I regained earth it seemed to be mine alone. I felt . . . intoxicated.'[6] Josephine was still imprisoned within a stereotyped sexualized fantasy, yet naked and exposed as she was onstage, she nevertheless sensed a new creative freedom.

Josephine couldn't understand exactly the terms in which Paris acclaimed her. To the eminent dance critic André Levinson she was the quintessence of 'African Eros', the 'black Venus who haunted Baudelaire';[7] to Picasso she was 'the Nefertiti of now';[8] to the novelist Paul Morand she was a pure physical force, *'une machine à danser'*.[9] These references meant nothing to her, and it was much easier for her to gauge her success by the number of journalists who were waiting outside her hotel the following morning, clamouring for a photograph and a quote from the city's new star. Also by the solid evidence of the box office, where there was such a run on tickets that the revue was rapidly extended beyond its initial two-week season. Out of superstition Josephine kept the first thousand-franc note that she received from her weekly wage tucked under her garter, where it eventually became too creased and faded for use. The rest she began to spend. She upgraded herself to a suite in the Hôtel Fournet, with two bedrooms and a private bathroom, which until recently would have been an unimaginable luxury. And she began to surround herself with the kind of treats she had longed for as a child: a flowered cretonne bed cover from Galeries Lafayette; a collection of baby dolls, which she named and laid out on her pillows, and a small menagerie of pets, including two baby rabbits, a snake, a parakeet and a pig named Albert.

It was not unusual for stars to surround themselves with an animal entourage. The size of Sarah Bernhardt's was legendary, and it was surely a mark of Josephine's sudden celebrity that the Hôtel Fournet allowed her to keep so many pets in her rooms, despite the mess, the noise and barnyard smells. Primarily, though, she sought comfort, not status, from her new pets. Being in Paris made her nostalgic for her sisters and brother, with whom she had shared a mattress at home, and having these grunting rootling animals helped to alleviate her loneliness. As she later admitted, 'I used to tell them everything, my joy's [and] my hurts.'[10]

Josephine was learning to spend her money in style, but another consequence of her success was the number of presents that started to arrive for her: flowers, poems, little items of jewellery and, above all, clothes. The city's couturiers – always a rapid register of fame – sent dresses, hats and shoes for her to wear, and while Josephine initially felt as thrilled as a child on her birthday, she was soon overwhelmed. She had no idea how or when to wear these lovely things, and she began to leave them lying on the floor where she'd unpacked them, crumpled heaps of exquisite, expensively cut fabric from Molyneux or Patou. The singer Bricktop, with whom she had become friendly, scolded her, suggesting she should at least ask a maid to hang them up, but Josephine shrugged helplessly, 'Oh no, Brickie, they are going to take them away tomorrow and bring me another pile.'[11]

One of the most magical aspects of her success was being able to live in a city with few blatant rules of segregation. She had been exaggerating when she told journalists that the revue's opening-night party was the first time in her life she'd been invited to sit at a table and eat with white people, but she genuinely found it extraordinary to walk through the streets of Paris without being called a nigger or having to shrink pre-emptively when she brushed against a white person. Although there were some shamefully racist reactions to the show, including Robert de Flers's complaint in *Le Figaro* that its 'lamentable transatlantic exhibitionism . . . takes us back to the apes quicker than we have descended from them',[12] these were lost in the wider adulation of the general public. As the dancer Mildred Hudgens recalled, 'Paris was like Christmas every day. People so crazy about you, you forgot you were black.'[13]

Even so, Josephine preferred to stick close to Montmartre and Pigalle. This neighbourhood felt like Harlem or St Louis, with music spilling out from hole-in-the-wall bars and voices that could be heard singing and chattering on the streets throughout the night. A reassuring number of those voices also sounded like home. The black American soldiers who had gravitated there after the war had settled into a colony and many were musicians: 'Any time you walked down the street you'd run into four or five people who had real talent to them,' recalled Sidney Bechet. 'Everybody had a kind of excitement . . . everybody was crazy to be doing.'[14]

The cast of the revue had identified the venues where they preferred to party after the show each night, including Le Rat Mort, a tough but thriving club owned by the Corsican mafia, and Le Grand Duc, known as Bricktop's in honour of its singer-hostess. Ada Beatrice Queen Victoria Louise Virginia Smith, nicknamed Bricktop because of the uncompromising red of her dyed hair, had become the matriarch of Montmartre's music scene. Like Josephine, she had learned her craft on America's black performing circuit, and in Harlem she'd been the hostess of the Barron Wilkins Club and a member of the celebrated Panama Trio, singing alongside Florence Mills. But it was in Paris, where she came in 1924, that Bricktop attained real influence.

Holding court at Le Grand Duc, she not only performed for her clientele, she also gave private Charleston lessons – among her students were the Cole Porters, the Fitzgeralds, Hemingway and even the Prince of Wales. By the end of the decade she would regard Josephine as a professional rival and a disloyal friend, but when Bricktop first adopted her as a protégée in the autumn of 1925, she was more than generous with her advice, and for a brief period the two women were lovers.

Another friend on whom Josephine came to depend was Jocelyn

Augustus Bingham, a black pianist and dancer who called himself Frisco. He'd arrived in France as a soldier, and had made a handsome living ever since, playing piano in the city's ritzier bars and clubs, and giving dance lessons in hotels and private houses. He could speak nine languages, including fluent French, and had made himself an expert in Parisian etiquette. During those early days it was to Frisco as much as to Bricktop that Josephine went begging for advice about how to conduct herself in this new city.

She was the first to admit that on her arrival she had looked and acted like a rube: 'I wore a checkered dress with pockets held up by two checkered suspenders over my checkered blouse. I wore a hat with feathers on the top of my head, and I carried a camera on my left hip and a large pair of binoculars on my right hip'.[15] When strangers asked for her autograph she wrote her name out as slowly and painstakingly as a small child (on Bricktop's advice, she acquired a rubber stamp made of her signature).

She was learning fast, though. Caroline Dudley began steering her towards a more Parisian image. The austerity of Chanel would not suit Josephine, but Caroline felt she would look marvellous wearing the more flamboyant plumage of Poiret, and the older designer, feeling under threat from a new generation of couturiers, was more than happy to be associated with a rising star. After Josephine was introduced to him at the art deco exhibition in Paris (at which Poiret's designs were showcased in two beautifully decorated river barges), he invited her to his atelier with the promise that he would create a new gown especially for her.

Back in America Josephine had found it difficult to walk into the most ordinary 5th Avenue store, but when she was ushered into Poiret's atelier she felt like a queen. Two assistants took away her clothes, and a third brought in a huge bolt of material 'beautifully silvery . . . like a flowing river'. As Poiret sculpted the fabric around her, tightened it around her torso and draped it around her legs, Josephine imagined herself 'like a sea goddess emerging from the foam'.[16] Yet she was not entirely overcome by the designer's largesse. Asking for paper and a pen, she drew the outlines of what, to her, would be the ideal dress, a Harlem flapper shift, fringed from shoulder to hem in shades of pink. Whatever Poiret truly thought of her design, he professed to 'adore' it, promising not only to make this 'Josephine Baker' gown for her, but to feature it in his next collection.

Soon there were no more sightings of Josephine in overalls or ankle socks. Caroline helped her pick through the couturier's offerings and select a daytime wardrobe of crêpe de Chine frocks, snakeskin shoes and cloche hats. She was sent to the Helena Rubinstein boutique for suitable make-up: a pale ochre foundation called Crème Gypsy and a dark red lipstick to balance the black kohl outline of her eyes. Bricktop recalled how good Josephine's urchin body looked in its elegant new wrappings: 'The French people loved all that chic, went out of their minds.'[17]

During these first transforming weeks in Paris, Josephine also settled into an affair with the artist Paul Colin. She had modelled for him when he was drawing sketches for the revue's posters, and he had been shameless in his pride at being the first Frenchman to make love to the 'Black Venus', but in return he was an affectionate, attentive and informative companion. He took her to the places where she needed to be seen, like the Salon d'Automne exhibition at the Grand Palais (where several of Tamara's paintings were hung) and Le Boeuf sur le Toit where she heard Jean Cocteau playing drums. (The latter claimed that jazz was the best intoxicant in the world, 'you feel yourself pushed about by twenty arms. You are the god of noise.'[18])

At the Bal Negre club in Montparnasse, Colin pointed out other people she needed to know – André Gide, Jules Pascin, Nancy Cunard – but his efforts to introduce Josephine to Paris were becoming redundant. The city's artists were already asking to paint or sculpt her, fascinated by the paradox of raw instinct and professional polish presented by her body. Others clamoured to meet her. The composer Darius Milhaud and the surrealists

Picabia and René Clair queued up at her dressing-room door, Ravel longed to know Josephine and 'soak himself in this bouillon of culture' and Princess Murat – the same Princess Murat whose dresses Diana had coveted at Belvoir – begged Caroline Dudley to bring Josephine to her house.

She had experienced nothing like this new celebrity, and while onstage she felt secure in the public's acclaim, she was unsure of who or what these clever Parisians saw in her. Sometimes when she was invited to yet another party among yet more strangers, she would suddenly freeze and run away, seeking out the security of her hotel room and her pets. She knew that people were beginning to talk and that she was getting a reputation for rudeness, and she went weeping to Frisco one day, convinced that Paris would turn against her. 'She looked very young still,' he remembered. 'She was such a baby then.' He would try and reassure her: 'Jo. I'd say, you're in the right country now. You just behave yourself, and you'll go far. Very far.'[19]

Behaving herself wasn't simple, though. Josephine could now see postcards of herself on the street stalls; posters of the revue were everywhere, and even though she continued to suffer panic attacks, the widespread attention was also making her arrogant. One adoring young student who invited her out to supper found himself handing over a thousand-franc note for the privilege. As he mournfully reported to Caroline, 'I've given Josephine all my money and she's given me nothing in return. Nothing.'[20] She knew it was wrong to abuse her new status – 'I was not only crazy but a nasty girl'[21] – but after nineteen years of craving love and recognition, she couldn't resist.

'Paris . . . turned my head a little,' she admitted, and she was beginning to give herself absurd professional airs.[22] Due to the revue's extended run at the Théâtre des Champs-Elysées, a season scheduled for Anna Pavlova and her company had to be postponed. The great Russian ballerina, now forty-four, felt the slight keenly, and in mid-November, when the *Revue Nègre* transferred to the Théâtre d'Etoile, Josephine turned the knife in Pavlova's humiliation by including a crude parody of the latter's signature solo, The Dying Swan, in her own act. It was hardly as if Josephine had a point to prove, for Paris was flocking to her performances – Cocteau, an exact barometer of trends, had returned to see her six times. Moreover, Caroline Dudley had lined up yet more cities to conquer during the winter and spring, with a tour of Brussels, Berlin and Moscow.

Had the troupe actually made it as far as Moscow, it's hard to fathom what their reception would have been. Jazz was not, in principle, banned under the new Soviet regime* – in 1923 Valentin Parnakh and his pioneering band, The First Eccentric Orchestra of the Russian Federated Socialist Republic, had been invited to play in front of the Comintern – but officials were always wary of any taint of 'rotten Western decadence'. While a few might have accepted Josephine's Danse Sauvage as an expression of revolutionary black feminism, it would have been more likely condemned as evidence of depraved colonial oppression.

Berlin would be the last stop in the revue's tour, and even there the performers were made aware of how vulnerable they might be outside the relative tolerance of Paris. Jazz had a huge following in Berlin and black musicians were not a rarity,† but when the troupe opened at the Nelson theatre in late December, an aggressive group of brownshirts gathered in the street outside. Chanting crude insults about black monkeys and their degraded music, along with slogans from Hitler's recently published *Mein Kampf*, they distributed pamphlets demanding the immediate closure of the revue. Before long these fascist ideologues would present a serious threat to Josephine, but in 1926 she was too excited by Berlin to pay them much attention.

The bright lights and the busy, brash hedonism of the German capital transfixed her. Women wore tuxedos and monocles in

---

* Sidney Bechet would tour Russia with Noble Sissle's band in the late twenties and early thirties.
† A version of *Chocolate Dandies*, the show in which Josephine had danced in America, had just concluded a triumphant run.

open view, while men flaunted lipstick and kohl. In contrast to Paris, where the raunchier clubs and brothels were herded into working-class neighbourhoods or hidden behind doors, Berlin advertised every kind of vice. Prostitutes and drug dealers traded on respectable streets; even on the grander boulevards like Unter den Linden, transvestite cabarets, pornographic cinemas and strip clubs operated next to crowded cafés and smart restaurants.

Weimar Berlin was dancing on the edge of an economic abyss. Post-war inflation and unemployment had reduced many to beggars, while a more recent bubble of stock market gains had induced a frenzied spirit of partying among the lucky and rich. When Louise Brooks came to the city to shoot the 1929 film *Pandora's Box*,* she would observe that everything and everybody was for sale. To Josephine, however, the city's problems barely registered. Its boarded-up shops, ragged war veterans and crowds of children scavenging through rubbish bins were like scenes from her childhood and irrelevant to the consuming thrill of her success. Her performances were receiving praise as highbrow as any review in the French press. The art magazine, *Berliner Illustrirte Zeitung* or *BIZ* hailed her as a 'figure of contemporary German expressionism', an embodiment of modern form and primitive vitality. She accumulated gifts of preposterous extravagance: 'Rings with fire as big as an egg . . . ancient earrings which belonged to a duchess from 150 years ago, pearls . . . bracelets . . . furs.'[23] Admirers queued to take her out to Berlin's most sought-after night spots: the Resi dance hall, where each table had a telephone to facilitate the making of assignations, and the Kuka, a club so fashionable it didn't even open until 3 a.m.

The most potent tribute, however, was the attention paid to Josephine by Max Reinhardt. Reinhardt was still the most influential man in German theatre, with four performance venues

---

* Pabst's film, an adaptation of two melodramatic dramas of vice and corruption by Wedekind, famously featured Brooks in one of mainstream cinema's first lesbian kisses.

under his management as well as his Berlin-based drama school. His genius for spotting talent was legendary – Marlene Dietrich and Greta Garbo had both been unconfident, blurry young women when he'd first accepted them as students. And when Reinhardt introduced himself to Josephine he spoke to her about the 'treasures' of her dancing, 'the spontaneity of motion, the rhythm, the bright emotional colour'.[24] He promised that he could teach her to 'portray emotion as it has never been portrayed'. She might perhaps have dismissed the director as yet another intellectual in love with his own voice and with his own inexplicable theories of her success. But she recognized real power, and Reinhardt's low, resonant voice and brilliant blue stare hypnotized her, just as they had hypnotized Diana. When he suggested to Josephine that he take her on as his new protégée, she was profoundly flattered and willingly complied with his desire to show her off to his Berlin friends.*

Reinhardt was genuine in his admiration of Josephine's art. However, his attitude towards her showed none of the consideration and respect with which he'd treated Diana. One of the first invitations he offered her was to a party held at the flat of Karl Gustav Vollmoeller, *The Miracle*'s librettist, and as soon as Josephine arrived it was evident to her that it was some kind of stag event, for which she, the black dancer, was expected to provide entertainment. Compliantly, she got on with her task, taking off most of her clothes and moving into an intimate, sexy duet with one of the other female dancers. She felt no particular sense of outrage: this was the way the world worked; girls like her serviced the men with money and power. She was also probably high, having acquired a temporary taste for cocaine in Berlin, which seemed to be on offer wherever she went.

But to one of the guests, Harry Kessler, it seemed that Josephine retained a curious ability to transcend her surroundings.

---

* Josephine may not have seen *The Miracle*, but she did incorporate some of the iconography of Diana's role as the Madonna into her later work, including a Folies Bergère number in 1949.

As she danced she made herself oblivious to the roomful of watching men, losing herself in the movements of her body. To Kessler, at least, she ceased to be erotic; rather, she seemed to have clothed herself in the unselfconscious grace and dignity of her dancing.

This transformation fascinated Kessler and it reminded him of the Shulamite Woman, in the Bible, who manages to retain her spiritual purity even when forced into King Solomon's harem. It seemed to him that Josephine's talents could be wonderfully showcased in a pantomime ballet based on that story,* and he invited her to his home to discuss the project. Josephine had assumed it would be another party like Vollmoeller's, and when she arrived she was mortified to discover that female guests were present. She explained to Kessler that to strip off in front of respectable ladies was demeaning, that it broke her own private code of honour. However, when he explained his motive for inviting her, Josephine's mood changed and without hesitation she agreed to improvise a solo for the Shulamite Woman, there in his drawing room.

Kessler thought her performance was remarkable. Showcased in the room was a large sculpture of a crouching woman by Aristide Maillol, and instinctively Josephine latched onto it for inspiration. She danced as though the sculpture were a sacred idol and she its rapt priestess; at the same time she seemed to absorb the shape of the sculpture into her own body, imitating its lines and mass as she moved. Afterwards Kessler added his pleas to those of Reinhardt, insisting that Josephine must remain in Berlin and achieve the true expression of her talents under their direction.

All this was tempting to Josephine. These men clearly had money and influence and could do important things for her career. She could also imagine settling in Berlin, whose street life

---

* He imagined casting her alongside Serge Lifar, the latest beautiful young man to star with the Ballets Russes.

and food reminded her a little of home. But as she smiled and nodded her acquiescence to Kessler and Reinhardt, she apparently failed to consider her other, competing commitments. One of these was obviously the revue, which Caroline Dudley planned to run for many more months. The other was a contract she had signed even before leaving Paris to appear at the Folies Bergère.

Paul Derval, owner-manager of the prestigious venue, had spotted Josephine's outstanding box-office appeal as soon as she had arrived in Paris and had approached her privately with an offer to star in his next spring production *Folies du Jour*. Without telling Caroline, or indeed anyone else, Josephine had signed up with Derval, then more or less forgotten about it. In her world legal documents were not serious: marriage certificates and divorce papers were worth little more than the paper they were printed on.

Now, with her plans for Berlin beginning to advance, Josephine carelessly talked to the press about her enthusiasm for the city, and inevitably her comments reached Derval. An agent was dispatched to Berlin to remind Josephine of her agreement and to demand that she return at once to begin rehearsals. When Josephine was forced to confront the muddle she had made, she tried to turn it to her advantage. Berlin was clearly not an option if Derval was going to insist on holding her to their deal, but she would at least make him pay for depriving her of the option and told his agent that she would only return to Paris if she was paid an extra four hundred francs per show, bringing her earnings to the equivalent of $5,500 a month – a staggering sum that made her, reputedly, the highest paid performer in Paris.

As for the *Revue Nègre*, that would have to survive without her. Caroline was horrified when she was told of Josephine's imminent defection and, confronted with the collapse of her project, she did everything she could to dissuade her. She tried to shame her into acknowledging everything the revue had done for her, and appealed to Josephine's professional instincts, warning that the commercial Folies stage would present her as nothing more than 'a trussed-up performing mannequin'. Josephine was unmoved, however. Caroline's emotional argument that moving to the Folies would 'hurt her soul' raised only a stony-hearted quip, 'Missus, I'm feeling fine.'[25] Caroline set in motion a suit for breach of contract, but didn't have the heart to pursue it. She understood Josephine well enough to know that the concept of loyalty was an abstract luxury to her: 'She was a child still, a street child, taking what she needed.' Josephine's fellow performers were not so understanding, however; just a week after she left, the *Revue Nègre* was forced to close. None of them had any money saved, and while some found jobs in Europe, others were forced back home. As for Caroline, she was left with $10,000 worth of debt, which, according to her daughter Sophie, precipitated the break-up of her marriage.

Caroline Dudley was not alone in predicting that Josephine's unique qualities would be commodified. When Nancy Cunard reviewed *Folies du Jour* for *Vogue* she complained that it had become much harder to experience 'the perfect delight one gets from [her dancing]'.[26] Yet for Josephine herself, the lustre of a show that cost half a million dollars to stage represented a fabulous milestone in her career. The Folies was the city's oldest music hall; it had been stage to Maurice Chevalier, Charlie Chaplin and, above all, to Mistinguett, the French chanteuse upon whom Josephine had now fastened as her principal ideal and rival. And while it used to have a seamy reputation, under Derval's management the prostitutes who traditionally traded at the back of the theatre had been cleared out and the Folies' trademark nude scenes were repackaged with modern technology and expensive design.

Each show was programmed around a theme. For *Folies du Jour*, Derval planned to showcase the 'primitive' vitality of Josephine's dancing against scenes that portrayed the frippery of 'artificial' civilization. All the other dancers in the show were to be blondes or redheads, cast as Louis XIV's mistresses in a spectacular Versailles routine, or as Parisian flappers in a skit on modern window shopping – '*lèche-vitrine*'. When Josephine appeared in her jungle dance, she looked like some fabulously vital creature, slithering down a tree branch, naked except for a tiny tutu of fake bananas,* while a man dressed as a hunter lay 'sleeping' at the back of the stage. But if Josephine was being presented, even more overtly, as the white man's erotic dream, the confidence she'd gained during the last six months in Paris and Berlin allowed her to spin her material into something both sophisticated and anarchic.

Her virtuosity in this number (preserved in some 1927 film footage†) was remarkable. In the Charleston 'fan' move her knees and hands criss-crossed with the flashing speeds of a conjurer's card trick, she made every dance phrase pop with an unexpected rhythmic wit, or with the startling punctuation of a deep splits or high kick. But the glitter of the performance came, principally, from its confident spirit of mockery: Josephine was playing with this jungle imagery, rather than letting it play her.

The routine became known as her 'banana dance' and it was her signature piece for several years. In 1926, however, Josephine was more interested in the novelty glamour the Folies had to offer, including the dance in which she made her entrance hidden inside a huge crystal ball, descending slowly from the flies. When the ball hinged open and she began to dance a Charleston, reflections of her nearly-naked body bounced off a series of mirrored surfaces, an ecstatic proliferation of angles and curves that was multiplied by a chorus of dancing shadows – Josephine recast as a live cubist artwork.

Just as Derval had promised, dancing at the Folies ramped Josephine's celebrity up to a new level. She was a true 'vedette' now, her name spelled out in electric lights above the theatre and her performances advertised by giant colour photographs. By Christmas, the first Josephine Baker dolls came out on sale

---

* The idea for this soon-to-become-famous banana skirt was credited to Jean Cocteau.
† In this 1927 fragment she wore a coconut-shell brassiere, in deference to American censors.

and with her image beginning to feature in advertising campaigns Josephine found herself being held up to white women as a template of modern beauty – an astounding aesthetic reversal. Nancy was one of the first to adopt her look, not only in the African jewellery she collected but the black skullcap she had made in imitation of Josephine's hair. A few months later Josephine was invited to endorse a glossy hair pomade called Bakerfix, her photo appearing on billboards all around Paris. The vogue for suntans, started by Chanel, Sara Murphy and the Riviera set, took on new momentum with her celebrity, and beauty columns advised that walnut oil should be rubbed into the face and arms to bring a glow to pale skins. Valaze Water Lily beauty cream made new profits from its promise to deliver a 'body like Josephine Baker', and one expensive shop in the Place de l'Opéra placed a large moving model of Josephine in its window, next to a display of the cream.

Josephine also gave impetus to the French embrace of the Charleston. While it was probably a white American dancer called Bee Jackson who first performed it in Paris in 1924, it was Josephine's astonishing body and rhythmic intelligence that clinched its popularity as *the* dance of the *années folles*. There were rich commercial pickings to be had from its popularity, and not only for professionals such as Bricktop, who charged $10 to teach individual Charleston lessons and much more for an evening party. Sales of the shoes, frocks and accessories associated with the dance – the beads and jangling bracelets – all rose. Even the makers of bath salts profited by re-advertising their product as the perfect soaking cure for feet left swollen from a night of jazzing.

As poster girl for the Charleston, and embodiment of a new contemporary chic, Josephine's popularity soared. By the time she was twenty-one she was reputed to have received over forty thousand love letters and two thousand proposals of marriage. Her earnings rose too, and over the next couple of years she moved several times, each new address smarter than the last, until she was living in an apartment on the very expensive

Avenue Pierre-Ier-de-Serbie. When she was out in public she took care to look nothing less than a star. Some of her most beautiful clothes and accessories were gifts, including, it was said, the new car in which she was driven around – a Voisin, painted light brown to match her colouring, and upholstered in snakeskin. But she was extravagant with her own money too, splashing out sums that would have kept Carrie and Arthur in rent for years.

During her first season at the Folies the poet Langston Hughes arranged to meet Josephine before the evening show. As she emerged from the back seat of her Voisin, he was taken aback by the sudden, deferential stir of activity that surrounded her. One maid took Josephine's cloak from her, while another took care of her gloves and handbag; inside the dressing room, Josephine had her shoes removed by one dresser, while another placed a towel around her neck in readiness for her make-up to be applied. 'Here indeed was a star,' Hughes wrote, 'treated as no star I have ever seen, white, black, green, grizzly or grey, treated in America.'[27]

Hughes stayed at the theatre to watch Josephine perform, and afterwards they chatted together. Despite her queenly behaviour around her staff, it was clear to him that she felt vulnerable still, stranded halfway between the life from which she had run away and the starry life she now enjoyed. Recently, Florence Mills had come to Paris, and Josephine had gone to strenuous efforts to prove herself the singer's equal, sweeping in late to watch Mills's performance, wearing a floor-length ermine coat and escorted by eight young men in white tie and tails. Afterwards she had talked insistently with Mills, but virtually ignored Johnny Hudgins, her dear friend from the Standard days, who was also performing in Mills's show.

Josephine not only longed to be accepted by her former stage idols, she also wanted to be included in smart Parisian society. She tried to teach herself French by reading a collection of *Contes de Fées*, her favourite fairy tales, and she was absorbing everything she could about Parisian culture, yet she remained helplessly ill-equipped for certain situations. Ordering from a restaurant menu and navigating a formal dinner was still an ordeal, and in conversation her lack of education could be humiliatingly obvious. Bricktop's comment that at this stage in her career Josephine could barely speak American let alone French was a caustic exaggeration, but in certain circles that was how she was perceived. Certainly the further she moved away from Montmartre, and its relaxed ethnic mix, the more conscious she was made to feel of her ghetto background and her colour. *Vogue* might bestow its lofty blessing on black artists, opining that 'the Negro . . . composes better than Beethoven, he dances better than Nijinsky',[28] but when Josephine was portrayed by Sem, the city's leading cartoonist, it was made offensively clear that to sections of Paris she was little more than a novelty black sex act.

Sem's caricature showed her in elegant evening dress but with a monkey tail swinging from her bottom and a fly buzzing obscenely around its tip. In the face of such hatefulness it was no wonder that Josephine still chased after any beauty fad that promised to magic away the darkness of her skin, rubbing herself with lemon juice, and bathing in a mix of goat's milk and bleach that, according to her fellow dancer Harry Watkins, 'burn[ed] her pussy' every time.[29] It was no wonder, too, that she began to yearn for a lover, a Parisian Prince Charming who would protect her from condescension and abuse.

For a few weeks she believed she'd found him in a rich young playboy called Marcel, who promised her both love and luxury. He installed her in a large apartment on the Champs-Elysées with an interior designed by Poiret, a marble swimming pool and a double bed that had once been slept in by a Venetian Doge. However, when Josephine began to hint at marriage, even to imagine herself having a baby with Marcel, his interest suddenly waned. With another of her lovers, Georges Simenon, she suffered a similar disappointment. Simenon (not yet famous as a crime writer) had offered to help Josephine with her unwieldy correspondence and she had fallen in love with him, drawn by the emotional sensitivity that lay beneath his gangsterish façade.

Their affair lasted long enough for her to hope that Simenon might leave his wife for her, but while Simenon liked to boast that Josephine was the only woman in Paris who could match his sexual energy, he never considered her marriage material.

To Frisco, Josephine's desire to be loved was very affecting. He observed how childishly happy she could be made by a thoughtful present or a simple romantic declaration. Yet no woman could take as many lovers as she did without acquiring a reputation, especially if she was black and if she danced as Josephine danced. There was no doubt, too, that many of the men who had affairs with her exaggerated her sexuality to enhance their own. A composer she met in Berlin claimed she was 'a beast for sex, looking for the perfect penis',[30] while an Austrian actor swore to the nightly queues of men outside her bedroom, all waiting to service her. It was even rumoured that some nights she worked in a bordello, simply to satisfy her remarkable appetite.

When Hemingway described dancing with Josephine at the Jockey Club in Montparnasse, it was as though he had bagged some fabulous prey. She was 'the most sensational woman any-body ever saw . . . Tall, coffee skin . . . legs of paradise, a smile to end all smiles . . . she was wearing a coat of black fur, her breasts handling the fur like it was silk'. Initially she had been dancing with a British officer, but when Hemingway cut in he boasted that 'she slid off him and onto me' and 'everything under that fur instantly communicated with me'.[31]

Josephine had, in fact, become part of the city's itinerary: wealthy American students in Paris were said to follow a well-beaten path, starting with Maxim's, going on to Le Bal Tabarin to watch the cancan girls and ending up 'wherever Mlle Bakaire was holding forth.'[32] And Mlle Bakaire was becoming ubiquitous. Despite Josephine's love affairs and her earnest attempts to penetrate Parisian society, she was now working an average of ten hours a day. She began at a *thé dansant* club called the Acacia, which had been recently taken over by the small, stout American socialite, Elsa Maxwell.* Maxwell prided herself on setting trends, claiming to have been the first to 'discover' Bricktop in Paris, and to have invented the scavenger hunts that had the youthful elite of London and New York racing through the streets in furious, nightly competition for clues. Now, in Paris, she focused her attention on women her own age, who were no longer young or slender enough to feel comfortable in fashionable nightclubs. The Acacia offered 'taxi' partners for hire, willing young men who would steer her clientele gallantly around the dance floor, and a special opportunity to watch celebrity dancers like Josephine away from the usual evening crush.

From the Acacia, Josephine moved on to the Folies, and then to a series of clubs and cabarets, where she danced from midnight until dawn. It was an exhausting regime but as she confided to the young writer Marcel Sauvage, it was only when she was performing that she felt sure of being loved. Sauvage had initially come into Josephine's life to help her write a short biographical preface to Le Tumulte Noir, a collection of lithographs by Paul Colin, including several of Josephine herself. He had stayed on, however, when he realized how many stories she had to tell, and what kind of market there would be for a full-length memoir of her life.

During the months on which Marcel collaborated with Josephine on this book he came to know her better than anyone else in Paris. She regarded him as her confessor and concealed little. Often, when he arrived at her apartment, she was wandering around naked (she always felt most comfortable without clothes). She made no attempt to clear up the muddle of newspapers, clothes, records and expensive objets d'art that lay in heaps around her, nor to regulate the noise. This, Marcel recalled, was constant: the parrot squawking, Albert the pig grunting, music

---

* It was previously owned by Maurice Chevalier.

playing from a gramophone and, at frequent intervals, Josephine chattering on the telephone in her mix of American and pidgin French.

When Marcel had first suggested to his publishers that he should write Josephine's memoirs they thought he was joking; in 1926, it was only the distinguished and the elderly who were regarded as appropriate subjects. But Josephine wasn't just a dancer, Marcel argued, she was 'a phenomenon'[33] – everything about her life would be of interest to the public – and in writing his book he prefigured the formula of the modern celebrity memoir. Alongside the story of Josephine's life he added the kind of random facts that he knew would fascinate her fans – lists of her most extraordinary presents and famous admirers; tips on beauty and lifestyle; even the recipe for her favourite meal, corned beef hash and hot cakes with syrup. Marcel also knew better than to challenge the fantasy logic of her recollections: he was her storyteller, not her historian and uncritically he wrote down everything Josephine invented for him, from her 'Romeo and Juliet' parents, who'd had to run away from their families in order to marry, to her own instant Cinderella transformation from starveling child to beautiful star. He allowed her to contradict herself at will. At one point in the memoir she boasted of her dedication to her art – 'To live is to dance, I would love to die breathless, exhausted at the end of a dance' – while at another she berated the 'artificial life' into which her talent had forced her, promising that some day she would turn her back on the 'sad choices' she had made and retire to the country: 'I'll marry simply,' she declared. 'I'll have children and lots of animals. I love them; I want to live in peace among children and animals.'[34]

This notion bore little relation to Josephine's actual life, however. Even as she painted this picture of imagined, saintly calm she was busy forming ambitious plans for her career, and doing so with the help of her latest lover, a man who styled himself Count Pepito de Abatino. She'd met Pepito through his cousin

Zito, an artist who drew caricatures at Zelli's bar. Somewhere in his late twenties or early thirties, he was a thin, sallow Sicilian, yet to Josephine's uncritical eyes he was the very image of an Italian count: his high forehead framed by dark, slicked-back hair; his expression given an air of intellectual dash by the monocle he affected. From a certain angle, Pepito reminded her of the film actor Adolphe Menjou (the handsome support to Rudolf Valentino in *The Sheik*). And his manners, too, seemed as polished as any movie star's as he gazed at her through his monocle as if she were an object of rare beauty, telling her she was the greatest dancer he had ever seen, writing her elaborate love letters and pampering her with exquisite care.

In reality Pepito's breeding was as much an accessory as the yellow and white spats he favoured. He'd invented his title after he abandoned his modest trade as a stonemason to make a new life for himself as a dance partner and gigolo. Josephine's friends saw through his façade. Bricktop dismissed him as a 'bum' and a 'fraud',[35] distrusting his over-perfumed pomade, his flashy rings and bright clothes, and assuming that his intentions were simply to fleece Josephine for money. However, Josephine herself wasn't too concerned about the truth of Pepito's pretensions; what mattered to her were his promises to advance her career.

It was precisely because Pepito was a self-made creation that he was able to understand and help her as he did. Unlike all the other Pygmalion figures in Josephine's life he knew, from experience, how precarious her transformation felt. She might look like a star, even act like a star, but she didn't yet have the confidence of one and she wanted guidance in refining the way she talked and conducted herself.

Peptio was ready to offer her that guidance, and even more ready to help Josephine expand the range of her performing options. She was growing tired of the Charleston and the 'banana dance' and impatient to progress in her ambition to become a singer like Mistinguett. So far, however, none of her producers had made good on their promises to give her voice a trial and it was Pepito who sat Josephine down and told her she needed to make her own way. She needed to hire herself a singing teacher and she needed to find herself an independent platform.

It was possibly not Pepito who engineered Josephine's debut appearance on record, singing a sentimental little number called 'Who'. The result was poor; she was accompanied by a mediocre band and her small soprano voice sounded weak and untrained. But it was he who organized Josephine into opening her own nightclub, where she could be fully in control of her material and image. Backed with cash from one of her admirers (a Dr Gaston Prieur who'd grown rich from colluding in medical insurance fraud) Pepito found and purchased a small premises on rue Fontaine, close to the heart of Montmartre, and on 14 December 1926, Chez Joséphine opened its doors to the public.

As so often in her career, Josephine's progress advanced on the wreckage of other people's expectations. Just a block away was the Imperial, a club that had just changed its name to Josephine Baker's Imperial after she'd signed a year-long contract to perform there. Not only had Josephine reneged on the deal, she'd also poached many of the Imperial's staff – and a sizable chunk of its clientele once her own club opened.

But Josephine felt justified by the superiority and originality of her project. She and Pepito had planned Chez Joséphine as a careful fusion of New and Old World styles. The menu created by their American chef offered chitlins, black-eyed peas and rooster combs alongside steak tartare and plover's eggs, and Josephine's own image was pitched somewhere between Harlem hostess and French diva. A report in *Vogue* described her sweeping into the club at around 1 a.m., with an entourage of some few favoured fans, her maids, chauffeur and little white dog. She wore a tulle dress with a blue snakeskin bodice and shoes to match, a diamond at her waist. Her dressing-room walls were covered with press cuttings and photographs of herself, and the dog bore the dark crimson imprint of her mouth where she'd kissed it.

Yet there was an element of homeliness mixed in with Jose-

phine's glamour. Trotting by her side as she progressed through
the club was her new pet nanny goat (Albert the pig wasn't
allowed to appear in public, but was given free rein in the
kitchen, growing monstrously fat on leftovers). As she moved
between tables she used tricks she'd learned back in St Louis,
singling out susceptible men; pulling their moustaches and whis-
pering coarse endearments in their ears. When she started to
sing, she mixed raw, poignant blues numbers in among her
repertory of romantic French ballads.

She worked very, very hard at finessing her new skills, her
own amibitions now driven by Pepito's. He would sometimes get
rough with her, his Sicilian machismo getting the better of him
when he considered she was slacking in her daily practice. Once
or twice he even hit her. But the regime worked. Patrons came
to Chez Joséphine as early as seven or eight in the evening in
order to secure a table, and they would wait patiently until the
early hours of the morning, when she finally arrived to perform.
The Aga Khan became a regular at the club, as did Colette, who
also joined the lengthening line of older women taking a semi-
maternal, semi-sexual interest in Josephine.

Colette sent affectionate little notes, written on the paper
doilies she picked up from her table at the club; she called
Josephine my 'little brown daughter', and for a while the two
women were rumoured to be lovers.[36] Whatever the exact status
of their relationship, it was a wonderful endorsement. Colette
was cherished as one of France's leading writers and her interest
helped mark Josephine as a true Parisian. In the months that
followed the opening of her club Josephine felt a distinct social
change; invitations began to arrive for charity balls, fêtes and
galas. She was asked to open the 1927 Tour de France, and she
inspired a new dish, 'Poulet Joséphine Baker', at the Tour
d'Argent restaurant.

She was no longer the novelty jazz babe from Harlem. Under
Pepito's instruction, she continued to perfect her appearance: a
vampish spit curl appeared in the dead centre of her forehead,
her skin seemed to grow ever paler and she insisted on the

accented 'é' of Joséphine whenever and wherever her name was written. When she opened in a new Folies show in April 1927, she was required to dance one retro ragamuffin number, but otherwise she was packaged in a far more classic Parisian style, her costumes including a skirt of marabou feathers and a metallic, low-cut bathing suit with rhinestone straps that followed the contours of her naked breasts. Even her trademark banana skirt was now encrusted with diamanté.

High on the success of his project, Pepito expanded Josephine's commercial potential and in addition to the Bakerfix endorsement he secured a mass advertising campaign with Pernod. Both of them were getting rich on the profits, but they were also in danger of over-reaching themselves. On 20 June 1927 they orchestrated a large press conference, in which they announced to the world that they had become man and wife. Josephine did most of the talking. She said that she'd agreed to marry Pepito on her twenty-first birthday and that her new husband had not only given her a huge diamond ring, but all the 'jewels and heirlooms that have been in the family for generations'. The Abatinos were, she assured her audience, the real thing. She'd had them checked out by a private detective and they had 'lots of coats of arms and everything. I understand they live in a big swell chateau.'[37] Smiling at the room with breathtaking deceitfulness, Josephine assured journalists that she had never been married before and that it was all 'so much fun'.

Of course there were no jewels and no chateau, and there hadn't been a wedding either – as Josephine wasn't yet divorced from her last husband, Billy. However, as she started to flaunt her new ring and title around Paris, she believed for a brief moment that the story might stick. In America, at least, it was uncritically accepted, with the *New York World* running the headline 'NEGRO DANCING GIRL BRIDE OF ROMAN COUNT', and informing its readers that 'Josephine Baker of Harlem adds a noble husband to conquests abroad'. According to *Variety* magazine, her 'tie up with the count' was being talked about everywhere. And if the white press gave the story prominence, the black papers ran with it for days, elaborating the grandeur of the match and even inventing quotes from Pepito's father about his delight in having Josephine as his daughter-in-law.

Rapidly the lie of her wedding became elevated into a story of black inspiration. The previous year some of the French-produced Josephine Baker dolls had appeared in Harlem shops – a source of local pride. Now the *New York Amsterdam Press* boasted that Josephine had 'made a more auspicious venture on the sea of matrimony than any number of American women within memory'.[38] Black girls across America began to dream of emulating Josephine; to them she was all that the movie stars in *Picture-Play* had been to Tallulah. The singer Bobby Short was a child at the time and recalled how mothers and daughters in his hometown of Danville, Illinois, loved to talk over the tale of Josephine's success, saying to each other, 'My God, she's conquered France and now she's married this count.'[39]

In Paris, however, reporters digging for extra information rapidly discovered that there was no trace of any wedding ceremony, nor of any noble family called Abatino. They didn't enjoy being duped, and they made their displeasure clear to Josephine in a spate of vitriolic comment. Some of the attacks in the press were so fierce that she feared she might be arrested, and frantically she began to backtrack, pretending it had all been a joke that had got out of hand: 'Since it's amusing to be married I let it out around town that I was – you know how false news spreads.'

It was, in the end, all good publicity. And perhaps that was all it was intended to be, given that Marcel's book, *Les Mémoires de Joséphine Baker*, was due to appear in the bookshops very soon. Three weeks later, Josephine's stunt was forgiven and forgotten as journalists mined the memoir for new gossip. La Baker was again the public's darling. However, hubris was always a besetting issue in Pepito's plans – the Josephine Baker magazine, which he launched, edited by Simenon and featuring photographs of

Josephine and her famous clientele, floundered miserably. And he again miscalculated when he judged that this was the moment to push Josephine into the movies.

Offers from Hollywood had been arriving regularly at Josephine's door, but up till now she had resisted them. Scriptwriters seemed unable to imagine roles for her beyond the black stereotypes she had worked so hard to escape, principally that of the comic plantation nigger girl. But Pepito was keen to persuade her that a film appearance would dramatically enlarge her audience – cinema was now very big business in France, with many of the traditional Boulevard theatres converting to large movie houses – and she finally yielded to his arguments when a script arrived from the French novelist Maurice Dekobra, which she was assured had been written especially for her.

La Sirène des Tropiques told the story of a young Antillean woman, Papitou, who falls in love with a French engineer and follows him back to Paris in the hope of marrying him. Diverted into a successful career as a dancer, Papitou fails to locate her engineer until after he has become engaged to another woman, at which point she heroically renounces her great love, assuring the audience and herself that 'sacrifice is the purest form of joy on earth'.[40] As a plot line it was hardly original – Tallulah had acted in a dozen similar stories about headstrong young women with hearts of gold – but what was important to Josephine was that the role of Papitou transcended race; ultimately, she was just a girl in love. Or at least that was how the film was presented to her. Later Josephine claimed the script had not been adequately translated for her and that she had been unaware of how many crude jokes about colour it contained. (One especially offensive, and extended, gag involved Papitou falling into a coal bin and causing a terrified elderly woman to believe she'd seen a black devil; then subsequently falling into a flour bin and causing the same woman to believe she'd seen a ghost.)

The crassness of the material was also exacerbated by Josephine's inability to transcend it. She hated being on set; like Diana, she was tormented by the blinding lights and interminable waits between shots. She was also usually exhausted, having sung at her club until dawn, managing only a couple of hours' sleep before she had to get up for filming. Fatigue and irritability not only made her behave badly, they also made her difficult to direct.* At the premiere on 30 December 1927, Josephine wept, unable to recognize herself as this 'ugly silly person' up on the screen. No one on set had been able to persuade her to mute her usual performance style, and her comic eye-rolling grin and vibrating energy came across as manic, even freakish.

Josephine was impatient for artistic maturity, and yet it seemed to take so much time and trouble. The divinity of the great stars still dangled unreachably above her. Florence Mills had recently died – officially from a botched appendectomy, but probably from tuberculosis – and most of Harlem had been on the street to watch her funeral cortège pass by and see the flocks of birds that were released from an aeroplane in tribute to *Blackbirds*, her signature show. In jealous anguish, Josephine wondered how she would ever attract such love. Although she was making progress as a singer, even the musicians who played for her thought her voice would never have sufficient power 'to throw the velvet', and she was still only performing to a very small, select audience at her club. By the end of 1927, Pepito decided that in order to accelerate her transformation (as well as put some distance between Josephine and her horrible film debut) it was time to leave Paris and go out on tour. In an emotional speech, Josephine announced to journalists that she was going away to be reborn: 'The Charleston, the bananas, finished.† Understand I have to be worthy of Paris, I have to become an artist.'

The tour Pepito arranged was monumental. Between early

---

* So bad were her tantrums that Luis Buñuel, who was working as assistant director, quit the film in disgust.
† She spoke a little prematurely. The bananas had become integral to her image whether she liked them or not, and in 1934, when she made the film *Zouzou*, she wore her banana skirt for all the publicity; labels printed with her picture were also offered to the greengrocers of Paris, to fix to the fruit on their shelves.

1928 and late 1929 Josephine sang and danced in twenty-four cities across Europe and South America; in each one she also performed in a local nightclub, temporarily renamed Chez Joséphine. Travelling with her and her entourage of staff were fifteen steamer trunks of equipment, including 137 costumes, 196 pairs of shoes, 64 kilos of face powder and 30,000 publicity shots to distribute en route. Exhausting as the schedule was, it gave Josephine intensive schooling in the skills required to be a star. As the centrepiece of the show, she had to be able to hold a performance together in the face of bad stages, inadequate bands or hostile audiences, and she had to learn tough lessons in the art of projecting her voice, body and personality. Offstage she worked with singing and dancing coaches; language tutors to improve her French and manicure her English; conversation classes to coax her into expressing herself more intelligently. Even at the end of 1927, a tang of the feral still lingered around her image; stories that she ate with her hands at mealtimes were untrue, but many believed them. Two years, however, would work a remarkable change, as revealed by the picture taken by *Vogue* photographer George Hoyningen-Huene in 1929. It wasn't just the sultry choreography of the photograph that registered her new sophistication – the fluid line of her body echoed by the fall of pearls and the silken material held delicately between her hands – what was remarkable was the composure of her gaze and the stillness of her presence. Of the dancer who'd been compared to a kangaroo, a boxer, a monkey and a savage, there was not a trace.

For Pepito, however, success came at a price. As Josephine shed her St Louis accent and social awkwardness, she inevitably began to outgrow her lover. He remained necessary to her in certain ways – as a professional advisor and a compliant ear to her worries and complaints – but she could no longer take seriously his flashy rings and spats, his carefully assembled stock of compliments and small talk. He began to seem almost pathetic in contrast to the men who were beginning to pursue her, among them Crown Prince Gustaf Adolf of Sweden, the irrepressible

Feodor Chaliapin, and Charles-Edouard Jeanneret-Gris, the Swiss architect who called himself Le Corbusier.

Josephine and Le Corbusier had met in South America and become lovers two months before the end of her tour. The architect was far from her usual type, with his thick pebble glasses and long, clever face, but she was both flattered and captivated by his brilliance, listening raptly to his vision of architecture as an agent of social transformation, and posing willingly for the erotic sketches he drew of her. They met again, by design, on the boat travelling back from Rio to Bordeaux, and it was during this voyage that Josephine developed the idea of one day using her money to build a village in the French countryside, where people of every colour and class could live in a Corbusian-style utopia.

That vision would resonate in Josephine's imagination, eventually inspiring the 'rainbow tribe' of orphans she began to adopt, and the home she made for them in a rural French chateau. She and Le Corbusier would continue to correspond affectionately on the subject, although in romatic terms their lives would separate; the architect was returning to his fiancée Yvonne and Josephine was returning to Paris, which she claimed was her one true love. To the journalists who clustered round her, she declared she had, as promised, made herself worthy of the city: 'I have grown up. I am a woman.'[41]

Now that Josephine considered herself fully formed as a performer, she was ready to stake her rivalry to Mistinguett – her idol and her nemesis. She no longer had the platform of her club; Prieur had failed to find a replacement singer to sustain the business at Chez Joséphine, and he subsequently went to prison, having finally been convicted of insurance fraud. However, the Casino de Paris, where Mistinguett had just been performing, was ready to offer Josephine a starring slot in its next production, *Paris qui remue* (Bustling or Swinging Paris). This show was being themed in response to the city's forthcoming

Exposition Coloniale, and Josephine was obviously a natural fit for its exotic, African scenes. But while she would be required to dance glossy variations of her old numbers like Danse Sauvage she was also, crucially, being allowed to sing.

The Casino's owners, Henri Varna and Oscar Dufrenne, had quelled their reservations about the ability of Josephine's voice to fill a theatre and commissioned the songwriter Vincent Scotto to provide her with a light romantic ballad. The result, 'J'ai deux amours Mon pays et Paris', turned out to be another milestone in Josephine's career as her Danse Sauvage. Scotto worked carefully to flatter her modest range, and Josephine sang the material with a poignant, yearning lift in her voice that transformed it into something intensely personal, the story of her own life. Audiences loved her, and not only did the song become one of the highlights of *Paris qui remue*, which ran for an exceptional thirteen months, but when it was recorded it sold three hundred thousand copies. Critics professed their amazement at this new Josephine: 'She left us a *negresse*, droll and primitive, she comes back a great artist'; 'The beautiful savage has tamed her instincts'.[42] Again, her transformation was registered by commerce, and high-quality products like de Sévigné chocolates and Vitus radios began to solicit her endorsement.

But for Josephine, the greatest affirmation of all was the reaction of Mistinguett, who now regarded her as a genuine threat. The fifty-five-year-old singer was beloved in Paris – Maurice Chevalier claimed she had become the city's 'symbol of gaiety and good humour and courage and heart'[43] – yet her growing hatred of Josephine was tainting her image. She insulted 'la petite nègre' to anyone who would listen, and when she saw Josephine at a film premiere she called out recklessly, 'Well, Pickaninny, why don't you come up and salute me?'[44] Josephine, reacting with instant fury, stalked over and lashed out with her nails, while Mistinguett, no less a street fighter, retaliated. But to the delighted crowds watching, it appeared to be the older singer who was having to battle hardest for her reputation.

There were crowds everywhere that Josephine went now,

drawn by her fame, but also by her spectacular new accessory, a tame cheetah with a gem-encrusted collar,* which she took around with her on a lead. Bricktop wryly commented, 'You couldn't get within blocks of her, everything stopped cold. The French men and the women too would come running up to her: Joséphine, belle Joséphine, brave Joséphine.'[45] Some, however, mourned the old Josephine. Janet Flanner wrote ironically, 'She has, alas, almost become a little lady. Her caramel-coloured body has become thinner, trained almost civilized . . . On that lovely animal visage lies now a sad look, not of captivity but of dawning intelligence.'[46]

But Josephine was moving in step with the times as well as with her own ambition. The economic uncertainties that had ended the Twenties and opened the new decade were dampening enthusiasm for the experimental and the exotic. The black, untamed garçonne of 1925 was no longer a fashionable look, and Josephine's new incarnation as a diva chanteuse proved far more to the taste of the 1930s public. Almost as significantly, it would provide Josephine with a stronger defence against a changing political culture.

As early as 1927, Josephine had become aware of a shift in Paris. The influx of a new type of American tourist, drawn more by the cheapness of the franc than by the rarity of the city's culture, was introducing an overt level of racism into public life. She began to hear 'nigger' on the streets; a hotel refused her and Pepito entry on the grounds that she might offend their other American guests. Most mortifying was the incident that occurred on the night of Charles Lindbergh's landing at Le Bourget, in May 1927. Paris was en fête – trams flew the Stars and Stripes, crowds gathered in the Place de l'Opéra, and at the Folies Bergère it was Josephine who joyfully announced the news of Lindbergh's safe arrival. Afterwards, however, when she went

---

* Later, during one of Josephine's recurrent periods of debt, she pawned the choker for $20,000.

to a celebratory dinner at the L'Abbaye de Thélème, an Ameri-can objected loudly to the fact that he was seated at a table next to her, calling out, 'At home a nigger woman belongs in the kitchen.'

Josephine later wrote, 'I thought if the floor could open up and swallow me it would be a blessing.'[47] But this insult was nothing compared to what awaited her when she left Paris to go out on her 1928–9 tour. In America the Ku Klux Klan had already begun to target any deviation from the white ideal – flappers, jazz musicians, communists and homosexuals as well as blacks. And in an increasingly reactionary Europe it wasn't only Josephine's colour that made her vulnerable to attack, but her reputation for promiscuity and nude dancing.

The first stop of the tour was Vienna, and days before she arrived protests were already being organized against Josephine and her 'brazen-faced heathen dances'. Church bells were rung to warn the pious off the streets when she appeared and sup-porters of Hitler prepared to demonstrate against her contami-nating presence. So effectively did the Church and the Nazi party combine their opposition that the wisdom of letting Jose-phine perform was debated both in the city council and in the Austrian parliament. Arguing in her favour was the liberal aris-tocrat Count Adalbert Sternberg, who appealed to the estab-lished German culture of naturism by claiming that to attack Josephine was to blaspheme against God, who had created the human body. Even though she was barred from performing in the theatre that had originally been booked, the Ronacher, she was allowed to transfer to the smaller Johann Strauss Theater, where she played for a month to packed crowds.

Still the controversy escalated. In Prague, Budapest and Zagreb, student agitators and Catholic protestors again joined forces, gathering outside the theatre to throw ammonia bombs and chant, 'Go back to Africa.' In Munich, Josephine was banned from making any appearance at all; in Berlin claques of Nazi sympathizers were in the Theater des Westens every night, and Josephine cut short her scheduled six months to just three weeks.

Even when she crossed the Atlantic to Argentina, in the spring of 1929, controversy followed, with both the Church and the President condemning her immorality. All this hardened Josephine's determination to leave the primitivist black imagery of her stage material far behind. Yet even though she was sometimes frightened, sometimes maddened, by these personal attacks, she began to relate them to issues larger than herself. Travelling around Europe she realized there was a world of hatred and evil outside the bubble of her success, a world that in some vague way it was her duty to address.

Josephine's political conscience was both uninformed and sentimental, but it was passionate.* It fed the vision of the utopian village that she planned with Le Corbusier and more immediately it inspired her to begin writing a novel about the injustice of race. *Mon sang dans tes veines (My Blood In Your Veins)* was eventually published in 1931, with the help of the ghostwriter Félix de la Camera, and if its literary value was trite, its creation was a revelatory process for Josephine, forcing her to address more directly the abuse of her childhood and the racism of the world she now inhabited. It was a Romeo and Juliet story about Joan, a young black girl, and her childhood sweetheart, a wealthy white boy called Fred. As adults, they are forced into divergent lives, but when Fred has an accident, Joan selflessly offers her blood for his life-saving transfusion. In that act of sacrifice, however, she also symbolically reclaims him, for back in the early 1930s, race was still thought to be 'carried' in the blood. There's an element of revenge as well as romance in the fact that, with Joan's gift, Fred has been turned into a 'white negro', one of her own.†

---

* It may even have made an impact on Crown Prince Gustaf given his subsequent, ardent support of the civil rights movement.
† That image may have resonated with an evening she spent with Le Corbusier on the ship bound for France. Dressing up for dinner at the captain's table, the two of them 'swapped' race, Josephine wearing a thick mask of white powder, Le Corbusier blacked up like a minstrel.

The past that Josephine had battled so hard to escape – the St Louis ghetto, the black touring circuit, the ignominy of the chorus line – was one she no longer wanted to ignore. Several months after she returned to Paris, she received a message from it in the form of a package from Dyer Jones, the St Louis trumpeter for whom she had worked when she was eleven. It contained a good luck charm – a rusty old nail wrapped around with a lock of Dyer's hair – and a note that said simply, 'I think of you. Your success has given me pleasure.'[48] A year or two earlier Josephine might have tossed away that token as an unwelcome and irrelevant reminder of her former life. Yet like Nancy and so many others of her generation, she was starting to see the world in larger, more politically exacting terms. Just at the point where she finally began to transcend the limits of her colour, and to be embraced as a Parisian chanteuse, Josephine also started to re-embrace her blackness – as both an essential part of her identity, and a cause.

EPILOGUE

On 15 April 1975, twenty thousand people stood on the streets of Paris to watch as Josephine Baker's coffin was driven in state across the city. Many thousands more watched on television, drawn by the congregation of famous names inside the Madeleine Church, and by the fact that for the first time in French history an American woman was being mourned with full military honours. Josephine had fantasized about such a funeral ever since the spectacular send-off Harlem had given Florence Mills back in 1927. And the fact that Paris staged it for her was a mark of the tenacity with which she had sustained the city's love during the course of her long career.

It was nearly half a century since she had first been embraced by Paris as its Black Venus. By the time she was fifty she had carefully transmuted her image into that of an ageless diva, armoured with false eyelashes and feathered headdresses. Even at sixty-eight, she was still working that image successfully, sing-ing her now classic repertory of songs into rhinestone-studded microphones and dancing a game vestige of the Charleston.

Offstage, however, Josephine might be unrecognizable. Years of toxic conk applications had burned off all but a few meagre tufts of her hair, and her long, chorus-girl legs required careful bandaging to protect them from cold and strain. But once she had put on her wig and her make-up, some alchemy of stage lighting and adrenalin still summoned up a spark of her youth-ful self. In her final revue, *Joséphine*, which opened in Paris on

8 April 1975, she was able to sing thirty-four songs and dance a few iconic jazz steps.* The reviews were almost uniformly ecstatic.

People spoke of the show as one of the triumphs of her career, and it was sold out for weeks to come, yet three days after its premiere Josephine failed to emerge from her hotel room at her usual time. When anxious staff entered, she was discovered unconscious in her bed, her reading glasses askew, around her an array of newspapers and magazines reporting her success. She died a few hours later. And while the official cause of death was registered as a stroke, those close to Josephine liked to think she had died of happiness.

Among the many telegrams of congratulation that she had received on 8 April was one from President Giscard D'Estaing, sent 'in the name of a grateful France whose heart so often beat with yours'.[1] The president's message was a tribute to a cherished star, but it also reflected Josephine's status as a patriot and a heroine of the Second World War.

When France went to war against Germany it was not surprising that she should have found the French cause so close to her heart. Her own hatred of the Nazi regime dated back to the treatment she'd received while on tour to Austria and Germany. Yet her patriotic commitment went far beyond that of most of her colleagues: for in addition to dancing and singing for the French troops, Josephine also worked as a low-level spy, trafficking secret information.

At the beginning of the war, when she was still being invited to embassy parties, she was recruited by the French military police to keep her ears open for relevant snippets of war gossip. In 1940, as the German army marched on Paris, the colour of her skin made it unsafe for her to remain in the city and she joined the mass exodus south. But it was from this point that her work became more crucial. Outside German-controlled territory,

---

* The revue had premiered in Monte Carlo in the winter of 1974.

Josephine was relatively free to move around, and under the cover of touring she travelled through neutral zones like Portugal, Spain and parts of North Africa. Accompanying her was an intelligence officer posing as her assistant, and secreted in her luggage was information from the Free French forces to their allies, much of it written in invisible ink on her sheet music.

Josephine's actual contribution to the war effort was hardly heroic compared to the dangers faced by members of the Resistance,* but it acquired a noble cast when set against the record of contemporaries such as Mistinguett and Maurice Chevalier, who remained in occupied Paris and entertained the enemy. When she returned to the city in 1944 she was greeted by cheering crowds, and in addition to a clutch of awards, including the Médaille de la Résistance, she received a handwritten note of thanks from Charles de Gaulle.

According to the jazz musician Alain Romans, Josephine came back to Paris 'more French than Louis XVI'.[2] Yet she was now determined to do more for those whom she continued to regard as 'her own people'– the American blacks. In 1936 she'd been given a salutary reminder of the conditions they endured when she was invited to perform in the New York *Follies*. Expecting to be greeted like a returning star, she was informed by the management of the St Moritz hotel that she was only permitted to use the service entrance and that she must stay away from the lobby as they didn't want to alienate any 'guests from the Southern states'.[3]

After the war, Josephine was determined to use her name to expose and challenge the racism of her birthplace. In 1948, commissioned by the French newspaper *France-Soir*, she travelled incognito around the American South, attempting to use public facilities that were reserved for whites. The arrests, assaults and threats she suffered were written up for the paper in a series of

---

* It was given an extravagant boost with the publication of *The Secret War of Josephine Baker*, written by Jacques Abtey, her intelligence officer.

colourfully indignant articles. Three years later, Josephine launched an even more public campaign: during an extensive cross-state tour, she refused to perform in any city that barred her from staying in first-class hotels, and she insisted on hiring black stage crews. She lobbied local businesses for more enlightened attitudes and when, inevitably, she started to receive threats from the Klan, she reported them straight to the press.

At a time when black celebrity activists were scarce, Josephine was embraced as a potent rallying force. Her activities were debated in Congress and, according to the *Chicago Examiner*, she orchestrated 'the best public race and press relations stunt of the century – if not for all time'.[4] On 20 May 1951, officially designated Josephine Baker Day, she was driven through Harlem in a motorcade.

Josephine was entranced by her success: but she was naive and stubborn. To the anxiety of black leaders, her campaigning grew increasingly disconnected from political pragmatism, and even from the truth. Some of the statements she made about America during the early 1950s were so fantastically intemperate, and some of her judgements (including her belief that the Argentinian dictator General Peron was a promoter of universal brotherhood) so bizarre that she became a liability to the very people she wanted to serve. It was only in 1963, when she returned to Washington to support Martin Luther King and the city's historic civil rights march that she was reaccepted as a beacon for the black cause.

If Josephine had difficulties reading the real world, it was partly because she had been cocooned for so long inside the fairy-tale logic of her career. As the heroine of her own Cinderella story, she thought that the rest of the world should fall into place around her. If she wanted something, or believed something to be true, there were few people capable of denying her. And just as her sense of entitlement distorted and inflated her political judgement, it also gave her an aggrandized, exaggerated view of her personal life, especially her mission to become a mother.

It's not clear what combination of factors prevented Josephine from having children of her own – she certainly suffered from acute gynaecological problems, and was ambivalent about encumbering her body with pregnancies. But she was nonetheless determined to create an alternative, adopted family, and do so on a grand scale. From 1954 onwards she toured the world, picking up babies and small children as she went. All were taken back to Les Milandes, the chateau she had bought herself in rural France, and by 1965 her 'Rainbow Tribe' numbered a dozen children, with her 'unofficially' adopted teenage son, and eventual biographer, Jean-Claude Baker, making a thirteenth.

The goodness of her intentions was never in doubt. Josephine had removed all of the children from impoverished conditions, and with this multi-ethnic family she believed she was laying the foundations of a community ruled by the principles of love and equality. Yet the entire project was also typical of her impulsive, narcissistic style. She gave little thought to the effect of uprooting her children from their African, Asian or South American homes, nor to the problems of maintaining a stable family life for them. How could she? She'd acquired no experience of domestic management, and what she knew about mothering she had learned from Carrie. Even though Les Milandes was overseen by Jo Bouillon, the fifth man to become Josephine's 'husband' (legal or otherwise),* the household was frequently in a state of turmoil. Nannies, teachers, gardeners and kitchen staff were hired and sacked in short order, and as Josephine came and went at unpredictable intervals, scattering love and presents, but also criticisms and punishment, her children were unruly, anxious and confused.

She had tried so hard to hold her family together when she was little – foraging for toys to give her brother and sisters, dancing for them in the cellar of Gratiot Street – but she had lost

---

* Pepito had died of cancer in 1936: Josephine's relationship with his much younger replacement, Jean Leon, was brief, and her marriage to Bouillon in 1947 was an arrangement of convenience rather than passion.

that capacity for simple love, and she'd been treated as a star for too many years to settle for the compromises of domestic life. It was symptomatic that her final, sixth 'marriage'* was both brief and symbolic; she and her 'husband', a playboy artist called Robert Brady, conducted most of their relationship by letter.

Yet if Josephine's experiment in family life was chaotic, her true family had long been her public. There were moments when she flirted with the idea of retiring, when she felt herself teetering on the edge of absurdity and irrelevance, but her fans had always kept faith with her. The funeral that was staged in Paris was the climax of the long and loving relationship she'd formed with the city since 1925, and over the following decades the splendour of that event became part of the legend that accumulated around her. Not even Josephine could have anticipated the resonance her story has subsequently acquired. A black ghetto girl who clawed her way to stardom; a free spirit and political activist; a chorus dancer who became more famous than Pavlova – she's been claimed as a role model by generations who never even witnessed her performances onstage.

Josephine's public life reached its apotheosis with one of the most elaborate funerals in living memory, but the political crusades to which Nancy Cunard dedicated herself led only towards her progressive isolation. When she collapsed in Paris in March 1965, Nancy was spectrally thin, delirious and alone and the small funeral service that was held for her at the British Embassy Church was reported by the *Evening Standard* to have been a 'sad, and lonely farewell to a toast of the Twenties'.[5]

In truth, Nancy had long since put the Twenties behind her. As she worked on the *Negro* anthology in the early 1930s, she was already turning her back on the frivolity of the previous decade – consumed instead by the feelings of righteous fury and

---

* They privately exchanged vows in a church, but didn't bother with an official ceremony.

disgust that had been roused by the black cause. Yet despite disassociating herself from her old friends and acquaintances she wasn't settling into an alternative niche in political circles. Her views were simply too maverick. Just as the contents of *Negro* were perceived as confusingly eclectic in their spread of cultural and political history,* so Nancy was regarded as an ideological loose cannon. Her growing support for Communism was problematic for American blacks, her sexual morality even more so. Nancy refused to defer to local sensibilities when she was travelling in the States and refused to restrict her interest in black men; like Josephine she was unable to acknowledge the delicate, pragmatic circumstances within which civil rights activists had to operate. She saw only her own blazing vision of right and wrong.

It was the outbreak of the Spanish Civil War that provided Nancy with a mission even more consuming than the civil rights cause. During the writing and research of *Negro* she had forged links with the Associated Negro Press, and in 1935 was commissioned by them to report on talks held by the League of Nations after Mussolini invaded Abyssinia. Reporting suited her, channelling both her literary and political passions, and the following year the ANP sent her to Barcelona as their official war correspondent in Spain.

The train journey to Barcelona in the autumn of 1936 marked a dividing line in Nancy's life – before Spain and after Spain. She fell in love with the country and even more with its people who, aside from Franco's forces, came to represent for her the world's struggle for freedom. During the two and a half years in which she reported on the Civil War she also had the exhilarating experience of feeling she was part of a unified movement. People like herself – writers, artists, journalists and idealists – were converging on Spain from all over Europe and America. Nancy was continually bumping into old acquaintances, such as

---

* It would be another thirty-five years before *Negro* was recognized as a pioneering feat of documentation and a prime resource for black studies.

Hemingway, and forging new and intense bonds with fellow travellers like the poet Pablo Neruda. All of them shared her belief that the battle against Franco would determine the course of the free world; and even though Nancy was frequently harrowed by what she saw – the hungry, wounded and dispossessed, the shattered towns and cities – she had rarely felt more purposeful and fulfilled.

Still she needed to do more. It was unbearable to her that anyone should remain unaffected or untroubled by the situation in Spain, and in 1937 she distributed a questionnaire among two hundred or so writers, demanding that they state their position on the Republican cause. Nearly one hundred and fifty complied, and the results were published in the *New Left Review*, under the title 'Authors Take Sides on the Spanish War'. Most supported the Republicans, but there was an inflammatory tone to the questionnaire that inevitably prompted a number of inflammatory replies. George Orwell's (unpublished) view was that the whole project was 'bloody rubbish' and the product of ignorant dilettantes. In his response he wrote, 'I was six months in Spain, most of the time fighting, I have a bullet hole in me at present and I am not going to write blah about defending democracy or gallant little anybody.'

Orwell had been dismayed by the factionalism that was undermining the unity of Republican forces, and rightly considered the black-and-white politics of the questionnaire to be naive. However, he was unjust in condemning it as ignorant. While Nancy was in Spain she was often first among those who went to the most dangerous and beleaguered places; she accepted cold, hunger and sleep deprivation as a matter of course. Even when the Republican army was routed, she stayed on to witness the suffering of the half a million refugees who fled Franco's army and were herded into temporary camps on the French border. Writing for the *Manchester Guardian* as well as for the ANP, Nancy's impassioned reporting helped to spark a relief campaign that brought in crucial donations of food, money and clothes.

Knowing she had done something, however small, to mitigate

the sub-human conditions of these camps brought Nancy an unusually solid sense of achievement. But Franco's triumph was a personal agony to her. After Spain, Nancy went to recuperate with friends in South America, and when the Allies went to war against Germany she initially had neither the energy nor the courage to confront this new fight against fascism.

It wasn't until 1941 that she finally returned to Europe and with much apprehension settled in London. Nancy had long felt an entrenched wariness towards her home city, and her antagonism towards Maud and the British establishment had precluded her from staying there for more than a few months at a time. The war, however, left her with no option, and despite the bombing and rationing, she was oddly at peace during the three and a half years that she lived there. For the first, and only, time in her adult life she found herself emotionally and politically in tune with the rest of the population. She was focused on useful work, mostly translating for the Free French forces, but also finding the time to write poetry and edit a volume of poems in celebration of her beloved, desecrated France.

The end of the war was, in some ways, a wrench, as Nancy was forced to reconsider her circumstances. Where should she settle? What should she do? The house in Réanville was out of the question. Returning to assess the state of it after the war, she was traumatized to discover that all her precious books and artworks had been looted or desecrated. Worst of all, some of the most viscious acts of vandalism had been committed not by the enemy, but by her French neighbours.

Nancy couldn't bear to stay, and instead travelled south, finding a small and very basic new home in a rural hamlet, Lamothe Fénélon. She was far from wealthy, but she was still independent, and for the next two decades she fell into a pattern of summering in France, then escaping the winter cold by travelling and visiting friends.

It was a life that allowed her to remain free, but it was often lonely. No new political activity had replaced the camaraderie she had found in Spain, and while she raged against Franco's continuing dictatorship, and against the world's continuing abuse of blacks, she lacked both the financial resources and the personal contacts that would have allowed her to embark on any concrete plan of action. She was not a natural joiner of formal groups or political parties, and just as she became more politically marginalized, so she grew more isolated in her personal life.

Nancy never lacked for company. She remained a charismatic presence – witty, informed, surprising to talk to and still astonishingly stylish. Aspects of her appearance might look eccentric in the 1950s – her armloads of bangles and flamboyant scarves – but her beauty was even sharper in middle age, and some men still found her mesmerizing. During her fifties she continued to find new friends – and lovers – wherever she travelled. Yet she was able to depend less on her older friends, as age, illness or geography unravelled the close communities she'd known in Paris and, at times, in London. When she and Iris Tree accidentally met in Rome, they both winced at the realization that it was twenty years since they had last seen each other. Iris, however, was far more shocked at the changes she saw in Nancy. She wrote to Diana that she feared their friend was living a life that was 'somehow malevolent, bereft of surrounding sympathy or love'.[6] Certainly the rift between Nancy and her mother had never healed. During the war, as Lady Cunard was driving through London she had caught sight of Nancy walking along the pavement but hadn't stopped the car. By 1948 it was too late. Diana contacted Nancy to tell her that her mother was dying and begged her to attempt a last reconciliation, but Lady Cunard had not asked for Nancy, and Nancy did not want to make any gesture of appeasement.* The only family she saw were her cousins Victor and Edward. Her unofficial father, George Moore, had died long before the war, in 1933.

---

* She didn't, however, refuse her one-third share of her mother's much dwindled estate. Another third was left to Diana who, although not averse to mocking Lady Cunard, had always remained fond of her, and was perhaps the daughter Maud would have liked.

Nancy wrote a loving memoir of Moore, which, along with the book she wrote about her old friend Norman Douglas, was one of her finest pieces of post-war work. She still wrote much of the time, never abandoning her poetry, even though she had given up expecting any acclaim for it. However, the one book that publishers and readers most desired, her autobiography, was one she felt unable to write. She wanted no part in reiterating old gossip about Paris and the 1920s, believing that there was something morally repugnant in writing about any of her close friends who were still alive. It would be a betrayal of their intimacy.

Nevertheless, Nancy was perfectly capable of undermining friendships by other means. Iris was right to observe that she wasn't living well in the Fifties, drinking too much, eating too little and obsessing over the political wrongs of the world. Strangers might fall under Nancy's spell, but to friends she could be taxing company. Even those who loved her best were nervous of inviting her to stay for extended periods, knowing that they would have to deal with the volatility of her alcohol-drenched mood swings and her inevitable, exhaustive grilling of their views on Spain.

That country still consumed her, and she visited it as regularly as she could. Yet captivated as she was by the people, the landscape and the culture, she could not give up her personal crusade against its fascist rulers, and anxious friends began to observe the corrosive effect this was having on Nancy's mental health. During the late 1950s her behaviour grew more aggressive; she insulted the Spanish police, picked political fights with complete strangers and made reckless public statements calling for the release of political prisoners. During one visit in 1960, her actions were so provocative that she was arrested and thrown out of the country.

In the old days Nancy would have been exhilarated by such a stand-off; now it acted as a destructive catalyst. As she travelled back to London, her always precarious mental state was disintegrating, and by the time she arrived she was emotionally fractured and deeply paranoid. Friends who tried to calm her down were accused of being fascist spies: unable to rest quietly she roamed the streets, insulting policemen and making outrageous sexual approaches to strangers. When she ended up in jail, it was evident to the doctor who was called to examine her that she was in desperate need of psychiatric treatment.

Nancy spent the summer incarcerated in the Holloway Sanatorium, a few miles outside London. The combination of rest, sedatives and proper nutrition stabilized her condition, but it left her pitifully bereft. In July she wrote to Janet Flanner, mourning how little her life seemed to have amounted to: she was proud of *Negro*, she said, and of her reporting in Spain, yet she had failed to find love and she had failed as a poet.

When she was released in September, it was with a regime of anti-depressants and strict orders to avoid alcohol. But while she regained her old responsive alertness, Nancy's physical health was now failing, and in 1963 she was diagnosed with emphysema. She had always depended on being fit, with a body that was responsive, light and free. As Michelet had observed, she needed to be able to outrun her demons. This new experience of being short of breath and unsteady on her feet was intolerable to her; and numbing her frustration with more and more alcohol, inevitably she took a bad fall in early 1965, when she tripped and broke her thigh. After being told by her doctors that she couldn't move for three months, she had to allow herself to be taken care of by an old friend, the French painter Jean Guérin.

Guérin's Riviera villa was delightful and he was a tender host, but Nancy was beyond taking any pleasure in either. Even before the fall she had been worrying about her independence: the capital she had inherited was fast diminishing and living costs were rising.* Now with her broken thigh she was terrified that she might never be able to travel again or to live on her own.

---

* Ironically, her assets would be valued at over $120,000 after her death – if she had ever deemed it acceptable to have her finances properly managed she would have been able to live her last few years in far more comfort.

And as she fecklessly mixed her prescribed drugs with consoling doses of alcohol, that fear pitched Nancy back towards madness.

She became impossible to care for, disobeying her doctors, refusing to eat and being vilely rude to those around her. After she had thrown one particularly distressing scene, Guérin suggested that she leave and Nancy, somehow impelled by the force of her own rage, managed to drag herself and her few belongings onto a train. She ended up on the doorstep of Solita Solano, who was living just outside Paris, but by this point she was raving and urgently in need of medical care. Solita had no room to accommodate her properly, and the next day arranged for her to go and stay with Janet Flanner in the centre of the city.

Nancy never arrived. For some reason she was determined to seek refuge with Raymond Michelet, even though his tiny apartment had even less room than Solita's little house. Michelet was shocked by Nancy's ravaged state, and with the help of Georges Sadoul (their mutual friend from the surrealist days), he begged Nancy to let him book her into a hotel where she could be properly examined by a doctor.

Sadoul doubted, however, that a doctor could do anything to help. Nancy seemed lost to them: 'Her mind was cracked, her beautiful intelligence had clouded over and she hardly knew what to do but insult her best friends, present and absent.'[7] She trusted no one, and that night worked herself up to the conviction that the doctor summoned by Michelet was part of a fascist conspiracy against her. On the morning of 12 March she set fire to the few papers she had with her and tried to make her escape. The taxi driver she hailed outside the hotel took one look at her dishevelled clothing, trembling limbs and wild expression and drove her to the nearest police station.

Two days later, in the ward of a public hospital, Nancy died. It was a small and pitiful death, and to those who had known her, a tragic one. Yet even in those desperate straits she remained oddly true to her nature. Throughout her life she had followed the compass of her own convictions; and even though her mind and body had been battered to a point where she was barely recognizable, she had refused to conform to what others had wanted for her; the terms on which she died had somehow remained her own.

For Zelda Fitzgerald, all hope of freedom seemed to be stolen from her with the onset of her first breakdown in 1930. Confined in the Prangins clinic in Switzerland, she was not only suffering the mental anguish of hallucinations and depression, but was also tormented by the eczema, which now flared across her face, shoulders and neck. During the periods when she was well enough to write, she sent long letters to Scott, trying to understand how she had arrived at such a pass, begging for his help as she tried to 'unravel this infinite psychological mess'.

She wavered between guilt and rage, sometimes berating herself for her 'hideous dependency' on Scott, sometimes railing against his drinking and self-absorption. He, in turn, was as gentle with her as he knew how: 'I love you with all my heart,' he wrote in one undated letter, 'because you are my own girl and this is all I Know.'[8] Yet because he was wretched – and exhausted – he could not prevent himself retaliating, writing letters in which he angrily itemized all of Zelda's crimes and derelictions. For more than a year, the two of them were in hell, stumbling and quarrelling through the wreckage of their past.

In the autumn of 1931, Zelda was well enough for them to sail back to America and, for a while, to live at home in Montgomery while Scott worked. But early in 1932 the shock of her father's death precipitated another breakdown, and she was admitted to the Phipps clinic in Baltimore. It would, however, prove a very different experience from her time at Prangins, for it coincided with an intense period of creativity. Even though the doctors at Phipps found Zelda silent and withdrawn, inside her head she was flying, working for hours every day on her autobiographical first novel *Save Me the Waltz*.

In purely therapeutic terms this was a critical project for her. She was narrating her own life in her own voice, rather than having Scott's version superimposed on her. And through the character of her heroine, Alabama, she was able to question who she was and what she had done. She puzzled over her youthful determination to reject her father's moral principles, his integrity and his work ethic; she also tried to imagine what it would have been like for her had she had been strong enough to accept Sedova's invitation to dance with the San Carlo ballet two years previously. In the novel, she took Alabama as far as a cheap boarding house in Naples and to the threshold of success, performing a repertory of solo roles. But it was perhaps an indirect comment on Zelda's own cowardice that she then invented an injury that terminated her heroine's career. By the end of the novel she puts Alabama back with her husband David, sitting amidst the frowsty remains of yet another party.

Far more important to Zelda than the novel's therapeutic logic, however, was the literary satisfaction it brought her. *Save Me the Waltz* may be technically flawed, its structure disjointed, its language both solipsistic and overwrought, yet it has passages of brilliantly visualized imagery and a precision of sensual detail that lends a near-hallucinatory clarity to some of Alabama's experiences. When Zelda sent it to Scribners, she dared to hope it would be published.

She hoped even more for her husband's admiration and support, but Scott was more anxious than he had ever been about his own writing, terrified that his talent was 'dead and buried' from the worry over Zelda's health, the expense of her medical bills and the cost of Scottie's education.[9] His agonizingly slow-burning fourth novel *Tender is the Night* was nearing completion, but the fact that Zelda's book overlapped with much of his, that key images and descriptions echoed passages of his own, convinced him that she had made a terrible pre-emptive strike, and he saw her novel only as a betrayal and a threat. Impervious to her delicate state, he fired off excoriating letters to her, her doctor and Scribners, lost to everything but his fear of failure.

His anxiety was completely out of proportion. Years later, *Save Me the Waltz* would be placed within a tradition of women's writing that encompassed the poetic narratives of Charlotte

Perkins Gilmour and Virginia Woolf. At the time, however, it barely registered. Fewer than 1,500 copies sold, and while one or two critics noted the originality of Zelda's voice, it was generally agreed that much of it was unreadable.

But even though the novel had no real power to hurt Scott professionally, it exposed, once again, the fundamental conflict of their marriage. The sparkling, money-making story on which they'd embarked in 1919 – the Fitzgerald love affair – had brought them opportunities and fame, but what had united them had, inexorably, imprisoned them. There simply wasn't enough space in the legend they had created for them both to flourish as individuals. At his bleakest moments Scott began to toy with the idea of divorce – if he could not save them both, he had to save himself.

By now Zelda could not be mistaken for anything other than an invalid. Despite the intensity of her imaginative life, her skin was lined and dull; her lips bitten raw, her expression frequently skewed into a meaningless smile. For limited periods of time she was well enough to live with Scott in a rented house, and for there to be days when their old intimacy was almost restored. But her speech and movements were marked by unnerving slippages – to one of their Baltimore neighbours she seemed like 'a broken clock'[10] – and between these periods of relative calm she was not only suicidal, but developed a new, and very unnerving, religious faith.

Scott's ledger entries for 1935 were starkly despairing: 'Work and worry . . . Debts terrible . . . Zelda in hell.' Yet the following year saw a significant change. Scott had begun spending recuperative periods in rural North Carolina, and when he decided he might settle there, in Asheville, he had Zelda transferred to the nearby Highland Hospital. This monastically run institution took a brusque line with neurotic, 'artistic' women, but if Zelda was forced into bracing physical activity she was also allowed to paint, and during 1936 developed a new direction for her work.

She'd taken up her brushes again in Phipps, and Scott, perhaps in unconscious reparation for his assault on *Save Me the Waltz*, had organized a small exhibition of her work in New York. Zelda was disappointed by the degree to which the press focused on her as a 'fabulous', 'almost mythical' star of the 1920s, but *Time* magazine greeted the show as 'the work of a brilliant introvert . . . vividly painted, intensely rhythmic.'[11] In Highland, she pressed forward, distilling the exaggerated mass and energy of her portraits and landscapes into visionary abstracts, trying to find shapes and colours that corresponded to the intensities of her inner life.

Scott, meanwhile, was in Hollywood, writing scripts for MGM and earning a much needed weekly stipend of $1,000. He was also happier, having met and fallen in love with a young British journalist. Sheilah Graham was pretty, blonde and athletic; she reminded him physically of Zelda, yet she possessed what was to Scott an incredible reserve of pragmatism and kindness. He described her wonderingly as 'one of the few beautiful women of Zelda's generation to have reached 1938 unscathed'.[12]

There was no question of Sheilah displacing Zelda from her central role in Scott's life, yet it had been evident for a long time that the Fitzgeralds could not healthily spend more than a few days or weeks in each other's company. When Zelda was finally allowed to leave Highland in the spring of 1940, it was to her mother's house in Montgomery that she went. Scott lived quietly with Sheilah, drinking more than he should but far more in control of both his mood and his energy, as he worked on his fifth novel *The Last Tycoon*.

He and Zelda wrote to each other every week – long, loving letters in which they lingered over their past and restricted most discussions of the present to the subject of Scottie, who had now finished boarding school and was a student at Vassar. Scott had fretted over their daughter during her adolescence, critical of any lapse in her studies or behaviour that might suggest she had inherited any of her parents' traits. But Scottie had survived the dislocations of her family life; mature for her age, she was already showing signs of a literary talent, about which Zelda and Scott could correspond with pride. Through their letters, at least, they sustained the illusion that they were a family still.

They had not seen each other for eighteen months when, on 21 December 1940, Zelda received a telephone call from Harold Ober, informing her that Scott had suffered a massive, and fatal, heart attack. It was news for which she was helplessly unprepared. Even though Scott had experienced a minor cardiac episode the previous month, he had assured her he was recovering well, and had confidently resumed the final stretch of his novel. She had not even begun to imagine what her life would be like without him. Zelda and Scott had known and loved each other for over twenty years, and even when she believed she hated him, even when their marriage had foundered, he had remained her 'best friend', her confidante. Above all, he had retained the talismanic power to make her believe that there was always a fresh start just around the corner. As Zelda wrote to Edmund Wilson, she could not bear the idea that he would never again come to her 'with his pockets full of promise and his heart full of new refurbished hopes'.[13]

She was not well enough to go to the funeral, but she got through the next few months as best she could, immersing herself in a quiet domestic rhythm of gardening and cooking with her mother. By early 1942 she had moved into another creative cycle, starting her second novel, *Caesar's Things*, and working hard on her art. Even though she still had to retreat to the Highland clinic for periods of time, she was well enough to sustain a new and careful relationship with Scottie, who got married in 1943 and, three years later, gave birth to her first child, Timothy.

Zelda had found stability of a kind. Yet a self-portrait that she painted in 1942 is evidence of what it cost both her and those around her. In that portrait her lips are clamped into a taut line of anguish, and her eyes burn as if the madness inside her is battling to get out – as it continued to do. She was back in Highland in 1948 when Scottie gave birth to her second child, a daughter, and on 9 March wrote a letter of poignant optimism, expressing the hope that she would be well enough to see them all very soon. The following night, however, a fire broke out in the hospital's kitchen, and while all of the patients on the lower floors were taken out to safety, Zelda and six others sleeping on the top floor were apparently locked into their rooms, and could not be rescued in time. When Zelda was found the next day her body was so badly burned that she could only be identified by the charred slipper that had got caught beneath her.

She was buried beside Scott in Rockville, Maryland, and after the funeral Scottie wrote to her grandmother that 'it was reassuring to think of these two high-flying . . . spirits being at peace together at last'. All she wanted now was to erase the recent memory of her parents' suffering and to 'think of them only as they must have been when they were young'.[14]

That is how the world wants to remember them, too. Yet the bleak and blighted years of Zelda's illness were in some ways more productive than the decade of her jazz age success. During the enforced separation from Scott, and from the trappings of their joint celebrity, she was able to channel her originality and energy into something other than column inches and material for Scott's fiction. It is impossible now to guess what work she might have produced if she had made other choices when she was young, or if her mental condition had been better managed. As it is, the letters, novels and paintings produced during the last eighteen years of her life remain as a strangely lucid, hauntingly lit portrait of a woman engaged in a heroic struggle for self-knowledge.

If Zelda and Scott had forged a Faustian pact with celebrity, so too had Tamara de Lempicka. Jean Cocteau always said of her that she 'loved art and high society in equal measure', and for a decade Tamara had seemed to serve both equally. Yet the forces of fashion and history that had swept her to eminence were changing course in the early 1930s, and while she was still much talked about in public, in private she felt that she had failed to catch the pulse of the new decade: 'I hate my life which is useless, without scope,' she wrote to Gino Puglisi in May 1935, confessing that she had spent the last few weeks immobilized by depression.[15] She was finding it increasingly hard to paint, and the lavish foreign holidays she took with her new husband Baron Raoul Kuffner, only exacerbated her sense of being out of kilter with the world. The following year she again wrote to Gino, 'I am an unhappy being, condemned, without a homeland, without a race always alone.'[16]

Inevitably the gathering political tensions in Europe fed her malaise. Visits to Austria and Berlin had revived memories of the Bolshevik terror still lodged in her imagination, and she was aware, too, that her and Raoul's Jewish blood could make them vulnerable. By 1938 she had persuaded Raoul to relocate to America, and by the time they were settled in Hollywood in early 1940, she believed, optimistically, it might be a new beginning for her. The concentration of money and success in Hollywood reminded her of Paris in its heyday; Tamara loved the mix of American old money and new movie-star aristocracy and she devoted much of her energy and a great deal of Raoul's money to hosting parties from their rented Beverly Hills mansion.

She was painting, too. And when, in 1941, the influential gallery owner Julian Levy offered her a one-woman show in New York, her confidence soared and she threw herself into the business of promoting the show. However, while her success at marketing herself in Hollywood society brought her a great deal of press attention, it was mostly the wrong kind. All that journalists wanted to write about were details of her Beverly Hills friends, her clothes, even her beauty regime. Disastrously, she became known as 'the Baroness with the brush', and her work was tagged '*tres* Hollywood'. The following year, when Peggy Guggenheim opened her new gallery, The Art of this Century, none of Tamara's work hung on its walls.

She had miscalculated badly, but she was also a victim of changing trends. A new wave of artists, led by Jackson Pollock, was creating expressive form out of the heroic, messy physicality of paint; by comparison Tamara's exquisitely invisible brush strokes looked old-fashioned and almost inert. After she and Raoul moved to Manhattan in 1942, she was forced to confront the gulf between her own art and that of the new generation. Although she tried hosting a weekly salon in her huge refurbished apartment, the Upper East Side was not Montparnasse in the 1920s; the creative centre of Manhattan was downtown, in Greenwich Village, and would remain there throughout the 1950s, among the beat poets and the post-war existentialists.

Tamara craved the society of interesting people; she needed the stimulus of youth. As she got older, friends observed her mounting frustrations, pent up with an energy that, despite her continuing productivity, she seemed unable to channel. Tamara was also haunted by a fear of death. Already she had lost two of the people who mattered most to her: Malvina had died in France in 1945 and Tadeusz had died of cancer in Poland in 1951. Then, in 1961, Raoul suffered a fatal, and very unexpected, heart attack.

For years he and Tamara had enjoyed the most civilized of marriages. They took lovers, dined at different times and even lived in separate buildings. When Tamara painted ten hours a day, Raoul didn't complain of being neglected as Tadeusz had done. Yet still they had remained deeply wedded, and while Raoul's death left Tamara a very wealthy widow, it also left her lonely and exposed. By 1963 she was unable to manage on her own and moved to Houston to be near Kizette, her husband Harold Foxhall – a Texan geologist – and their two daughters, Victoria Ann (nicknamed Putti by Tamara) and Christie (nicknamed Chacha).

It was not a move Kizette welcomed, however, since her relationship with Tamara had remained tense and conflicted. Even though Tamara had been distraught with worry while her daughter remained in Paris during the war, and had pulled every string she could to secure her safe passage to America, she had done little to welcome Kizette to her new American life. Busy promoting a youthful image among her Beverly Hills circle, she had rarely acknowledged Kizette's existence; and in truth she was disappointed in her daughter. Kizette had graduated from Oxford, she was good-looking and clever, but as far as Tamara was concerned, she lacked any distinguishing talent, and had apparently settled with Harold into the kind of bourgeois domesticity that she, herself, had always despised.*

Now, even when it suited her to move closer to Kizette, Tamara could not but criticize and interfere. If it was too late to save Kizette from mediocrity, she believed she could at least make something of her two granddaughters. She indulged Putti and Chacha with imperious extravagance, buying them beautiful clothes and even whisking them to Paris to see the newly famous Beatles. With equal imperiousness she also tried to take over the girls' upbringing, scrutinizing their performance in school, passing judgement on their looks and even their boyfriends. (In one 1963 photograph Tamara is tilting her granddaughter's face upwards with one finger: it could be a gesture of affection, but looks much more as though she's subjecting the girl's face to a severe and challenging scrutiny.)

Women like Tamara, who had achieved remarkable success and lived through remarkable times, might be excused some impatience with the mundane. Diana Cooper set exacting standards for her son John Julius, and Josephine could be unreasonably demanding of her Rainbow Tribe. But Tamara's need for control was considered by her family to be pathological. When Putti got engaged, Tamara flew into a tantrum because the young man had sought permission from Harold, not from her – she claimed that the money she poured into the household gave her the right to be considered its head.

Nor was it just the her family who saw her behaviour as extreme. Much of Houston took the same view. Tamara's European hauteur and dated glamour – she was now approaching

---

* In fact, Kizette was more like her mother than Tamara acknowledged, and had several extra-marital love affairs.

seventy – looked bizarrely anachronistic in this very American city. The pungent obscenity of her language and the nicotine stains on her teeth were considered unsavoury and the judgements of the Houston society were confirmed when she was invited to a party at the French consulate and was rebuffed, very publicly, by a group of visiting Parisians. These women, all around Tamara's age, were clearly discomfited by her presence, muttering, 'What are you doing here, Tamara?' before pointedly moving away. Later Tamara admitted to her hostess, one of her few friends in the city, that these Parisians had apparently not forgiven her for the 'obscene practices' that had made her notorious back in the 1920s.[17]

Despite regular trips back to Europe, Tamara felt that her social and her professional life had become stranded in 'this uncivilized location', as she contemptuously referred to Houston. But at the beginning of the 1970s the art world finally began to court her again. There was a revival of interest in the art and style of the deco era, and when the French historian and collector Alain Blondel stumbled across some of Tamara's early work, he regarded it as an extraordinary find. In 1972, he mounted an exhibition of her work – forty-eight paintings dating from 1925 to 1935 – in his Galerie du Luxembourg. And even though reviews were mixed, those which were positive exclaimed over the quality of her work and over its inexplicable neglect.

The interest snowballed and Tamara featured prominently in the major art exhibition that was part of the events marking 1975 as International Women's Year. Two years later a lavish new book appeared about her life and work, edited by Franco Ricci. Tamara was outraged to discover that Ricci had included letters exchanged by her and the poet D'Annunzio during their odd non-affair in the mid-1920s, along with sections of the lurid diary kept by D'Annunzio's housekeeper Aélis. Yet gossipy as the press coverage was, it could not undermine the fact that Tamara's paintings were now seriously back in style.

The 1920s were being exhumed as a golden age of glamour and high living: the clothes, interior design and music were all exhibiting a nostalgic return to the jazz age, and Tamara's work was emerging as a prime reference point. In 1976, when the Victoria and Albert museum staged an exhibition of early twentieth-century fashion, her paintings were centrally displayed. Two years later a reissued paperback of Huxley's *Point Counter Point* would use *Autoportrait* as its cover illustration. (This was the novel featuring Lucy Tantamount, one of several characters based on Nancy Cunard.) For years Tamara's reputation had suffered from her close identification with the Twenties, but now it climbed higher and higher, as her work became acknowledged as one of the decade's treasures.

Tamara was initially surprised that her 'old stuff' should receive so much attention: but she rapidly came around to capitalizing on it, even claiming that it was she who had launched the entire deco movement. She revelled in the attention, and to the many journalists who sought her out she was a funny, charming fund of stories. At home, however, her behaviour was far less accommodating. She was possibly suffering early symptoms of the arteriosclerosis that would kill her, and her moods were turning more violently unpredictable; she was exceptionally abusive to Kizette and her memory wandered.

Fortunately for her family she had now discovered a refuge away from Houston in the ritzy, cosmopolitan city of Cuernavaca in Mexico, a resort for the rich, the colourful and the dangerous since the days of Al Capone. Tamara was delighted by the number of artists and nomadic aristocrats who had settled there, and among whom she established her own court. One of her most attentive new friends was Robert Brady, the same playboy artist to whom Josephine had been briefly and 'platonically married'. Brady evidently had a taste for famous elderly women: he loved to call Tamara 'Baroness', fawning over her talent and begging stories from her. But Tamara took far more pleasure from Victor Contreras, the young Mexican sculptor. She was painting nearly every day, even as she turned eighty, and Contreras appeared to have an instinctive understanding and appreciation of what she was doing. With him she felt rejuvenated as a woman and as an artist, and after she had purchased her own house in Cuernavaca in 1978, she saw him constantly.

Cuernavaca might have bought a tranquil conclusion to Tamara's life, except for her health. Her lungs and arteries were wrecked; she developed emphysema and she was terrified by her prolonged lapses into confusion and forgetfulness. By the end of 1979 she was dependent on an oxygen tank and could barely shuffle from one room to the next. She lived on almost nothing but the cocktails she still stubbornly insisted on serving her few select visitors. She still insisted, too, on wearing her jewels, her hats and her brilliantly coloured dresses. Even so, by the time she died, in the early morning of 16 March 1980, she had wasted away to a tiny, brittle version of her former self.

Robert Brady delivered the eulogy at her funeral, proclaiming his delight that Tamara had lived long enough to see 'the incredible renaissance of interest in her art'.[18] His style of delivery may have been ingratiating, but no one believed more firmly than Tamara in the truth of her own resurrection. Her request to Contreras that her ashes be scattered over the summit of Mount Popocatépetl, the volcano that towered over the landscape of Cuernavaca, wasn't just because of her sentimental attachment to the place; she was already imagining herself as a phoenix rising from the fires of Il Popo.

And in fact, her reputation continued to soar. In 1981 the Canadian director Richard Rose staged an experimental play based on the story of her relationship with D'Annunzio. When *Tamara* transferred to Los Angeles in 1984, Anjelica Huston played the title role and the play acquired a cult status that sustained it through a further three-year run in New York. Simultaneously, the prices for Tamara's paintings climbed even higher. Celebrity collectors like Jack Nicholson and Madonna drove them through the $2 million mark, and Madonna staked her own claim to the eroticized glamour of Tamara's portraits by including several in her music videos. The art establishment might remain ambivalent, with *Time* magazine headlining its coverage of a 1994 exhibition, 'Who is right, the movie stars or the critics?'[19] Yet even if Tamara's work was not accepted into the canon, her deco paintings remain one of the most visible and charismatic reference points of the 1920s. Even as the debate continues over her artistic ranking, there are few painters who have left behind a more compelling register of period style, and of the women who embodied it.

Tamara had endured three decades of neglect before she and her art were rediscovered. When Tallulah Bankhead returned to America in 1931 she, too, became aware of how fickle the forces of taste and fashion could be. Paramount Studios had been determined to market her as the new Marlene Dietrich, calculating that her musky vocal tones and deeply hooded eyes would mimic the extraordinary mystique of the German star, both their timing and judgement, however, were badly flawed.

Firstly the studio had failed to understand that Tallulah's appeal was predicated on qualities very different from Dietrich's. It was her comedic vitality that made her adorable to fans, and despite her considerable gift for sexual insinuation, she was not the languid femme fatale the studio bosses wanted her to be. The essential disconnection between Tallulah and her new image was evident in the first three films she shot in New York, in which her performances came across as both tawdry and flat. The fact that the material didn't suit her also emphasized the lack of chemistry between her and the camera. Back in her teenage years, her features had been veiled by the magical but temporary dew of youth; now, in its starker adult form, her beauty looked almost caricatured on screen, as if the camera could find no mystery or nuance within it.

In early 1932, Paramount sent Tallulah out to Hollywood, hoping to restart her career. Gamely, she applied herself to the life of the studio star, buying a wardrobe of party frocks, renting a mansion and filling it with as many famous faces as possible. She flirted and flung out her best lines, was as outrageous as she knew how and, as always, ensured that the stories circulating about her, including a rumoured affair with Dietrich herself, were even more wicked than the truth.

All of Tallulah's most self-promoting efforts, however, could not alter the fact that her arrival in Hollywood was unluckily timed. By 1932, the sobriety of the depression era was ushering in a new culture of piety into cinema. Salacious stories of film-star life and uncensored sexual content, which had been key to the industry's rapid expansion, were now deemed inappropriate. A new Motion Picture Code had been introduced, determining the ways in which the studios should clean themselves up.

But Tallulah was incapable of moderating herself; in the late summer she gave an interview to *Motion Picture* magazine about her new life in Hollywood, and typically turned the conversation round to love and sex: 'I haven't had an *affaire* for six months,' she complained, 'the matter with me is I WANT A MAN!'[20] Even in the wicked old world of Hollywood, women were not expected to issue such frank declarations of need. And although Tallulah's line was quoted everywhere and the magazine's circulation prof-ited, she made the industry nervous. According to Douglas Fairbanks Jr, 'we were a little frightened, a little on edge. You never knew what she was going to do.'

Just as Tallulah's behaviour was out of key with the new Hollywood, so was the image that had been foisted on her. If sexual scandals were falling out of favour, so too were Dietrich-style sirens; already Paramount were seeking out more whole-some, fresh-faced starlets to sell to the public. Within a year it became evident to Tallulah that she had to leave – and when even the ubiquitous Elsa Maxwell failed to show up for her farewell party, she knew she was right to do so.

She travelled back to New York, and to what she considered her proper milieu, the stage. Aware that ten years was a very long time for an actor to have been absent from Broadway, she used her own money to fund and publicize her comeback pro-duction, *Forsaking All Others*. It was classic Tallulah material: a comedy about a spirited young bride and the adventures with which she consoles herself after being jilted at the altar. Yet while it attracted back many of her gallery fans, and some reassuringly good reviews, the play only ran for three months and lost Tallulah $40,000. These were hard times for the theatre, and even though she managed to keep her stage career active, it wasn't until 1939 that she secured a long-running hit.

With every year that passed, Tallulah was also becoming more aware of her age. She was getting a little too gamey, a little too worldly to sustain her image as the darling ingénue. In 1938, despite being widely tipped for the role of Scarlett O'Hara in the film *Gone With the Wind*, she lost the part to an unknown English actress, Vivien Leigh, who was nearly twelve years her junior. The tyranny of youth was a fact of professional life, Tallulah knew that, but still she felt herself being edged onto shifting, uncertain ground.

Possibly she would have minded less if she had acquired the buffer of a family life, which in her fantasies, at least, she'd always craved. When she had been forced to have a hysterectomy in 1933, after being diagnosed with an advanced case of gonorrhoea, it had felt like a tragedy. Rumours circulated that she had caught the disease from the 'divine' Gary Cooper, whom she claimed she had always been determined 'to fuck'. If so, this sexual conquest had deprived her of the beautiful babies she had imagined for herself, and for several months afterwards she was too depressed even to work.

She was still emotionally vulnerable in May 1937 when she visited London and re-encountered Napier Alington, newly single after the death of his wife. Cecil Beaton saw them together at a party and sensed her desperation. 'Tallulah danced frenziedly, throwing herself about in a mad apache dance with Napier Alington. After he left she wept and bemoaned the fact that he had never married her. Then she threw off all her clothes, performing what she called 'Chinese classical dances. In the midst of these outrageous situations one had to reluctantly drag oneself away.'[21]

Tallulah hated having to drag herself away, too, and in a

reversion to her old pattern she rebounded from Naps into the arms of another, very different man. John Emery, an actor possessed of pleasant charm and matinee-idol looks, appeared to be the perfect remedy against Naps's treacherous allure, and she was determined to have him. She met Emery at the end of July, proposed to him several days later and, on 31 August, they were married. Her impatience was driven not only by her hunger for love and stability, but also by the desire to offer her new life as a gift to her father. The previous year Will had been made Speaker of the House of Representatives, a position from which he might even aim at the Presidency, and Tallulah had long been conscious of the fact that her disreputable image was an embarrassment to him.

She wanted to present herself as the perfectly reformed daughter, and to that end she decreed that she and Emery would relaunch themselves as a classy, classic theatrical couple. There would be no more cheap comedies and sassy innuendo. Instead, in the autumn of 1937, she put together the finances for a production of *Antony and Cleopatra*, in which her husband would play Caesar and she, naturally, would be Cleopatra. Unfortunately, the critic who wrote that 'Tallulah Bankhead barged down the Nile last night and sank', summed up the general verdict that her acting skills were not remotely suited to Shakespeare. Nor, it turned out, was she suited to marriage.

Tallulah's relationship with Emery foundered principally over her own exhausting need for attention and company. When she rudely claimed that her husband had not been big enough to satisfy her in bed, he retorted that she had never stopped talking long enough to notice; and their marriage had disintegrated long before their divorce was finalized in the summer of 1941. But if Tallulah minded the public humiliation, it was nothing compared to the grief she suffered over two infinitely more dreadful losses. The previous September, weakened by a recent bout of influenza, Will had suffered a fatal abdominal haemorrhage; just one day later Naps, too, had died, contracting pneumonia while on active war service in Cairo. These two men had been the loves of Tallulah's life, and with their deaths she began to feel more deeply the chill of her own approaching middle age.

But, as always, distraction was provided by her career, which in 1939 had been given an unexpectedly successful new twist. She had been cast in *The Little Foxes*, a searingly political play by Lillian Hellman about the murderous struggle for money and power within a Southern family. Tallulah played Regina Giddens, a rapacious woman fighting for her rights, who was not only less sympathetic than any role she'd ever played, but also much older. New as this territory was, Tallulah recognized that Regina came with a complex history and a malevolent charisma that demanded real acting skills. Submitting herself to the discipline of her director, Herman Shumlin, she opened on Broadway to the most enthusiastic reviews of her career. The play not only survived twelve months in New York, but ran for a second year on tour.

Other significant roles followed, in Thornton Wilder's *The Skin of our Teeth*, Alfred Hitchcock's *Lifeboat*, and in a production of Noël Coward's *Private Lives*, which she financed herself. By the time Tallulah was approaching fifty – an age she had always dreaded – she had started to market herself not only as a mature actress, but as a wickedly mature woman of the world. In 1950 she was hired to host a new radio talk show, NBC's *The Big Show*, in which her self-parodying routine as a wise-cracking, hard-drinking roué gained her millions of devoted listeners. Two years later her memoir, *Tallulah*, topped the bestseller lists and was serialized in newspapers around the world. She was paid $20,000 a week to perform cabaret in Las Vegas, filling the house with her racy anecdotes and impersonations. Not only had Tallulah apparently survived the passing of her youth, she had become far richer and more famous than ever before.

Yet her new image had a brittle, almost desolate quality to those who knew her well. As she swaggered into a party or a bar yelling, 'Isn't anyone going to fuck me tonight?' repeating the same old stories of her outrageous youth, Tallulah's once bubbling mischief seemed shop worn.[22] She tried to maintain her glamour with cosmetic surgery and thicker applications of make-up, but she was trying too hard, and her once scorchingly vivid features began to harden into a drag queen's disguise. And because she was so successful at selling her public persona, she was also in danger of making herself less credible as an actor. Like Tamara courting Hollywood's admiration, Tallulah was seduced into selling an image that could only damage her.

The crunch came in 1956 when she was offered the role of Blanche DuBois in a revival of Tennessee Williams's *A Streetcar Named Desire*. It was the most important challenge of her late career, and Tallulah was determined to rise to it. However, her recent commercial antics had won her a new audience among young gay men, and it was they who crowded out the audience for *Streetcar*. It was a kind of tragedy for Tallulah that she had become a camp icon, for every line that she uttered became a prompt for laughter, and no matter what she or her fellow actors did, the audience was determined to treat Williams's play as a screaming farce.

It wasn't the death blow to her career, but after it she struggled. By the early 1960s she suddenly looked much older than her age. Some of the ravages of nicotine and alcohol could still be concealed by cosmetics, but they'd left her short of breath and inclined to clumsiness. Having once been so exhibitionist in her sexual demands, Tallulah now hated to be touched or even seen up close. There were no more lovers, only a series of tactful young men who could be hired or cajoled into taking care of her and escorting her to parties. She was still working, and there were nights when she could deliver a very competent perform-ance, but there were also nights when she looked dangerously uncoordinated, and when her once perfect memory deserted her – occasionally her fellow actors were startled to hear her delivering lines from a completely different play.

Pills and drink cocooned her from too stark a realization of her own loneliness and professional decline, but they also precipi-tated the rapid deterioration of her health. She was only in her mid-sixties when she began to suffer intermittent hallucinations, her lungs began to fail and she lost her appetite for food. In December 1968, when she contracted Asian flu, she weighed only 100 pounds and was far too weak to fight the infection. The pugnacious life force at which her grandfather John had marvelled was all played out.

Tallulah had lived her version of the flapper experiment with more public swagger than any of the other five women in this book. And by contrast, it was Diana Cooper who appeared to mellow into the most contentedly conventional old age. Certainly, once she had parted company with the theatre in early 1933, the trajectory of her life became more obviously pinned to Duff's political career. She hosted clever little dinners for his colleagues, and when he was appointed First Lord of the Admiralty in 1937, she stamped her own brand of glamour on the running of Admiralty House. During the Second World War she accompanied him on his foreign postings: to America to drum up support for the British cause; to India and the far East to assess the readiness of British troops, and to Algiers in 1944, where he was sent as British Representative.

By 1945, when Duff was appointed ambassador to Paris and Diana became mistress of the British Embassy, she had apparently slipped into a life of irreproachable respectability. And yet, although it might appear as if she had put aside her old hankerings for independence, she had still not conformed to type. Her marriage to Duff continued to evolve in unpredictable ways, and while some of his mistresses (including the persistent Daisy Fellowes) remained a thorn in her side, others, such as the writer Louise de Vilmorin, became absorbed into her life.

Duff had fallen in love with the delicate, sharp-featured Lulu soon after they arrived at the Paris Embassy. But it was Diana, in her idealizing way, who came to love her more. Putting aside a room in the embassy for the younger woman's personal use, she orchestrated a tender, rather joyous ménage between the three of them. And while she had always been convinced that she lacked any lesbian impulses, to her old friend Conrad Russell she acknowledged that Lulu was encouraging her to become 'a little unnatural' in her 'ways'.[23]

She also became fond of Susan Mary Alsop, another of Duff's Paris mistresses, who actually had a child by him.* Yet if some of Diana's acquaintances thought her bizarrely accommodating of Duff's affairs, she did provide her own compensations. Conrad Russell, the nephew of the Duke of Bedford, was one of them. She had got to know him well in the early 1930s, a quiet Englishman, who preferred farming to politics or society. He lavished presents on Diana and wrote her long romantic letters, offering the unstinting devotion that she needed, still, as a prop to her confidence. They loved each other, platonically, until his death in 1947, although in 1938 Russell was roused to a rare dissatisfaction with that arrangement when Diana had an affair with Carl Burckhardt, High Commissioner at the League of Nations, whom she met in 1938.

There was something almost destined about this relationship, given that as a child Burckhardt had been raised by Hugo von Hofmannsthal, the father of Raimond, her former 'child lover' back in the days of *The Miracle*. To Diana, Burckhardt appeared uncannily like Raimond's confident and very seductive older brother; she even wondered if Raimond had asked for 'lessons and tips' from Carl when he was younger, for both men inspired a very unusual erotic response in her. Certainly the affair developed a level of physical passion that caused a jealous Russell to enquire if Diana and Burckhardt planned to 'go off together'.[24]

Throughout all this, Diana's love for Duff remained unshakeable, and if she was restive, it was principally for adventures other than sexual. The 1930s had in some ways been a period of limbo for her. While a younger generation of rebels was turning to communism rather than cocaine, her own world had remained largely unchanged. Many of the people she knew were unaffected

---

* The child was passed off as her husband's and his parentage only made public in 2008.

by the economic depression: picnics, treasure hunts and parties continued, almost uninterrupted from the previous decade, and Diana was invited to scores of them. Yet even amidst the privileged fun and the secure knowledge of having Duff and John Julius at home, she despaired over her failure 'to love my life as it deserves to be loved'. Depression and hypochondria stalked her, as they had always done when she had no serious occupation. And while she could diagnose herself as suffering from 'introspection apprehension' [and a] lack of interest', she was unable to find any project to replace her acting career.[25]

It was war, yet again, that forced Diana out of herself. Initially she had been traumatized and tearful: with the grinding heartbreak of the Great War still lodged in her memory, she could only imagine that this second round of hostilities would be infinitely worse. But her most acute fears were for John Julius, and when he was sent to safety in America, she braced herself to do something useful. Periods of war would have to be given over to Duff's official travels, but when Diana was in England she set herself up as a subsistence farmer at her family's seaside cottage at Bognor. The work was hard and she knew nothing about agriculture, but she became as proud of the modest competence she acquired with her bees, chickens, ducks, cows and pigs as she had been of her nursing skills at Guy's. The idea that she was producing sufficient food to contribute to the war effort pleased Diana enormously.

In 1944, when Duff was posted to Algiers, she initially resisted the move, reluctant to engage with yet more upheaval. However, as the headquarters of the Free French forces, Algiers had become a fascinating microcosm of the world at war, populated by a rogue mix of politicians, journalists and refugees. Diana soon found herself playing hostess to Charles de Gaulle and Andre Gide, Evelyn Waugh and Martha Gellhorn, and she discovered a spirit of informality and improvisation in the tenor of her new life that reminded her of the years when she was on tour with *The Miracle*.

When the time came to move to Paris she again resented the

change. She imagined that life in the embassy would confine her to a diary of rigidly formal dinners, and to a style of relentlessly codified behaviour. But in this she seriously underestimated herself. As she drew up guest lists for embassy events she rode roughshod over political allegiances and old grudges; notoriously she ignored the taint of wartime collaboration that hung over some of the Parisian artists, including Jean Cocteau, whom she included in 'la bande', her special group of favourites. Her solution to boredom was to mix everyone up: orchestrating dinners where Clement Attlee, the new Labour prime minister, might find himself seated next to Cocteau, parties where the Tory aesthete Chips Channon might find himself playing charades with a young communist trade unionist to whom Diana had taken a fancy.

Sometimes the guest list failed to spark. Ernest Hemingway was judged by Diana to be 'the greatest bore to end bores', and she disliked having to receive the exiled Duke and Duchess of Windsor. Before the war she had been a reluctant member of the Fort Belvedere set that revolved around Edward, the former Prince of Wales, and had observed his developing relationship with Wallis Simpson with a degree of pity. Now in Paris she judged that he had become 'sillier and duller', while his 'Becky Sharp' of a wife had become 'more common'.[26]

Yet even the unsuccessful dinners added to the embassy's allure. People clamoured for invitations precisely because the outcome was so unpredictable. It was widely assumed among political circles that it was because of Diana's social astuteness that Duff retained his ambassadorial post as long as he did, surviving a year and a half under the new Labour government, despite his own staunchly Conservative affiliations. Success had been sweet for Diana, and when Duff's post was terminated in the autumn of 1947, it was she who suffered most. They continued to live near Paris, renting a romantic eighteenth-century house, Chateau de St Firmin, yet while Duff settled more or less contentedly to the writing of his next book, she could not let her disappointment lie. She was outrageously disparaging about the new ambassador and his wife, and established her own rival court at St Firmin, poaching visiting dignitaries or celebrities to her own parties, which she made sure were always unsurpassably stylish and interesting.*

Guests like Greta Garbo and Princess Margaret may have bolstered her ego, but Diana was unused to being ousted from anything and, as she wrote in her memoir, she 'felt much older after the dismissal'.[27] She also became depressed about the diminishing of her beauty. Even though it had been years since she'd depended on it professionally, she had always believed her looks were the basis of any love she inspired and any success she achieved. Now in her late fifties, she clung to what remained of her youthful appearance, experimenting with wigs, suffering through an eccentric variety of beauty treatments and submitting to a painful facelift. These battles were sympathetically reported by Duff in his diary – 'She hates old age and fears death' – and inspired sections of Enid Bagnold's 1951 novel *The Loved and Envied*.

But Diana had much more to lose than her looks. Duff's health, undermined by years of excessive eating and drinking, was in decline, and in May 1953 he suffered a severe stomach haemorrhage, vomiting quantities of terrifying, rusty black blood. He recovered sufficiently for Diana to take him on a convalescent cruise at the end of the year, but on board ship he suffered a second, fatal haemorrhage. He died on the afternoon of 1 January, Diana sitting crouched in the bathroom during his final struggling hours because she couldn't bear to witness the undignified convulsions of his body, nor the final departure of his spirit.

For a long time afterwards she withdrew into herself. She refused to go to Duff's funeral, feeling that to share her grief in public would be too unbearable and somehow too vulgar, and

---

* Her behaviour, which was considered both funny and scandalous, fed into the early chapters of Nancy Mitford's 1960 novel, *Don't Tell Alfred*.

in the months that followed she considered suicide. As she explained to Evelyn Waugh, she had no faith in her ability to survive alone. In public she might appear to have a certain 'incandescent aura', but inwardly she felt she had never been anything 'but a beating frightened heart built round and for Duff'.[28]

As always, though, Diana was stronger than she acknowledged, much stronger. Travel helped to save her, as did friends, and it was with Iris Tree that she travelled to North Africa and attempted to get high on hashish paste – Iris wrote wild poems all night, Diana was disappointed that she only had bad dreams. By 1955 she was sufficiently recovered to begin new projects, writing the first part of her trilogy of memoirs, and in 1960 moving back to London to be near John Julius and his family. From her little house in north-west London, she embarked on a new, and in some ways very contented, phase in her life. She discovered that the 1960s suited her; they reminded her of the 1920s: colourful, feckless, greedy for novelty and socially on the move. If Diana socialized with old friends and family, she also ended up at dinner parties with interesting young men such as Mick Jagger and Andy Warhol.

The irresponsibility of old age suited her, too. She had nothing more to prove and, as far as she could see, no occasion for guilt, even if to John Julius and his wife Anne she might often seem as demanding and irrational as her own mother had been. She was also just as capable of emotional blackmail. Anne had hoped Diana might settle in Clapham when she moved back to London, guaranteeing a few miles of family distance. Diana's wounded response was, however, worthy of the late Duchess, and the house she moved into was just a few hundred yards away from her son and daughter-in-law.

Much of the time though, Diana in old age was entertainingly subversive and funny. When parking laws were first introduced in London, she left cajoling notes on her car: 'Dearest Warden. Front tooth broken off, look like 81 year old pirate so at dentist 19a. Very old – very lame – no metres [sic].'[29] While she could be extremely grand, she could also be startlingly practical – when invited to a ball at Wilton House and finding there was no accommodation provided, she hired a caravan and camped in the grounds. By the time she reached her eighties she told everyone she kept a phial of poison by her bed in case old age became too hideous. Yet although her sight and hearing started to fail, and she was bedridden for the last two years, her life was a relatively benign falling away. Diana was ninety-three when she died, and her body was taken to Belvoir Castle to be buried with the rest of her family and next to Duff.

In the obituaries and reminiscences that followed she was celebrated as a wit, a society beauty and a loving wife; the turbulent years during which she had battled for Duff and for independence seemed to have been long buried and forgotten. These were, however, key to her story. Although Diana's palatial upbringing had been a world away from Josephine's ghetto childhood, she too had fought for her life against the destiny of her birth. She'd shown the same instincts of self-determination that had made Josephine run away from the ghetto when she was thirteen and carry on running until she became a star. And like Josephine's Diana's flight had been propelled by the restlessness of a generation.

Scott Fitzgerald observed that the flapper had been created by a spirit of emancipation that had been fermenting since the beginning of the century. But it had been the social derailment of the war years, combined with transformations in modern technology, that had driven the hopes and ambitions of these young women to new levels at the start of the 1920s. They were part of a collective surge in expectation that was carrying them far beyond anything their mothers and grandmothers could have envisaged.

It was not an easy transition. For Zelda, the process of shucking off her girlish habits of dependency for a more adult self was perplexing, painful and eventually crippling. For women who claimed their freedom in more provocatively sexual ways, it took a different kind of courage. Today we regard the Sixties and Seventies as a revolution in women's liberation, yet when we look at the unself-regarding stubbornness with which Nancy claimed sexual equality with men and the audacity with which Tallulah and Tamara conducted their erotic adventures, they were, in fact, anticipating that revolution by several heroic decades.

The six women in this book seem very modern to us in the way they broke taboos and in the way they puzzled out their notions of freedom. But they also seem very modern to us in the way in which they struggled to combine their public and private lives. The Twenties was a decade of celebrity, and its shiny international culture of cinema and radio, advertising, fashion and the popular press, precipitated all six to a heady degree of fame. Even Nancy and Zelda, with their comparatively limited professional profiles, were elevated into icons – photographed and painted, and given the status of modern fairy-tale heroines by those who wrote about them in the gossip columns and magazines. No less than celebrities of the twenty-first century, some of the women became victims of their own fame, as they grew habituated to the distorting reflections of their public image. But all six found themselves grappling with the quintessentially contemporary conundrum: how to combine career and family, self-interest, marriage and love.

Certainly if their experience tells us anything, it is that progress is rarely linear. Much of what this flapper generation wanted to become was stalled or deflected by events of the Thirties and Forties. A few brave souls, like Nancy, moved with those events and took the flapper spirit of insurgency to a wider political arena. But by the middle of the 1960s it was up to a new post-war generation to confront the issues that had been raised in the 1920s. Once again there would be male dandies and short-skirted young women ready to elevate sexual emancipation and freedom of spirit over the dutiful conservatism of their parents, ready to take drugs and dance to music that was designed as an assault on the middle-aged.

It's not surprising that Diana saw resemblances between the

Sixties and her own youth. But another half-century on, it's startling how closely we continue to identify with her and her peers. Nancy, Zelda, Diana, Tallulah, Tamara and Josephine belonged to a dissident, often brilliantly wayward generation of women. Even now their aspirations and battles have a resonance for us, and even now they hold up a standard against which our own vision and nerve can be judged.

NOTES

INTRODUCTION

1 Jean-Claude Baker and Chris Chase, *Josephine: The Hungry Heart*, Cooper Square Press, New York, 2001, p. 3.
2 Laura Claridge, *Tamara de Lempicka: A Life of Deco and Decadence*, Bloomsbury, London, 2001, p. 116.
3 Scott Fitzgerald, 'The Offshore Pirate' in *Flappers and Philosophers*, Serenity Rockville, 2009, p. 9.
4 Ibid, p. 27.
5 *The Times*, 5 February 1920.
6 Scott Fitzgerald, *The Great Gatsby*, Penguin, London, 1974, p. 36 (first published 1926).
7 *New York Times*, 4 June 1923.
8 Dorothy Dunbar Bromley, 'Feminist – New Style' in *Harper's Monthly Magazine*, October 1927, p. 560, cited Joshua Zeitz, *Flapper*, Three Rivers Press, New York, 2006, p. 112.
9 Robert A. Schanke, *That Furious Lesbian*, Southern Illinois University Press, 2003, p. 2.
10 Nicholas Murray, *Aldous Huxley: An English Intellectual*, Abacus, London, 2002, p. 157.

Chapter One – DIANA

1 'Expectation and hope' cited by Joyce Marlow (ed.), *Women and the Great War*, Virago, London, 1999, p. 1.
2 Cited by Philip Ziegler, Diana Cooper, Penguin, London, 1981, p. 145.
3 Cited by Juliet Nicholson, *The Perfect Summer*, John Murray, London, 2006, p. 68.

4 Cited by Ziegler, p. 53.

5 Diana Cooper, *The Rainbow Comes and Goes (RCG)*, Century, London, 1984, p. 156.

6 Ibid, p. 17.

7 Cited by Ziegler, p. 31.

8 Cooper, *RCG*, p. 73.

9 Ibid, p. 81.

10 Cited by Ziegler, p. 55.

11 Cooper, *RCG*, p. 61.

12 Cited by Ziegler, p. 33.

13 Jane C. Desmond (ed.), *Meaning in Motion: New Cultural Studies of Dance*, Duke University Press, 1997, p. 140.

14 Cooper, *RCG*, p. 77.

15 Ibid, p. 84.

16 Ibid, p. 88.

17 Cited by Ziegler, p. 93.

18 Cooper, *RCG*, p. 82.

19 Ibid, p. 106.

20 Ibid, p. 82.

21 Cited by Ziegler, p. 36.

22 Cooper, *RCG*, p. 96.

23 Artemis Cooper (ed.), *A Durable Fire: The Letters of Duff and Diana Cooper, 1913–1950*, Hamish Hamilton, London, 1983, April 1913, p. 6.

24 Cited by Ziegler, p. 59.

25 Ibid, p. 15.

26 Ibid, p. 16.

27 Ibid, p. 63.

28 Ibid, p. 22.

29 Cited by Nicholson, p. 78.

30 Cited by Marlow, p. 22.

31 Ibid, p. 49.

32 Cooper, *RCG*, p. 123.

33 Cited by Ziegler, p. 65.

34 Enid Bagnold, *A Diary Without Dates*, Heinemann, London, 1918.

35 Cooper, *RCG*, p. 131.

36 Cited by Ziegler, p. 65.

37 Cooper, *RCG*, p. 129.

38 Cited by Marlow, p. 4.

39 Cited by Ziegler, p. 114.

40 Ibid, p. 61.

41 *Daily Mail*, 6 September 1916, cited in Lois Gordon, *Nancy Cunard: Heiress, Muse and Political Icon*, Columbia University Press, New York, 2007, p. 63.

42 Cited by Ziegler, p. 71.

43 Cooper, *RCG*, p. 151.

44 John Julius Norwich (ed.), *The Duff Cooper Diaries*, Phoenix, London, 2005, 31 July 1916, p. 34.

45 Ibid.

46 Cooper, *RCG*, p. 96.

47 Ibid, p. 144.

48 Cited by Ziegler, p. 80.

49 Ibid, p. 79.

50 Cooper, *RCG*, p. 142.

51 Cited by Ziegler, p. 71.

52 Ibid, p. 46.

53 Ibid, p. 84.

54 *Letters D and D Cooper*, 3 May 1913, p. 7.

55 Ibid, 23 June 1914, p. 14.

56 Ibid, 2 July 1916, p. 29.

57 *The Duff Cooper Diaries*, 6 March 1916, p. 26.

58 Ibid, 27 August 1915, p. 14.

59 Cited by Ziegler, p. 82.

60 Ibid, p. 97.

61 Ibid, p. 98.

62 *Letters D and D Cooper*, November 1916, p. 31.

63 *The Duff Cooper Diaries*, 29 March 1917, p. 49.

64 *The Duff Cooper Diaries*, 17 May 1917, p. 53.

65 Cooper, *RCG*, pp. 152–3.

66 *Letters D and D Cooper*, 28 April 1918, pp. 49–50.

67 Cooper, *RCG*, p. 149.

68 *Letters D and D Cooper*, 27 September 1917, p. 39.

69 Cooper, *RCG*, p. 173.

70 Ibid, p. 156.

71 *Letters D and D Cooper*, 3 June 1918, p. 69.

72 Ibid, 5 June 1918, p. 70.

73 Cooper, *RCG*, p. 162

74 Cited by Ziegler, p. 123.

75 *Letters D and D Cooper*, 8 July 1918, p. 81.

76 *Letters D and D Cooper*, 4 July 1918, p. 80.

77 Cooper, *RCG*, p. 205.

78 Cited by Ziegler, p. 121.

79 *The Duff Cooper Diaries*, 31 October 1918, p. 85.

80 Cooper, *RCG*, p. 215.

81 Ibid.

Chapter Two – NANCY

1 Nancy Cunard, *GM: Memories of George Moore* (*GM*), cited by Gordon on p. 60.

2 *The Duff Cooper Diaries*, 11 July 1916, p. 33.

3 Cited by Gordon, p. 89.

4 Cited by Gordon, p. 63.

5 Cited by Anne Chisholm, *Nancy Cunard*, Penguin, London, 1981 (first published 1979), p. 31.

6 Cited by Gordon, p. 12.

7 Cited by Daphne Fielding, *Emerald and Nancy: Lady Cunard and Her Daughter*, Eyre & Spottiswoode, London, 1968, p. 24.

8 Nancy Cunard, *Album Amicorum* (*AA*) (unpub.), cited by Chisolm, p. 41.

9 Cited by Fielding, p. 20.

10 Cunard, *AA*, cited by Chisholm, p. 40.

11 Cunard, *GM*, cited by Chisholm, p. 32.

12 Christopher Hassall, *Edward Marsh, Patron of the Arts*, Longmans, 1959, cited by Fielding, p. 26.

13 Cited by Gordon, p. 22.

14 Cited by Chisholm, p. 51.

15 *Manchester Guardian*, 4 December 1913, cited by Paul O'Keefe, *Some Sort of Genius: A Life of Wyndham Lewis*, Jonathan Cape, London, 2000, p. 141.

16 Cited by Gordon, p. 25.

17 Cited by Chisholm, p. 55.

18 Ibid.

19 Iris Tree, 'We Shall Not Forget, for Nancy Cunard', in Hugh Ford (ed.), *Nancy Cunard*, p. 21, cited by Gordon, p. 59.

20 Cunard, *GM*, cited by Fielding, p. 59.

21 Cited by Juliet Nicolson, *The Great Silence*, Murray, London, 2009, p. 33.

22 Cited by Virginia Nicholson, *Singled Out*, Penguin, London, 2008, p. 23.

23 Cunard, unpublished diary, cited by Gordon, p. 76.

24 Ibid., p. 74.

25 Ibid, p. 75.

26 Ibid, p. 76.

27 Ibid, p. 73.

28 Cunard, diary (unpublished), cited by Chisholm, p. 72.

29 Ibid, cited by Gordon, p. 81.

30 Ibid, p. 83.

31 Cunard, diary, cited by Chisholm, p. 76.

32 Ibid, p. 79.

33 Ibid, p. 85.

34 Ibid, p. 76.

35 Cunard, diary (unpublished), cited by Gordon, p. 84.

36 Ibid, cited by Chisholm, p. 89.

37 Ibid, cited by Gordon, p. 87.

38 Ibid, p. 87.

39 Ibid.

40 Ibid, cited by Chisholm, p. 90.

Chapter Three – TAMARA

1 Cited by Claridge, p. 68.

2 Cited by Justine Picardie, *Coco Chanel: The Legend and the Life*, HarperCollins, London, 2010, p. 128.

3 Cited by Kizette de Lempicka-Foxall and Charles Phillips, *Passion by Design: the Art and Times of Tamara de Lempicka*, Phaidon, Oxford, 1987, p. 36.

4 Ibid, p. 22.

5 Cited by Claridge, p. 37.

6 Ibid, p. 41.

7 Cited by Stefanie Penck, *Tamara de Lempicka*, Prestel, London, 2004, p. 20.

8 Cited by Foxall, p. 38.

9 Cited by Lynn Haney, *Naked at the Feast: A Biography of Josephine Baker*, Robson, London, 1981, p. 51.

10 Cited by Claridge, p. 79.

11 Cited by Diana Souhami, *Wild Girls*, Weidenfeld & Nicolson, London, 2004, p. 60.

12 Ibid, p. 60.

13 Cited by Suzanne Rodriguez-Hunter, *Found Meals of the Lost Generation*, Faber, London, 1994, p. 94.

14 William Carlos Williams, *The Autobiography*, New Directions, New York, 1967, p. 229, cited by Brenda Wineapple in *Genêt: A Biography of Janet Flanner*, Pandora, London, 1989, p. 85.
15 Cited by Claridge, p. 89.
16 Cited by Foxall, p. 42.
17 Ibid, p. 172.

Chapter Four – TALLULAH

1 Cited by Joe Lobenthal in *Tallulah! The Life and Times of a Leading Lady*, Aurum, London, 2004, p. 16.
2 Tallulah Bankhead, *Tallulah: My Autobiography*, Victor Gollancz, London, 1952, p. 22.
3 Ibid, p. 32.
4 Ibid, p. 24.
5 Cited by Lobenthal, p. 10.
6 Bankhead, p. 22.
7 Ibid, p. 42.
8 Ibid, p. 45.
9 Frances Marion, *Off With Their Heads!*, Macmillan, London, 1972, cited by Tim Lussier, 'The Mysterious Death of Olive Thomas' on www.silentsaregolden.com.
10 Bankhead, p. 54.
11 Cited by Lobenthal, p. 34.
12 Bankhead, p. 57.
13 Cited by Lobenthal, p. 20.
14 Bankhead, p. 60.
15 Bankhead, p. 74.
16 Ibid, p. 57.
17 Cited by Lobenthal, p. 24.
18 Ibid.
19 Ibid, p. 21.
20 Bankhead, p. 58.
21 Cited Lee Israel, *Miss Tallulah Bankhead*, W.H. Allen, London, 1972, p. 56.
22 Cited by Lobenthal, p. 38.
23 Ibid, p. 30.
24 Bankhead, p. 56.
25 Ibid, p. 73.

26 Ibid, p. 70.

27 Ibid.

28 Ibid, p. 90.

29 Cited by Israel, p. 75.

30 Ibid, p. 72.

31 Cited by Lobenthal, p. 28.

32 Ibid, p. 17.

33 Ibid, p. 36.

34 Cited by Israel, p. 68.

35 Cited by Lobenthal, p. 43.

36 Cited by Israel, p. 66.

37 Cited by David Bret, *Tallulah Bankhead: A Scandalous Life*, Robson, London, 1996, p. 25.

38 Cited by Lobenthal, p. 50.

39 Ibid, p. 37.

40 Bankhead, p. 98.

41 Cited by Israel, p. 179.

42 Cited by Lobenthal, p. 55.

Chapter Five – ZELDA

1 Cited by Sally Cline, *Zelda Fitzgerald: Her Voice in Paradise*, John Murray, London, 2002, p. 85.

2 Edmund Wilson, *Letters on Literature and Politics*, p. 478, Farrar, Straus and Giroux, New York, 1977, cited by Matthew J. Bruccoli in *Some Sort of Epic Grandeur*, University of South Carolina Press, 2002 ed., p. 132.

3 Cited by Zeitz, p. 53.

4 Scott Fitzgerald, *This Side of Paradise*, first published 1920, Dover, New York, 1996, p. 44.

5 Cited by Nancy Milford, *Zelda Fitzgerald*, first published 1970, Penguin, Harmondsworth, 1974, p. 77.

6 Cited by Zeitz, p. 47.

7 Cited by Milford, p. 63.

8 Ibid, p. 63.

9 Barry Paris, *Louise Brooks: A Biography*, University of Minnesota Press, 2000, p. 33.

10 Zelda Fitzgerald, *Save Me the Waltz (SMTW)*, first published 1932, Vintage, London, 2001, p. 1.

11 Cited by Milford, p. 9.

12 Fitzgerald, *SMTW*, p. 28.

13 Cited by Milford, p. 9.

14 Cited by Cline, pp. 39–41.

15 Ibid, p. 40.

16 Cited by Milford, p. 18.

17 Cited by Cline, p. 33.

18 Ibid.

19 Ibid, p. 36.

20 Zelda Fitzgerald letters (ZFL), unpublished, cited by Milford, p. 54.

21 Ibid, cited by Cline, p. 67.

22 Fitzgerald, *SMTW*, p. 57.

23 Cited by Cline, p. 42.

24 Fitzgerald, *SMTW*, p. 35.

25 Cited by Cline, p. 47.

26 ZFL cited by Cline, p. 45.

27 Fitzgerald, *SMTW*, p. 37.

28 Scott Fitzgerald, *The Great Gatsby*, first published 1926, Penguin, Harmondsworth, 1974, p. 155.

29 Cited by Milford, p. 33.

30 Ibid, p. 44.

31 ZFL, cited by Milford, p. 45.

32 Ibid, p. 50.

33 Cited by Milford, p. 52.

34 ZFL cited by Milford, p. 53.

35 Ibid, p. 56.

36 Ibid, p. 61.

37 Cited by Zeitz, p. 51.

38 ZFL cited by Milford, p. 68.

39 Cited by Bruccoli, p. 111.

40 Fitzgerald, *SMTW*, p. 42.

41 Ibid, p. 45.

42 Scott Fitzgerald, *The Crack-Up*, first published 1945, cited by Cline, p. 84.

43 Cited by Cline, p. 86.

44 Cited by Milford, p. 75.

45 Zelda Fitzgerald, 'Caesar's Things', (unpublished), cited by Cline, p. 85.

46 ZFL cited by Milford, p. 85.

47 Cited by Milford, p. 90.

48 Ibid, p. 86.

49 Cited by Cline, p. 111.

50 Ibid, p. 109.

51 Zelda Fitzgerald, 'A Millionaire's Girl', cited by Cline, p. 31.

52 Cited by Cline, p. 116.

53 Ibid.

54 ZFL cited by Bruccoli, p. 109.

55 Cited by Cline, p. 126.

56 John Peale Bishop, *Collected Essays*, Scribners, New York, 1948, cited by Cline, p. 121.

57 ZFL cited by Milford, p. 50.

58 Cited by Cline, p. 123.

59 Cited by Milford, p. 102.

60 Cited by Cline, p. 124.

61 ZFL cited by Milford, p. 54.

62 Unpublished diary of Alec McKaig, cited by Milford, p. 90.

63 Cited by Bruccoli, p. 161.

64 Cited by Milford, p. 108.

65 John Doss Passos, *The Best Times*, New American Library, New York, 1966, p. 129, cited by Bruccoli, p. 171.

66 Cited by Cline, p. 99.

67 Cited by Bruccoli, p. 177.

68 Cited by Cline, p. 137.

69 Unpublished diary of Alec McKaig, cited by Milford, p. 88.

70 Cited by Cline, p. 138.

Chapter Six – JOSEPHINE

1 Cited by Phyllis Rose, *Jazz Cleopatra: Josephine Baker in Her Time*, Vintage, London, 1991, p. 55.

2 Cited by Baker and Chase, p. 55.

3 Ibid, p. 18.

4 Ibid.

5 Ibid, p. 19.

6 Cited by Lynn Haney, p. 17.

7 Cited by Baker and Chase, p. 24.

8 Ibid, p. 36.

9 Ibid, p. 42.

10 Ibid, p. xxi.

11 Haney, p. 38.

12 Ibid, p. 25.

13 Cited by Baker and Chase, p. 55.

14 Ibid, p. 57.
15 Cited by Paris, p. 72.
16 Cited by Baker and Chase, p. 63.
17 Ibid, p. 62.
18 Ibid, p. 70.
19 Cited by Haney, p. 40.
20 Cited by Baker and Chase, p. 74.
21 Lucy Moore, *Anything Goes: A Biography of the Roaring Twenties*, Atlantic, London, 2009, p. 49.
22 Jeffrey H. Jackson, *Making Jazz French: Music and Modern Life in Interwar Paris*, Duke University Press, 2003, p. 1.
23 Cited by Baker and Chase, p. 59.
24 Ibid, p. 91.
25 Ibid.
26 Ibid, p. 97.

Chapter Seven – DIANA

1 Cited by Ziegler, p. 123.
2 Ibid, p. 126.
3 Cooper, *RCG*, p. 219.
4 Cited by Ziegler, p. 129.
5 Cooper, *RCG*, p. 220.
6 Ibid, p. 221.
7 Ibid.
8 *Letters D and D Cooper*, 30 January 1929, p. 264.
9 *The Duff Cooper Diaries*, 2 June 1919, p. 103.
10 *The Duff Cooper Diaries*, 13 October 1919, p. 109.
11 D.H. Lawrence, *Aaron's Rod*, first published 1922, Penguin, Harmondsworth, p. 157.
12 Clement Scott, 1898, cited by Catherine Haill in *Women in the 19th Century Theatre*, V&A Museum.
13 Cited by Ziegler, p. 147.
14 *The Duff Cooper Diaries*, 2 June 1919, p. 102.
15 Cited by Ziegler, p. 146.
16 Ibid, p. 146.
17 *The Duff Cooper Diaries*, 22 July 1921, p. 148
18 Cited by Ziegler, p. 148.
19 Ibid, p. 149.

20 Ibid, p. 153.
21 *The Duff Cooper Diaries* (16.10.1923), p. 181.
22 Diana Cooper, *The Light of Common Day (LOCD)*, first published 1959, Century, London, 1984, p. 11.
23 *Letters D and D Cooper*, 30 January 1927, p. 249.
24 John Charmley, *Duff Cooper: the Authorized Biography*, Papermac, London, 1987, p. 33.
25 Cited by Ziegler, p. 134.
26 *The Duff Cooper Diaries*, 12 October 1925, p. 211.
27 Cooper, *RCG*, p. 172.
28 *The Duff Cooper Diaries*, 2 December 1923, p. 183.
29 Cooper, *LOCD*, p. 12.
30 Cited by Ziegler, p. 155.
31 Cooper, *LOCD*, p. 29.
32 *Letters D and D Cooper*, 8 December 1923, p. 149.
33 Cooper, *LOCD*, p. 13.
34 Ibid, p. 15.
35 *Letters D and D Cooper*, 3 January 1924, p. 153.
36 Cited by Ziegler, p. 158.
37 Cooper, *LOCD*, p. 26.
38 Ibid, p. 27.
39 *Letters D and D Cooper*, 13 February 1924, p. 166.
40 *The Duff Cooper Diaries*, 5 May 1924, p. 195.
41 Cited by Ziegler, p. 162.
42 Cooper, *LOCD*, p. 39.
43 Cited by Ziegler, p. 180.
44 Cooper, *LOCD*, p. 40.
45 Ibid, p. 34.
46 Ibid, p. 18.
47 Ibid, p. 33.
48 Cited by Ziegler, p. 159.
49 *Letters D and D Cooper*, 24 January 1927, p. 247.
50 Cited by Lyn Garafola, *Diaghilev's Ballets Russes*, Oxford University Press, New York, 1989, p. 250.
51 Cooper, *LOCD*, p. 46.
52 Ibid, p. 47.
53 Ibid, p. 51.
54 *Letters D and D Cooper*, 3 October 1925, pp. 202–3.
55 Cooper, *LOCD*, p. 50.
56 *Letters D and D Cooper*, 3 October 1925, pp. 202–3.

57 Cooper, *LOCD*, p. 20.

58 *Letters D and D Cooper*, 3 November 1925, p. 209.

59 Ibid, 10 October 1925, p. 206.

60 Ibid, 9 December 1926, p. 232.

61 Ibid, 8 January 1927, p. 244.

62 Ibid, 4 December 1925, p. 212.

63 Cooper, *LOCD*, p. 74.

64 Ibid, p. 76.

65 Ibid, pp. 43–4.

66 Ibid, p. 67.

67 *Letters D and D Cooper*, 14 December 1926, p. 234.

68 Ibid (19.12.26), p. 237.

69 Cooper, *LOCD*, p. 90.

70 *Letters D and D Cooper*, 28 January 1929, p. 261.

71 Ibid (30.01.29), p. 263.

72 Cited by Ziegler, p. 119.

Chapter Eight – TALLULAH

1 *Letters D and D Cooper* (08.12.24), p. 186.

2 Bankhead, p. 104.

3 Cited by Israel, p. 82.

4 Bankhead, p. 105.

5 Cited by Lobenthal, p. 56.

6 Ibid, p. 57.

7 Ibid, p. 70.

8 Cited by Israel, p. 81.

9 Bankhead, p. 145.

10 Cited by Israel, p. 84.

11 Bankhead, pp. 122–3.

12 Ibid, p. 122.

13 Cited by Lobenthal, p. 72.

14 Ibid, p. 89.

15 Bankhead, p. 145.

16 Cited by Lobenthal, p. 91.

17 Ibid, pp. 93–4.

18 Bankhead, p. 125.

19 Cited by Lobenthal, p. 96.

20 Ibid, p. 94.

21 Bankhead, p. 143.

22 Cited by Israel, p. 89.

23 Cited by Lobenthal, p. 84.

24 Ibid, p. 161.

25 Cited by Israel, p. 95.

26 Cited by Lobenthal, p. 97.

27 Bankhead, p. 127.

28 Ibid, p. 130.

29 Cited by Lobenthal, p. 91.

30 Bankhead, p. 131.

31 Cited by Lobenthal, p. 105

32 Cited by Israel, p. 112.

33 Bankhead, p. 110.

34 Cited by Lobenthal, p. 118.

35 Bankhead, p. 107.

36 Cited by Israel, pp. 116.

37 Cited by Lobenthal, p. 99.

38 Cited by Israel, p. 106–7.

39 Cited by Cline, p. 184.

40 Bankhead, p. 109.

41 Cited by Lobenthal, p. 101.

42 Ibid, p. 171.

43 Ibid, p. 95.

44 Ibid, p. 117.

45 Ibid, p. 111.

46 Ibid, p. 113.

47 Cited by Israel, p. 113.

48 Ibid, p. 114.

49 Cited by Lobenthal, p. 160.

50 Ibid, p. 164.

51 Cited by Lobenthal, p. 132.

52 Bankhead, p. 157.

53 Cited by Lobenthal, p. 108.

54 Ibid, p. 147.

55 Ibid, p. 123.

56 Ibid, p. 147.

57 Cited by Israel, p. 123.

58 Cited by Lobenthal, p. 148.

59 Bankhead, p. 149.

60 Cited by Lobenthal, p. 174.

61 Ibid, p. 142.
62 Ibid, p. 227.
63 Ibid, p. 156.
64 Cited by Israel, p. 126.
65 Cited by Lobenthal, p. 167.
66 Ibid, p. 168.
67 Ibid, p. 131.

Chapter Nine – NANCY

 1 Cited by Chisholm, p. 96.
 2 Ibid, p. 100.
 3 Nancy Cunard's unpublished diary, cited by Gordon, p. 131.
 4 Cited by Chisholm, p. 99.
 5 Ibid.
 6 Ibid, p. 98.
 7 Ibid, p. 142.
 8 Ibid, p. 101.
 9 Michael Arlen, *Piracy*, cited by Chisholm, p. 102.
10 Cited by Chisholm, p. 404.
11 *Daily Mail*, 17 September 1921, London, cited by Gordon, p. 119.
12 Cited by Gordon, p. 92.
13 *The Autobiography of William Carlos Williams*, cited by Gordon, p. 127.
14 Cited by Chisholm, p. 199.
15 Cited by Paul O'Keefe, p. 245.
16 Cited by Norman Murray, p. 183.
17 Cited by Chisholm, p. 112.
18 Aldous Huxley, *Antic Hay*, first published 1923, Vintage, London, 2004, p. 75.
19 Ibid, p. 78.
20 Cited by Chisholm, p. 118.
21 Cited by Murray, p. 146.
22 Cited by Chisholm, p. 120.
23 Ibid, p. 92.
24 Cited by Murray, p. 146.
25 Cited by Gordon, p. 127.
26 Cited by Chisholm, p. 123.
27 Ibid, p. 125.
28 Cited by Gordon, p. 101.

29 Cited by Chisholm, p. 141.

30 Cited by Chisholm, p. 223.

31 Cited by Gordon, p. 127.

32 Cited by Chisholm, p. 138.

33 Nancy Cunard (ed.), *Negro*, Wishart & Co., London, 1934, cited by Gordon, p. 90.

34 Cited by Gordon, p. 108.

35 Ibid, p. 124.

36 Ibid.

37 Cited by Chisholm, p. 232.

38 Ibid, p. 41.

39 Ibid, p. 143.

40 Cited by Gordon, p. 143.

41 Ibid, p. 143.

42 Ibid, p. 147.

43 Cited by Chisholm, p. 208.

44 Ibid, p. 233.

45 Ibid, p. 169.

46 Ibid, p. 163.

47 Ibid, p. 179.

48 Ibid, p. 169.

49 Ibid, p. 172.

50 Ibid, p. 171.

51 Ibid, p. 186.

52 Ibid, p. 176.

53 Ibid, p. 182/178.

54 Ibid, p. 174.

55 Ibid.

56 Ibid, p. 202.

57 Ibid, p. 205.

58 Ibid, p. 186.

59 Ibid, p. 264.

60 Cited by Gordon, p. 157.

61 Cited by Chisholm, p. 247.

62 Cited by Gordon, p. 160.

63 Cited by Chisholm, p. 223.

64 Ibid, p. 224.

65 Ibid, p. 250.

Chapter Ten – ZELDA

1 Cited by Moore, p. 125.
2 Fitzgerald, *SMTW*, p. 81.
3 Cited by Bruccoli, p. 191.
4 Ibid, p. 196.
5 Scott Fitzgerald, *The Great Gatsby*, p. 46.
6 Ibid, p. 70.
7 Fitzgerald, *SMTW*, p. 82.
8 Cited by Milford, p. 120.
9 Fitzgerald, *SMTW*, p. 91.
10 Cited by Milford, p. 193.
11 Ibid, pp. 123–4.
12 Ibid, p. 124.
13 Cited by Bruccoli, p. 217.
14 Cited by Cline, p. 157.
15 Ibid, p. 161.
16 Cited by Milford, p. 128.
17 Ibid, p. 126.
18 Cited by Bruccoli, p. 221.
19 Cited by Milford, p. 200.
20 Ibid, p. 138.
21 Ibid.
22 Cited by Cline, p. 168.
23 Cited by Milford, p. 127.
24 Cited by Milford, p. 117.
25 Cited by Cline, p. 166.
26 Ibid, p. 175.
27 Cited by Milford, p. 136.
28 Ibid.
29 Cited by Claridge, p. 98.
30 Cited by Cline, p. 173.
31 Cited by Milford, p. 267.
32 Fitzgerald, *SMTW*, p. 73.
33 Cited by Milford, p. 137.
34 Ibid, p. 267.
35 Cited by Cline, p. 184.
36 Cited in John Richardson, *A Life of Picasso*, Volume 3, Jonathan Cape, London, 2007, p. 287.

37 Cited by Bruccoli, p. 254.

38 Ibid, p. 253.

39 Cited by Milford, p. 139.

40 Ibid, p. 140.

41 Ibid, p. 144.

42 Cited by Cline, p. 210.

43 Cited by Milford, p. 150.

44 Ibid, p. 158.

45 Ibid, p. 148.

46 Fitzgerald, *SMTW*, p. 128.

47 Cited by Cline, p. 258.

48 Fitzgerald, *SMTW*, p. 128.

49 Cited by Milford, p. 157.

50 Ibid, p. 163.

51 Cited by Cline, p. 222.

52 Ibid, p. 281.

53 Cited by Bruccoli, p. 271.

54 Ibid, p. 294.

55 Cited by Cline, p. 229.

56 Cited by Milford, p. 204.

57 Cited by Cline, p. 274.

58 Cited by Milford, p. 172.

59 Fitzgerald, *SMTW*, p. 101.

60 Cited by Milford, p. 184.

61 Ibid, p. 175.

62 Cited by Milford, p. 168.

63 Ibid, p. 194.

Chapter Eleven – TAMARA

1 Cited by Milford, p. 185.

2 Cited by Claridge, pp. 117.

3 Cited by Foxall, pp. 58–9.

4 Ibid, p. 82.

5 Ibid, p. 81.

6 Ibid, p. 81.

7 Ibid, p. 43.

8 Cited by Claridge, p. 108.

9 Ibid, p. 136.

10 Cited by Foxall, p. 68.
11 Cited by Claridge, p. 140.
12 Ibid, p. 135.
13 Ibid, p. 145.
14 Ibid, p. 148.
15 Cited by Foxall, p. 172.
16 Cited by Claridge, p. 147.
17 Ibid, p. 147.
18 Ibid, p. 169.
19 Ibid, p. 170.
20 Janet Flanner, *Paris Was Yesterday*, Virago, London, 2003, p. 73.
21 Cited by Foxall, p. 138.

Chapter Twelve – JOSEPHINE

1 Cited by Baker and Chase, p. 116.
2 Ibid, p. 130.
3 Cited by Haney, p. 50.
4 Cited by Baker and Chase, p. 111.
5 Cited by John Kirby Abraham, *In Search of Josephine Baker*, Pen Press, London, 2001, p. 23.
6 Cited by Bennetta Jules-Rosette, *Josephine Baker in Art and Life: the Icon and the Image*, University of Illinois Press, 2007, p. 48.
7 Cited by Haney, p. 64.
8 Ibid, p. 64.
9 Ibid, p. 69.
10 Ibid, p. 103.
11 Cited by Baker and Chase, p. 120.
12 Cited by Abraham, p. 29.
13 Cited by Baker and Chase, p. 150.
14 Cited by Haney, p. 75.
15 Cited by Jules-Rosette, p. 142.
16 Ibid, p. 142.
17 Cited by Baker and Chase, p. 119.
18 Cited by Haney, p. 67.
19 Ibid, p. 80.
20 Ibid, p. 82.
21 Cited by Baker and Chase, p. 119.
22 Ibid.

23 Ibid, p. 124.

24 Cited by Rose, p. 85.

25 Ibid, p. 82.

26 Ibid, p. 100.

27 Cited by Haney, p. 115.

28 Ibid, p. 110.

29 Cited by Baker and Chase, p. 137.

30 Cited by Haney, 87.

31 Ibid, p. 104.

32 Ibid, p. 105.

33 Ibid, p. 111.

34 Cited by Jules-Rosette, p. 161.

35 Cited by Haney, p. 119.

36 Ibid, p. 126.

37 Ibid, p. 133.

38 Ibid, p. 134.

39 Ibid, p. 135.

40 Cited by Jules-Rosette, p. 78.

41 Cited by Rose, p. 141.

42 Cited by Baker and Chase, p. 171.

43 Cited by Haney, p. 160.

44 Ibid, p. 161.

45 Ibid, p. 163.

46 Flanner, p. 87.

47 Cited by Haney, pp. 130–1.

48 Ibid, p. 167.

EPILOGUE

1 Cited by Haney, p. 332.

2 Ibid, p. 236.

3 Ibid, p. 236.

4 Ibid, p. 253.

5 Cited by Chisolm, p. 441.

6 Ibid, p. 403.

7 Ibid, p. 438.

8 Cited by Milford, p. 181.

9 Cited by Milford, p. 296.

10 Ibid, p. 287.

11 Ibid, p. 322.

12 Ibid, p. 350.

13 Ibid, p. 388.

14 Cited by Cline, p. 43.

15 Cited by Claridge, p. 200.

16 Ibid, p. 206.

17 Ibid, p. 316.

18 Ibid, p. 363.

19 Ibid, p. 372.

20 Cited by Israel, p. 145.

21 Cited by Israel, p. 171.

22 Ibid, p. 259.

23 Cited by Ziegler, p. 272.

24 Ibid, p. 214.

25 Ibid, p. 201.

26 Ibid, p. 278.

27 Diana Cooper, *Trumpets from the Steep*, first published 1960, Century, London, 1984, p. 245.

28 Cited by Ziegler, p. 321.

29 Ibid, p. 359.

BIBLIOGRAPHY

Abraham, John Kirby, *In Search of Josephine Baker*, London: Pen Press, 2001.

Acton, Harold, *Memoirs of an Aesthete*, London: Methuen, 1948.

Adickes, Sandra, *To Be Young Was Very Heaven*, New York: St Martin's Press, 1997.

Arlen, Michael, *The Green Hat* (first published 1924), London: Capuchin Classics, 2008.

Bagnold, Enid, *A Diary Without Dates*, London: Heinemann, 1918.

——, *The Loved and Envied*, London: Heinemann, 1951.

Bailey, Catherine, *The Secret Room: A True Gothic Mystery*, London: Viking, 2012.

Baker, Jean-Claude and Chase, Chris, *Josephine: The Hungry Heart*, New York: Cooper Square Press, 2001.

Bankhead, Tallulah, *Tallulah: My Autobiography*, London: Victor Gollancz, 1952.

Barnes, Djuna, *Ladies Almanack* (first published 1928), Manchester: Carcanet, 2006.

Baughman, Judith S. (ed.), *American Decades: 1920–1929*, Detroit: Manley/ Gale, 1995.

Beaton, Cecil, *The Glass of Fashion*, London: Weidenfeld & Nicolson, 1954.

Benstock, Shari, *Women of the Left Bank*, London: Virago, 1987.

Blakiston, Georgiana, *Letters of Conrad Russell*, London: John Murray, 1987.

Brett, David, *Tallulah Bankhead: A Scandalous Life*, London: Robson, 1996.

Brittain, Vera, *Testament of Youth*, New York: Macmillan, 1933.

Bruccoli, Matthew J., *Some Kind of Epic Grandeur*, Second Revised Edition, Columbia: University of South Carolina Press, 2002.

Bryer, Jackson R., and Barks, Cathy W., *Dear Scott, Dearest Zelda: The Love Letters of F. Scott and Zelda Fitzgerald*, New York: St Martin's Press, 2002.

Charmley, John, *Duff Cooper: The Authorized Biography*, London: Papermac, 1987.

Cheng, Anne Anlin, *Second Skin: Josephine Baker and the Modern Surface*, New York, Oxford University Press, 2011.

Chisholm, Anne, *Nancy Cunard* (first published 1979), Harmondsworth: Penguin, 1981.

Claridge, Laura, *Tamara de Lempicka: A Life of Deco and Decadence* (first published 1999), London: Bloomsbury, 2001.

Cline, Sally, *Zelda Fitzgerald: Her Voice in Paradise*, London: John Murray, 2002.

Connolly, Cressida, *The Rare and the Beautiful*, London: Fourth Estate, 2004.

Cooper, Artemis (ed.), *A Durable Fire: The Letters of Duff and Diana Cooper, 1913–50*. London: Hamish Hamilton, 1983.

Cooper, Diana, *The Rainbow Comes and Goes* (first published 1958), London: Century, 1984.

——,*The Light of Common Day* (first published 1959), London: Century, 1984.

——, *Trumpets from the Steep* (first published 1960), London: Century, 1984.

Cowley, Malcolm, *Exile's Return: A Literary Odyssey of the 1920s*, New York, Viking, 1951.

cummings, e.e., *The Enormous Room* (first published 1922), London: Dover, 2002.

Cunard, Nancy, *These Were the Hours*, Southern Illinois University Press, 1969.

——, *Negro: An Anthology* (first published 1934), edited and abridged by Hugh Ford, New York: Frederick Ungar, 1970.

Desmond, Jane C. (ed.), *Meaning in Motion: New Cultural Studies of Dance*, Duke University Press, 1997.

Douglas, Ann, *Terrible Honesty* (first published 1995), London: Picador, 1996.

Fass, Paula S., *The Damned and the Beautiful: American Youth in the 1920s*, New York: Oxford University Press, 1977.

Fielding, Daphne, *Emerald and Nancy*, London: Eyre and Spottiswood, 1968.

Fitzgerald, Scott, *This Side of Paradise* (first published 1920), New York: Dover, 1996.

——, *Flappers and Philosophers* (first published 1920), Rockville: Serenity, 2009.

——, *The Beautiful and Damned* (first published 1922), London: Penguin, 1966.

————, *The Great Gatsby* (first published 1926), Harmondsworth: Penguin, 1974.

————, *Tender is the Night* (first published 1934), London: Penguin, 1997.

Fitzgerald, Zelda, *Save Me the Waltz* (first published 1932), London: Vintage, 2001.

Flanner, Janet, *Paris Was Yesterday*, London: Virago, 2003.

Ford, Hugh, (ed.), *Nancy Cunard*, London: Chilton, 1968.

————, *Four Lives in Paris*, San Francisco: North Point Press, 1991.

Garafola, Lyn, *Diaghilev's Ballets Russes*, New York: Oxford University Press, 1989.

Glendinning, Vitoria, *Edith Sitwell: A Unicorn Among Lions*, New York: Knopf, 1981.

Gordon, Lois, *Nancy Cunard: Heiress, Muse and Political Icon*. New York: Columbia University Press, 2007.

Gottlieb, Robert, *Sarah: The Life of Sarah Bernhardt*, Yale University Press, 2010.

Haney, Lyn, *Naked at the Feast: A Biography of Josephine Baker*, London: Robson, 1981.

Hemingway, Ernest, *A Moveable Feast* (first published 1936), London: Arrow Books, 2004.

Huxley, Aldous, *Antic Hay* (first published 1923), London: Vintage, 2004.

————, *Those Barren Leaves* (first published 1925), Harmondsworth: Penguin, 1951.

Israel, Lee, *Miss Tallulah Bankhead*, London: W.H. Allen, 1972.

Jackson, Jeffrey H., *Making Jazz French: Music and Modern Life in Interwar Paris*, Durham: Duke University Press, 2003.

Jules-Rosette, Bennetta, *Josephine Baker: the Icon and the Image*, Urbana and Chicago: University of Illinois Press, 2007.

Kurth, Peter, *Isadora: The Sensational Life of Isadora Duncan*, London: Little, Brown and Company, 2002.

Lawrence, D.H., *Aaron's Rod* (first published 1922), Harmondsworth: Penguin, 1950.

Lempicka-Foxall, Kizette de and Phillips, Charles, *Passion by Design: the Art and Times of Tamara de Lempicka*, Oxford: Phaidon, 1987.

Lobenthal, Joel, *Tallulah! The Life and Times of a Leading Lady*, London: Aurum Press, 2004.

Mackrell, Judith, *Bloomsbury Ballerina: Lydia Lopokova, Imperial Dancer and Mrs John Maynard Keynes*, London: Weidenfeld & Nicolson, 2008.

Marlow, Joyce (ed.), *Women and the Great War*, London: Virago, 1999.

Meade, Marion, *Bobbed Hair and Bathtub Gin*, New York: Doubleday, 2004.

Mellow, James R., *Invented Lives*: *F. Scott and Zelda Fitzgerald*, Boston: Houghton Mifflin, 1984.

Milford, Nancy, *Zelda Fitzgerald* (first published 1970), Harmondsworth: Penguin, 1974.

Moore, Lucy, *Anything Goes: A Biography of the Roaring Twenties*, London: Atlantic, 2009.

Murray, Nicholas, *Aldous Huxley*: *An English Intellectual*, London: Abacus, 2002.

Nicholson, Virginia, *Among the Bohemians: Experiments in Living 1900–1939*, London: Viking, 2003.

———, *Singled Out*, London: Penguin, 2008.

Nicolson, *The Perfect Summer* (first published 2006), London: John Murray, 2007.

———, Juliet, *The Great Silence*, London: Murray, 2009.

Norwich, John Julius (ed.), *The Duff Cooper Diaries*, Weidenfeld & Nicolson, 2005.

O'Keeffe, Paul, *Some Sort of Genius: A Life of Wyndham Lewis*, London: Jonathan Cape, 2000.

Paris, Barry, *Louise Brooks: A Biography*, Minneapolis: University of Minnesota Press, 2000.

Penck, Stefanie, *Tamara de Lempicka*, London: Prestel, 2004.

Picardie, Justine, *Coco Chanel*: *The Legend and the Life*, London: Harper-Collins, 2010.

Reynolds, Michael S., *Hemingway: The Paris Years*, New York: Norton, 1999.

Richardson, John, *A Life of Picasso*, Vol. 3, London: Jonathan Cape, 2007.

Rodriguez Hunter, Suzanne, *Found Meals of the Lost Generation*, London: Faber, 1994.

Roojen, Pepin van, *Art Deco Fashion*, Amsterdam: Pepin Press, 2007.

Rose, Phyllis, *Jazz Cleopatra: Josephine Baker in Her Time* (first published 1989), London: Vintage 1991.

Ryersson, Scot D., and Yaccarino, Michael Orlando, *Infinite Variety: The Life and Legend of the Marchesa Casati*, New York: Viridian Books, 1997.

Sauvage, Marcel, *Les Mémoires de Joséphine Baker*, Paris: Corréa, 1949.

Schanke, Robert A., *That Furious Lesbian*, Carbondale: Southern Illinois University Press, 2003.

Showalter, Elaine, *Daughters of Decadence*, London: Virago, 1993.

Souhami, Diana, *Wild Girls*, London: Weidenfeld & Nicolson, 2004.

Stein, Gertrude, *The Autobiography of Alice B. Toklas* (first published 1933), London: Penguin 2001.

———, *Paris France*, New York: Liverwright, 1940.

Stenn, David. *Clara Bow: Runnin' Wild* (first published 1998), New York: Cooper Square Press, 2000.

Taylor, D.J., *Bright Young People: The Rise and Fall of a Generation*, London: Chatto and Windus, 2007.

Troy, Nancy, *Modernism and the Decorative Arts in France: Art Nouveau to Le Corbusier*, New Haven: Yale University Press, 1991.

Vaill, Amanda, *Everybody Was So Young: Sara and Gerald Murphy: A Lost Generation Love Story*, Boston: Houghton Mifflin, 1998.

Wilhelm J.J., *Ezra Pound: London and Paris 1908–1925*, Pennsylvania State Press, 2008.

Wineapple, Brenda, *Genet: A Biography of Janet Flanner*, London: Pandora, 1989.

Zeitz, Joshua, *Flapper*, New York: Three Rivers Press, 2006.

Ziegler, Philip, *Diana Cooper* (first published 1981), Harmondsworth: Penguin, 1983.

INDEX

T